Product Safety Management and Engineering, 2nd Edition

Library of Congress Cataloging-in-Publication Data

Hammer, Willie
    Product safety management and engineering / Willie Hammer. — 2nd ed.
        p.   cm.
    Includes bibliographical references and index.
    ISBN# 0-939874-90-3 : $84.95
    1. Product safety.   I. Title.
TS175.H35   1993
658.5'6—dc20   93-7373
                                                           CIP

Managing Editor: Michael F. Burditt
Editorial Production: Johansen & Associates
Cover and Interior Design: Matthew Doherty Design
Development Editor: Louise Sheldon
Schematic CAD Drawings: Steve Pommer

The Society wishes to extend special appreciation to Robert E. McClay, Jr., Indiana University of Pennsylvania, Department of Safety Sciences, for his dedication in completing a technical review of this new edition.

Table of Contents

Preface

The growing concern about the increased complexity and magnitude of hazards, accidents, and costs, was commented on by Hollister and Traut of the Department of Energy, at the fourth conference of the International System Safety Conference, in July 1979, as follows:

During the past century we were concerned with hazards of the following type:

- Hazards that were simple and easily recognized.

- Hazards that impacted only individuals or small groups of people in fairly immediate ways.

- Hazards that were controlled to a large extent by the persons who might be harmed.

- Hazards that had associated benefits that were recognized and attained by individuals.

- This concern has gradually turned, however, to the following kinds of hazards:

- Hazards that are very complex and hard to recognize or understand.

- Hazards that may impact many thousands of people over long periods of time.

- Hazards that are controlled by persons other than those who may be harmed.

- Hazards that may have benefits whose value to persons at risk is only indirect and not easily measured.

During the past centuries, we have made tremendous progress in technological development, especially in the United States. As a result, actor Robert Redford asked in 1989, "Are we the beneficiaries of our progress and development or the victims?"

We are the victims when inadequately safeguarded technological progress causes the generation of accidents, fatalities, or injuries. More and more, the public has become concerned with the possibilities and the increasing frequency and numbers of accidents, and the fact that the products involved range all the way from automobiles to space vehicles.

Other countries have recognized the need for action and have increased their efforts to lessen the number of accidents through better safety standards and education. This desire for increased safety has taken place in Japan as well as in all of the Western European countries. The United States, however, has done comparatively little to provide and augment suitable controls and safeguards with similar mandatory standards, and has few additional consumer product safety standards with which to lessen accidents, and minimize mishap causes or their effects.

Increased improvements in foreign safety through better standards, designs, and manufacturing have produced benefits in quality, reliability, and especially in safety, for such products as automobiles and electronic equipment. An additional result of the foreign effort, prior to the undertaking of similar programs in the United States, was a massive desertion by the consumer of American-made products, causing a serious and often irrecoverable economic effect. Not only did the adverse affect caused by unsafe products result in reductions in sales in the United States, but in Third World countries as well.

Purchasers in all countries now want only those products that meet acceptable safety levels, and countries that formerly imported American products because they were cheaper, will no longer do so when the products are considered hazardous. Today, lowest price is only one criterion. Whether it is price or safety that is more important can best be judged by the affect on sales of our foremost American products, such as automobiles, where, when there is a recall because of an unsafe situation, sales drop dramatically. Today, even if it is only *rumored* that a product is unsafe, a similar sales decline will also take place.

It is little wonder that liability suits resulting from accidents have become one of the major reasons for the United States being the most litigious nation in the world.

Accidents are also one of the major causes for increased product insurance, legal costs, and the reason for proposed legislative action in many states to limit the size of awards resulting from product liability suits. But action to control awards for liability does not constitute the way by which designers can minimize the creation of unsafe products, or lessen the number of accidents, and the adverse affects that derive from them.

Based on my many years as a safety engineer, I have some suggestions on how to help overcome the safety problem. We need to develop better safety-oriented engineers and designers adequately knowledgeable in safety and the means of accident avoidance, thereby resulting in safer products and operations, and fewer injuries, fatalities, and losses. Most importantly, the achievement of safer products and their operation can be accomplished *at no cost to the general public, to the manufacturers, or to the government at all levels*. This wondrous feat can, however, be accomplished by raising the level of safety expertise in all practicing engineers, with the added effect of helping to increase the esteem in which they are held. In order to do this, my suggestions are as follows:

1. In order to practice, all engineers should be registered or licensed in the same manner that all medical personnel are. (Registration of engineers in the past, supposedly to protect the health, safety, and welfare of the public, has been a sham, a delusion, and a failure. At present, only a fraction of all engineers must now be registered.)

2. Prospective practitioners of engineering should be required to pass an examination oriented and limited to matters of safety, accident causation, analyses, and prevention. (Courses on new methodologies of design will continue to be taught in engineering schools as they are now.)

Furtherance of these efforts will produce engineers better able to analyze all aspects of safety with greater technical knowledge of the means and methods for accident prevention.

For the improvement of product safety, therefore, this second edition includes, among other things, the following:

(a) A new method for the study of accident analysis, causes, and minimization (Sneak Circuit Analysis).

(b) Additional examples of Failure Modes and Effects, and Fault-Tree Analyses of consumer products.

(c) Past efforts to find means to determine foreseeability of avoiding adverse events such as accidents with products and their concomitant litigation.

(d) The first reasons for the initiation of standards, arising from technical advances, and the development and rapid adoption of a new highly desirable product for transportation—the railroad and the equipment on which it operates.

(e) A new hierarchy of safety methods for control of accidents, or the minimization of injury and damage if accidents should occur.

In conclusion, I would like to acknowledge and thank the following for their contributions and assistance: Bob McClay of Indiana University of Pennsylvania, who provided suggestions and information on this revision; for information and published papers I used on Sneak Circuit Analysis, especially from Tyrone Jackson of TRW and later from Hughes Aircraft Company; John P. Rankin of The Boeing Company (Houston); and E. Lloyd and W. Tye for information from their book *Systematic Safety* published by Civil Aviation Authority in London. I would also like to thank Mr. Peter Perkins, Product Safety Manager of Tektronix, Inc., of Beaverton, Oregon, who gave me the impetus to update the first edition of this book.

To all, I not only extend my thanks, but my hope that this book will assist substantially in the furtherance of the safety efforts in which we are all involved and concerned.

Willie Hammer
Senior Scientist
Hughes Aircraft Company (Retired)

Introduction

Build a better mousetrap and the world will beat a path to your door. If the better mousetrap turns out to have a substantial risk for humans, someone from a government agency may come up the path with a legal document asking that you recall, repair, or replace it. If it has been involved in an accident, a personal injury lawyer may come up the path with a liability claim right behind the government representative.

A pratfall by a comic may seem funny (humorous) because it was intentionally done. An accidental fall by an elderly person, however, in a bathtub or shower, or because of an icy sidewalk, a high step, a curb, or a flight of stairs, might (and often has) caused injuries that are funny (unusual, odd, or strange) only in the way in which they may have occurred. It is also accidents such as these that often provide the basis for liability suits.

Falls and impacts were probably the first human accidents to occur during man's primeval days. But, accidents with products undoubtedly began when someone got hit on the head by a falling stone hammer, or mashed their fingers when the newly invented lever slipped, or when the first rolling wheel impacted with, or ran over, some unsuspecting prehistoric person's toes, causing injury. Although these comments may appear facetious, they really point out that it was the continued development of products such as tools, other devices, and structures that created new hazards, thereby adding to the original problems of falls, impacts, fires, and drownings that caused accidental deaths and injuries.

Hazardous products might be as small as the molecules of a gaseous toxic substance, or as large as a house or commercial aircraft; as simple as an everyday tool, or as complex as a vehicle launched to reach outer space and the planets. Today, because of the variety and number of potentially hazardous products, there is a growing concern for safety and accident avoidance, where formerly accidents may have been acceptable and, in fact, considered a part of the high cost of technical progress.

This increased concern for safety and accident avoidance has come about because of several serious matters: (1) It has been said that the United States has become the most litigious nation in the world, and accidents and lawsuits for liabilities have become the major reason (whether or not the defendant wins the case); (2) the constantly rising cost of insurance premiums (every person and organization with any assets is insured) because of the concern of possible involvement, either directly or indirectly, in an accident; and (3) the ever increasing possibility for the recall of products because analyses or accidents with similar but different products have generated fears.

To cover themselves economically in such situations, manufacturers (and others in the chain of commerce involved with products) use insurance. In the past few years the cost of insurance has skyrocketed to where it is either prohibitive to obtain or becomes a formidable part of doing business.

Insurance companies are accused of overcharging and of making tremendous profits, and thereby growing rich. The insurance companies claim that they are losing money on liability insurance. They point out that new interpretations of the common law have made it easier for and more probable that plaintiffs will win personal injury suits, juries have been making larger and larger awards, legal costs have soared, there are more "nuisance" claims, and new laws are imposing new requirements, restrictions, and penalties.

Personal injury lawyers are accused of being "ambulance chasers" and of pressing claims that have little validity because they can make tremendous amounts of money in personal liability cases. The contention is that the contingency fee basis used for such claims increases the number of cases, increases the amount of each claim, and therefore increases the insurance costs. The personal injury lawyers point out that if there were no such contingency agreements, injured parties generally would not be able to afford the legal fees involved.

Legislative bodies are accused of being ineffective and of doing nothing to correct the situation. Insurance companies and manufacturers request legislation that would restrict the length of time during which claims for injuries could be filed, how awards should be determined, the limits to the size of awards, the limits to the fees lawyers could charge, and other provisions that would assist them. On one hand, there are accusations that legislators are influenced by the "rich" insurance companies and "powerful" manufacturing associations to provide restrictive legislation. On the other hand, there are accusations that most of the legislators are lawyers themselves and do not want such restrictive legislation.

The point that seems to be lost in all these accusations and arguments is that people are being injured and killed and much damage is being done to property. Many products are inherently hazardous because of the purposes for which they are to be used, but safeguards can often be provided to minimize and control these hazards. In some cases, hazards can be eliminated entirely or their probabilities of causing accidents reduced to such a low value that they can be considered to have been eliminated. The problem has been that those who design and manufacture these products are too often uneducated in ways of providing safeguards.

Until a very few years ago there was no engineering school in the United States which taught principles and methods of accident prevention to undergraduate engineers. Yet these undergraduates were the people who would become the designers of products. At the time this is written, a few such elective courses have been initiated so that hundreds of engineers out of all the thousands graduated each year are receiving such training. It was been estimated[1] that every year 35,000 new products are developed. With so few safety-trained and safety-oriented engineers and designers, many of the products eventually marketed will be unsafe.

Nothing is perfectly safe. Safety is relative; it is not absolute. But much can be done to reduce the number of accidents by improving the products we use. Making products safer will reduce the number of recalls, liability claims, and insurance costs, and it will provide other benefits. Figure 3-1 indicates some of the costs to which a manufacturer may be subjected because of safety-related considerations.

Of these, insurance premiums are certain; any company in business will have to pay them unless the company is large enough to carry its own risks. The costs for payments of claims have been going up and the possibility of having to pay a crippling amount is uncertain but present for most manufacturers. The only way to reduce or eliminate such claims is to produce a safe product.

In the past, the forcing functions that have lead to safer products and practices have been court decisions and legislative actions. Therefore, it would be wise to learn about these first in order to understand why and how they have influenced product safety technically.

Notes

[1] *Newsweek*, advertisement: "What's a New Idea Worth?," Nov. 17, 1977, p. 95.

Product Liability

Bases for Product Liability Actions

According to a 1973 survey by Hackett and Turczak,[1] 42% of the product liability cases they reviewed were based primarily on strict liability, 40% on breach of warranty (30% implied warranty, 10% express warranty), and only 18% on negligence. Since more and more states have adopted the strict liability concept since 1963, the percentage of cases in which negligence must be proved has probably decreased to a lower level. In all states that observe the strict liability concept, negligence need no longer be claimed or proved in product liability cases.

It was only in 1963 that the concept of strict liability was set by the Supreme Court of California. The rapid acceptance by most of the states and the impact on industry make it advisable that everyone involved with the manufacture and distribution of products be knowledgeable in the development of modern laws on product safety and liability and the present status of those laws. Many of the terms and principles involved are contained in Figures 2-1 through 2-3. Some of the legal milestones in product liability are presented in Figure 2-4.

History of Liability Laws

In the rapidly expanding economies of the Industrial Revolution in Britain and the United States, common and statute laws and their judicial interpretations were oriented to assist individualism and the growth of commerce and industry. To help the growing industries, with their attendant hazards, it was not considered desirable to inhibit *all* dangerous activities and conduct, only those considered unreasonably dangerous.

Before the Industrial Revolution, claims for injury or damages were predicated on laws of contracts and on laws of trespass (see Figure 2-4). Under the laws of contracts, a person could sue another person if there was a breach of the provisions of expressly stated provisions of an agreement. According to the laws of trespass and, subsequently, the so-called *Action on the Case*, a person who caused injury to another was strictly liable, even if the hurt was unintentional and done without fault or negligence.

To further the growth and progress which were the Industrial Revolution, the government, the courts, and the industrialists were willing to compromise safety for economic advantage. The necessity of having to prove fault or negligence on the part of an employer or manufacturer when an injured person claimed damages became the means by which industrial progress would be impeded least while affording a show of consideration toward safety in that unreasonable risks were to be avoided.

The dividing line between what was unreasonable and what was reasonable has never been defined definitively and it has always been subject to the opinions of those who have the final, authoritative say-so. Managers of the hazardous enterprises considered anything to be reasonable which benefited their enterprises and did nothing to interfere with earning a profit. The courts of the time agreed with them. It was no coincidence that the concepts of a plaintiff's having to prove negligence on the part of the defendant to win a case and that of "privity" occurred almost at the same time and at this time.

The principle of liability embodied in ancient laws, which had come to stress compensation of victims, went into temporary decline. Under the principle of trespass, a plaintiff did not have to prove fault or negligence, but after the middle of the nineteenth century proof of negligence or other fault on behalf of the defendant became an essential requirement for recovery of damages. By 1850 (Figure 2-4) it was said that "the plaintiff must come prepared with evidence to show that the intention was unlawful, or that the defendant was in fault; for if the injury was unavoidable, and the conduct of the defendant was free from blame, he will not be liable."

Terms and Principles Commonly Employed in Product Liability

Care —   *Great Care:* That high degree of care that a very prudent and cautious person would undertake for the safety of others. Common carriers, such as airlines, bus companies, and railroads, must exercise a high degree of care.
Reasonable care: That degree of care exercised by a prudent man in observance of his legal duties towards others.
Slight care: That degree of care less than that which a prudent man would exercise.

Discovery —   The legal process of determining as many facts pertinent to a case as possible by permitting the plaintiff access to the defendant's records and personnel. The plaintiff can request a court order for all documents which a reasonable person would ask for with good cause for a particular purpose in mind.

Exercise of due care —   Every person has a legal duty to exercise due care for the safety of others and to avoid injury to another if possible.

Express warranty —   A statement by a manufacturer or dealer, either in writing or orally, that his product will perform in a specific way, is suitable for a specific purpose, or contains specific safeguards.

Foreseeability —   A manufacturer may be held liable for actions that result in injury or damage only when he was able to foresee dangers and risks that could reasonably be anticipated.

Foreseeability for safe design —   A manufacturer must be reasonably careful in designing and producing a product to avoid injuring others by exposing them to possible dangers, or he is liable for damages. Where hazards cannot be eliminated, he is obligated to warn any prospective user of inherent dangers or properties of the product.

Implied warranty —   The implication by a manufacturer or dealer that a product is suitable for a specific purpose or use, or is in good condition, or is safe, by placing it on sale. The implied warranty of safety is the principle that any product by being placed on sale is implied to be safe. The implied warrant of merchantability implies that the product sold is in as good condition as other products of its type normally are. The implied warranty of fitness implies that the product is suitable for the purpose for which it is sold.

Inherent danger of a product —   A manufacturer must employ reasonable care to warn all prospective purchasers and legal users of hazards involved and of any inherently dangerous conditions in the product.

Liability —   An obligation to rectify or recompense any injury or damage for which the liable person has been held responsible or for failure of a product to meet a warranty.

Negligence —   Failure to exercise a reasonable amount of care or to carry out a legal duty so that injury or property damage occurs to another.

Negligence per se —   No proof of negligence required since it involves acts or the omission of acts of which no reasonably careful person would have been guilty.

Privity —   Privity indicates a direct relationship between two persons or parties, such as between a seller and buyer.

Proximate cause —   The relationship between the plaintiff's injuries and the plaintiff's failure to exercise a legal duty, such as reasonable care. If A playfully pushes B in a crowded space so C is hit by B, and C loses his balance, falls, and is injured, A's push is the proximate cause of C's accident.

Res ipsa loquitur (The thing speaks for itself) —   The principle that occurrence of an accident is sufficient proof that negligence existed. For the principle to apply, the item causing the accident must have been under the sole control of the defendant; the accident would not have occurred if proper care had been exercised by the defendant; and there was no contributory negligence on the part of the plaintiff.

Responsibility for handling —   A distributor, wholesaler, or retailer must exercise reasonable care in the handling and preservation of a product in his possession so that it will not later cause injury to a user.

Standard of reasonable prudence —   A person who owes a legal duty must exercise the same care that a reasonably prudent man would observe under similar circumstances.

Strict liability —   The concept that a manufacturer of a product is liable for injury due to a defect, without necessity for a plaintiff to show negligence or fault.

Tort—   A wrongful act or failure to exercise due care for which civil legal action may result.

Figure 2-1. Terms and principles commonly employed in product liability.

Grounds for Injury and Damage Claims

Type Of Claim	Principle	Plaintiff Must Prove	Common Defenses
Breach Of Express Warranty	Defendant is liable if injury is caused by a breach of an oral or written promise that the product will perform in any specific way, it does not and an injury consequently results.	1. A contract (Privity) existed between Defendant and Plaintiff. 2. The Defendant made a specific promise. 3. There was a breach of the promise. 4. The breach of the promise resulted in the Plaintiff's injury.	1. There was no contractual relationship between the Plaintiff and Defendant. 2. There was no promise. 3. No promise had been breached. 4. The time limit of the promise had been exceeded. 5. The Plaintiff was negligent in use of the product, exceeding stipulated limits. 6. Disclaimers or limitations of warranties.
Breach Of Implied Warranty	Products put on the market must be reasonably safe and fit for the ordinary purposes for which they are marketed.	1. The product was not reasonably safe for the purpose for which it was marketed. 2. The product had caused the injury or condition which led to the injury.	1. The product was reasonably safe when it left the Defendant's control. 2. The Plaintiff's negligence had caused the accident and resultant injury.
Negligence	A Manufacturer is obligated to exercise reasonable care in the design and manufacture of his product so that injury does not occur to a user or other person.	1. The product had a defective or harmful condition when it left the control of the Manufacturer, such as: • A concealed danger. • Failure to include needed safety devices in the design. • The design called for materials of inadequate strength. • A manufacturing defect. 2. The defective or dangerous condition in the product caused the injury. 3. The harm was foreseeable to the Defendant 4. The Manufacturer did not take reasonable precautions to guard against the harm.	1. Due and reasonable care was exercised by the Manufacturer. 2. There was no negligence on the part of the Defendant. 3. The accident and injury were due to the actions of others. 4. The user had been warned or had known of the hazard but had assumed the risk in use of the product.
Strict Liability	The Manufacturer can better sustain the loss from an accidental injury resulting from use of a product that can injure the user, even if the Manufacturer was not negligent. No need for privity or for the Plaintiff to prove Defendant's negligence.	1. The product had a defective condition. 2. The defect existed when it left the Defendant's control. 3. The defect made the product unreasonably dangerous. 4. The defect was the cause of the accident and injury.	1. The defect was the result of action by another after it left the Defendant's control. 2. The accident was due to a fault of the Plaintiff such as abnormal use or contributory negligence. 3. Allergy or susceptibility. 4. Disclaimers.
Liability Without Fault	Limited liability imposed by statute compensates Plaintiff.	1. An injury occurred. 2. Injury arose out of a situation covered by "No-Fault" Compensation Agreement. 3. Injury occurred during a period covered by the agreement.	1. There actually was no compensable injury. 2. The injury was not of a situation covered by the agreement. 3. The agreement was not in effect.

Figure 2-2. Grounds for injury and damage claims.

The Common Law

Much of English law (and subsequently American) developed in the form of statutes, but a great mass is found in the so-called "common law". Development of the English common law began after the Norman Conquest when limited, local feudal laws were gradually replaced by the more widely applicable law of the Royal Courts. The Royal Courts derived the common law almost entirely from decisions of judges rendered in actual cases brought before them. When enough decisions and precedents had accumulated they became the common law. (Common law therefore develops in a haphazard manner, according to the social mindedness, backgrounds, biases, and whims of the court at the time a decision and precedent is made. Codified law, on the other hand, is established at a specific point in time by an organized effort by or for a governing body or person, taking into account current practice, custom, and the desires and aims of the governing body.) It became a practice to refer to previously decided cases for suits under consideration. This rule of *stare decisis* ("to stand by decided cases"), or "case law," provided a measure of guidance on how judges might rule in future cases involving the same set of circumstances.

Stare decisis is not absolute. It can be changed and limited by legislative action (statute law). For example: in common law the right to recover damages for negligence was a right of the injured party only. If his death occurred before completion of his lawsuit, his dependents could not recover. To remedy this, states and the Federal government enacted statutes which permitted dependents to bring suits for wrongful death and for injuries to the deceased and to the dependents (such as loss of companionship).

Courts can reverse themselves if they believe they were in error. By a change in membership of a court the minority may become the majority. In the United States laws of one state may differ from those of another state on the same subject, and interpretations may differ even more. Precedents which must be followed can be established only by decisions of the highest court involved. When the Supreme Court of a state renders a decision on a matter, a precedent is set for lower courts within that particular state but not for other states or for the federal courts. Lawyers in other states who feel that such a precedent may help their case may cite it but the court in which the suit is being contested need not accept it.

The limitation regarding "the same set of circumstances" must be emphasized. Even what a layman might consider as very slight differences may permit judges to circumvent precedents they believe are no longer in consonance with current social philosophy and conditions, technology, and changed ideas. More than a hundred years ago a judicial opinion regarding decisions which differ from precedents indicated: "It is not only the right but the duty of the judge to take note of fundamental changes in public opinion."

By distinguishing the facts in a case before him from the facts presented to the judge who had set a cited precedent, any judge can appear to differ. He will, however, in effect be establishing a new precedent. These potential differences of judicial opinion create uncertainties which plague lawyers and litigants. There can be no certainty in any case that anyone will know the outcome before a decision is rendered. A lawyer may indicate the merits of his case to a client but any position on the result must be uncertain. Melvin Belli, a noted personal liability lawyer, pointed out in his book *Ready For The Plaintiff*, that in March 1955 the Supreme Court of Pennsylvania handed down a decision from which one justice dissented. Three months later the same court made a contrary decision in another case involving the same facts. The opinion of the former lone dissenter became the unanimous opinion of the court, and in almost exactly the same words.

Figure 2-3. The common law.

Some Legal Milestones in Product Liability

Date	Name	Significance
1750 BC	Code of Hammurabi	The person who injures another is liable and will suffer punishment identical to the injury he caused, whether the injury was intentional or not.
200 BC	The Old Testament	A person who injures another unintentionally may find sanctuary in designated cities where he may remain without harm until the high priest dies; then he may return home.
1300	Law of Trespass and Action on the Case	Any person who trespasses on another's property or person and in so doing causes an injury, even though unintentional, shall be punished by death if his action caused the death of another, and by confiscation of his property. Action on the Case involved considerations of injuries or damages which resulted because the defendant failed to take a necessary action. The fact that a death was unintentional could be used in a plea for pardon by the king. (The pardon of the king usually required peace be made with the family of the injured, generally by a pecuniary settlement.)
1837	*Priestly* v *Fowler*	Assumption of risk bars an injured person from recovery for injuries.
1842	*Winterbottom* v *Wright*	A seller is liable for injury by his product only to the party with whom he has contracted to supply the product (Rule of Privity).
1850	*Brown* v *Kendall*	Imposed the necessity of the plaintiff proving negligence by the defendant for the purpose of imposing liability for accidental injury.
1852	*Thomas* v *Winchester*	Exception to the Rule of Privity: Products considered imminently dangerous to life because of the manufacturer's negligence makes the seller liable for injury to any user of the defective product whether there was a contract or not.
1868	Fourteenth Amendment to the U.S. Constitution	Due-Process Clause interfered with passage of state laws to protect workers and the public.
1903	*Huset* v *J.I. Case*	Exception to the Rule of Privity: The manufacturer who delivers a product without giving notice of a known dangerous condition is liable to anyone injured in using that product.
1910	Worker's Compensation Acts	"No-fault" liability which limited damages an employer had to pay for an injury at work and limited the right of employees to sue their employers.
1916	*McPherson* v *Buick Motor Company*	A manufacturer has a duty to inspect products for defects; failure to do so subjects him to a claim of negligence if it places life and limb in peril. Also, the lack of privity should not affect a plaintiff's right to recover for his injuries.
1960	*Henningsen* v *Bloomfield Motors*	Each product, by being put on the market for sale, bears an *implied* warranty that it is reasonably safe for use.
1963	*Greenman* v *Yuba Power Products*	A manufacturer is strictly liable when the article he places on the market, knowing it will be sold without inspection for defects, proves to have a defect that causes injury to a human being. Also, costs of injuries are to be borne by manufacturers who put such defective products on the market.
1964	*Noel* v *United Aircraft*	The supplier of a product can be found negligent (and liable) by failing to make a newly developed safety device available to owners of the product, or in failing to warn them of a dangerous condition discovered after the product is delivered.
1968	*Barth* v *B.F. Goodrich Tire Co.*	Contributory negligence of plaintiff or others is no defense in a strict liability action.
1969	*Elmore* v *American Motors*	The policies which apply to the rights of any user of a product which result in his injury also apply to any innocent bystander who is injured.
1970	*Thomas* v *General Motors*	The manufacturer is liable for any and all foreseeable unintended uses, misuses, and abuses of the product and even for abnormal uses which were foreseeable and could have been designed against or otherwise safeguarded.
1970	Occupational Safety and Health Act	Principally imposes by statute a mandatory duty on each employer to maintain a safe place of work, with safe tools to work with, and safe work rules. To a much lesser extent imposes requirements on the worker.

Figure 2-4.   Some legal milestones in product liability.

1972	*Cronin* v *J.B.E. Olson Corp.*	That a product is defective (without consideration of whether it constitutes an unreasonable danger) and results in an injury is sufficient to impose strict liability on the manufacturer. Further that the plaintiff's awareness of the defect is no defense under the strict liability doctrine.
1972	Consumer Product Safety Acts	Authorizes a Commission to protect the public against unreasonable risks associated with consumer products; the Commission sets and enforces mandatory standards; bans hazardous products; and conducts research, information, and education programs.
1973	Balido v Improved Machinery	Warnings and directions do not absolve the manufacturer of liability if there is a defect in design or manufacture.
1973	*Glass* v *Ford Motor Co.*	The burden of determining whether the defective part was a manufacturing or design defect is no longer imposed on the plaintiff.
1973	*Borel* v *Fibreboard Paper Products Corp.*	Established legal requirements on manufacturing and selling products containing asbestos. Serves as a precedent for other toxic substances.
1975	*Lee* v *Yellow Cab*	In California this set the precedent that although plaintiff's negligence (however minor) contributed to his injury recovery of damages is not eliminated. The degree to which such negligence contributed to his injury shall be used to prorate the damages which he is entitled to recover. (Other states have similar precedents using the comparative negligence principle rather than following the old one of recovery if there was contributory negligence.)
1976	*Highway Traffic Safety Administration* v *General Motors*	Actual proof of harm is not required for a safety defect to be considered to exist in a vehicle. The government can therefore order defective products to be recalled even if the defect had not caused a collision or injury.
1976	Toxic Substances Control Act	Required adequate data to be developed regarding the effects of chemicals and chemical mixtures on human health and the environment. Interpreted in Dow Chemical Co. v Environmental Protection Agency (1979).
1980	Comprehensive Environmental Response, Compensation, and Liability Act (CERLA) or "Superfund"	Created policy and procedures for the identification, containment, and removal of sites contaminated with hazardous substances. Provided a broad federal authority to respond directly to threatened releases of hazardous substances dangerous to human health or the environment.
1981	*N. Jonas & Co.* v *EPA*	The federal regulation of pesticides was broadened to include substances that a reasonable consumer would use as pesticides given the label, literature, advertisements, and circumstances.
1983	Hazardous Material Storage Ordinance	A model ordinance was promulgated in Santa Clara County, California, after an underground storage tank in San Jose leaked 43,000 gallons of a chemical and had contaminated a public drinking water well. In 1984, a federal underground storage tank regulation program was instituted.
1984	*Widson* v *International Harvester Co.*	Equipment furnished without a safety device may be considered defective even if the device is offered as optional equipment.
1987	Federal Clean Water Act	The original Federal Water Pollution Control Act (1948) was amended in 1972, 1977, and 1987. It identifies many toxic pollutants and hazardous substances.
1988	Lead Contamination Control Act	Attempts to prevent lead contamination from drinking water coolers. Also see Federal Safe Drinking Water Act.
1990	Hazardous Material Transportation Uniform Safety Act (HMTUSA)	The hazardous material transportation process includes the manufacture of transport containers, routing, shipment labeling, handling, and incident response. The federal Hazardous Material Transportation Act was amended to give the federal government preemptive responsibility in the transport of hazardous materials.
1990	Clean Air Act Amendments	The federal Clean Air Act, first enacted in 1955, was modified to improve air control pollution efforts. Many states have more stringent or supplemental regulations. See Pollution Prevention Act of 1990 relative to reporting efforts to recycle or reduce toxic releases to the environment.
1990	Corporate Criminal Liability Act	California provided for criminal charges if business managers fail to notify consumers of concealed product hazards or employees of dangerous working conditions.

Figure 2-4 (cont'd). Some legal milestones in product liability.

Privity

Even in those cases in which an injured party could prove negligence on the part of a defendant, the injured party sometimes couldn't even be heard in court. This was because of a decision made by Lord Abinger of England in 1842. His decision derived from the laws of contracts and involved the principle known as *privity*.

When A enters into a sales contract with B, privity exists between them. If B then resells the item to C, privity exists between B and C but not between A and C. Since there is no direct contractual relationship between A and C, C may not sue A, according to Lord Abinger.

Lord Abinger's decision in the case of *Winterbottom* v *Wright* was, in effect, rejected by later jurists. The consequences that Abinger indicated would result if he did not make that decision subsequently proved his foresight correct even though his decision may not have been.

Winterbottom was the driver of a mail coach that overturned because of a defective wheel. Winterbottom was injured in the accident. He sued the manufacturer of the coach (Wright) for damages. Lord Abinger ruled against Winterbottom on the ground that there had been no contract between the two and therefore there was a lack of privity.

In this case, Wright had sold the coach to the postmaster-general of England, for whom Winterbottom was driving. In effect, the only person who could sue Wright was the postmaster-general, and he had not been injured. Winterbottom could sue only the postmaster-general, who had not built the coach that had injured him. It was a *Catch 22* situation that affected not only persons injured in or by coaches but also workers injured in industrial plants. The machinery in those plants was built and sold under contract to the employers, who were rarely injured.

Lord Abinger's dismissal of Winterbottom's suit also stated that unless there was privity of contract, "every passenger, or even any person passing along the road, who was injured by the upsetting of the coach, might bring a similar (legal) action. Unless we confine the operation of such contracts as this to the parties who entered into them, the most absurd and outrageous consequences to which I can see no limit would ensue."

The precedent that privity must exist was later overturned, indicating that Lord Abinger was wrong, but the consequences to which he could see no limit have proved to be correct. Whether or not these consequences are absurd or outrageous is debatable, but the product liability situation does appear to have gotten out of hand. To understand what has happened, one must understand the legal changes that have occurred since then.

The first breach in the privity barrier occurred ten years after Lord Abinger's precedent-setting decision, but it applied only to products inherently or imminently dangerous to life, such as drugs, food, firearms, and explosives. The coverage of this decision was not well-defined. In 1903 another limited exception to privity was made in the case of a manufacturer who delivered a product that he knew had a dangerous condition but did not provide suitable notice of danger. The intentional concealment was considered to be a form of fraud on the part of the original seller and the seller was liable to the first buyer *and* to any other person injured while using the product. Of course, this decision affected only those cases in which it could be proved that the manufacturer had knowingly concealed information on dangers.

The decision that destroyed Lord Abinger's position by the almost unlimited scope of its applicability came in 1916 in an opinion made by Justice Benjamin Cardozo of New York. When the case was appealed, the appellate decision presented by Justice Kellogg included additional precedents. The decisions of the two courts involved three principles important to product liability cases.

In this case, McPherson bought a Buick automobile from a dealer. A wheel collapsed while McPherson was driving the car and McPherson was injured. He sued for negligence in that Buick failed to inspect and detect the defect in the wheel before it was released for sale. Buick contended a lack of privity existed since McPherson had bought the car from the dealer; therefore, Buick contended that McPherson could not sue. Justice Cardozo, speaking for the court, held that the manufacturer was liable for injuries resulting from the use of a product whether or not the product was inherently dangerous if there was evidence of negligence by the manufacturer in assembly of the product. Further, "If, to the element of danger there is added knowledge that the thing will be used by persons other than the purchaser, and used without new tests, then irrespective of contract, the manufacturer of this thing of danger is under a duty to make it carefully."

Although this decision began the general abandonment of the concept of privity Lord Abinger had established, the plaintiff still had to prove negligence on the part of the manufacturer and had to prove that the product was unreasonably dangerous at the time of manufacturer. If the thing was made with care, the manufacturer could be held blameless. A manufacturer did not have to make a product that was entirely safe and foolproof; the product had to be designed and manufactured with reasonable care and could expose the user to a reasonable risk.

The third significant aspect of this decision was that the suit can be directed toward a manufacturer for failure of a component produced by a subcontractor for installation in his equipment. For McPherson's case, the automobile was considered the dangerous instrument, not the wheel that collapsed. The plaintiff still may, and generally does, sue anyone in the chain of commerce who may be involved, leaving the court to decide where the blame lay when there is more than one party that could be held liable.

Implied Warranty of Safety

The decision which can be considered the modern beginning of the principle of strict liability also derived from an automobile accident. Automobiles may be sold with warranties which indicate that the manufacturer, through his dealers, will replace any part or assembly that proves defective during a stipulated period. This *express* warranty generally limits the manufacturer's liability to replacement of the defective part or assembly. Even more important is the *implied* warranty of safety that accompanies every product put on the market for sale.

Chrysler Motors sold a Plymouth to Bloomfield Motors, a dealer, from whom it was then purchased by Mr. Henningsen. While Mrs. Henningsen was driving the car a few days later the steering mechanism failed, the car hit a brick wall, and she was injured.

The car was so badly damaged that it was impossible to prove that the steering mechanism had been negligently manufactured. The Henningsens brought suit for damages and injury against the dealer and Chrysler Motors.

Chrysler contended that the express warranty limited its liability only to replacement of the defective parts. The company also claimed privity of contract as a defense. The court quickly overruled the privity aspect. It also ruled that any product put on the market for sale carries *implied* warranties. One of these is the implied warranty of safety: that the product, by being offered for sale, is reasonably safe for use. It became apparent that every product placed on sale will have such an implied warranty unless the purchaser agrees to the provisions of a suitable disclaimer.

A manufacturer's express warranty generally limits the time the warranty is in effect, the equipment or portions thereof covered, and the extent of replacement: labor, parts, or both. An implied warranty has no such limitations. (Other express warranties, such as those printed in advertisements or made in oral statements during a sales pitch, are similar to the implied warranties, but they are far more destructive to any defendant's case in which a breach occurs and a claim is taken to court.)

The court thus held *both* Chrysler and Bloomfield liable without having to prove there had been negligence. The court strengthened the position that there need be no privity of contract and added the comment that:

> The burden of losses consequent upon use of defective products is borne by those who are in a position to either control the danger or make equitable distribution of the losses when they do occur.

That losses should be borne "by those who are in a position to...control the danger..." engendered the concept that a manufacturer will be held to be as knowledgeable regarding his product as an expert in that field must be to provide a safe product.

The phrase "The burden of losses...is borne by those who are in position to...make equitable distribution of the losses when they do occur" did not express a new idea. This concept, that the manufacturer is better able to sustain losses than the injured party, is a reiteration of the view expressed by Sir Thomas Raymond in 1682.[2]

The theory is that manufacturers can recoup their losses by including them as business expenses, from liability insurance, by increasing their prices to customers, or by combinations of these.

That privity was not needed was based on Justice Cardozo's comment: "The dealer was indeed the one person of whom it might be said with some approach to certainty that by him the car would not be used. Yet the defendant (Buick) would have us say that he was the one person whom it was under a legal duty to protect."

Strict Liability

Until 1963 a plaintiff had to prove that a manufacturer had been negligent in a way that made him liable for the consequences of any accident resulting from such negligence. In that year the doctrine of *strict liability* was established by the California Supreme Court in the case of *Greenman* v *Yuba Power Products*.

Mrs. Greenman bought her husband a combination power tool as a Christmas present. He later bought another attachment to be used on the tool. While he was using it as a lathe, the block of wood on which he was working came loose and struck him on the head. Greenman sued for damages and won, but the manufacturer, Yuba Power Products, appealed and lost again. This time the California Supreme Court issued a statement that involved the concept of strict liability:

> ...A manufacturer is strictly liable in tort when the article he places on the market, knowing it will be sold without inspection for defects, proves to have a defect that causes injury to a human being.

Another part of the court's opinion again points out that accident costs must be borne by the manufacturer and not the injured party:

> ...The purpose of such liability is to ensure that the costs of injuries resulting from defective products are borne by the manufacturer that puts such products on the market rather than by the injured persons who are powerless themselves.

What is most interesting about this case is that the court, in other parts of its opinion, concluded that there was a defect in design that made the product unsafe for use. In effect, the ruling indicates that there is no difference between a design defect and a manufacturing defect when strict liability is imposed. Subsequent rulings, especially in other states, distinguished between the two but still indicated that strict liability applies for either one. Under the need to prove negligence, it is extremely difficult to prove that a product was unreasonably dangerous because a designer had been negligent.

The doctrine of strict liability has now been accepted by the courts of almost all the states. The doctrine provides a great relief to the plaintiff in that he need not prove negligence on the part of the manufacturer. It still must be proved that the injury or damage was attributable to a defect or unreasonably dangerous[3] condition of the product and that the condition existed when the product left the control of the manufacturer. The strict liability principle has practically destroyed negligence as a basis for suit in product liability cases in those states in which the principle has been adopted.

Bystanders

Lord Abinger's prediction that without privity of contract every passenger of a vehicle, or even any person passing along the road, who might be injured, might bring legal action against the manufacturer of the vehicle is now a fact of life for any product. In 1969 in the case of *Elmore* v *American Motors* it was ruled that any person, not only the owner or operator of a vehicle, could sue if injured. Mrs. Elmore was driving a car manufactured by American Motors Corporation when something on the underside of the car failed and caused it to swerve so that it hit an oncoming car. Mrs. Elmore was injured and a Mrs. Waters, in the oncoming car, was killed. Mrs. Elmore and the family of Mrs. Waters brought suit against American Motors. American Motors claimed that Mrs. Waters was not a user or operator of their car and therefore they were not liable for damages. The court not only ruled against the car company but did it in terms that extended the coverage to all such effected persons, or bystanders, and killed the privity rule forever in product liability cases:

> If anything, bystanders should be entitled to greater protection than the consumer or user where injury to bystanders from the defect is reasonably foreseeable. Consumers and users, at least, have the opportunity to inspect for defects and to limit their purchases to articles manufactured by reputable manufacturers and sold by reputable retailers, whereas the bystander ordinarily has no such opportunities.

Third-Party Suits

As a result of the accident indicated above, Mrs. Waters' family could have sued Mrs. Elmore, but instead the family sued American Motors. This is known as a *third-party suit*. Such suits are especially prevalent when the third-party is known to be capable of paying off large claims and judgments. (This is also known as the deep-pocket principle.) In other cases, the plaintiff might legally not be able to sue the party immediately responsible. This has become widespread in industrial accident cases. An injured worker covered by a worker's compensation law generally cannot sue his employer (see Figure 2-5) unless there has been gross and willful negligence. He therefore sues anyone else whose action might have contributed to his accident and injury. Such claims are often higher and the suits are fought longer because the injured person or his family receives worker's compensation which provides support for living expenses and, generally, all medical costs. In addition, the employer's insurer may be supporting the injured party's suit.

The insurance industry claims that on property liability insurance, of which product liability is a part, it lost $4.5 billion in one year. To recover some of their losses, individual insurance companies themselves are generating claims against other parties such as manufacturers or their insurers. One insurance company may be obligated to pay worker's compensation to an injured person. To recover its costs, this insurer will institute a suit on behalf of the injured party, generally against the manufacturer of the equipment involved in the accident. If the suit has merit and the worker's compensation insurer wins the case, the insurer collects the expenses and costs to which it was subjected and turns any remainder over to the injured person.

In many instances, the person covered by worker's compensation will bring suit but will be supported by his employer's insurer. In such suits the plaintiff can lose nothing and has much to gain. In 1977 a young man in California was awarded $1.1 million after he lost eight fingers in a press that had a defective safety switch. A person who would receive only worker's compensation for loss of *all* his fingers would have gotten slightly more than $40,000 plus a small lifetime disability pension. During the time until the case is tried and a verdict reached the worker receives an income from his worker's compensation. There is therefore not the urgency to settle a claim that there would be if the plaintiff had no income. These considerations are inducive to any person injured in an industrial accident in which he is covered by worker's compensation to make a third-party claim against a manufacturer, if he can. The American Mutual Insurance Alliance states that more than 70% of all cases over $100,000 involved industrial accidents, which constituted only 30% of *all* product liability suits. Industrial equipment manufacturers are therefore subjected to larger claims than most other product manufacturers.

Even insurance companies have been subjected to third-party suits. Insurance companies make inspections of the facilities and equipment of the companies they insure. There have been cases in which their inspectors or safety engineers have failed to detect deficiencies which later resulted in accidental injuries. The persons injured have subsequently sued the insurers. This precedent may someday to extended to product liability cases. If an engineer for a product liability insurer examines a product and

Worker's Compensation and Product Liability

Historically, an employer has been obligated to provide his employees with: a safe place to work and safe tools with which to perform the work; competent fellow workers and supervisors; rules by which all could perform safely, enforcement of the work rules; and knowledge of hazards which might be encountered in the work which were not readily apparent. If a worker was injured because of an obligation he believed was breached, he could sue for indemnity on the basis the employer had been negligent. The burden of proof was on the claimant, who frequently was reluctant or had great difficulty in proving the employer negligent. If he had been temporarily disabled, the injured person would not sue for fear he would not be permitted to return to his job or would not be able to find a similar one with another employer. In addition, fellow employees who knew of the employer's negligence would not testify for fear of losing their own jobs. Also, the courts of the time were heavily biased towards the employers. The employer (or his insurer) could successfully defend himself by showing the employee had been negligent himself (even to a minor degree), a fellow employee's negligence and not that of the employer had been the cause of the accident, or that the employee had known and assumed the risks involved in his work.

Alabama in 1885, Massachusetts in 1887, and other states passed employer liability laws which turned out to be totally ineffective in preventing or lessening accidents. The liability laws were predicated on reducing the employer's defense of using the common law principle of assumption of risk. If the employers could lose more cases, the theory went, they would do more to prevent accidents. Instead, the employers did little but increase their insurance coverage, whose rates went up. The existing system had five major drawbacks: (1) Insufficient compensation: injured workers generally received so little for an injury they were often impoverished and they or their dependents frequently became charity cases; (2) Inconsistency of awards: there was no consistent pattern to the awards, and one claimant might receive one-tenth that which another had received for similar injuries under similar circumstances, or nothing at all; (3) Delay: cases generally took six and sometimes twelve years to be tried and adjudicated, drawn out by insurers who knew that the injured worker and his dependents usually had no other source of income and would often settle for very little; (4) Employee-employer antagonism: the employer's insurer which took over his liability for accidents did its utmost to minimize payments and nothing to maintain good relations so that the employees grew resentful towards the organization they knew, the employer; (5) Wastefulness: the system did little to help employees, was of benefit only to the insurance companies and to participating attorneys, and was extremely costly to employers. Employees and employers therefore called for corrective action and new legislation.

The first state worker's compensation laws, passed by Montana in 1909 and New York in 1910, were declared unconstitutional on the basis that because they were compulsory, they violated the Due-Process Clause of the Fourteenth Amendment. The state of Washington passed a law calling for compulsory insurance which was upheld by its Supreme Court, Iowa passed an "elective" law in 1911, and New York passed a revised compulsory law, all of which were upheld by the Federal Supreme Court in 1917. Twenty-three states still have elective laws; the remaining states, the District of Columbia, and Puerto Rico each have compulsory laws; and the federal government has two compulsory laws: the Federal Employees Compensation Act and the Longshoremen's and Harbor Workers' Act. The provisions of each law are different and interpretations of even comparatively similar provisions are different.

Worker's compensation is "no-fault insurance"; the worker receives benefits as long as the injury resulted from an accident, the accident arose out of his employment, and it occurred during the course of his employment. The worker cannot collect if the injury was caused by his intoxication, arose out of an altercation in which he was the initial physical aggressor, or was one he intentionally caused. To receive these benefits, employees gave up most of their rights to sue their employers, who might be sued in cases of "willful negligence." Some states prohibit suits against fellow employees whose negligence caused the injury; others permit such suits to be instituted.

Even when the benefit schedules for injuries were originally established, the amounts paid were generally inadequate to maintain the workers and their dependents in the manner to which they were accustomed. Since then, with rapidly rising living costs, the situation in regard to worker's compensation has grown even worse. (Some companies, unions, and states provide additional insurance or assistance.) Whenever he/she can, therefore, the injured person attempts to sue a third party, such as the company (or companies) which made, sold, maintained, modified, or inspected the equipment which injured him/her. Successful suits almost always bring awards far higher than the injured person would receive from worker's compensation, and in some cases more than he/she would have received in earnings during his or her lifetime. (See text.) The number of third-party suits for industrial injuries has increased tremendously since the strict liability concept was first accepted and is increasing yearly in numbers and amounts of claims. Industrial equipment manufacturers are therefore asking for stricter and more frequent inspections by OSHA (Occupational Safety and Health Agency) personnel.

Figure 2-5. Worker's compensation and product liability.

fails to note any deficiency, the user is led to presume that the product is safe. If, however, the user is injured, the insurance company might be sued. Such suits have already been instituted, and in some cases won, against testing laboratories that have tested products, found that the products met their criteria, and implied that the products were safe by putting their labels on them. Users assume that the labels indicate that the products are completely safe when they are not. When the users are injured, they then institute third-party suits.

Product Accidents in the Military Service

Since 1946 any military person, or his or her survivors, is entitled to receive the same benefits to which any civilian, injured or killed in an accident, would be entitled, as the result of a liability suit. A suit can be directed towards any third party, except the federal government. At one time it was thought that because the military profession was such a hazardous one, persons in the armed services, or their families, were not entitled to sue for injuries suffered. Now, however, any accidentally injured military person can file a claim for liability against the maker of a product, the user of the product, or any part of the product that might have contributed to the accident.

Other Concepts and Liability Problems

The "Second Collision" Principle

For manufacturers, the product liability problem will probably continue to grow worse. Another new concept to plague them is that of "second collision." Under this concept, a manufacturer may be responsible for subsequent consequences of an accident which his product had not caused. Example: a motorcyclist skids on a slippery street and hits a projection on a truck which results in an injury to him. According to the "second collision" concept, the maker of the truck might be held liable; if the projection had not been there, the motorcyclist might not have been injured.

Engineering Advances

For many years rulings of the courts in matters of accident prevention and liability were used as guidance by engineering personnel. Now safety engineering has been moving ahead of the courts in certain areas. When the courts learn of these technical advances, their decisions may be influenced. For example, the courts have held that a manufacturer has a duty to warn of any hidden defect. Engineers contend that if the manufacturer knew enough to realize there was a defect about which he must provide a warning, the manufacturer should have done something

about it. In one case a worker was operating an industrial vacuum cleaner when its rotating impeller burst, pieces tore through the casing, and the worker was injured. His claim, with which the court agreed, was that the manufacturer had failed to provide an adequate warning. Engineers would also have found the manufacturer guilty, but on the ground that the design was defective. The casing should have been strong enough to contain within itself the pieces of the burst impeller. At some future date a court may find a product defective even when it has a warning which today would be considered adequate.

Class Action Suits

In a class action suit litigation is initiated on behalf of anyone who could suffer from a deficiency in a product which caused injury to one of them. Because of this there have been claims in amounts of $100 million or more. However, courts have narrowed the number in a suit to those who have agreed to become party to the suit. Even so, a claim which individually might be small could assume tremendous size.

Comparative Negligence

It was previously held that if a plaintiff's negligence in any way, even to the slightest degree, contributed to his injury, he would not be compensated. Many felt this to be an injustice. In *Barth* v *B. F. Goodrich Tire Co.* the precedent was established that contributory negligence of the plaintiff or others is no defense in a strict liability action. The plaintiff could recover even if his negligence had in part (generally less than 50%) contributed to his injury (comparative damages). The degree to which such negligence contributed is used to prorate the liabilities. Thus, if the liabilities were assessed at $15,000 and the plaintiff's negligence were found to be 10% of the cause of the accident, he/she would recover $15,000 − 0.10 x 15,000, or $13,500. The significance of this ruling is, of course, that where defendants formerly paid nothing if the plaintiff had been negligent, now they will have to pay. This will increase the number of awards and consequently the costs of insurance.

Reasonable and Unreasonable Care/Risk

The dividing line between what was considered reasonable and what was unreasonable[4] has never been defined definitively. As a result, managers of the hazardous enterprises considered anything to be reasonable which benefited their enterprises and did nothing to interfere with earning a profit. The courts of the time agreed with them. As a result, not only was the general public endangered but working conditions in industrial activities grew to be abominable. Attempts were made to control the situation by passing corrective laws. In the United States the Fourteenth Amendment of the Constitution, passed after the Civil War, unexpectedly proved to be a severe obstacle to such corrective action. Its Due Process Clause[5] was interpreted so that it was boon to employers and a detriment to passage of state laws which attempted to eliminate unsafe working conditions. Any state law attempting to regulate occupations violated "the liberty of the individual in adopting and pursuing such calling as he may choose." Such laws were considered to be "meddlesome interference with the rights of the individual."

Use of the Due Process Clause as a basis for declaring state laws regarding working conditions unconstitutional was ended by the Federal Supreme Court in 1937. The new laws which required improved working conditions required safer industrial equipment and other products. At about the same time, federal regulatory agencies began to blossom in number and authority. Standards which they and the courts considered "reasonable" began to be far higher than those which industry considered "reasonable," and these agencies had the power and authority to enforce their concepts. So-called "consumerism" also demanded improved levels of safety of both the manufacturers and of the regulatory agencies. Thus, the courts, the economic impact on manufacturers, and the regulatory agencies have all tended to increase what should be considered as reasonable care in the manufacture of products and to reduce the risks to which the public is exposed.

Foreign Markets and Liabilities

Companies that do business outside the United States are no longer restricted to giant multinational corporations. Moderate and small-sized companies might find their products sold in other countries, even if they had never intended such sales. An exporter or other dealer could buy a quantity of a product from a manufacturer and send it abroad. The manufacturer may then become liable for any injuries which result.[6] The trend in product liability laws in other countries is toward increasingly severe restrictions. The European Economic Community (EEC) has prepared a draft directive whose adoption is expected in the near future to standardize product safety and liability measures. At the present time, the requirements and legal aspects of product safety differ from country to country. France and Luxembourg have, in effect, established no-fault liability, similar to worker's compensation, in which the injured party has only to show that any injury or damage was caused by the defective product. Some countries *presume* fault on the part of the manufacturer unless he can show he exercised due care. Most of the other countries require the plaintiff to prove fault on the part of the manufacturer. In 1975 Britain passed an industrial safety law which laid the onus for equipment safety directly on the manufacturer of the equipment and not on the employers as the Occupational Safety and Health Act (OSHA) of 1970 does in the United States. The new EEC draft directive[7] indicates, among other measures, that: (1) the producer of an article shall be liable for damage caused by a defect in the article, whether or not he knew or could have known of the defect; (2) the producer shall be liable, even if the article could not have been regarded as defective in light of state-of-the-art development when the article was put into circulation; and (3) a product is defective when it

does not provide for persons or property the safety which a person in entitled to expect. The directive indicates that any person who imports an article into the EEC for resale shall be treated as its producer. With a united European Community becoming a reality in 1992, these tough product liability restrictions will become universal throughout all European member countries.

An article in *The Wall Street Journal* (March 3, 1977, p. 28) indicates that the EEC proposals are based on the "strict liability" concept now prevalent in the United States; the exception is that the defendant producer must prove that the product was not defective when it left his control. In the United States the *plaintiff* must show that the product was defective at such time. The article also points out that the 17-nation Council of Europe is also considering a product liability code, which, however, may not be mandatory.

Notes

[1] Hackett and L. Turczak, *Analysis of Basic Causes of Product Liability Losses*, Proceedings of the 1976 Product Liability Prevention Conference, New Jersey Institute of Technology, Newark, New Jersey, 1976.

[2] "In all civil acts the law doth not so much regard the intent of the actor, as the loss and damage of the party suffering." Sir Thomas Raymond, in *Bessey* v *Olliott*, 1682.

[3] The terms "unreasonably dangerous," "reasonable care," "foreseeable," "state-of-the-art," and numerous others can only be ill-defined and must be resolved by the court or jury in each individual case. In effect, they are not as the manufacturer or designer consider them but as they will be considered by the judges or jury.

[4] Judge Learned Hand gave his opinion that "unreasonable risk" is a function of three variables: (1) the probability that the risk will result in harm, (2) the gravity of injury if that should occur, balanced against (3) the burden on the manufacturer to take adequate precautions to prevent such an occurrence.

[5] "No state shall make or enforce any law which shall abridge the privileges or immunities of citizens of the United States, nor shall any state deprive any person of life, liberty, or property, without due process of law; nor deny to any person within its jurisdiction the equal protection of the laws."

[6] In 1971, when hearings on the Consumer Product Safety Bills were being held in Congress, the Special Counsel to the Electronics Industry Association commented on why such an act should not apply United States standards to exported products: "If the countries to which the products are being exported have standards of their own, the products would have to meet them before they enter the country. If the country has no such standards, that is its affair, and the

United States standards should not be imposed." If foreign standards were as bad as those of most of the electronics industry at the time, there would have been problems. If there were no standards, and United States standards were not used, there would have been two problems: (1) liability in case accidents occurred and (2) the resentment of the countries importing the equipment that they were being treated as second-class persons, with the implication that the lives and well-being of their citizens were of less importance than those of Americans. The drop in sales for the second reason could have been far more damaging than any liability suits.

[7] Alan St. John Holt, "New International Requirements for Product Safety," *Hazard Prevention*, November/December, 1977, p. 16.

Questions

1. In accordance with what legal principle can a manufacturer be held liable for an injury caused by an unintended use of his product?

2. What is an express warranty? Explain if it must be in a contractual agreement or if it can be imposed by other means.

3. What is an implied warranty of safety? For how long after a product has been sold is it normally in effect?

4. Define negligence. What must a plaintiff prove in order to collect damages where negligence is claimed?

5. What is the concept of strict liability? What is a plaintiff not required to prove in a strict liability case that he must prove in a negligence case?

6. Define privity. Explain how privity used to affect liability claims.

7. What is a third-party suit? Why is a third-party suit frequently used with industrial injuries?

8. Why are industrial equipment manufacturers asking for stricter enforcement of OSHA standards?

9. Discuss whether or not a product designer who has never had formal instruction in accident prevention principles and methods can be said to be using "reasonable care" in the design of a product.

10. Discuss whether or not a designer can be held liable for injuries resulting from an accident due to an error he made in design.

11. How would Justice Cardozo's comment in *McPherson* v *Buick Motor Company* regarding the relationships between Buick, the dealer, and McPherson have applied to *Winterbottom* v *Wright*?

12. Discuss what is meant by negligence in design and production of a product. How can a lack of foreseeability generate a safety problem; would this lack be more liable to occur in design or production?

13. Many of the legal milestones listed in Figure 2-4 were originated because of injuries with automobiles such as *McPherson* v *Buick Motor Company*, and *Henningsen* v *Bloomfield Motors*. Discuss which of these two might have been a production or design problem or both.

14. Discuss how maintenance, or its lack, will affect the possibility of failure and the occurrence of an accident. Show how all the factors indicated will affect warranties, sales, and recalls.

15. Indicate what you believe are the major reasons for recalls of modern automotive products. Do you believe these recalls are justified? How will recalls affect product safety?

3

Safety Costs and Losses

Courts have held that the cost of making a product safe must be included in the cost of the product itself. Manufacturers are in business for the purpose of making money, and they want to keep their production costs as low as possible. Few manufacturers understand all of the cost factors involved, and many take a short-sighted view of the actual situation in regard to costs for safety.

Many manufacturers considered that once their product left their plant and was in the hands of the ultimate consumer, it was no longer their responsibility. If anything did happen for which they were liable, their insurance coverage would take care of the problem. The cost of insurance was minor.

The cost of insurance has risen tremendously. A company can usually obtain insurance but sometimes only at a prohibitive or very high cost, and often, punitive damage costs are uninsurable. The subject of costs of providing safety in a product is being reconsidered to include not only the immediate costs in providing safeguards by design but also the various costs and benefits which might be engendered over the life cycle of the product. A small savings by elimination of a safety device might prove financially disastrous if an accident occurs in which someone is injured because the safety device was lacking.

In 1983, a decision resulting from another accident, this time with a Ford Pinto, resulted in a final award of $12.4 million, after many appeals and re-appeals. The initial award was $10.1 million to a young driver injured in 1970, after the brakes on his car failed, and he suffered major injuries resulting in lifelong brain damage. After the verdict, Ford asked for, and was granted, a new trial. Once again the plaintiff won, but this time the award was reduced to $9.2 million. Ford appealed, yet again, this time to the State Court of Appeals, which ruled in favor of the company. The California Supreme Court, however, disallowed the findings of the lower court, whereupon Ford appealed to the U.S. Supreme Court which refused to stay payment of the award. By the time this ended, and Ford withdrew its appeal, 13 years had passed and accrued interest had raised the total amount now due the driver to $12.4 million.

After many demands by the public and a ruling by the Department of Transportation regarding the use of air bags or other types of automatic restraining devices, automobile companies finally were required to provide such safeguards to protect the occupants of automobiles against severe impacts and rollovers. Although air bags will protect the faces and chests of drivers, and often of front seat passengers, against impact with the windshield, it is also necessary that some type of seat belt or shoulder harness be worn because of the possibility of severe impact against the side of the vehicle, or in the event of rollover.

An example of an automobile accident in which air bags for front seat occupants might not have been of great use is in the case of *Gosper* v *Toyota*. On June 9, 1990, a jury awarded $5.37 million to Cynthia Gosper when her Toyota Sr5 pickup truck rolled over after being rear-ended while she was driving it on vacation in Arizona. Gosper suffered severe injuries resulting in her becoming a quadriplegic, and the money awarded was to be divided between her two children.

The jurors found that there was a defect in the truck's design that caused it to topple out of control from a paved highway, also causing the driver's side door to pop open, thereby throwing Gosper from the truck. A question also arose regarding the truck's stability. Gosper had been driving about 55 mph when she was hit by a station wagon traveling at between 70–90 mph. After the impact, the truck skidded off the highway, swayed on two wheels, and rolled over several times. Gosper was thrown through the opened door and suffered a broken neck. It is doubtful, however, that air bags alone would have prevented her from falling from the truck when it rolled over, or that they would have prevented the injuries that resulted.

Jurors initially came back with an award of $6.2 million, but reduced the damages by 15% because of the belief that her failure to wear a seat belt contributed to the extent of her injuries. The jurors agreed, however, that the truck's design was flawed, but were split in their decision on whether the defect was in the truck's stability, or in the door latch that opened.

Ralph Nader and the Center for Auto Safety said, "Studies show that the Toyota four-wheel drive truck does have a high roll-over rate." According to the Fatal Accident Reporting System for model years 1984 to 1986, 30 out of 35 roll-overs involving Toyota four-wheel drive trucks resulted in fatal accidents. Liability attorneys say the Gosper verdict will spur others on to file lawsuits, and the decision is to be appealed.

Another accident of interest, involved the question of foreseeability. According to the law, prudent persons should be able to anticipate the risks, harm, and adverse affects to which they may be subjected because of their conduct. According to this, people must act reasonably in order to prevent accidents with injury or damage, and if a person fails to behave in a reasonable manner, the deficiency may be considered to be one of negligence on that person's part.

This means that a person who operates a motor vehicle and fails to anticipate the adverse consequences of motor vehicle operation may be liable for any injury resulting from a lack of foreseeability. The vehicle operator must, therefore, foresee the hazards that might exist on the highway, such as hazards from other vehicles and pedestrians, and from fixed items on, in, or near the road or adjacent to it, such as traffic signal stanchions, advertising signs, and street lights.

On June 4, 1990, the *Los Angeles Times* reported that Mary Elizabeth Henderson of Grenada Hills had sued three companies and the County of Los Angeles, alleging that she was severely injured when a car in which she was riding struck a traffic pole in June 1989. The Los Angeles Superior Court suit, which seeks unstated damages, maintains the pole was not designed to minimize injuries in collisions. The defendants included Pomco Inc., American Corporation, and the Pacific Metal Division, as well as the county.

Life Cycle Safety Costs

The life cycle of any product ranges from the time the product is conceived until it is finally properly disposed of. The life cycle durations of products differ. That of toys may be very short; that of heavy industrial equipment may be very long.

Failure to consider the various phases its products will pass through has plagued heavy equipment manufacturers. Equipment, after being sold to its original purchaser, has sometimes been modified, resold, and remodified, and then many years later it is involved in an accident. The original manufacturer was then sued, sometimes 15 to 18 years after the equipment was originally built.

Measures to control and minimize safety problems must be initiated at the start of the life cycle of any product, planned for its foreseeable life,[1] and exercised over its life. The costs to do so become part of the overall risk program costs.

Accident Prevention Program Costs

The product life cycle can be divided into phases during which specific tasks must be accomplished if the product is to be considered safe, if the probability of its having to be recalled is minimized, if accidents with their attendant claims are to be eliminated, and if insurance costs are to be reduced. These tasks, described in Chapter 12, require coordinated and cooperative managerial and technical activities if the product safety program is to be successful.

The cost of such safety programs at the time of manufacture in relation to other product costs varies. Affecting factors are the product's intended function and complexity, the severity of the injuries and damage an accident could generate, the participation of human operators, the size and status of the program, and numerous other factors. Unfortunately, it has been thought that product safety programs add unduly to the costs of a product. Usually this is not true. To a great extent the added costs of making a product safe, over what a product will normally cost, become imposingly high because of corrective changes that must be made to conform the product to the originally intended design and reasonable safety.

In many cases, these changes are made only after test failures, customer complaints, recalls—either voluntary or forced by regulatory agencies, or accidents have occurred. The new philosophy is that a good product safety program can save money for a manufacturer.

If it is assumed that increased accident prevention program costs result in safer products, the program may pay for itself in reduction or elimination of design change tasks, recalls, and of accident and claim losses. In addition, a good product safety program can also support legal defense to prevail in alleged claims or litigations, and might help prevent high increases in insurance premiums.

Insurance Premiums

Insurance means that the cost of accidents is paid not only by the company involved in any claim action but also by other companies that have had no involvement. Insurance spreads the risk of doing business. The companies that perform well, have safe products, and are subjected to no or few claims are, when purchasing insurance, actually paying for those whose products are less safe and are involved in accidents. One manufacturer pointed out that in 1974 the premium for liability insurance on his product was $1,210. In 1977 the same insurance cost $72,000, even though the product had never been involved in an accident and the company had never been subjected to a claim. The company could not do without the insurance because insurance was required by the large retailers through whom the product was sold. The higher cost of the premiums had to be reflected in the price of the product. The manufacturer did not feel that this would change his competitive position in relation to other manufacturers since they would be similarly afflicted. All would be affected by the increase because the buyers' market would probably be reduced by the higher cost.

An association of manufacturing press builders reported that in 1968 eleven of its members paid insurance premiums which totaled $274,000; in 1975 they paid just under $2 million. In subsequent years (figures currently unavailable) they probably paid far over that amount.

A manufacturer who had been subjected to numerous claims has pointed out that $10 of each of the $54 it charges for a football helmet is for product liability insurance. A manufacturer of heavy construction equipment stated that it would take $30 million in sales just to make a profit sufficient to pay the premiums for product liability and property damage insurance.

Companies that had been involved in accidents sometimes found it almost impossible to obtain liability coverage; when they could find an insurer, the premiums were impossibly high. One small-sized shop equipment company that had been involved in accidents and litigation found that its product liability premiums increased from $2,000 in 1973 to $10,000 in 1975; then its policy was canceled. Insurers who would quote cited premiums of $150,000 to $200,000, approximately 10% of the annual sales of the company. The directors of the company voted to liquidate at a loss and the firm went out of business.

An alternative to paying high liability insurance premiums is *going bare*, that is, not carrying any insurance. Some companies do this if they have good records and are capable of sustaining any losses imposed on them. They do not consider it reasonable that with their relatively safe products they must bear the burden of covering companies that produce unsafe products.

One company decided to go bare when its insurer indicated that it would no longer carry the company's product liability insurance. The company had an excellent record (44 years in business and only two claims, neither of which has been settled yet). Another insurer would provide insurance in 1977 at a cost 20 times that of 1976 with one-sixth the coverage. As the head of the company indicated: "Paying a premium almost equal to the amount of coverage seems to us to be against the whole idea of insurance."

A product manufacturer must therefore evaluate whether or not the use of his product embodies such a risk that his company will find it beneficial to participate in an insurance arrangement. If so, the manufacturer may have to decide the upper and lower limits of coverage he will need and whether or not he can afford the premiums. If he can't, he should consider the alternatives.

Recalls

The term *recall* is also intended to include items which may be repaired, replaced, or repurchased instead of being returned to the manufacturer. A recall may be required by a government agency which considers that the product has a defect that exceeds the agency's limit for the risk to which a user may be subjected. It is not necessary for the product to have already been involved in a mishap and to have caused harm before a recall action can be ordered. It only has to have a defect that could result in an accident. (See *Highway Traffic Safety Administration* v *General Motors* in Figure 2-4.)

Since the inception of motor vehicle recalls, a very high percentage of vehicles built in the United States have been recalled for one safety reason or another. In one year, 1972, more cars were recalled than were built (some of the defective cars had been built as far back as 1965). In 1977 a new record was set: 12.6 million cars were recalled.

Many of the items to be fixed were simple; occasionally the manufacturers mailed to the vehicles' owners the parts to be replaced or added along with instructions on how the parts were to be installed. It has been estimated that the cost of preparing and mailing notices, without any parts, is approximately $1.25 to $1.50 each. In 1977 approximately 12.6 million cars, both domestic and foreign, were recalled. The cost to prepare and send each notice and to make a change at a dealer's shop has been estimated to average $10 to $12. In that black year of 1972 General Motors had to recall almost 7 million Chevrolets at a cost of approximately $40 million. The fact which works to the advantage of the manufacturer is that even after having been notified many owners neglect to have the defect corrected.

During the same year the Ford Motor Company in one action had to recall and repair 436,000 vehicles at an estimated cost of $30 million, or more than $68 per car. The Ford Motor Company considered the expenditure advisable. More than 200,000 cars had to be recalled because there had been flash fires in the cars' engine air filters.

In 1975 and 1976 the Consumer Product Safety Commission took recall actions that affected approximately 10 million items in each of those two years. The individual costs of preparing and mailing recall notices are probably about the same for consumer products as they are for automobiles, but as a percentage of sales and profit they are far higher. The impact of a recall on a consumer product manufacturer might therefore be greater than that on an automobile manufacturer. The chief mitigating factor with consumer products is that large lots are often in the hands of wholesalers and dealers and can be easily withdrawn at slight cost in notices. Records are not kept of purchasers' names and addresses for most consumer products. It may be necessary to use the news media to warn owners of nonconforming items and to inform them what steps to take to have the item repaired, replaced, or repurchased. The rates at which purchasers return such items for repair or replacement are also generally very low.

Accident and Claim Losses

Figure 3-1 lists the types of losses that can result when a product is involved in an accident. Many of these costs can be accounted for directly and precisely; others can only be measured by the effects they generate. If the news media indicate that a product has been involved in an accident, a drop in subsequent sales is probable if there is an alternative product available. During 1971 sales of the Ford Pinto dropped 25% during a short period when the public learned that flash fires had occurred over a short period of time in the cars' engine air filters. Such sales drops are measurable.

In addition, many manufacturers are plagued with *nuisance claims*. Nuisance claims are claims which the insurance companies consider too small to justify the legal expense to contest. Many nuisance claims are not justified and some are outright false. Individually, these claims

---

Losses to a Manufacturer from an Accident Involving a Product Manufactured by the Company

There are numerous losses which can result from accidents. Not all of them apply to every specific product, and many of the costs are difficult to determine accurately, but even approximations will show that they can be financially damaging.

- Payments for settlement of injury or death claims, including awards to dependents and for plaintiff legal fees.
- Payments for property damage claims not covered by insurance. Such claims might also include:
  - Replacement costs for the product and other items damaged.
  - Loss of function and operations income.
  - Recovery and salvage costs of damaged equipment.
  - Expenditures of emergency equipment and supplies.
  - Costs of emergency assistance.
  - Administrative costs.
  - Plaintiff's legal fees.
  - Lost time and wages.
- Legal fees for defense against claims.
- Punitive damages assessed.
- Costs of accident investigation.
- Corrective actions to prevent recurrences.
- Slowdowns in operations while accident causes are determined and corrective actions taken.
- Penalties for failure to take action to correct hazards or defects or conditions which violate statutes.
- Lost time of manufacturer personnel, such as management and public relations people.
- Obsolescence of equipment associated with product which might have to be modified.
- Increased insurance costs.
- Loss of public confidence, and thus, revenue.
- Loss of prestige.
- Degradation of morale.
- Market share loss.
- Loss of company reputation for quality and safe product.

Figure 3-1. Losses to a manufacturer from an accident involving a product manufactured by the company.

may be small, but in the aggregate the total amount is substantial.

Because the cost to defend against a suit has increased, the threshold below which it is more economical just to pay off nuisance claims has also climbed. Insurance agreements generally stipulate that it is the prerogative of the insurer to determine which claims should be contested. A product manufacturer may believe that the claims are wholly unsupportable and, as a matter of corporate pride, oppose them; because of contractual stipulations the manufacturer may not be able to contest the claims.

The number of claims brought to court and the awards and settlements have also risen. The realization by the public that they can often collect for injuries or damages has increased the number of claims made. The increasing inclination of the courts and juries toward individuals instead of toward businesses has increased the number of decisions in favor of the plaintiffs. At the same time, the adverse attitudes of juries toward businesses and insurance companies has increased the sizes of the awards. In 1962 there was only one case in which the plaintiff won a damage suit of $1 million or more; there were two in 1963; as recently as 1969 there were only three; but by 1976 the number of $1 million plus awards ballooned to 43. By this time at least 250 Americans will have won damage suits of $1 million or more.

In the early 1960's there were approximately 40,000 product liability cases each year. Because of the strict liability concept and the lessened need to prove negligence in such cases, the number of claims and cases increased dramatically. The insurance companies indicate that there are now approximately 1 million product liability suits each year, but a report prepared for the federal government's Interagency Task Force on Product Liability puts the number at only 70,000. The true figure may be something in between, since many cases are settled out of court and only the insurance companies or the companies against whom the claims are made may have records.

The average award to plaintiffs has also been increasing steadily. In California the average verdict for 1972 was $94,000 (if the award of more than $14 million for the crash of a private aircraft is not included). By 1976 the average had more than doubled and was up to $200,000. Verdicts and awards throughout other parts of the country showed similar increases.

Losses to the insurance companies include the increased awards indicated and also legal fees, administrative costs, and other expenses. The insurance industry's Insurance Services Office (ISO) reported that:[2]

1. The insurers pay an average of $3,500 to defend against each product liability case involving bodily injury.

2. In addition to each dollar paid for claims, insurers pay defense costs of thirty-five cents in bodily injury cases and forty-eight cents in property damage. These costs are incurred no matter who wins the case.

3. The average payment is $13,911 per claim against each defendant and $26,004 per incident for bodily injury claims; and $3,798 per claim and $6,871 per incident for property damage cases.

4. Food products account for 56% of all paid product liability claims, but they constitute only 2% of bodily injury payments. Eighty-seven percent of the total claim dollars are paid for suits against manufacturers.

5. Less than 1% of the bodily injury claims make up more than 50% of the total bodily injury payments. Similarly, less than 1% of the property damage claims make up more than 45% of the dollars paid.

6. More than two-thirds of the claims paid are for less than $1,000.

Over 90% of product liability claims are settled before trial, even though a lawsuit is considered to have been involved. Some agreements between claimants and their lawyers stipulate that if a settlement agreement is reached before a case is brought to court, the legal fee will be a certain percentage of the total amount, for example, 33%. If the case must go to court, the percentage may rise to 40%. The plaintiff's lawyer may file the claim in court even when a settlement is imminent or foreseeable, make the settlement, and collect the larger fee.

Approximately 5% of bodily injury claims and 9% of property damage claims are settled by court verdicts. Data on settlement amounts are far less available than are data for court awards. Generally, the settlements are far smaller than awards for similar cases brought to trial; although it is difficult to compare the two, occasionally comparisons can be made.

The difficulty in establishing the costs of settlement is apparent from the following information published in the news media. On April 26, 1990, the *Los Angeles Times* described the reluctance of the Ford Motor Company to permit publication of the settlement amount in a lawsuit for $23 million, which resulted in an agreed upon settlement of $6 million. The hangup in the settlement came when Ford wanted the amount kept secret, but the Miller family, who had filed the suit, would go along with this only if Ford agreed to alert its customers to the need to equip its rear seats with shoulder harnesses. Ford refused to do this.

This case arose as the result of a head-on collision in a Ford Escort, in which one of the 11-year-old twin sons of James Miller was killed, and the other one left a paraplegic. It was the plaintiff's contention that there was a need for Ford to equip its rear seats with shoulder harnesses instead of lap seat belts only.

The bone of contention which prevented settlement of the suit was the argument by Ford that damage settlement suits are not the proper forum for setting seat belt policy—a rare breach in the increasing secrecy surrounding product and environmental safety cases, and medical malpractice matters. Ford, and other defenders of the push for silence, contend that making seven-figure settlements public can stimulate others to bring suit, and civil actions "are private matters" brought about by private litigants. Disseminating this information threatens privacy and property rights, according to secrecy advocates.

Justice Lloyd Dogget of the Texas Supreme Court told a conference, "I think many judges have shirked their responsibilities" in not seeing that suits over product liability have import far beyond the two parties involved. The majority decision of the Texas Supreme Court ruled for a presumption of openness for civil suits and sharply restricted the practice of sealing court records. This ruling was to take effect starting September 1, 1990.

Final settlements can be far less than the suit amounts which appear in the media. In 1968 a man was injured in a helicopter crash in Los Angeles. He sued the manufacturer of the helicopter for $500,000. In 1971 a jury awarded him $180,000. Unfortunately for the plaintiff, at almost the same instant that the jury announced its decision, he settled the suit outside the courtroom for $35,000.

In 1971 a young man was involved in a train accident in which his legs were so mangled that they had to be amputated. The railroad for which he worked offered him $700,000 to settle the negligence suit. The plaintiff and his attorney had asked for $2 million in damages, and a verdict for over $1 million was expected. The award by a superior court jury was for $200,000.

In 1972 the widows of three men killed in an aircraft crash sued the manufacturer and an aircraft dealer for $10 million. A few minutes before a jury reached a verdict, after a six-month trial in 1976, one widow accepted a settlement for her claim for $400,000. The jury reached a verdict rejecting the claims of all three.

In some cases, punitive damages may be assessed for the benefit of survivors when the defendant or his agent has committed an outrageous, malicious, or intentionally wrongful act. When a manufacturer has knowledge that his product is hazardous or has caused accidents and the manufacturer takes no corrective action to prevent further accidents, his conduct may be considered outrageous. When punitive damages are awarded, they are done so in addition to and separately from compensatory damages.

Early in 1978 a judgment of $2.84 million in compensatory damages and $125 million in punitive damages was made against the Ford Motor Company in California. The award was made to a young man who as a boy had been riding in a Pinto, made by Ford, when the carburetor malfunctioned and the engine quit. The car was hit in the rear by another car; this caused damages to the fuel tank from which gasoline leaked and was ignited. The boy was burned over 80% of his body; the woman driver of the car later died of burns (her family was awarded $659,680

in compensatory damages and $6,600 in medical costs). It was claimed that Ford could have provided a safe fuel tank for an additional $10 per car. The amount for punitive damages was based on the claim that Ford should not benefit by saving $10 per car which was unsafe. Since there were 12.5 million Pintos, the total savings was $125 million. The judge decided that the judgment was excessive and reduced the compensatory damages to $2.5 million and the punitive damage award to $3.5 million.

Today, more and more insurance companies are specifically excluding coverages for punitive damages from their contracts. Other contracts make no mention of whether or not punitive damages will be covered by the insurers. Some insurers are of the opinion that they are obliged only to pay compensatory judgments made against their clients and that actions of the courts to punish a manufacturer and force corrective action should not be negated by having the punishment absorbed by the insurers.

Notes

[1] The foreseeable life of a product may be far longer than its designed "useful" life. See Chapter 8. The manufacturer may consider a product has outlived its useful life, is worn out, and is obsolete in ten years. Maintenance, repairs, and modifications may make the product perform for someone many years more. The fact that the product may be operated for a period longer than for which it was originally designed should be considered by the manufacturer. (In some ways, this extra long life is a compliment to and verfication of the sound original design and manufacture as it relates to performance.)

[2] Insurance Services Office, Final Report - Technical Analysis (New York City, 1977).

Questions

1. Explain what would be meant by life cycle costs for safety. What types of costs would they include?

2. Discuss the types of activities during product development and manufacture which would be attributed to accident prevention and would require funds for accomplishment.

3. Why is the increase in insurance premiums more of a problem that should be resolved by an entire industry rather than by a single manufacturer?

4. What does "going bare" mean when applied to insurance? How is it done? Why are some companies doing this?

5. Why does the high cost of insurance sometimes punish manufacturing companies that have good product safety records?

6. Are all products subject to "recall" actions? Name some which are and some which are not. For those which can be recalled, are the numbers of items affected significant?

√ 7. List ten types of losses that can result when a product is involved in an accident.

8. It has been said that customers won't pay for safety in their products. Does there appear to be evidence that this is true or not true?

9. What have been the recent tendencies in court-imposed awards in product liabilities cases in regard to number of suits, who received the favorable decisions, and sizes or awards?

10. On the average, what additional percentage above the amounts paid for claims do insurers pay for legal defense costs? About what percentage of an award or settlement does a plaintiff usually pay his attorney? If a court award were for $10,000, how much would the legal costs cost the insurer, and how much would the plaintiff receive? What percentage of the insurer's cost does the plaintiff receive?

11. Is there any consistency in the amounts a plaintiff might receive from an award made by a jury and by an out-of-court settlement? Is either method fairer than the other?

12. What is the difference between compensatory damages and punitive damages? Why are punitive damages sometimes imposed? Discuss whether or not you think punitive damages should be paid by a company's product liability insurers.

13. Discuss the reasons for rising costs resulting from accidents.

14. What has been the effect on the cost of insurance premium?

15. Indicate whether the size of court awards by juries has risen in cases of product liability due to accidents. Has this also had an effect on out-of-court settlements and on the desire of injured parties to make claims and to sue?

16. Why has it previously been difficult to determine the amounts of settlements, and do you think this desire on the part of insurers of manufacturers will continue?

17. Discuss how, and if, the high costs of premiums and awards has led to increases in product safety. Cite some apparent changes in the design of the automobile.

4

Regulatory Agencies and Statute Laws

The first federal regulatory agency was the Interstate Commerce Commission (ICC). This agency was created toward the end of the nineteenth century principally to curb the abuses of the railroads. Roosevelt's administration, starting in 1933, saw a tremendous increase in the number and power of regulatory agencies. In 1938 the first agency responsible for product safety came into existence when the Food, Drug, and Cosmetic Act was passed. Figure 4-1 indicates some of the federal laws passed since that time. Figure 4-2 lists most of the federal organizations concerned with safety. All are involved with product safety in one way or another; many are also involved with operational safety.

The Interstate Commerce Commission originally had comparatively little power. Many of the current federal regulatory agencies have been given so much power that they virtually have life-and-death authority over the businesses they were created to regulate. In effect, a regulatory agency has legislative, executive, and judicial authority and functions. It can establish rules, regulations, and standards that have the force of law behind them without having been passed by a legislative body. In the case of *National Nutritional Foods Assn. v Weinberger*, a U.S. Court of Appeals ruled in 1975 that Food and Drug regulations developed in accordance with the Food, Drug, and Cosmetic Act, which authorizes such regulations, have the binding force of law. Challenges of regulations of other agencies would probably result in similar decisions.

In its executive capacity a regulatory agency ensures that its rules, regulations, standards, and the provisions of the enabling act are carried out. If they are violated, the agency can assess fines and penalties as would a court. If the action is contested, the action would be reviewed and adjudicated by a board established by the agency. In many cases, the agency and its board are not as impartial as the courts would be. The members are often persons who were appointed because they believed in the necessity for the legislation which created the agency and they are antipathetic toward those who violate the rules and regulations established.

Supporters of such regulatory systems point out the following benefits:

- Reduce litigation cost
- Maintain high priority for safe products
- Save taxpayers money
- Allow cost/benefit analysis for new proposals

The effectiveness of each such agency is generally dependent on the person in charge. Unfortunately, the top positions are filled by political appointees. The appointees are so different in their views, capabilities, interests, and relations with Congress and business that their accomplishments differ widely.

Since the activities of these governmental agencies have such impact on product safety and on the commerce related to products, it is advisable to review the principal agencies.

Food and Drug Administration (FDA)

Even in the very early practices of law, derived from even earlier common usages and practices in England, a vendor of tainted food or drink might be held strictly liable for any injury to a consumer. Thus in 1971, when the Bon Vivant Company of California, makers of gourmet soup, caused injury due to the presence of botulism in its vichyssoise, the amount of money awarded by the court because of this injury, and the subsequent loss of sales,

Federal Laws Addressing Product Safety

1927	Federal Caustic Poison Act
1938	Food, Drug, and Cosmetic Act
1947	Federal Insecticide, Fungicide, and Rodenticide Act
1953	Federal Fabrics Act
1956	Refrigeration Safety Act
1957	Poultry Products Inspection Act
1958	Federal Aviation Act
1960	Federal Hazardous Substances Labeling Act
1965	Federal Cigarette Labeling and Advertising Act
1966	National Traffic and Motor Vehicle Safety Act
1966	Highway Safety Act
1967	Wholesome Meat Act
1968	Radiation Control for Health and Safety Act
1968	Wholesome Poultry Products Act
1968	Fire Research and Safety Act
1969	Child Protection and Toy Safety Act
1970	Lead-Based Paint Poison Prevention Act
1970	Egg Products Inspection Act
1970	Poison Prevention Packaging Act
1970	Occupational Safety and Health Act
1970	Public Health Cigarette Smoking Act
1971	Federal Boat Safety Act
1972	Consumer Product Safety Act
1976	Toxic Substances Control Act
1976	Consumer Product Safety Commission Improvement Act
1977	Saccharin Study Labeling Act
1981	Consumer Product Safety Act Amendment
1983	Federal Meat and Poultry Inspection Act
1984	Toy Safety Act
1986	Asbestos Emergency Response Act
1990	Fire Safety Cigarette Act
1990	Consumer Product Safety Improvement Act

Figure 4-1. Chronology of federal laws addressing product safety.

drove the small company into bankruptcy. Despite the fact that the company pointed out that only a very small number of cans of soup, out of millions, had been found to be tainted, the adverse effect that this had on the public's trust in the company's products resulted in a massive financial loss, and its subsequent demise.

Similar instances of botulism in products from large companies (Campbell's Soup) have been found by the Food and Drug Administration, but the contaminated soup was withdrawn before the product was distributed and could cause injury, liability suits, and insurmountable publicity.

The Food and Drug Administration is one of the few pre-Roosevelt agencies having safety responsibilities. Certain of its functions were first initiated under the Food and Drug Act of 1906, but the Administration was first provided for in the Agricultural Appropriation Act of 1931. Since its first organization, its activities have varied in effectiveness depending on its director. The fundamental purpose of the FDA is to protect the health of the public against impure and unsafe foods, drugs and cosmetics, medical devices, and potentially harmful related products. Another area for which it has responsibility is in radiological health where it develops and stipulates safe limits and control standards for exposure of personnel to radiation. Because of its dissatisfaction with the standard for classifying and using lasers as issued by the American National Standards Institute (ANSI), the FDA has issued a standard of its own.

The FDA identifies health hazards of foods and drugs, sets standards for industry, and monitors to ensure that these standards are met. The FDA approves licenses for the manufacture of biological products and drugs to be marketed to ensure their safety. It checks observance of food standards, but it has neither the staff nor the capability to inspect all products put on the market.

Because the process of testing, reviewing, and confirming the results of tests of drugs, biological products, and medical devices is a lengthy process, there has been much criticism of the agency for its delay in granting marketing approvals. Approvals have taken as long as seven years, which is about twice as long as in some European countries. This criticism has been blunted somewhat in the past when the FDA refused to license production and sale of the drug thalidomide without a complete investigation. Thalidomide caused birth defects in babies whose mothers had taken the drug (obtained from foreign sources where its use was legal) during pregnancy. Recently the seven-year period has been reduced to two or three years, especially for drugs dealing with life-threatening diseases, such as AIDS (AZT). The agency also monitors not only the quality of biological products, drugs, and food on sale but also the manufacturer's, processor's, and distributor's facilities and quality control capabilities.

The FDA now tries to follow a policy of "deterrence" by preventing nonconforming products from reaching the market instead of finding violations after products have been distributed. In addition to keeping hazardous biological products and drugs from the market by not licensing or by forbidding their manufacture, distribution, or sale, the FDA can require that products it considers unsafe by withdrawn. It has the authority to seize products it considers potentially harmful to humans which are not withdrawn by the manufacturer (either the original

Federal Organizations Concerned with Safety

Organization	Address	Area of Concern
Consumer Product Safety Commission (CPSC)	1111 Eighteenth Street NW Washington, DC 20207	All consumer products except foods, drugs, cosmetics, medical devices, motor vehicles, boats, airplanes, radiation devices, tobacco, firearms, explosives, alcohol, and pesticides.
Department of Transportation (DOT)		
Coast Guard, Office of Boating Safety and Office of Merchant Maritime Safety	400 Seventh Street SW Washington, DC 20590	Boats and related equipment, ships and marine safety equipment, operation of ships, boats, and other vessels.
Federal Aviation Agency (FAA)	800 Independence Ave. SW Washington, DC 20591	Aircraft and their operation, airways.
Federal Highway Administration	400 Seventh Street SW Washington, DC 20590	Boats, highways, streets, terminals, and related equipment.
Federal Railway Administration (FRA)	400 Seventh Street SW Washington, DC 20590	Railroads and related industry equipment, facilities, and operations.
Hazardous Materials Transportation (Formerly, Materials Transportation Bureau)	400 Seventh Street SW Washington, DC 20590	Hazardous materials, pipeline safety.
National Highway Transportation Safety Administration (NHTSA)	400 Seventh Street SW Washington, DC 20590	Automobiles, trucks, buses, recreational vehicles, motorcycles, bicycles, mopeds, and all related accessory equipment.
Urban Mass Transit Authority (UMTA)	400 Seventh Street SW Washington, DC 20590	Subways, street railways, bus lines.
Environmental Protection Agency (EPA)	401 M Street SW Washington, DC 20460	Pesticides; air, water, noise pollutants; solid wastes; toxic substances which may affect the environment.
Food and Drug Administration (FDA)	5600 Fishers Lane Rockville, MD 20852	Foods, drugs, biological products, cosmetics, therapeutic devices.
Housing and Urban Development (HUD)	451 Seventh Street SW Washington, DC 20410	Mobile homes.
National Transportation Safety Board (NTSB)	800 Independence Ave. SW Washington, DC 20594	Accident investigations and recommendations for improvement of safety for all types of transportation equipment and activities.
Nuclear Regulatory Commission (NRC) (Formerly, Nuclear Regulatory Agency)	Washington, DC 20555 Street name not necessary	All nuclear facilities, equipment, materials, and their operations.
Occupational Safety and Health Administration (OSHA)	1825 K Street NW Washington, DC 20006	Industrial and construction equipment and workplaces, except for mines, nuclear facilities, and railroads, and their operations.

Figure 4-2. Federal organizations concerned with safety.

manufacturer of a product which comes under the Act or a product in which the seized product is incorporated).

The regulatory actions the FDA can either undertake or require are as follows:

- *Recalls:* correction or removal from the market of hazardous products. A Class I recall is invoked when there is a reasonable possibility that the use or exposure to the product will cause adverse health consequences or death.

- *Seizure:* withdrawal of hazardous products by means of a court order.

- *Prosecution:* criminal proceedings against an individual or firm for violation of the Food, Drug, and Cosmetic Act or its supporting regulations.

- *Injunction:* a court order that restrains an offender from continuing a violation.

- *Citation:* a notice that there is an apparent violation of the law which gives a firm or individual an opportunity to show at a hearing why there should not be a criminal prosecution.

National Highway Transportation Safety Administration (NHTSA)

The NHTSA was established principally to reduce the increasing number of injuries and deaths and economic losses resulting from traffic accidents. (It has other non-safety functions, such as protection of motor vehicles from having altered odometers, providing standards for improvement of gas mileage, etc.) It issues and ensures compliance with Federal Motor Vehicle Safety Standards which prescribe safety features and levels of safety performance. Motor Carrier Safety Regulations stipulate vehicle design features for trucks which affect the safety of drivers, their qualifications, hours of service, and recording and reporting of accidents. The Bureau of Motor Carrier Safety conducts road checks of vehicles and drivers. If a vehicle is found imminently hazardous, likely to result in an accident, or be in such condition that it might break down, the vehicle can be declared "out of service" immediately. Drivers can similarly be immediately forbidden to drive if the daily log shows that they have been driving in excess of permitted hours so that they might be fatigued and more than ordinarily prone to accident involvement.

The NHTSA investigates reports of safety-related defects in motor vehicles and can require their manufacturers to correct these defects if they were caused by design or manufacture. The NHTSA can require correction of safety-related defects even if such defects have not caused an accident or injury. This was affirmed in the case of *Highway Traffic Safety Administration* v *General Motors* (see Figure 2-4). Thus, the Administration is actively and strongly pursuing an accident-preventive policy of deterrence by anticipation and resolution of hazards rather than of reaction to accidents. The law that established the NHTSA requires that a manufacturer notify the Agency of any defect that it has found in its vehicles and the corrective action it intends to take. One of the commonest actions is to recall the affected cars and to have the defect corrected by a dealer. As mentioned on page 19, in 1972 numerically more cars were recalled than were built and sold. The agency has the authority to fine and penalize those who violate its regulations and standards. Each defective vehicle a company builds is considered a unit against which a fine can be assessed. As a result of *HTSA* v *General Motors*, the company was fined $400,000.

Occupational Safety and Health Agency (OSHA)

Under common law, an employer is obligated to provide employees with the following: a safe place to work and safe tools with which to do the work; competent fellow employees and supervisors; rules by which everyone can perform safely and assurance that the rules are observed; and information on any hazard not immediately obvious that might be encountered during work. From the high numbers of injuries and deaths occurring during the 1960's in industry, it was evident that corrective measures were needed. Control of working conditions by the states was deemed inadequate to relieve the problem.

The fundamental aim of the Occupational Safety and Health Act was to ensure, "so far as possible every working man and woman in the nation safe and healthful working conditions and to preserve our human resources." The law imposes as mandatory duties the common law obligations of employers. To a far lesser extent it imposes requirements on workers.

OSHA philosophy has been in agreement with modern safety concepts of deterrence by anticipation before the adverse effects become apparent from accidents. OSHA has required that places of work be made safer by eliminating or controlling hazardous conditions instead of through the use of personal protective equipment.

The largest number of complaints about OSHA and the standards it has issued have come from companies having the highest injury rates, companies employing from 20 to 250 people. The large companies are generally far more safety conscious, have taken accident-preventive measures even before the OSHA standards were imposed, have their own safety staffs, and find the economic impact of meeting the OSHA requirements far less burdensome.

The Occupational Safety and Health Act and the standards developed by the agency impose no direct requirements on equipment manufacturers. The requirements are imposed on the employers who purchase the equipment. A manufacturer may *expect* a purchaser of industrial equipment to install the necessary safety devices, but if an employee of that purchaser is injured because the purchaser failed to install the safety devices, the equipment manufacturer can be held liable (*Bexiga* v *Havir Mfg. Co.*).

Equipment manufacturers have been subjected to an extremely large number of third-party suits which they contend to be more the results of unsafe conditions permitted or created by employers. Therefore, equipment manufacturers tend to be in favor of stricter enforcement of OSHA standards. Any action that will reduce the number of accidents will also reduce the number of third-party suits.

Statute Law Versus Common Law

Statute law can overturn or limit the common law. Manufacturers have therefore requested, and in some states already gotten, slight relief in the form of restrictive legislation which, it is hoped, will reduce the product liability problem. There are, however, very few manufacturers of considerable size whose products do not cross state boundaries. When the products cross state boundaries, the companies are engaged in interstate commerce and are obligated to observe all pertinent federal laws. In addition, their products are subject to the statutes and common laws of the other states into which their products are shipped.

Some of the restrictive legislation that has been requested or has already been passed by states include:

- Abolishing or restricting the use of the doctrine of strict liability.

- Statute of limitation that restricts suits to specified periods from the time the product was purchased or manufactured.

- State-of-the-art defense that permits the defendant to show that the product was produced in accordance with the accepted state-of-the-art at that time. Also, the fact that any improvement was made in the product would not be held as a proof of deficiency of the discarded design.

- Amendments to worker's compensation laws that would place more responsibility on employers and minimize or eliminate third-party suits.

- Liability of a manufacturer to be nullified if it could be shown that the product met government safety standards at the time of manufacture.

Almost all of this legislation, proposed or already enacted, is directed toward helping the manufacturer. It includes little to protect the public by solving the fundamental problem that some products are defective and unsafe. The last piece of legislation on government safety standards is in itself a farce since for most consumer products there are no adequate government safety standards (see Chapter 5).

Consumer Product Safety Commission (CPSC)

The Consumer Product Safety Act of 1972, which has subsequently been amended a number of times, was originally passed because of the generally recognized need for an agency to protect the public against unsafe consumer products not covered under other laws.

The need for such legislation to safeguard the pubic against injury from consumer products was studied by the National Commission on Product Safety, appointed by President Johnson. The results of this study, released in 1970 in the Commission's Final Report, estimated that every year 30,000 persons were being killed in or around the home, 110,000 were permanently disabled, 585,000 were hospitalized, and 20 million were injured seriously enough to require medical treatment or were disabled for a day or more. The figures did not cover either vehicular or occupational accidents, only those resulting from consumer products. Many of these, however, were accidents involving the same kinds of tools and products used in occupational activities, often producing similar accidents and injuries.

The Final Report identified as causes of past accidents, 18 categories of consumer products with hazardous characteristics that had led to injurious accidents and claims for liability and compensation. Most of the injuries in these categories had been due to deficient product design, not to inadequate production quality, or products malfunctioning. Notable examples of these deficient products were:

- A toy bazooka which deafened the user's playmate.

- A wringer washing machine which killed a little girl, and crushed the fingers, hands, and arms of users.

- Baby furniture that strangled infants.

- Floor furnace grills on whose hot surfaces children were burned.

- Power tools which injured users because of a lack of effective guards for rotating blades, gears, or chains.

- Rotary lawn mowers which caused deep cuts or amputation of toes and fingers, and other injuries resulting from thrown rocks, pieces of metal, or other solid objects.

Because the Committee's Final Report indicated a critical need to protect the public against the risk of unreasonably hazardous products, Congress initiated legislation which resulted in the passage of the Consumer Product Safety Act in 1972. The Act's purpose, briefly stated, was to protect the public against unreasonable risk of injury from consumer products by assisting in evaluating the safety of these products; to develop safety standards; to promote research into product-related injuries. Federal authority over hazardous products was deemed necessary because prior control by state and local government was inadequate and because the distribution of most consumer products was national, and even worldwide in scope. Provisions of the Act defined the term "consumer products," and established the Consumer Product Safety Commission as a separate and independent agency.

The new Agency was given the authority to collect and disseminate data about hazards and other information pertinent to the safety of products, and to ban or recall for repair, replacement, or repurchase any product considered unreasonably hazardous. This in itself, it was reasoned, would force accident prevention measures to be taken by manufacturers of consumer products in order to avoid facing penalties for violations of the Act's provisions.

Subsequent to the creation of the Consumer Product Safety Commission, and the appointment of staff personnel, the Acting Director of the CPSC's Bureau of Information, William White, summarized the Commission's powers, indicating that it had been given the authority to:

1. Collect, analyze, and disseminate relevant injury and hazard data.

2. Conduct product safety investigations.

3. Test products and develop test methods.

4. Develop standards governing a variety of product characteristics.

5. Inform consumers of product hazards.

6. Ban products found to be unreasonably hazardous and not susceptible to any feasible safety standard.

7. Classify, ban, and seize hazardous products.

8. Require marketing notice and descriptions of new products.

9. Require certification that a product complies with the appropriate safety standard, plus notification as to the date and place of production.

10. Require manufacturers, distributors, and retailers to give public notice of deficient products (i.e. those products that fail to meet applicable standards or contain substantially hazardous defects).

11. Require manufacturers, distributors, and retailers of deficient products to:
    (a) bring the products into conformance, or
    (b) replace them with other products meeting the applicable standard free of charge to the consumer, or
    (c) refund the purchase price.

12. Inspect manufacturing plants, warehouses, or conveyances at reasonable times and only in product-related areas.

13. Require record keeping by manufacturers, labelers, and distributors of data that the Commission considers necessary for implementation of the Act. These records must be available for Commission inspection.

14. Refuse entry, test, seize, and destroy deficient imported products.

15. Subpoena records, documents, or witnesses.

16. Conduct hearings, file, and litigate suits; issue formal notices of noncompliance.

17. Obtain free samples of imported consumer products where necessary, and purchase, at cost, domestically-produced consumer products.

18. Construct and operate research and test facilities.

19. Establish a Product Safety Advisory Council of five members from consumer groups, governmental agencies, and consumer product industries. (This Council was eliminated by the 1981 amendment to the original Act.)

20. Establish federal-state cooperative programs.

Despite being the most comprehensive piece of safety legislation ever passed to that date by Congress, the Act failed to address an important underlying cause for the design of unsafe products. The Act provided no impetus to change the education received by engineers who ultimately became product designers. Traditionally the instruction for students and graduates of engineering schools has been oriented toward engineering science, and the development of new materials, processes, and technology. Seldom do design engineers receive formal instruction in the principles of product safety. Engineering education is traditionally directed toward designs that will produce performance under ideal conditions, but seldom are designers called upon to consider the consequences when products operate under less-than-ideal circumstances. Specifically lacking are strategies for producing designs that will minimize the opportunities for operator error. Although there are engineers experienced in safety matters and oriented toward strategies for safe product designs, those available are too few in number.

Another major obstacle faced by the CPSC in 1972 was the almost total lack of acceptable product safety standards. Though much attention has been devoted to developing new standards and strengthening existing ones, this process has proceeded at an agonizingly slow pace.

Efforts of the CPSC to a great extent are directed at providing information for the consumer about product hazards. The Commission has continually had to contend with the outmoded concept of most manufacturers, design engineers, and managers that accidents are primarily due to unsafe acts (errors or misuse) on the part of the product user. This mind-set causes the designer to often leave the products' hazards intact and to rely heavily on providing the operator with information in the form of warnings about hazards, and with long, detailed operating procedures for products being distributed in the marketplace. Many of these warnings and instructions often go unheeded by the product user.

That this concept is flawed has been evidenced by the arguments and court decisions in cases which occurred after the ruling by the California Supreme Court in 1963 regarding strict liability. These cases indicated that manufacturers had been negligent and liable for injuries caused by the design or production of products, be they for automobiles, consumer, or industrial use.

In and before the 1970's, product users could do little to change the design of unsafe products already being marketed, except to decline to buy them or to observe all warnings. Frequently, however, product manufacturers avoided the use of explicit product warnings. Warnings noted before sales might convince consumers to avoid the product since such warnings might indicate a severe hazard and the danger of injury. Economic actions by consumers concerning defective products are generally effective when a hazard, and the possibility of accidents, become widely known through news media coverage. In the 1980's the news media became much more aggressive in publicizing product hazards, often using CPSC data and product information.

Safety engineers have long held the concept that in order to have an accident, a hazard creating an unsafe condition must exist. If unsafe conditions could be eliminated or adequately controlled, even a totally inappropriate act, such as an error or the misuse of a product, would produce no accident. Intrinsically safe design makes products far safer than do attempts to eliminate accidents through consumer education by warnings about hazards and examples of accidents. Unfortunately, CPSC has met with only limited success in getting consumer product designers to adopt this philosophy.

Caught between political pressures from business desirous of less government regulation and consumers unaware of the agency's critical role, CPSC has experienced a steady decline in requested appropriations by administrations in office since 1972. However, many in Congress still believe that there is a critical need to regulate product safety, in an effort to reduce the number of injuries, deaths, and monetary losses from unreasonably dangerous products. Congress to date has given the Consumer Product Safety Commission a reprieve from dissolution, but the agency has never been funded as the drafters of the enabling legislation might have hoped.

Through more aggressive action on hazardous products, the CPSC could have been more helpful to both the public and to industry in improving consumer product safety. On the other hand, a more aggressive stance in the 1970's might well have resulted in the elimination of the CPSC in the 1980's when more conservative administrations took office. As a separate, independent agency, the CPSC is not a part of any department in the executive branch and has no cabinet officer to defend it when threatened by business lobbyists. To some safety observers, it appears that the CPSC in its early years should have focused more consistently on positive accident *preventive* designs and production control measures, rather than on warnings to alert consumers, or by resorting to recalls *after* products had caused injuries. Nevertheless, this agency today has many achievements to which it can point.

The Consumer Product Safety Commission, which had been confirmed as an independent regulatory agency, was assigned enforcement power under other legislative acts previously enforced by other federal agencies. Among these acts were: The Federal Hazardous Substances Labeling Act, The Child Protection and Toy Safety Act, The Flammable Fabrics Act, The Poison Prevention Packaging Act, and The Refrigerator Safety Act. The enforcement powers set forth in The Consumer Product Safety Act were also assigned to the CPSC, as stated earlier.

The CPSC has, for many years relied, in its enforcement strategy, on the mandates set forth in the 1972 Act requiring businesses to report product hazards. Failure to report them places the manufacturer, distributor, or retailer in a vulnerable legal position if the product is later found to be involved in accidents resulting in death, injury, or damage. In such situations, businesses are more willing to recall defective products without extensive and time-consuming litigation. Under the 1990 Consumer Product Safety Act Amendment, reports to the CPSC are required when:

1. The product fails to comply with a consumer product safety Rule, *or* a voluntary standard on which the CPSC is relying.

2. The product contains a defect which creates a substantial product hazard.

3. The product creates an unreasonable risk of serious injury or death.

4. The product is the subject of three or more civil actions where it is alleged to be involved in accidents producing death or grievous bodily injury, and where judgments for the plaintiff are found in three of these cases within a one-year period.

The CPSC has been successful in getting hazardous products removed from the market. In January 1985, the Honeywell Corporation agreed to pay a fine of $800,000, and to spend an additional $4.2 million, to inspect and replace valves that might be faulty on liquid petroleum gas furnaces and heaters. The company took these actions despite denying that anything was wrong with the valves.

One might still argue that it would be better if hazardous products were not allowed on the market in the first place. Under the CPSC's product recall strategy, action will only be triggered after a multiplicity of accidents and injuries have occurred and been reported. By the time corrective action, such as a recall, has taken place, many additional items will have been sold, and more consumers will have been injured or killed.

Mandatory Product Standards and Rules Enforced by the Consumer Product Safety Commission

Product Type	Legislation Under Which the Standard Is Enforced
Architectural Glazing	Consumer Product Safety Act
Asbestos Bearing Emberizing Materials	Consumer Product Safety Act
Asbestos Bearing Patching Compounds	Consumer Product Safety Act
Baby Cribs	Federal Hazardous Substances Act
Bicycles	Federal Hazardous Substances Act
Carpets and Rugs	Flammable Fabrics Act
Cellulose Insulation	Consumer Product Safety Act
Children's Sleepwear	Flammable Fabrics Act
Clothing Textiles	Flammable Fabrics Act
Coal and Wood-Burning Appliances	Consumer Product Safety Act
Electrically-Operated Toys	Federal Hazardous Substances Act
Extremely Flammable Contact Adhesives	Consumer Product Safety Act
Fireworks	Federal Hazardous Substances Act
Household Refrigerators and Freezers	Refrigeration Safety Act
Lawn Darts	Consumer Product Safety Act
Lead Containing Paint	Consumer Product Safety Act
Matchbooks	Consumer Product Safety Act
Mattresses and Pads	Flammable Fabrics Act
Omnidirectional CB Base Station and TV Antennas	Consumer Product Safety Act
Packaging—Child Resistant	Poison Prevention Packaging Act
Rattles and Pacifiers	Federal Hazardous Substances Act
Self-Pressurized Products Containing Chlorofluorocarbons	Consumer Product Safety Act
Small Toys and Toy Parts	Federal Hazardous Substances Act
Swimming Pool Slides	Consumer Product Safety Act
Unstable Refuse Bins	Consumer Product Safety Act
Vinyl Plastic Film	Flammable Fabrics Act
Walk-Behind Power Lawn Mowers	Consumer Product Safety Act

Figure 4-3. Congressional legislation and applicable product types for enforcement of Standards and Rules by the CPSC.

In an effort to go beyond sole reliance on a recall strategy, the CPSC has accelerated the dissemination of product safety methods through conferences and the production of product safety publications. The increasing effect of the CPSC, with its recall, rules, and litigation, has made most manufacturers aware of the effects of putting hazardous products on the market. Once, many safety specialists believed that common law suits in cases of product liability were more effectively instrumental in creating safer products than were the actions of the CPSC. A lawsuit for product liability due to consumer injury, leads top management, executives, lawyers, designers, and others to study similar products of their own as well as those of other companies, in order to determine whether or not *their* product could contain a similar defect that might result in an accident, injury, and liability suit. To a great extent today, the actions of the CPSC and the publicity given these actions by the media, have replaced the effects of liability suits.

To act as an effective deterrent, however, the requirements of the law must be understood by those who must comply. Terms like "substantial product hazard," "unreasonable risk," and "unreasonably hazardous" have legal mean-

ing, but have no agreed upon definition among safety professionals, much less designers and engineers unschooled in safety science. The CPSC has attempted to provide clearer guidelines about hazard degree, such as those in its *Product Recall Handbook* published in 1986. The 1990 amendment of The Consumer Product Safety Act also attempted to provide clearer criteria upon which product hazards could be judged.

In the 1970's, few mandatory consumer standards were available as guides for designers or as criteria with which the CPSC could judge products. As a result, many hazards were built into products and these were not recognized before the products were put on the market. Today, more mandatory standards, rules, and voluntary standards are available. Figure 4-3 lists mandatory CPSC standards and rules enforced by CPSC. With additional changes, withdrawals of defective products, and the economic failure of many offending producers, the safety level of remaining products will improve. The Law of Safety Progress (which I first expounded in 1972) says: "An unsafe product will either bring on corrective action or drive its producer out of business, thereby raising the safety level of all such products."

Another major CPSC effort consists of epidemiological studies to learn where consumer safety problems exist. This is done by recording and counting the numbers of accidental injuries reported to hospitals through the National Electronic Injury Surveillance System (NEISS), a system first devised by the staff of the National Commission on Consumer Product Safety. One hundred nineteen emergency rooms in hospitals throughout the country were originally contracted to submit data to the CPSC on consumer product related injuries on a daily basis. The results from this statistically significant sample can be projected to represent the whole country. The situations in which these injuries occurred are then analyzed to determine where additional data are needed, and where future regulatory activity should be directed. This information is also made available to the public.

Because of budgetary restrictions, the number of hospital emergency rooms reporting through NEISS had been reduced to 64 data reporting hospitals; however, in 1991 this number was again increased to 91. Figure 4-4 represents the data flow in the original hospital emergency room surveillance system. Today computers have simplified this process, but the essential features remain the same.

The data provided by NEISS indicates numbers and severity of injuries associated with product types, but gives little information as to whether the mishaps are caused by the products involved or whether these products are defective. The specific product involved and the casual factors leading to the accident are identified only in follow-up investigations by the CPSC. Special studies are also funded by the CPSC to gain additional information about specific product hazards and injury mechanisms. These investigations and studies essential to support the regulatory activity of CPSC have been impacted by budget cuts since the 1992 legislation was enacted.

The number of products over which CPSC has jurisdiction is staggering and is thought to exceed 10,000, partially explaining why such a sophisticated injury data collection system is necessary. Figure 4-5 shows products regulated by the CPSC and the Act which established this jurisdiction and enforcement powers. With so many products to regulate, it is also easy to understand why CPSC has not been able to develop safety standards for all of them. Out of necessity, existing voluntary standards are often used for enforcement purposes.

Many believe the use of voluntary standards to be far less beneficial to the general public than are the mandatory standards. The CPSC has, however, since its inception utilized many voluntary standards along with those which are mandatory. These standards indicate to the designer what features are needed to reduce the risk of accidental injury to an acceptable degree. By the use of voluntary standards, the CPSC has encouraged standards of development by numerous organizations, including manufacturers, technical societies, technical staffs of academic institutions, product testing companies, and government agencies. But as pointed out by David Pittle, in

Chapter 5, the accident preventive effort would have been far more effective if a policy of mandatory standards had been followed. Voluntary standards have been prepared for such products as: aerosol containers; bathtubs; shower stalls; camping tents; catalytic heaters; gas appliances; children's playpens; highchairs; home playground equipment; snowmobiles; and many others. The CPSC in 1989 continued its support for the generation of voluntary standards such as those on: all-terrain vehicles; arts/crafts materials; children's hook-on chairs; child-resistant closures; formaldehyde in pressed-wood products (particle board); glass bottles for carbonated drinks; pools, spas, and hot tub covers; indoor air quality; toy chests; audio-visual carts; and unvented gas room heaters.

The Customs Service assists the CPSC by examining imported products from other countries intended for sale in the United States, especially products for children. Importers are considered by the Consumer Product Safety Act to have the same responsibilities for product safety as do manufacturers and distributors.

The CPSC currently continues to provide information to manufacturers and the public and to press litigation through federal court actions. These actions include injunctions, seizures, criminal actions, civil penalties, inspection warrants, and subpoena enforcements. Over the years, significant reductions have been cited by CPSC in the numbers of accidental deaths and injuries from certain specific product types. On March 20, 1990, the CPSC claimed that since 1974, when child-resistant closures on specified products were mandated, an estimated total of 340 lives of children have been saved. This claim was based on the number of accidental ingestions occurring in the period from 1964 to 1986.

In 1989 there were 110 corrective actions by the CPSC where products were voluntarily withdrawn from the marketplace. For example, in that year, the San Diego Superior Court found Honda Motors Company not responsible in the case of a nine-year-old boy who received brain injury when he fell from a Honda ATV. Despite the outcome of this trial, Honda and other manufacturers of ATVs have decided to take them off the market.

In retrospect, the effectiveness of the CPSC and the federal effort to improve product safety in the U.S. can be given mixed reviews. Despite many achievements supported by the CPSC's unique and effective injury data collections system, some will point out that the full potential of the most comprehensive federal safety legislative act has yet to be realized. Several possible reasons have already been cited but a final one has to do with the Commission itself.

The 1972 Act authorized the appointment of five commissioners to direct the efforts of the CPSC. A variety of capable and talented individuals have been appointed by the President to these posts, and at times one or more of the Commission seats have remained vacant. Individuals so appointed have had backgrounds in government; have been consumer activists; have had experience as attor-

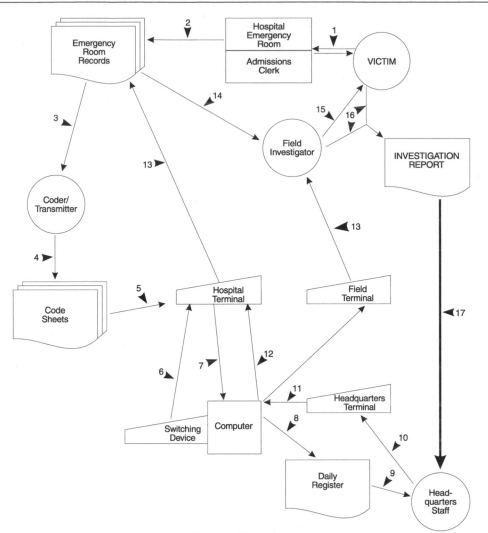

Key for Figure 4-4

1. An injured person is admitted to the hospital emergency room for treatment.

2. Basic information is obtained about the accident by the admissions clerk and is written on the emergency room record.

3. A hospital employee designated and trained as a coder/transmitter reviews records daily for those injuries involving consumer products.

4. This person transcribes coded equivalents for all relevant data to a code sheet.

5. At the end of each day's coding, the coder/transmitter types the coded data into a teletypewriter installed for this purpose.

6. During late night hours of low telephone line traffic, a special switching device attached to the headquarter's computer in Washington automatically polls each of the hospital-based terminals.

7. The computer edits the data for accuracy and completeness, and records the data.

8. The central computer then prepares a daily summary register.

9. The central computer also prepares detailed case printouts for headquarter's review each morning.

10. Headquarter's Staff type into their terminal hospital identification and case numbers for any items to receive a field investigation.

11. This is transmitted both to the appropriate hospital and

12. also to the CPSC field terminal.

13. Hospital personnel check the records for name, address, and telephone number of the victim.

14. This information is then given by telephone to the CPSC field investigator.

15. The field investigator initiates contact with the victim or family to conduct an investigatory visit.

16. He/she is visited at the earliest practicable time, usually within three days of the injury. A comprehensive interview is undertaken to verify surveillance data; identify make and model of the product; and to diagram, photograph, or collect a sample where appropriate.

17. Complete data on the product-related injury are collated then to form the investigation report which is sent to headquarters in Washington for confidential staff review and analysis.

Figure 4-4. Data flow in the original National Electronic Injury Surveillance System (NEISS).

Scope of Products Regulated by the Consumer Product Safety Commission

1. Apparel and non-apparel fabric regulated under the *Flammable Fabrics Act of 1953* (as amended).

2. Products which meet any of the below criteria are regulated under the *Federal Hazardous Substances Labeling Act of 1960* (as amended).

   - Toxins
   - Corrosives
   - Irritants
   - Flammable or Combustible
   - Strong Sensitizers
   - Radioactive
   - Those which can generate pressure through decomposition
   - Toys
   - Children's Furniture

3. Packaging, which is child resistant due to the hazardous nature of the materials within, is regulated under the *Poison Prevention Packaging Act of 1970* (as amended). The following materials may require such packaging:

   - All substances listed under item 2 above
   - Hazardous Foods, Drugs, and Cosmetics
   - Fuels

4. Under the *Consumer Product Safety Act of 1972* (as amended), consumer products are regulated and this has been defined to include:

   - Household Products
   - Products used in Education
   - Products used in Recreation

   (Exceptions under item 4 include Motor Vehicles, Pesticides, Foods-Drugs-Cosmetics-Medical Devices, Aircraft, Boats, Firearms/Ammunition, and Tobacco Products.)

Figure 4-5. Scope of products regulated by the Consumer Product Safety Commission.

neys, engineers, and homemakers; and have been qualified in the medical sciences. However, unlike other safety regulatory agencies such as OSHA, the Commission has never been served by a Commissioner recognized as a Safety Professional having certification either as a Professional Safety Engineer (PE) or a Certified Safety Professional (CSP).

Questions

1. How does a federal regulatory agency derive its responsibilities and powers?

2. Explain why it is considered that a regulatory agency has legislative, executive, and judicial authority and functions.

3. Which is the oldest federal regulatory agency having responsibility for ensuring safety of products?

4. What are some of the functions and responsibilities of the Food and Drug Administration (FDA)? What regulatory actions can it take?

5. What are some of the functions and responsibilities of the National Highway Transportation Safety Administration (NHTSA)?

6. What are some of the functions and responsibilities of the Occupational Safety and Health Agency (OSHA)? Tell how concern for safety in the workplace ties in with product safety.

7. In some European countries there are laws that make the manufacturers of industrial equipment responsible for the safety of the equipment. How does this differ from the OSHA requirements? Which would appear to be more effective?

8. What are the functions and responsibilities of the Consumer Product Safety Commission (CPSC)? List five of the most important functions, and the reasons you consider these more important than the others.

9. What authority does the CPSC have to correct a situation in which a marketed product is considered unreasonably dangerous?

10. What is meant by "deterrence by anticipation"? Do you think that agencies which follow such a policy are more effective in accident prevention than those which do not?

11. What is NEISS? What are the inadequacies of accident information received this way when the information is to be used by product manufacturers?

12. Discuss the difference between statue law and common law. Which has precedence?

13. What legislation has been either enacted by states or proposed to reduce litigation and the liabilities of product manufacturers for accidents?

14. Compare some of the effects resulting from actions by the CPSC and those of court decisions on liability due to accidents with products.

15. Express opinions on: (a) whether observance of standards should be voluntary or mandatory, and (b) whether standards should be prepared by product manufacturers.

16. The *Product Recall Handbook* issued by the CPSC calls for manufacturers, importers, distributors, and retailers to report a substantial hazard in a product. Why do manufacturers, importers, wholesalers, or retailers often fail to do so?

17. In what time period were most of the safety legislative acts passed by Congress? What historical reasons can be cited for this phenomenon?

18. Select five items in the room, determine if their safety is regulated by the CPSC, and, if so, under what Act would enforcement occur?

19. How might the CPSC respond differently to product hazards if it had members formally educated in Safety Science or certified as Safety Professionals?

5

Standards and Criteria

Although the dictionary indicates a number of meanings can apply to the word "standard," only two will be used in this book; one as the basis for a measure of distance, weight, or capacity, and two as the norm for common or accepted practice. The first usage is directed towards its technical aspect, while the second, under the section "Standards and the Courts" is indicated later.

The need for standards arose from the necessity to find the means for overcoming the chaotic conditions that existed, almost two centuries ago, because of the fierce entrepreneurship and individuality in calls for design and operation of new products, much of it unsafe. This situation was due mostly to the use of the new steam-driven equipment.

Railroads and Standards

In the late eighteenth and early nineteenth centuries, the magic phrase was *laissez faire*. This phrase not only meant freedom of choice, it also meant freedom from interference by decisions from the judiciary and government, and freedom from liability by employers, thereby permitting everyone to do as they wished. Standards not only did not exist as such, but any requirements that were followed were generally those of benevolent and compassionate factory owners who believed and accepted dicta from ancient biblical admonitions as guidance.

A prime example of the difference of the free inventive enterprise under laissez faire, combined with the latent conservatism of the time, and the desire to follow ancient customary usages, can be used to describe the effects on standards which had to be developed as a result of the birth of the new products of transportation, namely, railroads and the equipment on which they ran.

The width of the wheels used by the ancient Romans became that of the English equipment, 4′ 8-½″. In America, however, the situation was worse, because there was no agreed on standard at all, and in many cases the British usage was followed. Because of the individuality and laissez faire (combined in some cases with an inherent dislike, at the time, of the British), there was confusion, and companies in this country built railroads with differing track widths (gauges). And, even though rail types, sizes, and weights had been standardized by 1850, rail gauges still varied. By 1860, six gauges were in common use: the British standard that was used exclusively in eight states, and common in nine others, along with a variety of other rail widths that ran all the way up to six feet.

Entrepreneurs in California had already decided on a five-foot gauge, also approved by President Abraham Lincoln, in order to authorize a projected plan to build a railroad from the Mississippi, across the barren plains and mountains, to meet California's proposed railroad. Protests to Congress from other states that already had railroads, caused a veto after Lincoln's assassination, and led to the adoption of the British standard. Equipment being manufactured in Europe, for shipment around Cape Horn for use in California, had to be changed, causing long delays and higher costs. This was an early example of the effects of the lack of a common and definite standard. The use of these different standards within the United States often severely hampered shipments and interstate travel, because people, products, equipment, and supplies had to be transferred at various junction points. (Many inland towns became famous and were named after these railroad junction points.) It was said that during the Civil War, the lack of uniformity and standardization created serious military problems because massive numbers of soldiers had trouble reaching their positions.

Other problems with steam equipment, due to the lack of standards, were the differences in sizes, the threads of the fitting, and the thicknesses of pipe, thus creating difficulties in making good joints. Because of these differences in thickness, the strength and safety of the equipment also varied tremendously. In steam-powered equipment, for example, the boilers of steamboats, locomotives, and whole industrial plants blew up constantly; reportedly four to five every day, including Sundays. More than 1500 violent ruptures were reported each year, not only destroying the facilities, equipment, and plant operations, but also causing fatalities, injuries, tremendous damage, and loss of jobs. On October 8, 1894, 27 boilers blew up, one after the other, in Shamokin, Pennsylvania.

A standard to minimize the number of these accidents was needed, but it was two decades later, after the beginning of the twentieth century, that such a standard was produced, and the standardization of the design, production, operation, maintenance, inspection, and testing of steam-pressurized products was finally accomplished. The standard, in this case called a code, generated by the American Society of Mechanical Engineers (ASME), has been considered one of the foremost achievements of American engineering.

In the United States, laissez faire and the lack of use of a uniform standard, accepted elsewhere in the world still constitutes a serious economic problem. The rest of the world uses the metric system, while the United States uses the decimal system, thus products made in the U.S. often will not fit elsewhere unless specifically custom made. Sales of American products have, therefore, suffered greatly as a result.

Another example of the outmoded concept of laissez faire is the way in which nuclear power plants have been built: the same way railroads were hastily thrown together according to no one organized standard, resulting in differences in design, costs, construction, operations, maintenance, safety, and the need to make changes nationwide.

In France, use of a standard design avoided most of the American problems, both technical and economic, for such plants. This standard not only reduced costly designs and construction throughout the country, but also permitted greater ease in improvements for either those mandated by government authorities in the standard design or operation, or those made voluntarily in order to improve safety, or operational control in order to lower costs.

Objection to Standards

Gore Vidal once wrote, "The American has always reacted to the setting of standards the way Count Dracula responds to a clove of garlic or a crucifix." It was the thought of the conservative, outmoded man who still lived in the nineteenth century and who believed firmly in the concept of laissez faire.

That is the way many corporate personnel and engineers often feel when the provisions of a mandatory safety standard must be met. Any such requirement may be greeted with reluctance, since designers must first study and understand the new criteria in order to apply them properly and adequately. This is especially objectionable when observance could mean delay, inconvenience, or added cost, as well as loss of freedom to do as one wishes. Obsolescence of already prepared designs, parts, or even whole products could result, and there could be litigation if there is failure to meet the provisions of the new standard. For these reasons, designers and managers do not have the reaction referred to by Gore Vidal when the standard is voluntary, and thus can be ignored or accepted as desired, for these people accept what they might consider the low probability that a serious accident will occur.

Benefits of Standards

Despite all the reasons designers and others might give to the imposition of mandatory or voluntary standards, observance of a standard is beneficial to designers in a great many ways. A standard (using the term as a general designation for all types of criteria) often contains much useful technical information which engineers would be foolish to ignore and not use. A standard not only promotes consistency, but also basic levels of safety and dependability in similar equipment, materials, or operations. It helps eliminate the need for designers to search for information that is already available in a standard, because its initiation was based on an accumulation of past experience, both good and bad. The criteria or other requirements standards contain were originally generated to avoid the recurrence of accidents or the existence of hazards which indicated the potential for accidents. Standards were prepared to avoid situations that careful consideration showed could develop into problems unless suitable precautions were taken. In effect, they often indicate to designers what must *not be done*.

Standards help decide whether or not any proposed design is safe or taboo, and assist in making decisions regarding safeguards to be provided. They help lessen differences in opinion between designers, manufacturers, managers, and others regarding levels of safety, types of equipment, precautionary measures to be observed, and safeguards to be incorporated.

Benefits in the use of standards can be listed briefly:

1. Lessens the possibility of accidents.

2. Reduces the possibility of liabilities, lawsuits, and other legal actions. Proof that an accepted standard was observed can be an accepted and viable defense in a lawsuit for product liability.

3. Its provisions often indicate it is the accepted practice in an industry.

4. Presents previously evaluated methods of safe design.

Documents Which May Contain Criteria for Safe Product Design

Act —
A formal decision or law passed by a legislative body. Example: The Child Protection and Toy Safety Act of 1969 (Act of November 6, 1969, Public Law 91-113, 83 Stat. 187). An Act may contain authority to set up a regulatory agency, and indicate its purpose and authority. It may contain such information as technical requirements whose observance is mandatory, by whom such requirements should be prepared, by whom they must be observed, who should ensure their observance, and penalties for noncompliance.

Code —
A collection of laws, standards, or criteria relating to a particular subject such as safety, Examples: *National Electric Code*, registered trademark of the National Fire Protection Association, or California Vehicle Code.

Regulation —
A set of orders issued to control the conduct of personnel within the jurisdiction of the regulating authority. Federal Air Regulations, originally issued for this purpose, now also contain design criteria for aircraft.

Standard —
A rule or principle (or set of rules or principles) used as a requirement or as a basis for judgement. Example: Underwriters' Laboratories Standard UL 696 for Electrical Toys. A military standard, such as MIL-STD-454 (General Requirements For Electronic Equipment) frequently fulfills the same purpose as a military specification.

Specification —
A detailed description of requirements. A specification may be issued by anyone interested in procurement of a product, system, or facility. Example: Military specification MIL-B-5087 (Bonding, Electrical, and Lightning Protection, For Aerospace Systems).

Practice —
A series of recommended methods, rules, and designs, generally on a single subject, usually prepared for voluntary observance by representatives of an industry, and published by an association or technical society representing that industry. Example: American Petroleum Institute (API) Recommended Practice RP 2003, Protection Against Ignitions Arising Out of Static, Lightning, and Stray Currents.

Design Handbooks, Guides and Manuals —
Contain nonmandatory general rules, concepts, and examples of good and bad practices to assist a designer or operator. May contain pertinent information and discussions on all other types of standards; warnings and cautions; and operating and maintenance instructions.

Figure 5-1. Documents which may contain criteria for safe product design.

5. Ensures proper adherence to laws, codes, and other legal criteria.

6. Observance lessens cost of insurance premiums.

7. Ensures compatibility of parts, materials, and processes.

8. Ensures similarity of suppliers and reduces quotations for, and costs of, equipment and supplies.

9. Permits worldwide interchange of products and parts.

Standards and the Courts

The second meaning of the word "standard," when applied to matters of product safety, is commonly used to indicate whether the actions of a litigant have or have not been those of a "reasonably prudent" person. Courts have indicated a reasonably prudent individual will adhere to an acceptable level of conduct. This standard is in most cases what others, for example as in a jury trial, believe to have been a normal and acceptable level of conduct. Violation of that acceptable level of conduct may, in a court of common law, lead the court to assume that, under the circumstance, there had been negligence and lack of due care on the part of the defendant.

The results may determine whether performance of the defendant has been less than what might be considered an acceptable standard of conduct, with foresight and consideration to avoid injury to others. Even less prudent, and liable for penalty, would be someone who failed to meet a required code of conduct through violation of a stipulated mandatory criterion for the protection of others, such as a provision of an OSHA standard.

It has been said that the United States has become the most litigious nation in the world. Accidents and suits for

Comparison of Safety Standards

A capacitor or capacitive circuit can retain a high voltage charge even after power is shut off. A person who touches it and acts as a ground can get a nasty shock. The requirements for eliminating this problem with different equipment should be the same since the hazard, cause, and the effects are the same. The following list shows how five standards differ:

STANDARD	REQUIREMENTS
1. Military Standard 454	The capacitor or circuit must discharge to 30 volts in 2 seconds.
2. IBM Product Safety Criteria (Company Manual)	Discharge to less than 60 volts within 10 seconds after the circuit is opened.
3. *National Electric Code*, Registered trademark of the National Fire Protection Association. Art. 460 (ANSI Std C1).	Discharge to 50 volts or less within one minute after disconnect for capacitors rated 600 volts or less and in 5 minutes for capacitors rated more than 600 volts.
4. Underwriters Laboratories Std #478, Electronic Data Processing Units and Systems (ANSI Std C33.107)	A. Discharge to less than 50 volts within 1 minute. B. Where necessary to remove a panel with tools, provide instruction on the panel it is not to be removed for whatever time it takes for discharge (5 minutes maximum).
5. American National Standards Institute (ANSI) Std Z136.I (1973) For the Safe Use of Lasers.	If servicing of equipment requires entrance into an interlocked enclosure within 24 hours of the presence of high voltage within the unit, a solid metal grounding rod shall be utilized to assure discharge of high-voltage capacitors.

Figure 5-2. Comparison of safety standards.

liabilities have become the reasons (whether the defendant wins the case or not), for the rising cost of insurance premiums. Everyone and every organization with any assets is insured because of the possibility of involvement of some sort, direct or indirect, in an accident. Possible recalls of products generate fear of being found guilty of negligence and liability. Even when the defendant manufacturer has been found innocent, the costs of defense may be massive.

To cover themselves economically in such situations, manufacturers (and others in the chain of commerce involved with products) use insurance. In the past few years the cost of insurance has skyrocketed to where it is either prohibitive to obtain or becomes a formidable cost of doing business.

The courts have held that a manufacturer must be as knowledgeable about his/her product as any expert in that field. The manufacturer must know all the requirements that have been imposed by statute, issued by government agencies, published by technical and industry associations, and even those things known as "good engineering practices" that change with the state-of-the-art. When a designer or manager wants guidance on how to produce a safe product or on how to know the limitations that must be observed, the designer should be able to look to standards to provide the necessary information.

Attempts have been made to classify and define some of the types of documents that might contain information with which a manufacturer might be concerned. Figure 5-1 is another such attempt, but even it expresses generalities to which there might be contradictions. For example, *Federal Register*, Vol. 36, No. 75, April 17, 1971, Part II is entitled Safety and Health *Regulations* for Construction, but *Federal Register*, Vol. 37, No. 202, October 18, 1972, Part II is entitled Occupational Safety and Health *Standards*, even though the types of requirements are the same. Even though they may bear other titles, most of the documents in Figure 5-1, except the specific enabling acts or laws, are generally referred to as *standards* and the requirements in the standards are referred to as *criteria*.

Standards are intended to provide guidance but, unfortunately, sometimes they are contradictory, difficult to understand, lacking in specific details, incomplete, and frequently so innocuous that they are useless. Different standards may have different criteria for the same hazard (Figure 5-2). It is not a new problem. Noah probably had trouble with some of the divine guidance he received to populate the Ark. Genesis 6:19 says, "...two of every sort shalt though bring into the Ark...." But Genesis 7:2 says, "Of every clean beast thou shalt take to thee by sevens, the male and his female...."[1] There is no explanation of what a "clean" beast is until it is mentioned by Moses

(Deuteronomy 14:6), many begats and many years later. It omits important details, as do many of our present standards, such as how Noah is to collect and select the beasts and how he is to make the lion lie down with the lamb.

Manaker[2] pointed out that

> [In] a New York City case, *Sicurauza* v *United Crane and Shovel Company*, there was found to be two separate standards setting forth the minimum requirements for wire rope to be used on boom cranes. The conflict between the standards set by the Wire Rope Manufacturers and the Power Shovel and Crane Industry demonstrated the manner in which each industry seeks to establish standards which corresponded to its self-interest. In this case, the Wire Rope Manufacturers had an interest in standards which provided good and safe products for many applications, while the Power Shovel and Crane Industry sought standards which corresponded to the interest of the manufacturers of such equipment; and its decision in this regard was clearly based upon economics.

Also,

> It should be noted that existing codes do not always represent a safety practice of due care in an industry but rather they may represent an industry's attempt to "maintain profits by balancing the cost of formulating and complying with adequate codes with the cost of liability for failure to exercise due care....They do represent industry's attempt to maintain and maximize profit....Due care has historically been only an instrument of profit and loss and in the interval, millions have been injured and killed."[3]

The Problem with Standards

In 1970 the Final Report of the National Commission on Product Safety commented on 1,000 industry standards applicable to safety:

> Unfortunately, these standards are chronically inadequate, both in scope and permissible levels of risk. They do not address themselves to all significant foreseeable hazards. They give insufficient consideration to human risk...

> For many consumer products there are no applicable voluntary standards. Specifically, we found:

> Of the 44 categories of products which are the highest in estimated annual injuries, according to the Department of Health, Education, and Welfare, 26 are not covered by industry-wide safety standards.

Of the 18 products and product categories that are covered by industry-wide voluntary standards, review by the Commission staff and outside experts of seven selected standards indicates that each is deficient in many aspects of safety.

The report went on to point out that products that had met the Underwriters Laboratories standards had resulted in accidents or were unsafe:

1. Thousands of television sets that had caught fire.

2. A vaporizer cited for scalding children.

3. A lethal charcoal igniter.

4. A toy oven with a temperature of 660°F inside and 300°F on top.

5. Fifteen out of 29 portable electric heaters rated by the Consumers Union as "not acceptable" for being unsafe.

Although the above report was issued in 1970 and the Underwriters Laboratories has taken corrective measures, there have been numerous cases of inadequacies of standards:

1. In 1977 it was reported that home smoke alarms that used house current (as distinguished from battery power) and that were listed as having met the UL standards were themselves starting fires.

2. In March 1978 the Consumer Product Safety Commission announced: "In another labeling action, CPSC is encouraging Underwriters Laboratories (UL) of Chicago to upgrade their labeling requirements for hand-held hair dryers to warn consumers against using these dryers while in or around a bathtub. CPSC has learned of 29 deaths from electrocution by hair dryers since 1973; 26 of these occurred when hair dryers came in contact with the victim in a bathtub."

3. In April 1978 the Consumer Product Safety Commission announced the recall of an automatic coffeemaker because of a potential fire hazard. The CPSC indicated that some of the coffeemakers could be identified by a metal plate on which was etched: UL LISTED 429E, MADE IN SINGAPORE.

Many governmental agencies stipulate that the provisions of the *National Electrical Code*®[4] will be adhered to during building design and construction to minimize electrical injury accidents. The *National Electrical Code*® was written by the National Fire Protection Association in order to reduce the possibilities of electrically caused fires in buildings and associated structures. Provisions to protect personnel against shock were almost totally absent until a few years ago. At that time, a few requirements regarding shock protection in wet areas, such as around swimming pools, were added.

Voluntary or Mandatory Standards

In addition to problems with the requirements themselves, there has been much discussion on whether or not standards in which they are contained should be voluntary or mandatory, specification[5] or performance, or horizontal versus vertical.

Mandatory standards are issued by governmental agencies: federal, state, county, or municipal. Violations are treated as criminal acts and the violators are subject to fines and/or imprisonment. In some instances, a governing agency may make a voluntary standard mandatory by imposing the standard on all users in the areas over which it has jurisdiction. For example, use of the ASME (American Society of Mechanical Engineers) Code for Power Boilers and use of the Code for Unfired Pressure Vessels are often so imposed. A city that uses these codes will not permit boilers or pressure vessels that do not meet the codes to be installed, or will require that they be repaired or replaced if any deficiency arises so that there is noncompliance. Boiler and pressure vessel inspections are made periodically to ensure that the boilers and pressure vessels still meet the Code requirements. Insurance companies might not write coverage for boilers and pressure vessels that do not meet the requirements or are not inspected regularly.

A manager may weigh a safety requirement of a voluntary standard against the increase in the sales price of a proposed product, or the manager may believe that a competitor will forego that requirement and undersell him. With mandatory standards there is no option for refusal; all manufacturers must meet the same requirements.

Standards are "voluntary" on two bases and both generate problems: (1) Participation by all parties interested in preparation of a standard is voluntary and (2) It is entirely voluntary whether or not a company will use the standard after it has been prepared. Many companies will not.

Preparation of a voluntary standard is usually supposed to include representatives from industry, the government, and the general public. Representatives of the general public are frequently unavailable at meetings held to prepare and discuss standards because of the unavailability of funds. Representation by government personnel is sporadic. Representation by industry personnel and other organizations representing industry is generally overwhelming because these people attempt to protect their own interests. Acceptance of the standards must generally be approved by all or almost all of those present or their organizations; therefore, such voluntary standards are *consensus* standards. Consensus standards usually specify only the lowest common denominator performance acceptable to the members of the industry concerned. Recently the requirements of some of these standards have been made more stringent because of the requirements' inadequacies to minimize accidents and to protect defendants who had used them as guidance,

because of the number of suits against the organizations themselves that had issued the requirements, and because of the published adverse comments on the inadequacies of the requirements.

A voluntary standard indicates the lowest safety level an industry or manufacturer intends to meet in the product it supplies. A mandatory standard indicates the lowest safety level the government will accept. The two may not be, and generally are not, the same. If they were, there would be no need for the mandatory standard.

At one time a very common defense in personal injury liability suits consisted of the manufacturer showing that industry standards had been met. A plaintiff's lawyer could always produce an expert witness in a personal injury case who could cite the inadequacies in a consensus standard. Even if the jury might be hazy about any highly technical provisions or differences, the jury readily understood that the plaintiff had suffered the injury which had brought the case to court and that the expert was pointing out that the standard was inadequate to prevent injury.

There have even been cases in which a whole industry has been sued because of the lack or inadequacy of standards. In May 1973 the Federal Trade Commission instituted a class action suit against 26 plastics manufacturing companies, the Society of Plastics Industry (SPI), and the American Society for Testing Materials (ASTM). The standard issued by the ASTM (and the British Standards Institute) defined a "self-extinguishing" plastic as one that will not continue to burn after the ignition source is removed. The test required the plastic to be held in a horizontal position, but when the material was held in a vertical position or after a fire was initiated, the material continued to burn. From this architects would wrongly assume that materials that passed the test could be used to eliminate or minimize fire hazards.

Government action is needed when an agency believes that corrective action must be taken but the industry is reluctant to take such action because of the economic costs involved. In some cases, a voluntary standard may be technically adequate but industry members will not follow its provisions. It is therefore the government's task to force adherence to the standard. In some cases, the more safety conscious companies may find themselves at an economic disadvantage in relation to companies that do not follow the standard and market cheaper and less safe products. Mandatory standards will eliminate this inequity. Lastly, mandatory standards frequently set more stringent requirements which force manufacturers to develop new techniques, materials, and processes and to eliminate unsatisfactory ones.

Another inadequacy of voluntary standards is that testing is often biased. A manufacturer will send to the testing laboratory samples of products which he/she believes represents the quality of normal output. Unfortunately, samples of normal output may vary over time with regard to quality. Thus, the test results of even independent laboratories are influenced by the selection of samples. Under mandatory standards, samples are selected randomly. Test results may be different under voluntary and mandatory standards even if the tests were conducted using the same criteria and under the same conditions by the same laboratories.

In 1970 some of the problems with voluntary industry standards were brought out by Admiral Hyman Rickover in testimony before the Congressional Joint Committee on Atomic Energy.[6]

> To forestall the intrusion of Government, the industry concerned will usually propose voluntary safety requirements. These requirements represent the minimum all are willing to accept. This is not enough. There are more accidents. Only after the lapse of much time are laws finally enacted. Much harm will have been done in the interval—harm which could have been prevented.

> The typical industry-controlled code or standard is formulated by a committee elected or appointed by a technical society or similar group. Many of the committee members are drawn from the manufacturers to whom the code is to be applied. Others are drawn from engineering consulting firms and various Government organizations. However, since near unanimous agreement in the committee must generally be obtained to set requirements or to change them, the code represents a minimum level of requirements that is acceptable to industry.

> In a subtle way, the use of industry codes or standards tends to create a false sense of security. Described by code committees and by the language of many of the codes themselves as safety rules, they tend to inhibit those legally responsible for protecting the public from taking the necessary action to safeguard health and well-being. Many states and municipalities have incorporated these codes into their laws, thus, in effect delegating to code committees their own responsibility for protecting the public.

Dave Pittle of the Consumer Product Safety Commission said in 1977: "In some cases an existing voluntary standard may be entirely adequate to prevent or reduce an unreasonable hazard associated with a product, but is ineffective in protecting the public because it is not widely accepted by industry or because the promulgating agency lacks authority to require adherence to its terms. In such cases, government's role may simply be to ensure that all segments of the industry adhere to the standard. Even widespread membership in a trade association which has adopted a voluntary safety standard may not be sufficient where the trade association has no mechanism for ensuring compliance."

Because voluntary standards are prepared by parties who, in many cases, are interested in doing only the minimum of what is economically justifiable, their provi-

sions might not contain *all* requirements that would be desirable, because the majority does not elect to include them. And, even when a desirable provision is included, manufacturers may choose not to observe it because it is nonmandatory. There is need for economic justification of standards.

Japan has two sets of standards: the Japan Engineering Standards (JES), similar to ANSI, and the standards called for and approved by the Ministry of International Trade and Industry (MITI). The first, which is used internally, is similar to the voluntary standards in the United States. For the other, representatives of an industry prepare a standard which is submitted to MITI, and officials there either accept or reject its provisions. Once accepted, the manufacturers of the product must produce it in accordance with the standard, test it so that it meets all stipulated requirements, and then include certification with the product. If the standard is not met, the manufacturer is not permitted to export the product, thereby ensuring that standards and quality are kept high.

Performance Versus Specification Standards

The Old Testament again can be used to illustrate the difference between these two types of standards.

Deuteronomy 22:8 is a performance standard: "When thou buildest a new house, then thou shalt make a battlement for thy roof, that thou bring not blood upon thine house, if any man fall from thence." The performance standard indicates the end result to be achieved and leaves to the responsible party the details of how it is to be achieved. Manufacturers prefer performance standards over specification standards, if mandatory standards are to be imposed, since performance standards restrict them less.

Specification standard requirements include dimensions which must be observed, materials requirements which must be met, and other detailed criteria. The instructions Noah received for building his Ark, and later those for construction of the Ark of the Covenant in Exodus (so many cubits long, wide, and high, etc.) would constitute a specification standard. Such a standard permits little or no deviation.

Both types of standards have advantages and disadvantages. A specification standard provides a designer with a guide that obviates the need for *him* to determine what dimensions will make a product safe in regard to any specific feature. Figure 5-3 presents the maximal clearance that can exist between a guard and the feed table on a mechanical power press. If these clearances had not been indicated and there had been only a performance requirement that a guard be provided, the designer would have to determine what dimensions would make his design safe. From the author's experience, both types of standards are needed.

Horizontal Versus Vertical Standards

The difference between these two standards is of lesser interest to most product manufacturers and designers. Horizontal standards apply to similar hazards as they might exist in different industries or operations. Vertical standards are specific for a specific industry or operation, such as construction or shipbuilding. Thus, a horizontal standard for electrical protection would apply wherever electricity is used and a vertical standard for protection would apply only to those pieces of electrical equipment found in the specific industry covered.

SCRAT

Most standards are prepared for specific products or types of products. The standards-making organization will not prepare a standard for a new product until there

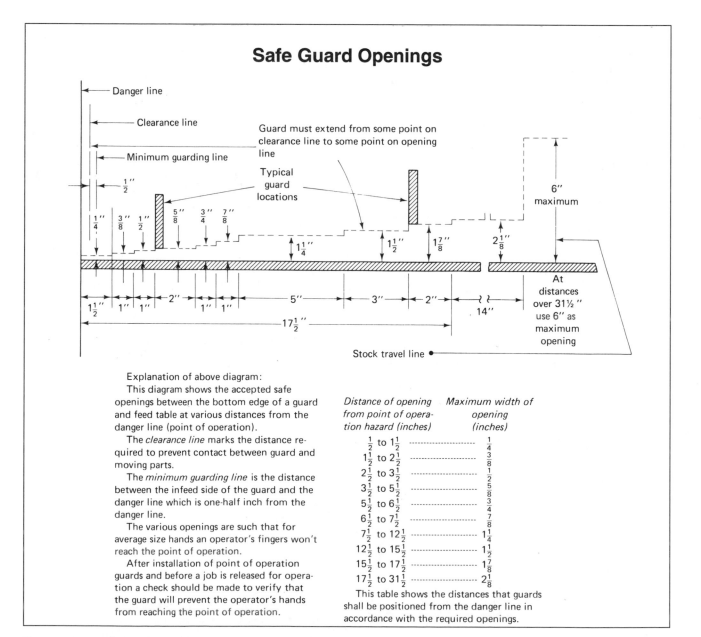

Figure 5-3. Safe guard openings.

is demand for the standard. By the time there *is* a demand and by the time the lengthy standards-making and acceptance process is completed, there are many new products on the market that have not been developed in accordance with any accepted requirements. In some cases, this may lead to a problem. A state or municipal requirement may stipulate that the equipment be certified as safe by a testing laboratory. The testing laboratory may not want to certify that the product is safe because the laboratory has no standard against which to test the product. The equipment therefore may not be installed.

It is now possible to develop standards based primarily on hazardous characteristics (Chapter 7) rather than on type of product. For example, the measures to prevent electrical shock in various products using 115-V power should be uniform. If it is known at the time the product is first conceived that 115-V power is to be used, the preventive measures against shock will be known immediately.

This is the concept behind a new method known as SCRAT (Safety Criteria Retrieving and Tabulating). Developed by and for a company involved with the safety of numerous products, many of the products so new that there are no adequate standards, SCRAT uses a computer to assemble the criteria pertaining to the product to be designed. All safety criteria pertaining to the products the company develops are entered on a computer tape. (These criteria were taken from government specifications, applicable industry standards, and good engineering practices.) A form lists the types of assemblies and subassemblies which might be hazardous. If it is an electrical product, there are design criteria that will apply to *all* electrical products; in addition, electrical switches and other devices might have specific criteria that must be observed. The person who is preparing the new company standard selects all of the items which might apply to the product to be developed. The computer prints out the criteria for those items, thereby synthesizing a new standard within minutes.

The Need for Standards

In spite of the adverse comments about the current situation in standards, good[7] standards are highly desirable and provide numerous benefits.

1. As indicated above, standards provide designers with guides so that they do not have to develop guides themselves. Thus the designers save time and effort.

2. Standards provide uniformity (the original purpose for the development of all standards), so that different engineers will provide approximately the same level of safety in their products.

3. Standards will provide designers with safe designs and thereby deter the designers from repeating errors

previously made by others. Figure 11-3 illustrates a requirement for power boilers. Before the requirement was imposed on how a boiler feedwater valve should be oriented there were explosions because boilers were depleted of water because of valve failures.

4. Standards alert designers to potential problems of which they may not have been aware. Otherwise, the safety characteristics of designs produced will depend on the experience, background, and capabilities of the individual designers. Accumulated over the years, standards indicate the types of hazards which could be present and the safeguards which could, should, or have been used. The criteria in the standards were originally generated to prevent reoccurrences of accidents or to avoid occurrences of situations which careful consideration showed could develop into problems unless suitable precautions were taken.

5. In trade-off studies against cost or other considerations, the designer and his managers are more influenced when it is known that a requirement of a standard, especially a mandatory one, *must* be met.

Company Standards

Because of the inadequacies of many consensus standards, many companies have developed their own standards. This is especially true of large companies that have many product lines, have large staffs of engineers, or have many different subdivisions in which different products are developed. Having its own standards imposes some degree of uniformity to all the company products, maintains a general overall safety level higher than the norm for those companies which follow the consensus standard, and gains all of the advantages of having standards, such as saving time and effort discussed in the above paragraphs. The Final Report prepared for the U.S. Interagency Task Force on Product Liability[8] reports the following: "Fifteen of the twenty firms visited are using their own standards or similar criteria."

A company that can show that it maintains higher safety standards than normal for the industry can better indicate its observance of due care in any case which might come to court. Even better, use of high safety standards will tend to produce safer products which might reduce the number of recalls, accidents, injuries, and resultant claims. The imposition of effective criteria by a manufacturer on his own operations and on supplies provided by vendors and subcontractors will also reduce the number of items returned as defective, even when no other safety problem arises.

Conversely, the issuance of standards by a company is not, in itself, evidence that the products it produces are safe. The company must ensure that the standards are observed by anyone involved with the design and manufacture of the company's products. If a company's own standards were not observed and there is an accident, a plaintiff might be able to use this to prove his or her case. He/she might be able to show that the manufacturer had produced a product that was faulty since it had not met even the company's own standards.

Company standards can be used to form the basis for checklists. These checklists can be used to analyze or study the products for the existence of hazards and their safeguards. How to prepare such checklists is described in Chapter 14.

Small companies generally do not have large staffs to prepare lengthy or complex standards. These companies may feel that the cost to prepare the standards are too high if they are developing only one or a few products. In such a situation, it may be a better procedure to upgrade a consensus standard. An existing standard can be reviewed by experienced engineers before design begins. There are certain fundamental criteria which should be in every standard. If they are not already in the standard being upgraded and if they relate to the products the company will manufacture, these criteria should be added. Some of these are shown in Figure 5-4. Insurance company or industry association engineers sometimes assist in such a task. (Since accidents even of a few companies affect the insurance rates of all companies within an industry,[9] it is advisable for industry associations to upgrade their standards to achieve the best practicable safety level rather than the minimal level. Since, however, some companies may opt for the less stringent requirements, some criteria which may be acceptable to more conscientious companies may be omitted. The association engineers may have information on these criteria and be able to disseminate it to all association members.)

Standards and Analyses

Even with good standards it is necessary to make safety analyses of the completed designs and product. Not only are these analyses to ensure that the criteria of the standards have been met, but also because hazards frequently exist even within the limits of the criteria. As shown in some of the following chapters there are four general categories of hazards: dangerous characteristics of a product, malfunctions and their effects, environmental effects, and operator errors. Thus, a design of a product may meet all pertinent criteria, but it would have to be examined to determine whether or not the environment could degrade its operation, whether or not operators could make errors and what the effects of those errors might be, or whether the end results of failure of a specific part could result in an accident. Figure 13-8 illustrates five coffee mills produced by five different manufacturers. Each coffee mill has a different degree of safety, cost, and convenience.

When performance standards and criteria are used, it is more necessary to make analyses than when specification standards are used, for it is apparent that when performance standards are used, more latitude is given to designers and there are more possibilities of deviations from good safety practices.

Some Basic Safety Requirements

1. Sharp corners, projections, edges, and rough surfaces which can cause cuts, scratches, or puncture wounds will be eliminated unless required for a specific function.

*2. Surface temperatures of exposed metal surfaces and parts, including equipment enclosures, will not exceed 60°C (at an ambient temperature of 25°C) where an inadvertent contact might occur, and 43°C where the part or equipment must be handled.

3. Materials used will not liberate, when installed and subjected to service conditions: (a) toxic, corrosive, odorous, or otherwise harmful gases; (b) gases which combine with the atmosphere or its moisture to form corrosive acids, alkalis, or flammable or explosive mixtures.

4. A warning will be provided if any material in contact with another, or under any specific foreseeable condition, will produce any product which is toxic, corrosive, odorous, or otherwise harmful. The purchaser will be notified of the hazard and must approve the warning label to be provided prior to its use.

*5. The following materials will be used only when less hazardous substitutes are not available for the required purpose and only with the approval of the purchaser: (a) magnesium or magnesium alloys; (b) zinc where its protective treatment may adversely affect any electrical circuitry; (c) cadmium; (d) radioactive materials; (e) (the purchaser may add any other materials whose use he/she might want to control).

6. When a material is rated as nonburning or self-extinguishing the standard used to qualify it will be indicated. The purchaser will be notified of any material, such as insulation, which does not meet a standard for nonburning or self-extinguishing materials.

7. Accesses (panels, covers, doors,…) will be marked with a warning of any imminent hazard which exists beyond the access. Warnings will be clear, direct, and attention-getting; will indicate the hazard; the injury or damage which could result; and measures to be observed to avoid injury or damage.

8. Protection will be provided against contact with moving parts, such as rotating gears, fan blades, belts or other pinch points, or rotating couplings when the product is in operation.

9. Items containing a high-speed rotating device will be designed to contain any fragments which might be produced by a failure of the device.

*10. Pressure vessels will be proof-pressure tested to 150% of the maximum expected operating pressure (MEOP) without permanent deformation.

11. Where reversed or rotated mounting of a part cannot be tolerated (result in damage), asymmetrical or other preventive mounting arrangements (polarization, keyways, pins) will be used to ensure proper orientation.

12. Design will protect against damage to parts due to accidental use of screws or bolts that are too long.

13. Parts will be secured in a manner such that failure of a single fastener will not free them completely if damage or injury could result. Friction between mating surfaces will not be employed as the sole means of preventing fixed parts from rotating or shifting.

14. Equipment which could be damaged if it is inverted or otherwise improperly positioned will be marked with arrows and notations: "This Side Up" or other distinctive instruction. Containers of such equipment will also be marked.

15. Equipment which could be damaged by rough handling will be marked "Handle With Care." Containers of such equipment will also be marked.

16. When a chassis, assembly, or other large unit is to be removable form its normal position or housing for maintenance or repair, it will be possible to place it on a smooth, flat surface without causing damage.

17. Where mechanical or power lift may be required, hoist or lift points will be provided and clearly marked.

18. Enclosures to hazardous portions of products will be strong enough to prevent exposure of a person through any forseeable abuse.

19. All electrical assemblies with live conductors will be securely enclosed to avoid accidental shock.

20. Switches, motors, and other components will be securely mounted to prevent unintended movement.

21. Containers of hot or corrosive liquids will be designed to prevent accidental spills. They will not deform, crack, or break when filled, nor react with the liquid they are intended to hold.

22. All potential hazards will be brought to the attentionof the purchaser with safeguards to be incorporated. No product will be delivered unless each of these safeguards has been approved.

*Values or materials in these paragraphs can be changed, added to, or deleted as the purchaser believes advisable.

Figure 5-4. Some basic safety requirements.

Notes

[1] Genesis 7:9 says they "went in two and two" or in pairs, but how many pairs of "clean" beasts went in?

[2] Ralph Manaker, *Standards—Effects on Liability*, Proceedings of the 1974 Product Liability Prevention Conference (Syracuse, N.Y.: Law Offices of Irwin Birbaum), p. 203.

[3] *Lawyers Desk Reference* (New York: Lawyers Cooperative Publishing Company, 1968), p. 948.

[4] National Electric Code is the registered trademark of the National Fire Protection Association. It is revised triennially. Revision years are 1978, 1981, 1984, etc.

[5] "Specification" standards are also called "design" standards. I prefer and use specification because even performance standards are met by design.

[6] Extracted from testimony before the Joint Committee on Atomic Energy, Congress of the United States, Washington, D.C., March 19 and 20, 1970.

[7] It has been said there is no "bad" standard; that any standard which presents even minimal requirements is better than none. I take issue with this. Many persons rely on statements that a product has met a specific organization's standard. They therefore believe it is safe and may not take adequate precautions when it actually is unsafe because the standard to which it was made was inadequate. Thus, a minimum standard can permit accidents to occur and the manufacturer to be sued. The manufacturers of this country conscientiously try to make safe products and believe they are doing so if they meet the requirements of consensus standards. Unfortunately, these standards are often inadequate. Representatives of standards-setting organizations sometimes indicate that they try to set standards which are practical and economically justified. Actually, the standards are neither if they still permit accidents to occur due to designs which could have been eliminated by more stringent requirements.

[8] Product Liability: Final Report of the Industry Study—Volume I, ITFPL-77/04, Interagency Task Force on Product Liability, U.S. Department of Commerce, PB 265 542.

[9] "Ask not for whom the bell tolls; it tolls for thee." John Donne.

Questions

1. Name five documents that may present safety criteria to be observed by manufacturers and designers.

2. Why is reliance on standards generally inadequate to provide a completely safe product?

3. In what two ways can standards be considered "voluntary"?

4. The preparation of a "voluntary" industry standard is supposed to be done by representatives of industry, the government, and the public. Discuss why this generally does not occur.

5. What are consensus standards?

6. Explain the difference between a performance standard and a specification standard.

7. What are some of the advantages to having good standards?

8. Discuss why it is important that a manufacturer impose his standards on vendors and subcontractors who furnish supplies to him.

9. Give five criteria that should ordinarily be observed in order to control mechanical hazards.

10. Give three criteria that provide requirements on warnings.

11. Indicate how the existence, or nonexistence and observance of standards affect a jury, judge, or the decision in a court case brought about because of liability for an accident.

12. Can failure to observe provisions of a standard be considered negligence? What if the defendant was unaware of the existence of a standard or of all its provisions?

13. Would a company that showed there was a real attempt to observe a standard be in a better legal position than a company that had failed, for any reason, to observe provisions?

6

Modern Concepts of Accident Prevention

The ways in which we live change, the new products we use are more complex and dangerous, and the hazards to which we are exposed grow greater each year (Figure 6-1). Each decade since the Industrial Revolution began has brought some major development or invention with new means for injury or death. Outstanding examples (with rough approximate dates) include: railroads (1830), operations in compressed air (1840), high explosives (1860), commercial electric power (1880), automobiles (1890), submarines (1900), airplanes (1900), chemicals and plastics (1910), high-energy electronics (1930), nuclear reactions (1940), helicopters (1940), and lasers (1950). It has been said that a new chemical is developed approximately every 20 minutes. Each one may or may not be dangerous. All of these must be added to the pre-Industrial Revolution hazards: falling, vicious animals, being struck by lightning, sports, fires, being run down by a horse or wagon, collapse of a structure, drowning, or accidental discharge of a gun. The fewer number of accidents with horses and horse-drawn vehicles has been over-compensated by the far greater number of automotive accidents. Falls are still a major cause of mishaps, constituting more than one-third of all non-transportation accidents.

The number, diversity, and severities of the dangers to which the modern person is exposed are tremendous and they will increase. Some operations now being undertaken only on experimental bases, but with significant attendant hazards, may become common. Ultrasafe safeguards will be required. To provide these safeguards consistently and with minimal added cost, erroneous concepts of accident prevention must be discarded.

Old and New Concepts of Accident Prevention

There is time to adapt to changes that come slowly; when technological change occurs rapidly, we must adapt rapidly. False or outdated concepts of accident prevention that could interfere with adequate and timely responses to problems must be eliminated. Even now, many persons who should know better hold to concepts on accidents and accident prevention which are no longer or never were technically, economically, legally, or morally valid.

Some of these concepts can be touched on here. The erroneous idea will be given first and then the modern view will be given. These concepts are discussed more fully in later, more appropriate chapters.

Safety won't sell. A person who buys a product expects, and the law requires, it be reasonably safe. A customer therefore may not pay more for safety, but he will not buy the product if there is any indication that it is unsafe.

Operator error and negligence are the principal causes of all accidents. For an accident to happen there must be a dangerous condition. Eliminate that condition and an accident from that cause is impossible; control that condition and the possibility of an accident is reduced. Figure 6-2 shows how fatalities of trainmen dropped after the government required that automatic couplers be installed on all railroad cars over a five-year period. Coupling accidents had been one of the principal causes of injury or death to trainmen. Railroad managers had claimed that such accidents were only due to errors and negligence on the part of the trainmen. Installation of the automatic couplers minimized that problem.

Figure 6-1. Times change.

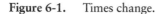

Almost all accidents are caused by accident-prone persons. There are a few people who have more accidents than other people do (sometimes they may be in more hazardous activities), but they are comparatively few in number. Most accidents involve persons who have no more tendencies toward accidents than persons who are not involved in accidents.

Engineers have been educated and can therefore be depended on to design safe products. At the present time, only a handful of engineering schools in the United States teach safety principles and methods to undergraduate engineers. These courses are electives and each course has from 15 to 20 students. Thus, of all engineers graduated each year, only a very small percentage has been exposed to any instruction on safe design methods. Before 1970 there was no such instruction.

Failures are the principal cause of accidents. Many injuries and much damage are the results of nonfailure causes. There are probably more injuries because products have dangerous characteristics.

A product which bears a seal of approval or label from an accredited testing laboratory is a safe product. The seal or label only indicates that the product has met the requirements of the laboratory. The requirements, however, may be inadequate to ensure that the product is safe.

A product designed and manufactured in accordance with the standards issued by the entire industry concerned with that product will be a safe product. Industry standards are very often less than adequate to make a product safe since the standards are usually minimal standards. Company standards are generally far better than industry standards since any company that produces its own standards is probably highly concerned about the safety of its products.

Making a product or operation safe increases costs. It often costs no more to make a safe product if the product is designed correctly in the first place. Changes increase the cost. Also, it may appear that safety increases costs to a specific organization or person, but when *all* costs over the entire life cycle and use of the product are considered, a safe product and its operation are less costly than a dangerous product.

Increasing safety slows operations. Experience has shown over a sustained period that a safer operation is generally more efficient and can be accomplished more rapidly. Stoppages and delays are eliminated.

Safety cannot be legislated. The Refrigerator Safety Act was passed because children were being trapped and suffocated in refrigerators. No child has died in a refrigerator that was designed within the provisions of the Act.

It is impossible to determine the safety problems of a new product before it is built. With the methods of analyses developed by safety engineers, the hazards that might be present in any product can be established before work is begun to physically make the product.

Corrections can be made if and after an accident points up where a danger exists. The consequences of an accident may be disastrous to the persons injured and, financially, to the manufacturers. Accidents, as sources of information on potential safety problems, have become economically unjustifiable.

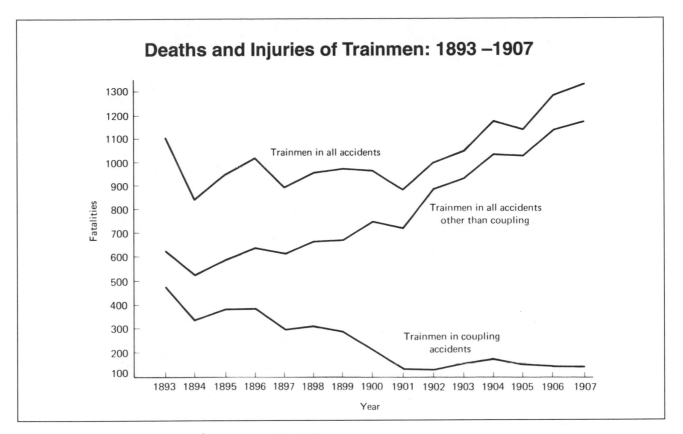

Figure 6-2. Deaths and injuries of trainmen: 1893 -1907.

The time to check a new product for safety is when the first prototype or model is tested. Safety considerations must begin when the product is first conceived and must be maintained throughout the life cycle of the product.

Ensuring that a product is safe can be accomplished by making a detailed analysis and test after the prototype of the product is developed. Since many problems are hidden by the time the prototype is built, the problems are not apparent. If any problems are found, there is a reluctance to make changes because changes are costly. Accidents during tests of prototypes have sometimes destroyed the prototypes and injured personnel. Analyses should be made continually as the product is developed.

If a product is used in a way the manufacturer did not intend, the manufacturer cannot be held liable if an injury results The courts have held that a manufacturer should be able to foresee all possible reasonable uses of his product. If an accident results from a use which the manufacturer did not intend, but which a jury considers reasonable, the manufacturer is liable.

Warning of a hazard is an adequate defense against a claim resulting from an injury due to the hazard the manufacturer warned against. A warning is an indication that the manufacturer knew the hazard existed. The warning is justifiable only after the manufacturer has done his utmost to eliminate or control the hazard and the hazard still remains.

It is cheaper to cover losses with insurance than to spend money making products safe because the probability of an accident is low. Not only doesn't insurance cover all losses, but the cost of insurance has increased so rapidly and to such heights that coverages have been reduced. A company that has a poor safety record may be able to obtain insurance only at extremely high cost. In addition, it is not now necessary to have an accident to suffer a monetary loss: to be subjected to a recall action when a product is found to be unsafe can also be economically devastating.

Designers make safety one of their primary considerations. In addition to design, designers must consider performance, cost, weight, size, reliability, maintainability, and other requirements. Designers pay most attention to those items which their managers choose. If the manager is safety-oriented, the product will be relatively safe. Managers generally stress those items which make their products sell, and safety is usually not one of these items.

System Safety Engineering

Many of the misconceptions cited above have always been erroneous and were excuses to attribute shortcomings to persons other than those making the statements. Some concepts have changed because conditions have changed, for example, the potential losses that can occur and the

System Safety

After World War II proposals were made which were later included in system safety concepts, but as an engineering discipline system safety actually developed as a result of the missile programs of 1950 and 1960. The liquid propellant missiles blew up frequently, unexpectedly, and devastatingly. In addition, the highly toxic and reactive propellants were sometimes more lethal than the poison gases used in World War I, more violently destructive than many explosives, and more corrosive than most materials used in industrial processes. They used cryogenic liquids with temperatures down to −320°F and pressurized gases at 6000 pounds per square inch. (A hurricane wind exerts a pressure of about a quarter of a pound per square inch.)

Under the concurrency concept in use at the time, the missiles and the facilities in which they were to be maintained in ready conditions for launch were built at the same time that tests of the missiles and training of personnel were going on. Air Force officers and commanders objected to the fact that they were being given complex systems capable of causing injuries to both military and civilian personnel and heavy damage to their property.

Missiles at test sites blew up often. Within 18 months after the fleet of 72 Atlas F intercontinental ballistic missiles became operational, four blew up in their silos during practice operations.

The Air Force had long had problems with aircraft accidents (from 1952 to 1966 it lost 7,715 aircraft in which 8,547 persons, including 3,822 pilots were killed). Until missiles were developed, aircraft losses were generally blamed on the pilots. Since there were no pilots aboard the missiles, no blame could be put on them. It became apparent that the causes of accidents were due to defective concepts, design, manufacture, maintenance, or other activity prior to use. The philosophy developed that safety programs had to be planned and initiated almost as soon as a new system was conceived and carried on through the system's life cycle and up to the time where it is finally eliminated.

Requirements for system safety programs for new hardware were initiated by the Air Force. The Army, because of the many personnel it lost in helicopter accidents, and the Navy adopted the concept. The Department of Defense issued a single directive requiring system safety programs be undertaken for all systems to be developed or modified.

Initially, there was a lack of methodologies which could be used for these complex systems; therefore those who worked in this discipline were forced by necessity into organized approaches to accident prevention. Little by little new concepts and new methodologies were developed; old ones which were still valid and useful were refined; and scientific, technical, and management techniques from other activities were adapted.

The concepts, safety program activities, hazard analysis methods, and control measures in this book were basically drawn from system safety experience. They are equally valid for product safety. The difference between the two is in scope; system safety being broader than product safety. If transportation on our highways is considered, the automobile can be regarded as a product, but with other products and affecting factors involved: the roads and highways themselves, traffic signals and signs, guard rails, the drivers, the laws and their enforcement, and a multiplicity of other items. All of these products, people, procedures, and their interrelationships make up a system.

Figure 6-3. System safety.

failure of insurance to cover these losses. One of the major causes of change in concepts has been the influence of system safety engineering (Figure 6-3) developed by the Armed Services and their weapons development contractors.

Some of the ideas in system safety engineering were also developed independently by others outside the Armed Services. The integration of these ideas into the concept that safety management and engineering is a continuing process that begins with the first steps in the development of a product is a system safety concept.

Another contribution of system safety engineers to safety engineering has been in the development or improvement of methodologies. The development and first applications of fault-tree analysis, an extremely useful investiga-

tive method described in Chapter 15, can be attributed to early system safety efforts. Other types of analyses, less well-known and not so widely used, such as fault-hazard analysis and sneak circuit analysis, were also developed for system safety activities.

Organized approaches have been used to determine, eliminate, and control hazards. Hazards have been divided into the following four categories:

1. Dangerous properties or characteristics of a product, which may be inherent, the result of a design error, a production defect, or some other deficiency.

2. Material failure, which may also be the result of design errors, production defects, environmental stress, or operator error.

3. Operator error, which may be due, to a great extent, to design errors.

4. Environmental stresses, which indirectly or directly can cause injury or damage. Environmental stresses can be controlled or eliminated by good design.

The following chapters will deal with these various categories of hazards and with the designs and means of avoiding accidents or controlling the injury or damage they might incur.

Questions

1. Why does the modern concept of accident prevention disagree with the idea that operator error and negligence are the principal causes of accidents?

2. What is an accident-prone person? Do you believe that there are persons who are accident prone? Are such persons the major cause of most accidents?

3. Are equipment failures the principal cause of most accidents?

4. What condition is required for an accident to occur?

5. Discuss whether or not increasing the safety of a product or an operation always slows its operation. Would making a product safer sometimes help speed up operations?

6. Why is it inadvisable to begin to determine whether or not a product's design is safe when the first prototype is tested?

7. Why is it inadvisable to determine through accidents whether or not a product is hazardous and then to make corrections based on the problem which has revealed itself?

8. Why can a manufacturer be held liable if an injury is due to a person's use of the manufacturer's product in a way which was not intended?

9. Discuss the implications of the use of warnings on equipment.

10. Why is it inadvisable to rely on insurance to cover all losses that might result with a new product?

11. Discuss why designers sometimes may not fully consider safety in their product designs.

12. Into what four categories are hazards divided?

13. Have modern concepts regarding accident causes and accident prevention changed?

14. Have common law decisions regarding accident causation and liabilities changed?

15. Discuss the long-held concept of non-liability because of environmental "Acts of God."

7

Hazardous Characteristics of Products

Nothing is completely safe. Take as an example a solid material:

If it is large enough, a person might fall off it.

- Smaller, a person might run into and collide with it.
- Smaller, a person might trip over it.
- Smaller, it might fall and hit a person.
- Smaller, he might choke on it.
- Smaller and in sufficient quantity, it might suffocate a person engulfed in it.
- Smaller and in sufficient quantity, it might be a dust which could form an explosive mixture.
- Smaller (microscopic), it might be toxic if a person inhaled it.

Origins of Hazardous Characteristics

There are three major causes of hazardous characteristics in products:

1. An inherent characteristic in the product or in one of the materials used in the product.

2. A design deficiency.

3. A manufacturing defect.

There are also lesser causes, such as poor or incorrect maintenance, but the three causes listed above constitute the overwhelming majority of reasons. The design prob-lem is probably the most significant aspect of all of these causes. Designers are not only responsible for the design deficiencies that they incorporate into their products which generate hazardous characteristics, but the design-ers are often also deficient in not properly controlling inherent hazardous characteristics of the product or its materials. In some cases, the designers contribute to manufacturing defects.

Inherently hazardous materials may be substances such as explosives, flammable gases or liquids, or toxic sub-stances. If any such material is to be used in or with a product, it is up to the designer to provide a controlling safeguard.

Many hazardous characteristics in products result from manufacturing defects that are due entirely to poor pro-duction practices, but in some instances the defects may be due to poor design. One of the commonest examples is rough or sharp edges and sharp corners. If the designer did not specify that these be eliminated, the designer was in error; if he did, but the specification was not observed, it is entirely a production defect.

In 1945 I took off in a fighter aircraft in which a mainte-nance man had cross-connected the aileron control wires. When I moved the stick to the right, the left wing instead of the right went down. The plane had been given a hazardous characteristic. This could probably also have happened during the initial assembly at the aircraft plant. Then it would have been considered a production defect. Today it would be considered a design defect: the designer should have foreseen the possibility of this happening and should have designed the connections so that the wires could not have been connected incorrectly.

Hazardous Characteristics

Most hazardous characteristics of products are energy-related. The most serious consequences will result when there is an uncontrolled or unintended release or transfer of energy in large amounts. Thus, explosives and substances that can cause explosions are inherently hazardous and can generate the most severe injuries and damage. From accident investigations and analyses it has become apparent that the greater the magnitude of uncontrolled energy present, the greater the hazard.

Lists of hazardous conditions have been developed based on experience and on theoretical considerations. Some hazards are common and have often resulted in accidents; other hazards are less common; and some hazards, such as an accidental nuclear explosion, have never occurred. The existence of certain hazards has been determined from theoretical studies or from small-scale tests. The causes, effects, and measures for their elimination and control are known, have been tabulated, and in many cases have been included in standards.

The information in Appendices A and B on hazards has been prepared from both experience and theory. It is presented for the use of designers and analysts in order to enable them to recognize potential problems and their effects. Figures 7-1 and 7-2 can be used as checklists in reviewing any product, component, task, or operation for hazards. Figure 7-1 indicates the hazardous characteristics that could be present or could be generated. The product, component, task, or operation is entered at the top as a column heading. A reviewer puts a mark in the appropriate box. On another sheet the reviewer lists the coordinates of the box, such as A7 or B9, and then notes what the hazardous relationship is. The same could be done with the types of injury that could occur (see Figure 7-2).

Appendix A provides information on the various hazardous characteristics that might be present. The checklist that accompanies each hazard can be used by designers and analysts to ensure that they cover all possibilities. Checklists such as these also may be used for accident investigations in which the cause of the accident is not readily apparent but the effects are. Appendix B consists of postdesign checklists that can be used after a design is completed to determine whether or not any desirable safety feature has been omitted or to ensure that hazards have been controlled, if any are present.

Familiarization with the types of hazardous characteristics that can exist with any specific phenomenon (such as electricity) or material (such as an explosive) or with any other destructive characteristic or property will permit the designer or analyst to determine immediately whether or not the product has or will have any hazards that could be eliminated or that must be controlled. As an example, a review of Figure 7-1 shows that when electricity is used, there can be only a limited number of hazards: possibility of shock, heating which could cause burns or fire, arcing or sparking which could cause fire or related damage, inadvertent operation of equipment whose operation could cause injury or damage, loss of power which in a critical situation could cause an accident, and electrical explosion. A product that uses electrical power should be analyzed to determine whether or not any of these hazards could or do exist.

Any material to be used in a product can be examined to determine whether its hazardous characteristics are indicated in more than one of the figures in Appendix A. For example, in Chapter 14 the discussion on interface analysis points out that a leak in a pipe might release fluid which could be hazardous because of its flammability, toxicity, corrosiveness, lubricity, contamination effect, odor, or degrading effects it could have on product operation. Every fluid used in a product could and should be reviewed to establish its hazardous characteristics.

Hazardous characteristics that can exist in products are generally proscribed and can be controlled by standards. The presence of many hazardous characteristics can be determined by reviewing the criteria in standards, in addition to using the material in Appendix A. Less overt problems, such as the causes and effects of malfunctions, are less susceptible to control by standards and may be present even when the good requirements are met. The best way to uncover such problems is by analysis. Checklists on malfunctions, environmental problems, and operator error are presented in the chapters on those subjects.

The presence of some hazards in products, such as sharp points and edges, has to wait until the items have been completed so that they can be inspected. Other hazardous characteristics may be discovered only after the product, either its prototype or its production models, have been tested or used. Even though designers may have observed all of the required safety criteria, the product may have been thoroughly analyzed, good manufacturing practices and quality control may have been exercised, the new product might vibrate badly, be hard to control, or be unstable when used under field operating conditions. A program to determine the presence of hazardous characteristics during prototype verification is of prime importance. It is one of the major tasks of the product safety engineer in verification operations. Requirements for verifying either the absence of hazards or their control if they are present should be included in tests plans. The provisions of the plans can be based on the various possibilities indicated in Appendix A.

Potential Hazards

	A	B	C	D			A	B	C	D
ACCELERATION	1					PRESSURE HAZARDS	49				
INADVERTENT MOTION	2					DYNAMIC:	50				
SLOSHING OF LIQUIDS	3					COMPRESSED GAS	51				
TRANSLATION OF LOOSE	4					COMPRESSED AIR TOOL	52				
OBJECTS						PRESSURE SYSTEM EXHAUST	53				
						ACCIDENTAL RELEASE	54				
DECELERATION	5					BLOWN OBJECTS	55				
IMPACTS (SUDDEN STOPS)	6					WATER HAMMER	56				
FALLS	7					FLEX HOSE WHIPPING	57				
FALLING OBJECTS	8										
FRAGMENTS OR MISSILES	9					STATIC:	58				
						CONTAINER RUPTURE	59				
CHEMICAL REACTION (NONFIRE)	10					OVERPRESSURIZATION	60				
DISASSOCIATION	11					NEGATIVE PRESSURE EFFECTS	61				
COMBINATION	12										
CORROSION	13					LEAK OF MATERIAL WHICH IS:	62				
REPLACEMENT	14					FLAMMABLE	63				
						TOXIC	64				
ELECTRICAL HAZARDS	15					CORROSIVE	65				
SHOCK	16					SLIPPERY	66				
BURNS	17					ODOROUS	67				
OVERHEATING	18										
IGNITION OF COMBUSTIBLES	19					RADIATION	68				
INADVERTENT ACTIVATION	20					IONIZING RADIATION	69				
UNSAFE FAILURE TO OPERATE	21					ULTRAVIOLET LIGHT	70				
EXPLOSION, ELECTRICAL	22					HIGH INTENSITY VISIBLE LIGHT	71				
						INFRARED RADIATION	72				
EXPLOSIVES AND OTHER EXPLOSIONS	23					MICROWAVE RADIATION	73				
EXPLOSIVE PRESENT	24										
EXPLOSIVE GAS	25					TOXIC HAZARD	74				
EXPLOSIVE LIQUID	26					GAS OR LIQUID	75				
EXPLOSIVE DUST	27					ASPHYXIANT	76				
						IRRITANT	77				
FLAMMABILITY AND FIRES	28					SYSTEMIC POISON	78				
PRESENCE OF FUEL	29					CARCINOGEN	79				
PRESENCE OF STRONG OXIDIZER	30					OTHER ADVERSE PROPERTY	80				
PRESENCE OF STRONG IGNITION	31					COMBINATION PRODUCT	81				
SOURCE						COMBUSTION PRODUCT	82				
						POTENTIATION	83				
HEAT AND TEMPERATURE	32					SYNERGISM	84				
SOURCE OF HEAT, NONELECTRICAL	33										
HOT SURFACE BURNS	34					VIBRATION	85				
VERY COLD SURFACE BURNS	35					VIBRATING TOOL (RAYNAUD'S	86				
INCREASED GAS PRESSURE	36					PHENOMENON)					
INCREASED FLAMMABILITY	37					HIGH NOISE LEVEL SOURCE	87				
INCREASED VOLATILITY	38					METAL FATIGUE CAUSATION	88				
INCREASED REACTIVITY	39					FLOW OR JET VIBRATION	89				
REDUCED ELECTRONIC EQUIPMENT	40					SUPERSONICS	90				
RELIABILITY											
						MISCELLANEOUS HAZARDS	91				
MECHANICAL HAZARDS	41					CONTAMINATION	92				
SHARP EDGES OR POINTS	42					LUBRICITY	93				
ROTATING EQUIPMENT	43					VIOLENT ODOR	94				
RECIPROCATING EQUIPMENT	44										
PINCH POINTS	45										
WEIGHTS TO BE LIFTED	46										
STABILITY/TOPPLING TENDENCY	47										
EJECTED PARTS OR FRAGMENTS	48										

Figure 7-1. Potential hazards.

Possibilities of Injury

TYPE OF INJURY			UNIT OR TASK	A	B	C	D
MECHANICAL	CUTS	1					
	PUNCTURES	2					
	BRUISES	3					
	BROKEN BONES	4					
	PARTICLES IN EYES	5					
	CRUSHING	6					
	STRAINS	7					
BURNS	ELECTRICAL	8					
	THERMAL, HEAT	9					
	THERMAL, COLD	10					
	RADIATION	11					
	CHEMICAL	12					
PRESSURE	ACCELERATION	13					
	CRUSHING, FLUID	14					
	CRUSHING, SOLID MASS	15					
	PINCHING	16					
	NOISE AND VIBRATION	17					
	DYSBARISM (INTERNAL GAS EFFECTS)	18					
SHOCK	ELECTRICAL	19					
	IMPACT	20					
	PRESSURE WAVE	21					
	COLD IMMERSION	22					
TOXICITY	ASPHYXIATION	23					
	ORGANIC DAMAGE	24					
	RESPIRATORY SYS. DAMAGE	25					
	CIRCULATORY SYS. DAMAGE	26					
	DERMATOSIS	27					
	CANCER	28					
	NERVOUS SYS. DAMAGE AND EFFECTS	29					
OTHERS	HEAT EXHAUSTION	30					
	WIND CHILL	31					

Figure 7-2. Possibilities of injury.

Questions

1. Describe five hazardous characteristics which might be present in a mechanical product.

2. Describe five hazardous characteristics which might be present in an electrical product.

3. List eight hazardous characteristics of automobiles by which they could cause injury or death.

4. What are the three principal causes of hazardous characteristics in a product?

5. Describe four hazardous characteristics which might be the result of inadequate design.

6. Describe four hazardous characteristics which might be the result of poor manufacturing practices.

7. It has been said that all hazardous characteristics are energy-related. Discuss whether this is always true.

8. List five products which are inherently hazardous.

9. Describe how a maintenance person doing improper maintenance or repair work can cause a hazardous condition or characteristic in a product.

10. A new type of liquid solvent is being developed. What hazardous characteristics might it have?

11. Describe how the presence, absence, or adequate control of hazardous characteristics in a product can be verified.

12. Within a few years after Lord Abinger indicated the need for privity for liability suits resulting from accidents, the privity barrier was breached in cases involving inherently dangerous products such as firearms, fuel, and explosives. Based on these facts, discuss whether all items such as fuel, firearms, and explosives, should be severely controlled, or their use prevented. Indicate where each can be used beneficially and without injury. What controls are advisable?

13. In 1617, even before Lord Abinger's decision, a manufacturer of firearms was held liable (in *Weaver v Ward*) for an injury. Discuss whether firearms are, or are not, hazardous. Is the product more hazardous than the persons who use them? Is it their inherent characteristic that makes them hazardous, or only their misuse?

8

Malfunctions

There is only one way a product will work correctly as its designer created it to work, but there are multiple ways in which the product can malfunction. These malfunctions can be categorized into:

1. Failures, which constitute by far the principal type of malfunction.

2. Unprogrammed operation of an assembly.

3. Premature activation of an assembly.

4. Erroneous outputs.

5. Failure of a component or assembly to cease operating at a prescribed time.

Causes of Malfunctions

Causes can be of five types:

1. *Faulty design.* Faulty design is the major cause of malfunctions. Malfunctions may be caused by erroneous calculations, failure to include all known affecting factors, inadequate knowledge of the loads to which parts are to be subjected, poor choice of materials to be used, and poor approximations of intended operating conditions of which little is known.

2. *Manufacturing defects.* Figure 19-3 indicates how manufacturing processes can affect the strength of metals. Thus, even though the designer may have calculated the required strengths correctly, his designs may have been degraded by poor production practices. Manufacturing problems are discussed in greater detail in Chapter 19.

3. *Maintenance.* Most products, especially those that have moving parts, require maintenance, but often the products receive no maintenance, improper maintenance, or maintenance at inadequate intervals. With consumer products this especially becomes a problem since maintenance generally requires time and money. Many consumers are do-it-yourselfers who frequently lack the know-how to do such work properly. Maintenance is very often neglected because the owners believe that as long as a product is operating satisfactorily there is nothing wrong with it and nothing need be done. Materials and parts degrade so that they fail even under conditions for which they were designed. Maintenance problems are discussed in greater detail in Chapter 20.

4. *Exceeding specified limits.* A designer may have predicated the design on operation within specific speed, temperature, or load limits. If the operator exceeds these limits, the equipment may fail. A product that is designed for intermittent, short-term use, such as an emergency power generator, will not withstand continuous heavy loads.

5. *Environmental effects.* Environmental factors that cause malfunctions are common. Rain or other sources of water can cause equipment to be so flooded that it will not operate or so overloaded that it collapses; electrical equipment can short-circuit; and steel parts can rust, weaken, or seize. Ice (which results from moisture in the presence of low temperatures), dirt, corrosion, or contamination can cause parts or equipment to jam. Low temperatures can cause freezing of lubricants so that the equipment will not start and can cause water to freeze so that it bursts pipes and other containers. Vibration can cause metal fatigue and surface roughness.

Minimizing Failures

Probably the earliest method of minimizing failures was to overdesign a product or structure. The amount by which it was overdesigned was called the safety factor. Safety factors were to take care of faulty design, unknown factors, manufacturing defects, and degradation of the product over the years. The idea was that making an item two, three, or five times as strong as was actually necessary

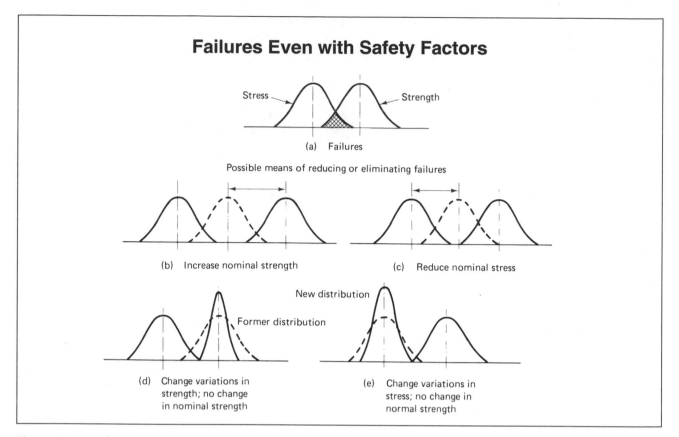

Failures Even with Safety Factors

Stress — Strength

(a)   Failures

Possible means of reducing or eliminating failures

(b)   Increase nominal strength

(c)   Reduce nominal stress

New distribution

Former distribution

(d)   Change variations in
strength; no change
in nominal strength

(e)   Change variations in
stress; no change in
normal strength

Figure 8-1.   Failures even with safety factors.

to withstand the stress which was to be imposed would reduce failures and accidents. Theoretically, a structure or component that had a safety factor of 4 would have twice the strength and would fail half as frequently as one that had a safety factor of 2.

In practice, this idea did not turn out to be true and led to another concept: the *margin of safety*. Several steel rods, for example, may be required in which each rod must have a nominal strength of 10,000 lb. per sq. in. (psi). There are, however, differences in the materials in each rod, in manufacturing workmanship and processing, and in handling or other activities. Some rods will fail under test at less than 10,000 psi, others at more, and the remainder at the stipulated nominal strength. If the number of failures were plotted against the stresses at which failures took place, the result would be a distribution function such as a normal curve. The result might look like the strength curve in Figure 8-1. If a similar plot were made of the stresses imposed, another curve would result which might overlap the first curve. Where failures would result is shown where there is an overlap [the shaded area in Figure 8-1(a)]. Thus, failures might result even though the nominal strength is greater than the stress that caused the rod to fail. Theoretically, the tails of the curves stretch to infinity so that there is always the possibility of an overlap where a stress may be greater than the strength.

To overcome this problem, the safety factor may be designated as the ratio between the minimum probable strength (S_{min}) to the maximum probable stress (L_{max}):

$$Safety\ factor = \frac{minimum\ strength}{maximum\ stress} = \frac{S_{min}}{L_{max}}$$

In some cases, safety margins are now used to indicate the difference between minimum strength and maximum stress. In terms of minimum strength, the safety margin can be expressed as:

$$Safety\ margin = \frac{minimum\ strength - maximum\ stress}{minimum\ strength}$$

The value for a safety margin should always be positive. If the value is negative, the stress and strength overlap and a situation such as that in Figure 8-1(a) exists.

Safety factors are sometimes expressed in other ways. For example, for aircraft a widely accepted practice is to design to a safety factor of 1.25 times the yield strength. Standards often require that pressure vessels be tested to 150% of the maximum expected operating pressure (MEOP) without permanent deformation (exceeding the yield strength). Other pressure vessels may have to be designed to withstand four times the MEOP without bursting, or in effect, requiring a safety factor of 4 based on ultimate strength.

Figure 8-1 illustrates how failures can be eliminated or their frequencies reduced:

1. Increase the nominal or mean strength of the component by selecting materials that have better properties. Instead of using steel that has a yield point of 30,000 psi, select one that has a yield point of 50,000 psi [Figure 8-1(b)].

2. Reduce the nominal stress that will be imposed on the part by increasing the area stressed by the load. For the same load, use a $\frac{3}{8}$-in. bolt instead of a $\frac{1}{8}$-in. bolt [Figure 8-1(c)].

3. Reduce the variations from the nominal strength by better workmanship, better finishes, and closer control of the production processes, materials, assembly, and handling. This will require no change in nominal strength, only in the deviations [Figure 8-1(d)].

4. Reduce the variations from the nominal unit stress by more rigid control of loads that could be imposed. Use of shock and vibration-absorbing devices will decrease deviations without changing the nominal value itself [Figure 8-1(e)].

5. Use of combinations of the above methods.

Reliability Engineering

Reliability engineering is the discipline principally concerned with failures and failure rate reduction. The basic concepts are indicated in Figure 8-2. There is an overlap between reliability and safety. Reliability is concerned with all malfunctions; safety is concerned with malfunctions that can result in injury or damage. (Only certain highlights of reliability are touched here to show applications to safety. For further details and applications, consult a good text on reliability.) Reliability engineers use a variety of methods to minimize the problems of failures of components and, thereby, of more complex equipment.

Derating

Derating is the equivalent in electronics to the use of safety factors in structures and mechanical equipment. Parts are failure rated by their manufacturers. Failures will occur under specific conditions and stresses. Reducing the stresses under which components must operate will reduce their failure rates. One of the principal stresses that adversely affects the lives of electronic equipment is increased temperature. In one method of derating, therefore, cooling is provided in order to reduce the operating temperature to the lowest level feasible even when the components operate at their normal capacities. The effect of temperature on capacitors is shown in Figure 8-3.

It can be seen in Figure 8-3 that the second affecting factor is the ratio of actual load to rated load as measured by voltage. As the load factor decreases, so does the failure rate.[1]

Redundancy

The reduction in failure rates obtainable by derating is generally far less than can be obtained through redundancy. There are a number of types in common use.

In parallel redundant designs the same functions are performed by two or more components, circuits, or subassemblies at the same time even though the combined outputs are not all required. Thus, if one unit fails, the remaining units can still carry on the product's function. This type of redundancy is generally applied to equipment that requires continuous operation. (Parallel circuits are not necessarily redundant; therefore, the correct terminology is *parallel redundance* or *replication*.) In the most common designs involving replication, there are generally only two components, circuits, or subassemblies in parallel, each of which could carry the entire load, such as the replication of single components in parallel circuits *A* and *B* (Figure 8-4).

If a configuration involves three parallel components, the unit will operate when one, two, or all three of the circuits operate. The three circuits will be load-sharing so that when all three circuits operate (the normal, designed condition), they are all derated and will have longer than normal lives.

If one circuit does fail, the other circuits have the capacity to assume the entire load until repairs can be made. Here again the most common design is to permit successful operation with only one operating unit.

The reliability of a triple redundant arrangement in which at least two circuits must be operative for the unit to provide the required output can be determined through the use of binomial probabilities. If the reliability of each component is R_c, the probability of at least two working is P(at least two working) = P(two working) + P(three working) or

$$R_{product} = 3R_c^2 (1 - R_c) + R_c^3$$

If the redundant circuits have different reliabilities, the equation would have to be modified.

Circuits involving more than triple redundancy are rare. The increase in reliability from more than three circuits is offset by the increased probabilities of loss of the more numerous components, and therefore increased maintenance, and by the increase in weight. A notable exception is the Boeing 747 airliner, which has four redundant flight control systems.

Decision Redundancy

With some triple redundant circuits each circuit is monitored and one is selected for operation. An additional unit monitors these individual outputs and decides which one is to be used. There are a number of techniques by which this decision can be made:[2]

Fundamentals of Reliability

Reliability is the probability that a piece of equipment or component will perform its intended function satisfactorily for a prescribed time under stipulated environmental conditions. Unreliabilty is the probability of failure. Reliabilities are expressed either as decimals or percentages. When reliability (R) is expressed as a decimal, unreliability (Q) is its complement and equals 1 - P. The reliability of an operation or test can therefore be established from: R = 1 - (No. of failures/No. of items at the start of the operation or test).

The frequency at which malfunctions occur is called the failure rate, λ. It is measured by the number of failures for each hour of operation or number of operations. Five failures in 1,000 hours of operation would constitute a failure rate of 0.005 per hr. The reciprocal of the failure rate is the mean time between failures (MTBF). The mean time between failures for a failure rate of 0.005 per hr. is 200 hr.

Equipment failures are of three types: (1) Early failures, which occur during the "debugging" or "burn-in" period due to poor assemblies or to weak, substandard components that fail too soon after the startup of a system. These are gradually eliminated with decrease in the early failure rate until the overall failure rate reaches a fairly constant level. This fairly constant level is attributable to random failures. (2) Random, or chance, failures result from complex, uncontrollable, and sometimes unknown, causes. The period during which malfunctions are due chiefly to random failures is the useful life of the component or system. (3) Wearout failures begin when the components are past their useful life periods. The malfunction rate increases sharply due to old age and to some random failures. Failure rates plotted against time for a large number of similar components produce the bathtub curve. Although reliability determinations are usually predicted on the useful, or random, failure period, the use of a constant failure rate concept is an oversimplification that has been undergoing modification lately.

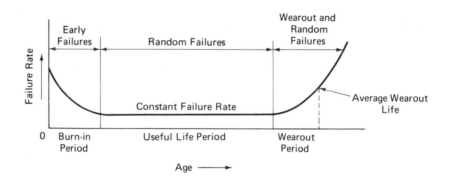

BATHTUB CURVE

According to the concept of constant failure rate, during the useful life of a large number of similar components, approximately the same number of failures will continue to occur in equal periods of time if failed items are replaced continually. The constant failure rate can be described mathematically by an exponential function. When failed items are not replaced, the number of failures during any period will decrease since there are fewer remaining items that can fail. The mathematical expression indicating the probability (or reliability) that components in a constant failure rate system will operate successfully to the end of a time period is the exponential law of reliability: $R = e^{-\lambda/t} = e^{-\lambda/T}$ where R is the reliability, e = 2.718, λ is the failure rate, t is the operating time, and T is the mean time between failures (MTBF).

The ratio, t/T, between required operating time (t) and mean time between failures (T) is of extreme importance according to the exponential law of reliability. When t equals T, whether each is one minute or 1,000 hours, reliability is 0.368 (36.8%). To increase reliability, it is necessary that the t/T ratio be decreased. When the mean time between failures is increased, the failure rate (which is its reciprocal) is also reduced.

The reliability of a complex system depends on the individual reliabilities of its components. If the operation of the system requires that all components operate satisfactorily at the same time, it is said to be a series system. In a series system, overall reliability is equal to the product of the individual reliabilities of the components:

$$\text{System Reliability, } R_5 = R_1 \times R_2 \times R_3 \times R_4 \ldots \ldots$$

This is called the Product Law of Reliability. In the event that each component of a six-component system has reliability of 90%, the overall reliability is: $R_5 = 0.9^6 = 0.53$ (53%). A system made up of 24 such series components would have an overall reliability of only 8%. Complex electronic systems are made up of thousands of components. To keep the reliability as high as possible and to minimize the effect of the Product Law, other means are employed, such as the use of extremely high reliability components, parallel redundant systems, standby systems, and operations under optimum conditions.

Where components are numerous, increasing individual reliabilities even a small amount can increase the overall reliability tremendously. A piece of equipment having 50 components in series, each having a reliability of 0.98, has an overall reliability of 0.36. Increasing each individual reliability to 0.99 raises the overall reliability to 0.60, an increase of 66.7%. However, the cost for each item with the higher reliability may be 600% to 1,500% greater.

Figure 8-2. Fundamentals of reliability.

Parallel redundant arrangements perform the same function at the same time even though the output of only one is required for the system to operate successfully. Both components must fail for the system to fail. The probability of simultaneous failures is the product of the individual failure probabilities of each operable arrangement. For example a component has a reliability of 81%; the probability of failure is 1 - 0.81, or 0.19. The probability of two failures in a parallel redundant system is (0.19)(0.19), or 0.36. System reliability is then 1 - 0.036, or 0.964 (96.4%). A doubly redundant system using three similar components in parallel would have an overall reliability of 99.3%. Redundant systems also have disadvantages. They increase cost, weight, volume, complexity, and maintenance. To retain the advantages of such systems, there must be a means to detect failed items and a system to ensure that they are replaced as soon as possible after failure.

Another means to increase reliability is to have standby or idling units that take over only when and if an operating units fails. To be effective, failure detection and switchover devices are necessary to activate the standby unit at the proper time. The little-used duplicate unit wears out at a much lower rate than the operating unit and does not require replacement as often. One unit may sometimes be the standby for any one of many components.

This method also has disadvantages. The failure detection and switchover devices do not have 100% reliability, so there is a possibility switchover may not be accomplished successfully. The standby unit itself may fail. Like parallel redundant systems, standby systems increase cost, weight, volume, maintenance, and complexity. Standbys are used in critical systems, especially for such facilities as electrical power for hospitals. Standby generators back up commercial power supplies or operating generators, and batteries sometimes back up the standby generators. Overall reliabilities of such electrical systems are extremely high.

Improving environmental operating conditions can also increase reliability. Parts are rated for specific conditions and stresses. Failures of electronic equipment increase with increased operating temperatures. Reducing operating temperatures prolongs the lives of electronic parts and thereby increases their reliabilities. Many computer units are provided with cooling units for this reason. Other environmental conditions that can be controlled to reduce failures are: humidity, shock, vibration, corrosive atmospheres, erosion, radiation, and friction.

Tests to establish reliability, especially of complex components or systems, are usually expensive, making a minimum of tests desirable. On the other hand, true probabilities are based on results from infinite or extremely large-sized samples. When only a few items are tested, the results may not be truly representative. Tossing a normal coin two or three times may result in heads each time. This may lead to the erroneous assumption that the result will always be heads. The next three tosses may all be heads again, all tails or combinations of heads or tails. With more and more tests, the average probability of a head (or tail) will be found to approach 0.50. The problem then arises as to how much confidence can be placed on past results to predict future performance. The term confidence level is used for this purpose. If it is believed that any prediction of future performance will be wrong no more than five times out of a hundred, the confidence level is 95%. Tables have been prepared to indicate the relationships between test results, reliability, and confidence. One such table is shown below in abbreviated form:

Number of Tests That Must Be Performed Without a Failure to Provide a Specific Minimum Reliability at Any Confidence Level

Minimum Reliability (%)	Confidence Level				
	90%	95%	97.5%	99%	99.5%
75	8	11	13	16	19
80	11	14	17	21	24
85	15	19	23	29	33
90	22	29	35	44	51
95	45	59	72	90	103
96	57	74	91	113	130
97	76	99	122	152	174
98	115	149	184	229	263
99	230	299	370	460	530

It has been found that most assemblies and systems actually do not have constant failure rates, especially when the systems does not have many components that are similar or have similar characteristics such as large mechanical units. Instead of being exponential, the distribution of failures may be Gaussian, Weibull, gamma or log normal. The chief difference is in establishment of failure rates. Means of improving reliability as indicated above remain the same.

In a constant failure rate system, the probability of failure of a component near the end of its useful life is no greater than at the beginning or any part of that period. Where the cause of failures is wear-out, the probability of a malfunction increases with the life of the component. Reliability decreases progressively and depends on the exact time that wear-out begins. In a constant failure rate system, the reliability decreases with overall time of use but not during the period of use, of the component. In many systems, the failure rate is assumed to be almost constant since continuing, regular maintenance is supposed to keep equipment in optimal operating condition. Components are not supposed to operate longer than their useful life periods, so that wear-out failures will not occur. By this concept of regular maintenance and replacement, the life of the equipment is endless; reliability is not degraded; and there will be no increase in failures. However, it has been found that components and equipment begin to wear out as soon as they begin to operate. Because of this fact, modification of the concept of constant failure rate and use of other failure distribution is necessary.

Figure 8-2 (cont'd). Fundamentals of reliability.

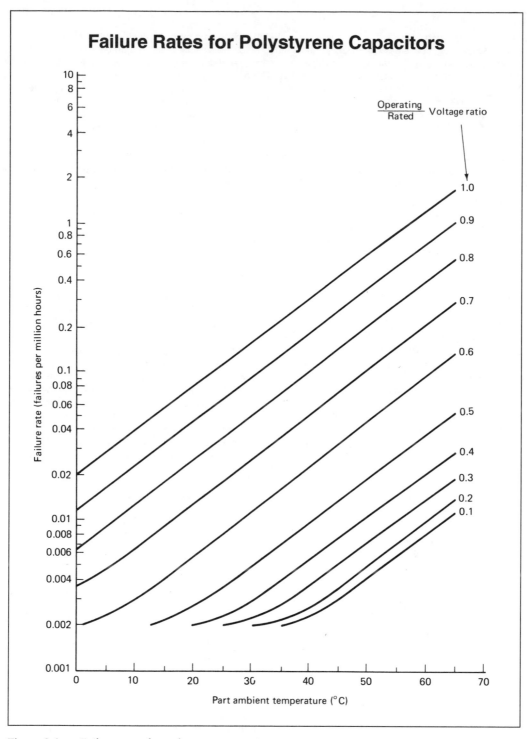

Figure 8-3. Failure rates for polystyrene capacitors.

1. *Majority vote.* With this technique the units operate on three input signals from parallel redundant systems. When one of the signals differs from the other two, the decision unit (voter) accepts the two similar signals as being correct. The probability of having two failures at the same time is possible but remote. If, however, this does happen or the voter fails, an error will result. Methods have been suggested by which even this problem can be lessened by replica-

tion in the voters.[3] With only one voter present, the probability of successful operation (P) is:

$$P = q[p^3 + 3p^2(1-p)] = qp^2(3-2p)$$

where
q = probability that the voter is working correctly;
p^3 = probability that all three logic units work;
$3p^2(1-p)$ = probability that two logic units work and one unit fails.

Redundancies

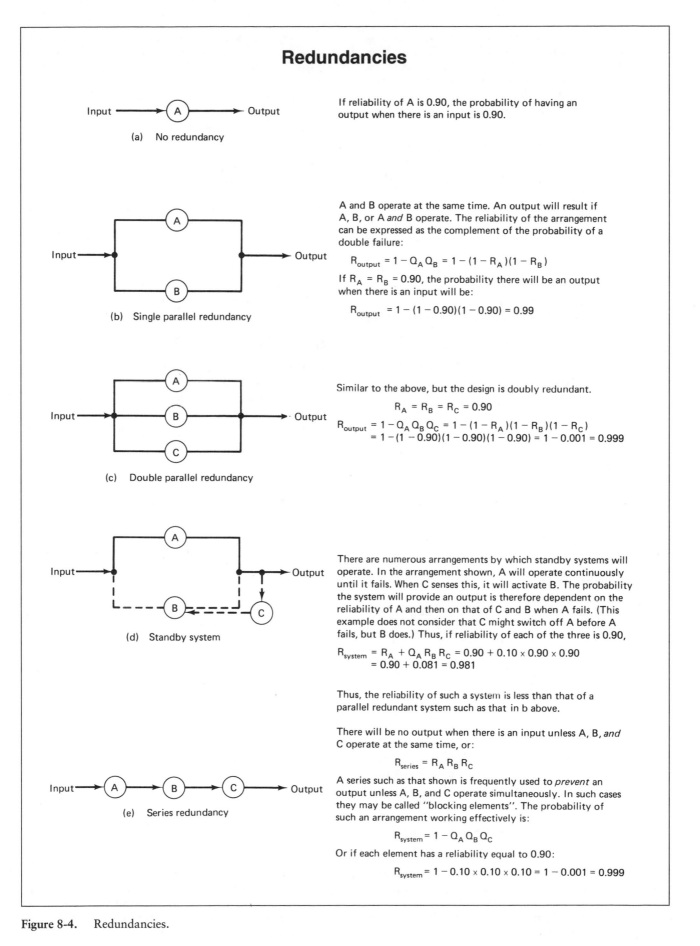

If reliability of A is 0.90, the probability of having an output when there is an input is 0.90. (shown with (a) No redundancy)

A and B operate at the same time. An output will result if A, B, or A *and* B operate. The reliability of the arrangement can be expressed as the complement of the probability of a double failure:

$$R_{output} = 1 - Q_A Q_B = 1 - (1 - R_A)(1 - R_B)$$

If $R_A = R_B = 0.90$, the probability there will be an output when there is an input will be:

$$R_{output} = 1 - (1 - 0.90)(1 - 0.90) = 0.99$$

Similar to the above, but the design is doubly redundant.

$$R_A = R_B = R_C = 0.90$$

$$R_{output} = 1 - Q_A Q_B Q_C = 1 - (1 - R_A)(1 - R_B)(1 - R_C)$$
$$= 1 - (1 - 0.90)(1 - 0.90)(1 - 0.90) = 1 - 0.001 = 0.999$$

There are numerous arrangements by which standby systems will operate. In the arrangement shown, A will operate continuously until it fails. When C senses this, it will activate B. The probability the system will provide an output is therefore dependent on the reliability of A and then on that of C and B when A fails. (This example does not consider that C might switch off A before A fails, but B does.) Thus, if reliability of each of the three is 0.90,

$$R_{system} = R_A + Q_A R_B R_C = 0.90 + 0.10 \times 0.90 \times 0.90$$
$$= 0.90 + 0.081 = 0.981$$

Thus, the reliability of such a system is less than that of a parallel redundant system such as that in b above.

There will be no output when there is an input unless A, B, *and* C operate at the same time, or:

$$R_{series} = R_A R_B R_C$$

A series such as that shown is frequently used to *prevent* an output unless A, B, and C operate simultaneously. In such cases they may be called "blocking elements". The probability of such an arrangement working effectively is:

$$R_{system} = 1 - Q_A Q_B Q_C$$

Or if each element has a reliability equal to 0.90:

$$R_{system} = 1 - 0.10 \times 0.10 \times 0.10 = 1 - 0.001 = 0.999$$

Figure 8-4. Redundancies.

2. *Median select.* In this arrangement the middle value of three signal outputs is selected. Variations are comparatively small when all three channels are working properly. Design still permits discrimination and acceptance of the middle-valued signal. This also occurs if one or two channels fail, even if failures occur with opposite outputs.

3. *TRISAFE (Triple Redundancy Incorporating Self-Adaptive Failure Exclusion).* Three amplifiers are connected at a common output point from which feedback gain is provided. If one channel fails, gain in one of the other amplifiers varies to compensate while the third continues to operate normally. The system will function unless all three signals to a voting point fail.

4. *Self-Organizing Concept (SOC).* This involves selection of an alternate signal path in event of a failure. It is analogous to the capabilities of the human nervous system in carrying out its functions. A detection unit determines when a failure has occurred and selects a new signal path until output is correct.

Standby Systems

Another method of increasing product reliability through redundancy is to have inoperative or idling standby units that take over when and if an operating unit fails. There must be failure detection and switchover devices to activate the standby unit at the proper time. The inoperative or idling redundant unit wears out much more slowly than does the operating unit and it requires much less frequent replacement. The operations of the units are sometimes alternated for this reason. In some cases, one unit can provide standby capacity for four or five operating units.

Activation of the standby unit may be manual, automatic, or both. A common example is the braking system on an automobile: If the hydraulic system fails, a hand brake is available. In this case, the driver is the detecting and activating agent. In other usages the failure could be detected and indicated to the operator so that he can activate the standby system if and when he wants. In fully automatic systems, detection and activation are interlocked so that failure of the operating unit causes activation of the standby equipment with a minimum of delay.

Hospitals that normally depend on commercial power frequently have an alternate backup source to furnish power for operating rooms, incubators, and intensive care units. Diesel generators may be standbys for commercial power supplies and batteries for diesels. The criticality of the potential loss of power determines what backup should be used and whether switching should be manual or automatic.

The detecting and switching devices do not have 100% reliabilities and may malfunction. Thus, the standby units may fail to activate when required or they may activate erroneously. Generally, the latter does not have any adverse effect, but the possibilities should be investigated

when the arrangement is designed. In some instances, the standby units, especially those that are rarely used or tested, may fail. As a result, the fact that the detection, switching, and standby units may themselves fail limits the reliability attainable by this method.

Series Redundancy

Multiple units arranged in a series in which *all* must operate to permit an output to occur create a *series redundant arrangement* (Figure 8-4). Generally, these arrangements are used to prevent inadvertent outputs that could be damaging if they occurred prematurely. In a series arrangement, all of the elements must be converted from safe open or off states to activated states before the device can be energized by the output. With series redundancy all the units in the series must fail if the device is to activate inadvertently; therefore, the probability of occurrence is generally low. As an example, see the discussion on coffee mills on page 148.

Screening

As pointed out on page 63, one means of reducing failures is to narrow the dispersion of strengths through good manufacturing practices and quality control. Components whose strengths are inferior are rejected. Screening attempts to eliminate components that may pass operating tests for specific parameters but with indications that they will fail within an unacceptable time. Screening requires four steps:

1. The parameters whose limits are not to be exceeded must be selected.

2. The limit for each parameter must be established. When product requirements are known, the limits can be based on expected operating conditions.

3. The components must be inspected and tested to verify that they meet the established limitations.

4. Items that fail to meet any limit may be rejected.

In one type of reliability screening both lower and upper limits may have to be observed. The lower limit is constrained to the highest possible level so that the margin of safety becomes a maximum. Limits can be prescribed for (1) extremely high-reliability items, (2) less critical applications, and (3) noncritical items.

Lower and upper limits are required for devices such as pressure diaphragms, which must not fail at less than a specific pressure but must rupture at another, higher level. In most cases, however, the upper limit need not be controlled; extremely high-strength values merely indicate extremely high abilities to withstand stresses.

Screening may also be done by operating the component or assembly over the time when burn-in failures may be expected to occur. If we refer to the bathtub curve in Figure 8-2, this type of screening consists of eliminating those items that would fail before the constant failure-rate portion of the curve begins. This type of screening is based on the fact that defects in manufacturing or assembly will become apparent immediately or soon after use begins. Substandard components can be eliminated or replaced so that the customer's problems will be reduced.

Burn-in testing requires that the stresses to which the components or assemblies are to be subjected and the criteria they must meet first be established. The levels of stress and their durations are specified so that substandard items will be detected but that no damage is done to satisfactory items. Visual inspections are made immediately after the tests are completed to determine if other damage has resulted not indicated by test equipment.

Accelerated-life testing shortens the time to determine how long long-lived components will last. It involves testing the items at much higher stresses than they would be subjected to under normal operations. Accelerated-life testing may be considered the reverse of derating. It involves testing a group of components by destruction of a sample. It therefore cannot be used as a 100% method of screening and therefore differs from the other types of screening described previously.

Accelerated-life testing has other weaknesses, the principal one being that there may be a change in the mode of failure. An increase in temperature may cause soldered connections to melt and fail when such failures would not occur at the usual operating temperature. The processes by which components wear out may be altered, producing conditions resulting in many more failures than usual. There may also be difficulty in determining the true relationship between the relative increases in stress and failure rate. An exponential increase in stress may only produce a linear increase in failure rate. Some types of stress may not be time dependent so that increasing stress levels may not accelerate the effects. Careful selection of test parameters is necessary to ensure that they are suitable for accelerated testing.

In the basic type of accelerated-life testing, constant-stress testing, groups of components are stressed at constant levels for each group. The number of components in each group must be large enough to make the test statistically significant. The results are then plotted and analyzed to determine whether there are abnormalities and failures. Whenever they are justified, extensions of values for predictions can be made.

The other two types of accelerated-life testing are step-testing and progressive-stress testing. In step-testing increasingly higher levels of stress are applied to the components, with each level of stress imposed for a specific duration of time. In progressive-type testing, different groups are started at different stress levels which are increased at a constant, regular rate.

Timed Replacements

In order to maintain a constant failure rate, components should be replaced before they wear out. In addition, some operations are so critical that it is necessary to keep failures to an absolute minimum. Replacement too soon is wasteful and creates an unnecessary maintenance and supply workload. In addition, excessive use of new units can result in burn-in failures.

Timed replacements can be made in two principal ways. The more common method uses manufacturer's failure data such as that shown in Figure 8-5. When these data are used with the expected operating time, the number of operational cycles after which wear-out failures can be expected to begin can be approximated. Replacements can then be programmed at shorter intervals. This is the premise on which maintainability programs are generally based.

The second means of determining the optimum time to make replacements in operating systems is by noting component *degradation* or *drift*. Most components in electronic and electrical products deteriorate gradually. An assembly can be tested for a specific characteristic, such as current flow through a specific circuit under a specific voltage. The results of the tests are plotted. At specified time intervals, the same tests are made and the changes, or drift, are noted. As the characteristics of the assembly near the points at which changes will become failures, the components involved will be replaced. Plotting the characteristics this way permits calculation of the time at which the components will no longer perform their functions adequately. The entire lot can then be replaced at the most opportune time.

Noting degradation to establish when replacements should be made was developed for aircraft use. For example, the SOAP (Spectrometric Oil Analysis Program) procedure to determine when aircraft engines should be overhauled (see page 108) is finding other applications. Automobile brakes now have indicators which indicate wear incorporated in the brake linings. From these it is possible to estimate the remaining useful life of the brakes.

Reliability Versus Safety

It has generally been assumed that reliability and safety are synonymous. This is true only in special cases. It has been pointed out that a product can be perfectly made and still be hazardous. A very common example of a very highly reliable but frequently unsafe product is the pistol. A special example was the nonpropulsive attachment (NPA) formerly used on the Navy's Sidewinder missile. The NPA looked like an automobile piston with four equidistant holes bored around its side and made to fit on the end of the Sidewinder's rocket motor. If the motor accidentally ignited while the missile was in storage, while it was being transported, or while it was being hung under the wing of a launch aircraft, the NPA would direct the exhaust gases out at right angles rather than straight back. In these cases the missile could not move. The NPA had almost perfect reliability; there was no case in which it did not work. Unfortunately, there were occasions

Generic Failure Rates

The failure rates listed below were taken from the *Nonelectronic Reliability Notebook*, Rome Air Development Center, Griffis Air Force Base, New York, January 1975 (AD/A−oo5 657). The *Notebook* contains failure rates from military systems, including ground, aircraft, space, and submarine equipment. The values selected for this table were taken almost entirely from the ground (stationary) or ground (mobile) categories. For further information, including other components and the mathematics of reliability, the *Notebook* should be consulted. The reliance which can be placed on the values shown will vary, depending on the actual experience data which was received from the field, and the reliability levels to which the equipment in which they were used was designed.

PART	FAILURE RATE (Failures per 10^6 Part-hours)
Batteries, rechargeable	27.027
Bearings, general	21.921
Bearings ball	9.142
Blowers and fans, centrifugal	9.542
Boards, printed circuit	0.003
Connections, solder	0.0039
Connections, welded	0.0017
Connections, wire wrap	0.000014
Connectors, rectangular	0.0065
Engines, diesel	1733.111
Engines, gas turbine	577.397
Gaskets and seals, gaskets	1.433
Gaskets and seals, O - rings	1.182
Gaskets and packing	0.24
Heater, electrical	2.151
Hoses, general	0.240
Instruments, meter	0.366
Instruments, indicator, air press	1.020
Instruments, indicator, fuel qty.	78.811
Instruments, indicator, liquid level	11.905
Instruments, indicator, temperature	62.016
Instruments, indicator, velocity	97.096
Mechanism, power trans, coupling	4.662
Mechanism, power trans, fan belt	4.007
Mechanism, power trans, gear box	11.726
Mechanism, power trans, pulley	39.279
Motors, electrical, induction	14.774
Motors, electrical fract. hp, ac	7.552
Motors, electrical 2 hp, ac	2.413
Motors, electrical 5 hp, ac	4.825
Motors, electrical 10 hp, ac	1.206
Motors, electrical motor generator set	27.778
Generators	9.34
Generators, turbine driven	11.925
Pumps, boiler feed	0.422
Pumps, centrifugal	12.058
Pumps, fuel	23.121
Relays, general	0.166
Relays, latching	0.569
Switches, pushbutton	0.270
Switches, rotary	1.329
Tanks, fuel	7.745
Valves, check	3.014
Valves, globe	0.185
Valves, relief	1.514
Valves, solenoid	2.404

Figure 8-5. Generic failure rates.

when ordnancemen failed to remove the NPA's after they had hung the missiles under the aircraft. When the pilots attempted to launch the missiles in flight, the hot gas discharge hit the wings and caused damage so severe that the planes had to be abandoned. After the third loss of an aircraft for this reason, the Navy eliminated the use of the NPA.

Because of factors such as hazardous characteristics, human error, and environmental stresses, reliability is only one factor in product safety that must be considered. Reliability is a large aspect of safety, but it is generally not synonymous with it.

Malfunctions Versus Damage

Insurance companies, except under special coverages, do not pay to correct malfunctions. They *do* pay for the damages or injuries that result from malfunctions. For example, if a resistor or condenser in a TV set malfunctions and the set ignites producing a fire, the insurer pays for the damage caused by the fire but does not pay for replacement of the resistor or condenser. More and more, however, cause-and-effect relationships are being established, both by analyses and by events, even when the relationship seems remote. In the case of the Ford Pinto mentioned on page 22, the carburetor malfunctioned. The usual effect of such a malfunction is that the car will not run. In the case cited, the failure of the carburetor on a busy highway exposed the car and its occupants to the danger of collision. If a car has power steering, the loss of power while the car is in motion could make the car hard to steer, perhaps with catastrophic consequences.

Whereas hazardous characteristics can generally be proscribed by suitable design criteria, malfunction consequences are usually determined by analysis. This can be done by methods indicated in later chapters. For example, fault-tree analysis reverses the procedure: A consequence is selected and then the circumstances, including malfunctions, that can cause the consequence are determined.

Categories of Malfunctions

In addition to categories of malfunctions listed in the first paragraph of this chapter, malfunctions can be categorized into:

1. Structural failures.

2. Mechanical malfunctions.

3. Power source failures.

4. Electrical malfunctions (from the power source to and including the load).

Some of the causes and effects of malfunctions and failures are listed in Figure 8-6. Certain of these categories overlap so that assignment of malfunctions or failures to one category or another is rather arbitrary. For example, lack of electric power could result from or be considered an electrical malfunction or it could be considered a power failure. In Figure 8-6, if the loss of power were within a transmission or distribution system or in the connecting equipment, it would be considered an electrical malfunction; if the loss were at the power source, it would be considered a power failure.

Malfunctions and Failures

Possible Effects	Possible Causes
Structural damage or failure	
Bending, distortion, or breakage that causes a product to fail in: • its structural function • mating with another part • alignment of parts • inability to disassemble from another part	Inadequate design strength for expected loads Inadequate care of metal surfaces during manufacture or handling Reduction of strength by corrosion Crimping of metal sheet Poorly fitted or inadequately tightened parts Loss of strength with temperature Loss of ductility, and brittleness produced by cold Fatigue due to vibrations Fatigue due to thermal cycling
Cracking or initial surface or edge failure that causes: • stress concentrations which lead to complete failures • irregular and rough surfaces • places where contaminants can accumulate • regions were corrosion can take place	Overloading Overpressures due to internal or external fluid Excessively high centrifugal force Rough handling Overtorquing of nuts and bolts Inadvertent exposure to aerodynamic loads High accelerations and decelerations
Breaking or complete failure of an object by separation into two or more parts: • cable, chain or sling failure • rupture of pressure vessels • tearing of thin materials • shearing of metal or plastic parts or their connections • twisting and shearing of shafts, nuts, belts, or pins • shattering of brittle materials • splitting away of a portion or of an extension of a body from its main mass	Impacts between moving vehicles or vessels or with structures Hard object dropped on a vulnerable part Moving object hitting a vulnerable part Rotating part hitting a stationary object Cutting or punching by sharp pointed objects Bird strikes Grounding of ships Blast overpressures
Crimping or creasing or cutting into a metal sheet, wire, cable or pipe: • reducing cross section and strength, permitting easy breakage • reducing or blocking flow of fluid • leakage of fluid • creating a high resistance point in an electrical wire or cable	Stress concentrations due to: • residuals due to manufacturing processes • scratches and gouges due to lack of care in handling • sharp corners • surface treatment • assembly stresses due to torquing or fits • surface roughness due to corrosion, chemical action, abrasion, or erosion • openings such as rivet or bolt holes • sharp bends or crimping • welding arc starts or other spark marks
Crushing or collapse of containers or structures delaminations of layered materials	Stress reversals due to: • vibrating or oscillating equipment • flexing panels • cyclic changes from tension to compression • temperature changes due to starting and stopping thermal equipment, or diurnal changes • pressure changes on containers

Figure 8-6. Malfunctions and failures.

Possible Effects	Possible Causes

Mechanical malfunctions
- Equipment will not operate
- Vibration and noise
- Bearing problems

Broken part
Separation of couplings
Separation of fasteners
Failure to release holding device or interlock
Binding due to heavy corrosion or contamination

Misalignment of parts
Misaligned, loose, or broken rotating or reciprocating
   equipment or parts
Broken or worn out vibration isolators or shock absorbers

Bearings worn due to overloading
Bearings too tight or too loose
Lack of lubrication

Power source failure
- Complete inactivation of power dependant systems
- Lack of propulsion during a critical period
- Guidance failure of a moving vehicle
- Failure during flight of airborne systems
- Inability to activate other systems
- Failure of life support systems
- Failure of safety monitoring and warning systems
- Failure of emergency or rescue and warning systems
- Failure of emergency or rescue systems

Prime mover failure
- Internal combustion unit
  - Fuel exhaustion or lack
  - Oxygen exhaustion or lack
  - Lack or failure of ignition source for chemical reaction
  - Interface with reaction
  - Mechanical malfunction
  - Failure of the cooling system
  - Failure of the lubricating system

Blockage of steam, gas or water used to drive turbines

Excessive wear of power equipment
Mechanical damage to power equipment
Poor adjustment of critical device

Failure of connection to electric generator
Excessive speed due to lack of control

Loss of electrolyte for battery or fuel cell

Electrical system failure
- Entire system inoperative
- Specific equipment will not operate
- Interruption of communications
- Detection and warning devices inactivated
- Failure of lighting systems
  - Release of holding devices

Faulty connector or connection
Failure to make connection
Conductor cut
Fuses, circuits breakers, or cutouts open
Conductor burned out
Switch or other device open or broken
Short circuit
Overloading

Figure 8-6 (cont'd). Malfunctions and failures.

Notes

[1] Nonelectronic items appear to act the same. For example, R. J. Will points out that the reduction in life of a speed reducer can be approximated by $L_r = -10^7/(P_o/P_r)^{10/3}$, where L_r is the reduced life; P_o is the overload; P_r is the rated load; and 10 million cycles is the normal operating life. [See Will's article, "Selecting Speed Reducers," *Machine Design* (Sept. 7, 1977), pp. 116-120.]

[2] F. R. Taylor, *Impact of Reliability Requirements on Flight Control Development* (Wright-Patterson AFB, Ohio: Air Force Flight Dynamics Laboratory, March 1967).

[3] M. Longden, L. J. Page, and R. A. Scantlebury, "An Assessment of the Value of Triplicated Redundancy in Digital Systems, *Microelectronics and Reliability* (Oxford, England: Pergamon Press, 1966), pp. 39-55.

Questions

1. What are the various malfunctions that can occur with products?

2. What are five types of malfunction causes?

3. What is meant by a safety margin? What would a safety margin of 0.25 mean? If calculations show that the safety margin is –0.25, what does this indicate?

4. When a code or regulation cites a safety factor of 4, what is generally meant? What would a safety factor of 1.25 mean?

5. What is the definition of "reliability" of a product or component?

6. Describe the "bathtub" curve and the various periods along the age axis.

7. What does "derating" a component mean?

8. Describe a parallel redundant arrangement and explain why it is used.

9. Why is a standby system frequently less reliable than a system that has active parallel redundance?

10. What is series redundancy often used for?

11. Discuss why quantitative reliability figures generally cannot be used as measures of safety. Discuss when they can be used.

12. List ten causes of structural failures, eight causes of mechanical malfunctions, five causes of power source failures, and five causes of electrical system failure.

13. Discuss the statement that claims that because a warranty is a contractual relationship between a manufacturer and a purchaser, it is the manufacturer or dealer that is protected from liability not the purchaser. The statement maintains that warranties were not designed with the customer in mind, since they spell out the limits to which the purchaser will be restrained in performance, time, extent, and rapidity by which a malfunctioning product should be repaired or replaced, and warranties therefore become important in cases of malfunctions.

14. Using automobiles as an example, discuss why and how warranties affect initial costs, as well as the cost of repair and replacement of malfunctioned products.

15. What is a "lemon" when referring to a mechanical product? Discuss the effects on a company which produces a product claimed to be a "lemon." What would you say was the difference between a malfunction and a "lemon"? Is one actionable in court?

9

Environmental Factors in Product Safety

Before the Industrial Revolution the environmental conditions that affected humans were those generated by meteorological and climatological conditions. There were ancient beliefs that certain adverse environmental conditions were directed specifically at individuals who had offended the gods. Lightning strikes were the weapon of the chief of any hierarchy of pagan gods; winds, storms, and other effects were used by gods lower in the hierarchy. Today, environmental problems are considered to include not only those of the natural environment but also those generated by humans. Figure 9-1 indicates some of the safety problems produced by the environment and their causes. Where similar conditions exist in man-made environments, similar effects can be generated.

For an orderly review of other problems, environments can arbitrarily be divided into the following categories:

1. Natural environment.
2. Induced environments.
3. Controlled environments.
4. Artificial environments.
5. Free environments.
6. Closed environments.
7. Combinations of the above.

The Natural Environment

A *natural* environment is one unaffected by the actions of humans. Environmentalists love to illustrate the natural environment by pictures of clear-flowing streams; white, undisturbed beaches and shorelines; or grass-covered meadows and forested areas inhabited by animals and birds. They do not show the adverse effects of such environments, such as the crash of a Lockheed Electra which occurred shortly after taking off from the airport at Boston, killing 62 of the persons aboard and wrecking the aircraft. The probable cause: birds ingested into the engines and oil coolers so that there was a power failure.

Each area of the United States (and of the world) is subject to one or more environmental hazards that can be catastrophic on a broad scale: earthquakes, flood, hurricanes, lightning strikes, blizzards, and so on. The natural environment sometimes displays other characteristics of wind, heat, and cold which could result in damage to products. Most products are not made for use in the most extreme weather conditions, but those extremes can be cited in order to show how adverse the environment can get: temperatures as low as −127°F (−88°C) (Antarctica, 1960) and −90°F (−68°C) (Siberia, 1892 and 1933); temperatures as high as 126°F (58°C) (El Azizia, Libya, 1922); wind speeds up to 225 mph (362 kmph) (Mt. Washington, New Hampshire, 1934); change in temperature from −4°F to 45°F (−20°C to 7°C) in 2 min. (Spearfish, South Dakota, 1943); and hailstones 5.4 in. (14 cm) in diameter (Potter, Nebraska, 1928). Men occupied those places when those measurements were made. Products they took there had to be made to cope with such conditions or the products failed. Most products are not subjected to and are not manufactured for these extremes; they are made for lesser conditions. Even under these lesser conditions many products have failed.

In December 1967 the bridge over the Ohio River at Mt. Pleasant, West Virginia, collapsed, dropping 75 cars and trucks into the water below, resulting in the deaths of 46 persons. Among the possible causes of the structural failure were two environmental factors. Changes in temperature, both diurnal and seasonal, would have caused almost continuous cycles of metal expansion and contraction over the years and eventual failure of an eyebar

Environment and Weather Problems

Possible Effects	Possible Causes

High humidity conditions

Loss of visibility due to fog, clouds, or condensation
Possibility of or acceleration of corrosion
Short circuits, inadvertent activations, or disruptions
of electrical systems by moisture condensation in
electrical devices
Skidding and loss of control of vehicle caused by wet
surfaces
Surface friction for traction reduced by wet surfaces
Flooding of facilities, shops, vehicles, and equipment
Loss of buoyancy of boats and other vessels
Washing away of foundations and equipment
Drowning of personnel
Warping and sticking of wood doors, drawers, and
similar items
Swelling of water absorbent materials
Icing of equipment
Personnel discomfort

Moisture and humidity

Rain, clouds, fog, dew, snow
Tides and floods
Lakes, rivers and other natural water sources
Vegetation and animal respiration
Temperature decrease without removal of moisture
Condensation on cold surfaces
Flooding and immersion in water
Naturally high atmospheric humidity
Personnel perspiring in inadequately ventilated
enclosure, equipment, or impermeable covering
Presence of humidifying equipment

Low humidity conditions

Drying out and cracking of organic materials
Generating dusty conditions
Increased tendency for creation of static electricity
Easier ignition of accidental fires
Increase in airborne salts, sand, dirt and fungi

Low relative humidity
Hot weather with little moisture
Heat in a closed room in winter
Moisture removed by airconditioning

Radiation

Ultraviolet radiation effects of sunlight
Infrared radiation effects
Snow blindness
Difficulty in guiding a vehicle or in reading dials and
meters caused by strong sunlight

Sunlight

High and low temperature effects

Weather and climate changes

Contamination

Sand, dirt, moisture, fungi...
Concentration of toxic gases, smog or particulate
matter caused by inversions
Electrical conductivity of water increased by salt, thus
reducing insulation value and permitting galvanic
coupling and deterioration of adjacent dissimilar
metals

Airborne salts, dusts, sand, dirt,...

Wind effects

Wind chill
Structural overloads, movement, or toppling caused
by pressure effects of wind
Sudden accelerations due to turbulence and gusts
Energized power lines blown down by wind

Meteorological and micrometeorological conditions

Electrical effects

Shock to personnel
Overloading of electrical circuits and equipment
Ignition of combustible materials
Other electrical effects

Lightning

Mechanical effects

Impact damage
Implosions and crushing of closed vessels
Pressure vessel ruptures
Dysbarism and bends

Hail
Water pressure, atmospheric pressure
Reduced atmospheric pressure
Changes in pressure

Figure 9-1.　Environment and weather problems.

which helped sustain the bridge structure. In addition, the extremely low (although not abnormal) temperature of the Ohio winter could have made the steel brittle, causing the steel to crack and fail under the load and vibration of the crossing vehicles. Increased knowledge in effects of extremely low temperatures and of temperature cycling will result in improved designs and materials to mitigate these problems and eliminate such disasters.

During and immediately after World War II there were numerous cases of welded ships breaking in two because of similar problems. Extreme cold made the welds brittle. In heavy seas the hulls of the ships were subjected to stresses which caused the welds to fail. Cold can be equally as detrimental to other products. Equipment and welded structures were subjected to intensive thermal stresses in Alaska during construction of the oil pipeline. Automobiles, even in the other 48 mainland states, have freeze plugs in their cooling systems to protect their cylinder blocks. If the water coolant freezes, the plug ruptures, preventing damage to the block.

In Hawaii the moderate heat and high humidity create another environmental problem for many products. These products must be protected against rust which could cause failures of mechanical equipment or structures. Moisture absorption can cause nonmetallic materials to expand and bind. Accumulations of moisture can cause electrical shorts and malfunctions.

Generally, the adverse effects of the natural environment, such as lightning, storms, heavy rains or similar disasters, were considered "Acts of God" for which no one could be held liable. In March 1962 the Pennsylvania Supreme Court ruled that any event formerly termed an "Act of God" would no longer be considered an acceptable defense against claims for liability. The fundamental reason appears to be that for each foreseeable hazard a safeguard can generally be provided. (It is doubtful that this ruling would be maintained if the adverse environment exceeded by far extreme conditions which could reasonably be expected.)

For example, the damaging effects of lightning strikes can often be avoided through the use of protective devices. Lawrence[1] points out that in the 50 years following the start of the British–French wars in 1793 more than 250 ships were struck by lightning and were damaged. During one 16-year period there were 150 cases which resulted in more than 70 seamen being killed and 133 being wounded, and in masts and spars being damaged. In 10 percent of the cases the ships were so disabled that they had to return to port for repairs. The Show Harris system of lightning protection for ships was patented and adopted in 1853. It eliminated almost totally the high incidence of death and destruction caused by lightning striking the ships.

More mundane items in the natural environment can also result in accidents, injury, and damage. Rocks hidden in snow through which a snowmobile is traveling can result in a smashing impact or in overturning of the vehicle with injury to the occupants. Streets wet with rain can be inducive to skidding of automobiles, loss of control, and damaging impacts.

Induced Environments

The activities of humans have resulted in conditions not normally found in a natural environment or found to such a meager extent they could be disregarded. Exhaust from automobiles, heating plants, refineries, and other industrial processes can cause smog that irritates the eyes and lungs, reduces visibility, and annoys people so that they are more likely to make errors and cause accidents.

A piece of electronic equipment can generate heat which may cause rapid deterioration of components so that they malfunction. The heat has induced a change in the environment immediately surrounding the components. Reliability engineers consider not only temperature but also vibration, shock, and radiation as environmental conditions that could have an effect on the products they are analyzing. Most of these conditions are induced by humans. Differentials on automobiles were failing at an abnormally high rate in the northeastern states. The severe natural winter conditions had been considered in the selection of metals used, but the selection had not included the consideration that salt would be put on the roads to melt ice. The salt then caused corrosion and failures of the differentials.

Controlled Environments

One or more aspects of the natural environment may be modified or limited for a specific purpose. Air may be heated or cooled, filtered, or dried or humidified to make it suitable for occupancy. Gas masks remove harmful gases, vapors, or particulate matter that might be present in the atmosphere around the wearer, leaving the person breathable air to use.

Artificial Environments

An artificial environment neither derives from nor is part of the natural environment. It is created for a purpose for which a controlled environment is inadequate. To exclude the air that could combine with some of the metals being arc-welded, helium is used to create an extremely localized artificial environment that encompasses only the spot being welded.

Other examples include:

1. Nitrogen or other inert gas in a container for long-term protection of a material that deteriorates in the presence of air.

2. Nitrogen in tanks of fuel or other highly combustible liquids to exclude the oxygen in air which permits fires to be started.

3. Underwater storage of substances that react in air, such as phosphorous, lignite, or sub-bituminous coal.

Free Environments

A free environment is one in which the movements of masses of air are unrestricted. Natural or man-made obstacles may divert the flow of air but they do not prevent the air from intermixing with other masses. A free environment is not necessarily a safe environment. Structures, equipment, and vehicles have been damaged by winds sweeping across open areas and blown away. A liquid oxygen plant was subject to reboiler and compressor explosions. Investigation determined that small amounts of acetylene released from a nearby plant were wind-borne to the compressor intakes. The acetylene accumulated until it reached amounts that exploded under the concentration, pressure, and heat generated by the compressors.

Closed Environments

A closed environment is one in which movement of air is restricted. Humans have probably had problems with closed environments since they built the first fire in a cave. A closed environment can become extremely hazardous because of the presence of even small amounts of toxic gas. Housewives have died because they mixed household cleansers which together produced chlorine gas. In a free environment the amounts of chlorine generated would have been comparatively small and the movement of air would have dissipated the gas. In the close confines of a space as small as a bathroom, the concentrations became fatal. In 1964, 53 men died as a result of a fire in a Titan II silo in which only 93 gallons of hydraulic oil were involved. Millions of gallons of petroleum products have been burned in above-ground tank farms without injury to anyone. In the silo, carbon monoxide killed the 53 men within minutes.

Closed environments have resulted in heavy concentrations of flammable vapors from liquids that were being used for cleaning reaching gas heater pilot lights. The pilot lights ignited the vapors so that flash fires, and sometimes explosions, resulted. Carbon monoxide poisoning in closed, parked automobiles in which engines were kept running to provide heat has killed the occupants. Even in moving cars, carbon monoxide that has leaked into the occupied space has overcome the occupants. If the gas itself didn't kill them, it made the drivers drowsy so that they lost control of their cars and were involved in accidents. Children have suffocated in refrigerators and trunks in which they hid while playing. (Such tragedies were the cause of the passage of the Refrigerator Safety Act.) Children (and animals) have also been suffocated in closed cars in which they were left while their parents went shopping.

Long-Term and Short-Term Effects

Environmental effects can be immediate or long-term. Immediate effects include interference with operations or material damage. Heavy rain can damage electrical equipment by causing it to short out. High humidity can cause environments to become unbearable for personnel.

Long-term effects can involve slow reactions that generate damage or loss of ability to function. Moisture can cause corrosion over varying lengthy periods so that equipment is ruined. Ultraviolet light from the sun can cause deterioration of rubbers, plastics, fabrics, and paints.

Changes in environment can also produce long- and short-term effects. Changes in temperature can cause expansion and contraction of metals so that fatigue failures result. Campus[2] pointed out how very large steel beams, some of them 30 ft. in length, failed longitudinally through their webs, even while not loaded externally, because of changes in temperature while still in a warehouse. The temperature changes caused them to fail along lines of maximum residual stress produced internally during manufacture.

Changes in temperature, due to solar heating and the cold of night, with their attendant stresses occur in both the external structure and in the interior bulkheads of ships. More gradual effects occur when a ship moves from a tropic to a frigid zone or vice versa. The complex inter-relationships between stresses due to changes in temperature, structural loads on the hull, vibration, brittleness, and rigidity of welds as compared to riveted joints, produced a rash of hull failures of welded ships built during World War II.

Various environmental factors have been investigated as the causes of personnel errors and accidents. Most common of the factors investigated have been temperature, humidity, pressure, vibration, and combinations of these. A study at Sandia Laboratories in New Mexico investigated whether or not there were correlations between accidents and time of day, magnetic influence, lunar or solar influence, or annual cycles. (Preliminary data showed no correlations between most of these, but the findings indicated that more research was required for others before decisions on correlations could be made.)

Analyses and Tests

Environmental factors in combination may generate effects totally different or of different magnitudes from what they would individually. For example, corrosion is a problem in which moisture is present but temperature may affect corrosion in different ways. High temperature accelerates corrosion, but it may reduce environmental relative humidity. Low temperature may lessen the corrosion rate and absolute humidity, but the relative humidity and condensation of moisture may increase. Therefore, it is necessary to explore these factors and the stresses they generate individually and in combination with all other factors and stresses.

Environmental considerations and analyses are predicated heavily on tests and experience because of the multiplicity of variations that could exist in almost every situation. In addition to the temperature and humidity aspects, corrosion may also depend on such factors as the composition of the metal, the size and arrangement of its crystals, the heat treatment to which it was subjected, the surface finish, presence of any stress concentrators, any stresses imposed, length and duration of vibrations to which it was subjected, protective coatings or films, presence of salt air to which it has been exposed, orientation of a crack or other surface defect to moisture or dirt, and numerous other factors. Rather than evaluate each of these factors and their interrelationships separately, it is frequently much simpler to make tests of the products in question under environmental conditions approximating those expected during operation. If there are enough tests, minor differences between similar products become unimportant and can be disregarded. Major affecting factors and their end effects will then become apparent and decisions on material suitability based on these factors can then be made.

Any technique or process that can minimize environmental testing costs is highly desirable. Tests under actual field conditions require that the product and the test personnel and equipment be transported to desert, arctic, or tropical sites. Then they have to wait until environmental conditions are suitable. This is extremely time-consuming and expensive, especially if tests must be conducted in more than one type of climate. Some field testing must undoubtedly be done, but anything to reduce its necessity or duration may save time and money.

Computer simulations have been used to make initial determinations. Arnold has described how information on actual or stipulated environments is used in a computer simulation process.[3] Environmental factors, listed in Figure 9-2, are plotted against some of the material or process parameters that might be affected. The two are compared by computer techniques. Figure 9-2 relates the action that a single environment factor (SEF) will have on a simple unit parameter (SUP). The factors and parameters shown here were chosen for a specific case (ordnance material), but others can be used where required.

This simulation is predicated on two basic facts. First, materials and parts will react in definite ways to environmental stresses. Second, those stresses can be established that will reflect the environments encountered by the materials or parts. Natural environments have certain general characteristics of temperature and humidity; for example, a desert is hot and dry. Other characteristics, like pressure change with altitude, are common to all climates. Induced environments can be established from theoretical considerations or past experience. The computer is furnished data on real environments, such as a desert and its related single environmental factors: high temperature, low temperature, solar radiation and mechanical interference (sand, dirt, dust), and other conditions. The computer is programmed to compare information on the environment to the physical and chemical characteristics of the material and equipment. Effects are then established.

The computer can also be programmed to form all possible combinations of environmental factors acting simultaneously to affect each unit parameter. In such cases, each of the single environmental factors is analyzed by the computer for effects on each simple unit parameter. Another matrix is then prepared to indicate whether or not there are any mutual effects. If one of the effects is 0, there will be no combined effect; two I terms or an I and D will indicate a possible, but not certain, effect; whereas two D terms means that a combined effect will occur. This methodology can be extended to as many environmental inputs as desired. Results may then approximate those shown in Figure 9-2.

Such simulations are valuable in eliminating materials being considered for use in a product. Testing of components, subassemblies, and assembled prototypes can be conducted in environmental test chambers. As in any laboratory tests, the validity of the results will depend to a great extent on how well actual field conditions have been reproduced. Test planners must therefore ensure that chamber tests are made as realistic as possible.

Effect of Environmental Stress on Specific Parameters

SIMPLE UNIT PARAMETERS (SUP)

SIMPLE ENVIRONMENT FACTORS

		Thermal state	Chemical state (composition)	Electric-magnetic state	Rheological state	Elastic state	Structural state (crystal structure, polymerization)	Strain state	Cleanliness state (dirt, corrosion products, etc.)
		Ther	Chem	Em	Rheo	Elas	Str	Stn	Cln
High temperature	Th	D	I	I	D	D	O	I	I
Low temperature	Tl	D	I	O	D	D	D	I	I
Changing temperature (thermal shock)	Tc	D	I	O	O	O	I	D	O
High pressure	Ph	I	I	I	I	O	I	D	I
Low pressure	Pl	I	I	I	O	O	I	D	I
Changing pressure (pressure shock)	Pc	I	O	I	O	O	O	D	O
Ionizing radiation	Ri	I	I	D	I	I	I	O	O
Mechanical interference (sand, dust, ice)	Im	I	O	I	I	I	I	I	D
Relative acceleration, steady or cyclic (includes vibration)	Ar	I	O	I	O	O	I	D	O
External electric or magnetic fields	Fd	I	I	D	O	O	O	I	O
Abnormal chemical surroundings	Cs	I	D	I	I	O	I	O	I
Aging	Zt	O	I	O	I	I	I	I	O

O. SUP unaffected in all cases. Example — age on thermal state.

I. SUP affected in some cases. Example — electric field on thermal state.

D. SUP affected in all cases. Example — temperature on thermal state.

Figure 9-2. Effect of environmental stress on specific parameters.

Notes

[1] Derek Lawrence, "Nature's Artillery," *Engineering*, August 1972, p. 764.

[2] F. Campus, "Effects of Residual Stresses on the Behavior of Structures," in *Residual Stresses in Metals and Metal Construction*, ed. W. R. Osgood (New York: Reinhold Publishing Corp., 1954), pp. 1–21.

[3] J. S. Arnold, "Computer-Calculated Environments," *Machine Design*, 25 April 1963, pp. 126–130.

Questions

1. List at least six environmental problems that can affect a product or its operation.

2. List the different types of environments that might be encountered and how they might interrelate.

3. What specific problems could occur with each type of environment?

4. Give five environmental problems that could affect automobiles or their operation.

5. Discuss some of the conditions humans have induced in the environment. Can you cite any beneficial ones?

6. Why did a Pennsylvania court refuse to accept the plea that an "Act of God" had occurred as a defense against a claim?

7. Why is the release of a comparatively small amount of toxic or flammable gas in a closed environment more than usually dangerous?

8. Describe five means by which products have been protected against adverse environments or the effects they could cause.

9. Why is it generally necessary to make environmental tests? Why is testing more effective than making analyses or simulations for environmental problems?

10. Discuss the benefits that can be derived from analyses and simulations.

11. A large missile was manufactured in Denver, sealed to keep it clean, and shipped by plane to Cape Kennedy. The missile was damaged by an environmental problem. What do you think happened?

12. Discuss whether environmental accidents should be considered as "Acts of God" or is there an increasing need for protective measures for accidents because of adverse environments?

13. With people becoming more environmentally conscious, the EPA and many federal laws regarding the environment are increasing in number and scope. Discuss whether product manufacturers and operators must be more alert in order to forestall by better designs the possibility of accidents to and from adverse environments.

14. What might have been done to prevent the environmental disaster because of the accident in Alaska with the Exxon Valdez?

15. Name other instances where there have been accidents involving the environment which might have been prevented by safer designs.

10

Operator Error

Compared to a machine, the human is a wonderful creation, in many ways able to outdo by far the machine's capabilities. The human can reason inductively and mentally outreach any computer's ability. The human can adjust to unusual situations; programmed equipment cannot.[1] The human can decide whether to go over, under, or around an obstacle, and then do it; a machine cannot do this. In emergencies the human can outdo his or her own normal performance to a degree that would cause any machine to blow a fuse or pop a gasket. Unfortunately, the human also makes mistakes which lead to accidents.

One somewhat questionable theory is that personal capabilities vary "biorhythmically" in 23, 28, and 33- day cycles. Days when two or three of these cycles are coincident may be "bad" days for the persons involved and they would do well to exercise extraordinary care. One transportation company in Japan used a computer to determine daily which of 500 drivers were schedule to have bad days. Those drivers were given cards urging them to be especially careful. In 1969, the first year the system was in use, the drivers' accident rate dropped 50 percent. Whether the issuance of the cards at any time, good or bad days, to indicate to the drivers that their performance was being monitored, would have had the same result has not been investigated.

Still another aspect of the error problem is determining *who*, that is, what kind of person, makes errors and is involved in accidents. Data on British World War I industrial workers led to a concept that the majority of accidents were caused by a small minority of persons who were "accident prone." Studies have shown that although there are certain persons who are involved in more accidents than others, these people do not cause the "majority" of accidents. Many people are involved in more accidents than is the average person because of their occupations, the hazardous conditions under which they must work, or other factors. See Figure 10-1 for a more scientific analysis of factors affecting human performance.

Persistent and Random Errors

Error is considered to be any personnel action that is inconsistent with normal, programmed behavioral patterns and that differs from prescribed procedures. By one method of classification, such errors can be considered as either *persistent* or *random*.

Persistent errors are those which experience has shown will occur and reoccur under similar conditions. For example, it is known that a person will generally tend to follow those procedures which involve minimal physical and mental effort, discomfort, or time. Any task which contravenes this basic principle is certain to be ignored or modified by the person who is supposed to accomplish the task.

Random errors are events that happen so rarely or are so unpredictable they are generally considered non-repetitive. For example, a person may be a highly competent operator but may be annoyed by a fly or a mosquito. Swatting at it, the operator hits a critical control or piece of sensitive equipment. If swatting flies or mosquitoes occurs often enough, it may become a persistent problem for which suitable precautionary measures can be provided. The consequences of even some random errors may also be so devastating that it may be advisable to provide a safeguard.

Errors in products and their detection might occur during design, production, testing, assembly, handling, or during servicing for maintenance or repair. And, an error can initiate a long line of possible effects.

Reliability values for task elements are listed later in this book; these are probabilities that the individual task elements will be accomplished correctly. An assumption might be made that calculations to determine the probability of the error's effect would simply consist of subtracting the probability of successful task accomplishment from 1.000. However, other considerations fault this idea:

Performance Shaping Factors

Extra-Individual

Situation Characteristics

Situation characteristics
Temperature, humidity, air quality
Noise and vibration
Degree of general cleanliness
Manning parameters
Work hours/work breaks
Availability/adequacy of supplies
Actions by supervisors
Actions by coworkers and peers
Actions by union representatives
Rewards, recognition, benefits
Organizational structure (e.g.,
   authority, responsibility,
   communication channels)

Psychological Stresses

Task speed
Task load
High jeopardy risk
Threats (of failure, loss of job)
Monotonous, degrading, or
   meaningless work
Long, uneventful vigilance
   periods
Conflicts of motives about job
   performance
Reinforcement absent or
   negative
Sensory deprivation
Distractions (noise, glare,
   movement, flicker, color)
Inconsistent cuing

Intra-Individual

(Organismic) Factors

Previous training/experience
State of current practice or skill
Personality and intelligence
   variables
Motivation and attitudes
Knowledge of required
   performance standards
Physical condition
Influence of family and other
   outside persons or agencies
Group identifications

Task and Equipment Characteristics

Perceptual requirements
Anticipatory requirements
Motor requirements (speed,
   strength, precision)
Interpretation and decision
   making
Complexity (information load)
Long- and short-term memory
Frequency and repetitiveness
Continuity (discrete vs
   continuous)
Feedback (knowledge of results)
Task criticality
Narrowness of task
Team structure
Man-machine interface factors:
   design of prime equipment,
   job aids, tools, fixtures.

Physiological Stresses

Fatigue
Pain or discomfort
Hunger or thirst
Temperature extremes
G-force extremes
Atmospheric pressure extremes
Oxygen insufficiency
Vibration
Movement constriction
Lack of physical exercise

Job and Task Instructions

Procedures required
Verbal or written
   communications
Cautions and warnings
Work methods
Shop practices

Figure 10-1. Representative listing of factors that shape human performance.

1. The operator might recognize the error and correct it, or it might be caught by a watcher, such as the operator's supervisor.

2. The error might immediately prevent the operation from proceeding (for example, by an interlock or by a computer-controlled system).

3. The error might be caught by quality control personnel.

4. The error might go undetected until after test or installation in a subassembly.

5. The error might be found when an attempt is made to use or test the assembly in a completed product.

6. The error might be found after the product has left the manufacturer's plant, possibly by maintenance personnel.

7. The error might be found during investigation because of an accident which might lead to claims and recalls if the cause generates a problem serious enough and often enough.

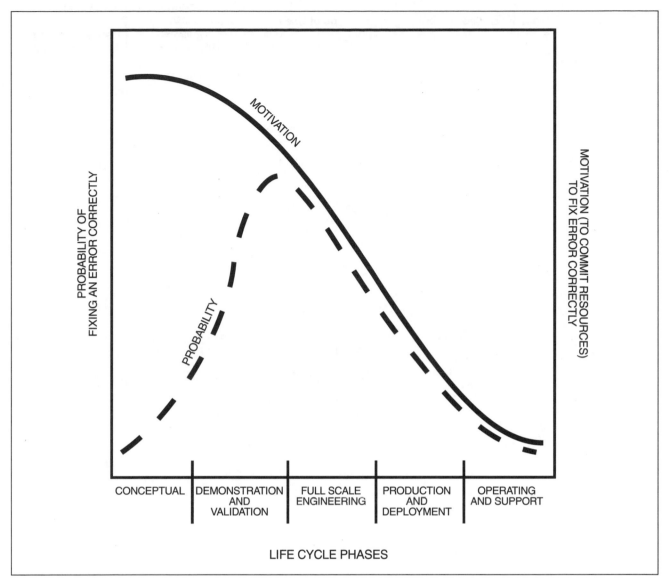

PROBABILITY OF FIXING AN ERROR CORRECTLY

MOTIVATION

PROBABILITY

MOTIVATION (TO COMMIT RESOURCES) TO FIX ERROR CORRECTLY

| CONCEPTUAL | DEMONSTRATION AND VALIDATION | FULL SCALE ENGINEERING | PRODUCTION AND DEPLOYMENT | OPERATING AND SUPPORT |

LIFE CYCLE PHASES

Figure 10-2. Motivation for early detection and probability of correctly fixing design errors.

Errors can be found through use of the Critical Incident Technique explained on page 139.

The motivation for correction of errors is generally the cost to correct it. Another major factor affecting correction is the delay involved in redoing work previously done, and the loss of material. A diagram indicating motivation for correction of errors is presented in Figure 10-2.

During the two world wars, and the conflicts in Korea and Viet Nam, and also in civilian use, it was found that pilots tended to commit errors often. Studies on pilot errors show their tendencies are similar to those committed by other personnel, such as drivers, workers, and users or operators of any type of product in any activity. These errors, and their corrective actions, may be classified as:

1. *Omission or forgetting errors.* These can be avoided by making it impossible to proceed further until corrective action has been taken.

2. *Substitution errors in selecting a wrong control or errors in identification.* Both of these can be mitigated by the arrangement of controls, including adequate separations (see Figure 10-3), shape-coding of control knobs, texture, lights to indicate position, and use of detents and interlocks.

3. *Adjustment errors.* These can be avoided by detents, computerization, and sound or light warnings of incorrect adjustment.

4. *Reversal errors.* Avoiding these can be done by use of uniform, standardized, and "natural" direction movements for controls of products.

Control	Measure of Separation	Type of Use	Edge to Edge Separation	
			Desirable Minimum for Stationary Situation	Desirable Distance for Moving Vehicle Situation
Cranks	0.5 MIN.	One hand individually	2"	4"
		Two hands simultaneously	3"	5"
Push Button		One finger individually	.50"	2"
		One finger sequentially	.25"	1"
		Different fingers individually or sequentially	.50"	.50"
Toggle Switch		One finger individually	.75"	2"
		One finger sequentially	.50"	1"
		Different fingers individually or sequentially	.62"	.50"
Lever Lock Toggle Switch		Finger and thumb individually	1"	2"
Knobs		One hand individually	1"	2"
		Two hands simultaneously	3"	5"
Pedals		One foot - randomly	d 4" D 8"	6" 10"
		One foot - randomly	d 2" D 6"	4" 8"

Figure 10-3. Controls design criteria.

5. *Unintentional activation of controls*. This can be minimized not only by separation, but also by the means shown in Figure 10-4.

Human Engineering

Human engineering or ergonomics is a technical discipline concerned primarily with the interrelationships between human beings and equipment. There are problems whenever the two come in contact. Human engineering attempts to minimize these problems and to provide maximal effectiveness by integrating human capabilities with equipment characteristics.

Studies by human engineers since World War II have indicated that errors are generally the result of the following:

1. *Failure to perform a required function (omission)*. Either a step is left out of a procedure, intentionally or inadvertently, or there is a failure to complete a necessary sequence.

   In some instances, intentional omissions may be due to procedures that are too lengthy, badly written, or in defiance of normal tendencies and actions. Omissions may be due to designs which overburden the operator so that he or she is incapable of performing all the necessary tasks. A complicated product that has numerous instruments to be monitored while controls are exercised may require an operator with two heads. In an emergency, additional workloads are superimposed and the operator may be overwhelmed by all the tasks he or she must undertake simultaneously.

   A human engineering study of fire department equipment mentions "it was discovered that collisions of fire trucks with cars while firemen were answering a call were all too frequent. Further investigation revealed that the accidents usually occurred at corners or curves in the road because the siren button (which must be kept depressed to sound the siren) was installed on the floor for foot operation. When turning a corner or rounding a curve, the driver had to remove his foot from the siren button to use the brake, the clutch, and the accelerator; consequently, cars were not being warned of the high-speed cornering of the fire engine."[2]

2. *Performing a function that should not have been performed (commission)*. A procedure or procedural step may be added unnecessarily or the person may substitute a procedure or procedural step with one of his or her own.

   Some of the most common cases in which persons take such actions which lead to accidents occur when they act reflexively. A person may have been warned repeatedly not to put his or her hands within the pinch area of a press or cutting machine. However, when operating rapidly the person or the feeding device may improperly place the item to be stamped or cut. The operator then reaches to correct the placement before the head of the press or the blade descends. If the operator isn't lucky, he or she loses fingers, a hand, or an arm.

   Sometimes included in this category are acts of substitution. In performing a procedure the operator changes a step in a prescribed procedure to one he or she has originated.

3. *Failure to recognize a hazardous condition*. The situation may require corrective action or there may be a latent hazard which the operator should avoid. Courts have held that it is the duty of a manufacturer to warn of any latent hazard in his product. The distinction between latent and obvious hazards has blurred because some people fail to recognize hazards that are readily apparent to other people.

4. *Wrong decision in response to a problem*. If a problem arises unexpectedly, the operator may not have time to think about the correct action to take and may respond erroneously. This matter is discussed more fully in the next chapter. One aspect is the capability and design of monitoring and warning systems. If a hazard suddenly occurs, these systems must give the operator the maximum time possible to decide what actions he or she must take to prevent the situation from turning into a contingency situation (the stage before an emergency); and if it does become an emergency, to avoid an accident.

5. *Inadequate response to a contingency*. A hazardous condition that has developed into a contingency may have been recognized and corrective action initiated, but the magnitude of the action is inadequate to prevent the contingency from progressing into an emergency and mishap.

6. *Poor timing*. The response in an adverse situation may have been correct and adequate, but it may have been too late or, in some cases, even too soon. On one hand, a person in a burning vehicle may try to save the vehicle and delay his or her exit until it is too late to do so successfully. On the other hand, fire-fighting may be abandoned while the fire could still be controlled.

To permit operators to respond in time when a situation calls for a response requires that designers consider reaction times. Reaction times will vary with numerous factors, such as the training, individual characteristics (age, physical disabilities and handicaps of the operator), and the concentration of the operator on the task. An operator may have a short reaction time in the laboratory when being tested to respond to lights on a panel. But when the operator is involved in a real emergency, the operator is in a state of shock, the degree varying with the individual, and his or her reaction time may be greater. The reaction time of a trained person will be less than that of an untrained person.

Figure 10-5 represents an indication of time required to react when the various senses are stimulated. Here

Methods for Prevention of Accidental Activation

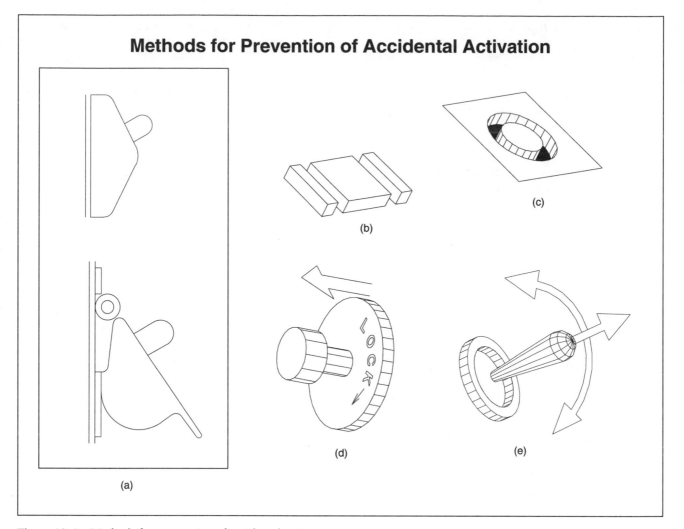

Figure 10-4. Methods for prevention of accidental activation, (a-e).

again it is pointed out that many of these time data were obtained from laboratory tests and may vary from actual times under field conditions. Under field conditions, response times may vary depending on whether or not the operator is "startled." For example, very loud auditory signals may cause a lengthy increase in response times.

Design Versus Procedural Safeguards

The attention of designers, manufacturers, insurance companies, and certain governmental agencies has been far too long held by the idea that the number of accidents can be reduced only by "safe usage" rather than by safe design. The attitude in such cases is that each person is responsible for his or her own safety. Any injury to an operator is therefore the result of an inadequacy on the operator's part. Before the Industrial Revolution the causes of accidents were few and simple and everyone knew the hazards of the products and operations with which they were involved and the precautionary measures which had to be taken. But products became more complex and there are more and more hazards that are not readily apparent. If the designer or manufacturer does not recognize a hazard before the product is marketed, the designer or manufacturer lacks foreseeability[3] and can be held liable if an accident results. If the designer or the manufacturer had recognized the hazard and did not use reasonable care to control it, they could also be held liable. It is therefore a legal necessity that a manufacturer do his/her utmost to uncover these hazards and that a safeguard be provided for each one that cannot be eliminated from a product.[4]

Safeguards can be of either of two types: (1) designed into the product or (2) procedural, in which operators are instructed to take or avoid specific actions. Designed safeguards are far more effective and satisfactory than procedural safeguards.

Swain points out:

> Hazards can be drastically and permanently reduced through design action in modifying the

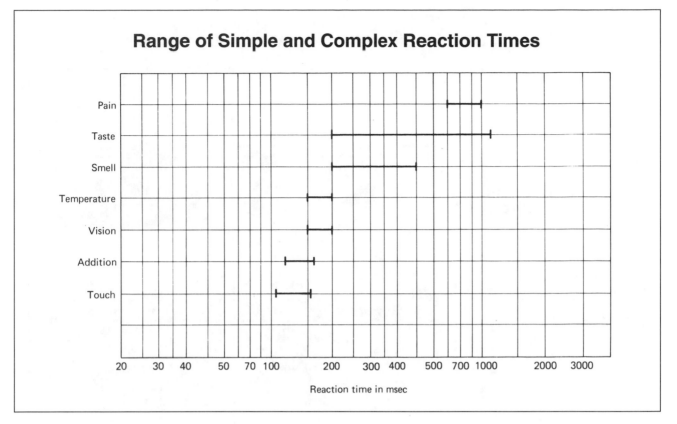

Figure 10-5. Range of simple and complex reaction times.

hazardous situation, whereas reduction through modifying people is limited and requires continuing reinforcement. Moreover reinforcement gets exceedingly more difficult to achieve because of the human tendency to "tune out" stimuli a person comes to consider as noise. Safety is a design problem, one to be resolved by objective engineering techniques.[5]

Incompatibilities between products and their operators must be eliminated or minimized. If the design of a product is not suitable for an operator, the propensity for errors and accidents is enhanced (see Figures 10-6 and 10-7). The designer must consider the physical characteristics of the operators who will use the product. Most books on human engineering have such tables for average-sized men and women. Figure 13-6 (upper left) shows an example of such information. Information of extraordinary persons, very large or small, very tall or short, paraplegic or otherwise handicapped, would probably have to be obtained from specialized sources or researched in the field.

Designing a person out of a system because he or she makes errors is generally impossible except in limited cases. Steps must therefore be taken to use design to the maximum possible and to use procedural safeguards only when hazards cannot be controlled by design. For example, the error of activating the wrong control can be minimized through proper separation of these controls, as shown in Figure 10-3. If the design is such that an error

cannot result in an accident, the need for procedural safeguards is eliminated. In the past, however, designers have relied too much on procedural safeguards to lessen their own problems.

Procedural safeguards are inadequate because:

1. Operators and maintenance people will not always follow instructions except as a last resort.

2. Any task that can be done incorrectly, no matter how remote the possibility, will someday be done that way.[6]

3. People generally will not believe that an accident will happen to them and therefore they ignore procedural safeguards.

4. Designers frequently contend that people should use "common sense" in using their products. Designers assume that the users have specific knowledge which they possess only infrequently.

Eliminating Errors

In many situations, designs can be such that an error will not result in an accident since, in most cases, for an accident to occur requires a dangerous condition and an error. However, it is sometimes impossible to eliminate or control the dangerous condition adequately; at such times an error could be disastrous. Safeguards are designed into

Figure 10-6.   Design deficiencies affecting aircraft operations.

equipment in order to minimize injuries to operators, but design safeguards (examples of which are shown in Figure 10-8) are less usual for maintenance personnel. Maintenance personnel are supposed to be more knowledgeable of the products they have to repair, and often they must remove or deactivate the operator safeguards for access to assemblies on which they must work.

In either case, the causes of errors are generally known and for each a countermeasure can be provided as a safeguard. Figure 10-9 lists some of the causes of errors that could result in errors and the measures which designers, who would develop the design safeguards, or methods engineers, who would provide the instructions and procedural safeguards could use to prevent or minimize errors. For the product safety engineers or for the design or methods engineers who want to review their own work, Figure 10-10 is provided.

Figure 10-7. Design deficiencies affecting aircraft maintenance.

Warnings

Manufacturers are required to inform users of their products about any but obvious dangers. Failure to warn is in itself considered a defect by the courts. Therefore, a product can be considered to be defective by design, manufacture, failure to warn, or any combination of these three. In Chapter 11 numerous methods are described for alerting and warning personnel of dangers. In this case, however, the use of warnings is more to alert prospective purchasers and users that *potential* dangers

exist in a product, generally through the use of labels (or other markings on the product). Effective warnings may reduce errors and accidents by focusing the attention of operators on conditions in which specific actions should be taken.

In the past there was no consistent method of preparing warnings. The key words to attract attention, CAUTION, WARNING, and DANGER, were often used indiscriminately to indicate different degrees of urgency. There is now a consistent method proposed for use of the

Design Safeguards for Maintenance Personnel

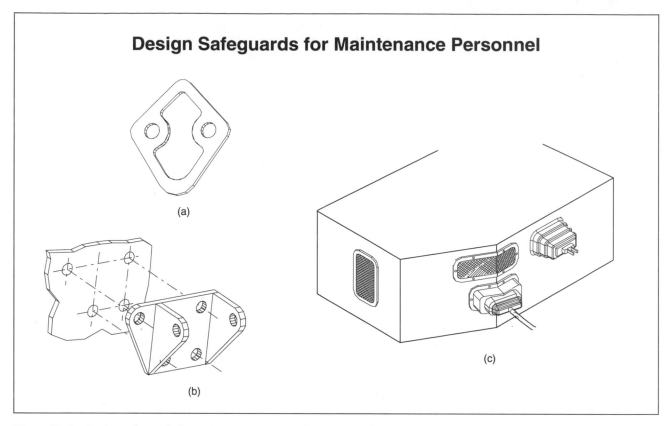

(a)

(b)

(c)

Figure 10-8. Design safeguards for maintenance personnel: unique configuration/alignment (a) (b); screened access panels (c).

three signal words that designate a degree or level of hazard seriousness.

1. DANGER indicates an imminently hazardous situation which, if not avoided, will result in death or serious injury. It is to be limited to the most serious situations.

2. WARNING indicates a potentially hazardous situation which, if not avoided, could result in death or serious injury.

3. CAUTION indicates a potentially hazardous situation which, if not avoided, may result in minor or moderate injury. It may also be used to alert against unsafe practices. It is permitted for property-damage-only accidents.

These definitions are taken from the American National Standard ANSI 2535.4-1991, "Product Safety Signs and Labels."

A warning is, in effect, a procedural means of alerting operators to the fact that there has been a failure to eliminate, or adequately control by design, a hazard that might lead to an accident, injury, or liability claim. To warn is considered a duty by law, in order to lessen the possibility of an accident. Labels are a major type of visual warning, but in many cases their content is deficient, and often are considered inadequate in the event of a trial. Warnings should be written in languages under-

standable to all potential users, and if the distribution of a potentially hazardous product is extremely widespread, labels should be multilingual.

Use of the signal word alone is inadequate; each warning label must contain at least two other items of information. The labels should indicate:

1. The action to be taken to avoid injury or damage.

2. The consequences that might result if the indicated action is not taken.

In addition, other information might be required for specific hazardous products. For a substance that might be fatal if taken internally, information on antidotes or actions to be taken should be provided. If the product might be used by an illiterate person, a person too young to read, or a person not capable of reading English, a warning symbol should be provided. If the user can read another language, another label in that language should be provided. Or, the alerting word and the necessary information should be provided in the foreign language. If a government standard prescribes that specific warning symbols, color, and wording be used, they must be on the warning.

The warning must be placed in a location where it will be immediately seen by the persons who use the product and who might be affected. The location should be as close

Minimizing Operator Errors

CAUSES OF PRIMARY ERRORS	PREVENTIVE MEASURES (TAKEN BY DESIGNER OR METHODS ENGINEER)
1. Inability to concentrate because of unsafe condition or equipment	1. Ensure that personnel must not work close to unguarded moving parts, hot surfaces, sharp edges, or other dangerous condition.
2. Critical components installed incorrectly.	2. Provide designs which permit components to be installed only properly. Use assymetric configurations or polarization on electrical connectors or mechanical assemblies; use female and male pairs which can be assembled in only one way or different sized connections on critical valves, filters, or other components in which flow direction is vital.
3. Untimely activation of equipment.	3. Provide interlocks or timer lockouts. Provide warning or caution notes against activating equipment unless disconnected or disengaged from load or other damaging condition. For critical functions provide controls that cannot be activated inadvertently. Use torque types instead of pushbuttons. Provide guards over critical switches.
4. Controls activated in wrong order.	4. Place functional controls in sequence in which they are to be used. Provide interlocks where sequences are critical.
5. Error or delay in reading instruments.	5. Ensure that most critical instruments are the most prominent or located in the easiest to read area. Ensure that instruments are labeled and designed for easy understanding. Do not require reader to turn head unduly or to move body. Avoid visibility problems due to lack of light or glare, legibility, viewing angle, contrast, or reflections. Provide direct readings of specific parameters so operator does not have to interpret.
6. Failure to note critical indication.	6. Provide auditory or visual warning that will attract operator's attention to problem.
7. Vibration and noise cause irritation and inability to read meters and settings and to operate controls.	7. Provide vibration isolators or noise elimination devices if source of vibration and noise cannot be eliminated or minimized to acceptable level.
8. Error or delay in use of controls.	8. Avoid similarity, proximity, interference, or awkward location of critical controls. Locate control close to readout. Locate readout above control so hand or arm making adjustment does not block out readout instrument. Ensure that controls are labeled prominently for easy understanding. Ensure that controls do not require much force for use. Ensure that controls and equipment respond fast enough for foreseeable usages. Provide warnings of potential safety problems as early as possible to give maximum reaction time.
9. Control setting by operator not precise. enough.	9. Provide controls that permit making settings or adjustments without need for extremely fine movements. Use click-type controls.
10. Controls broken by excessive force.	10. Provide controls adequate to withstand maximum stress an operator could apply. Provide warning and caution notes for those devices that could be overstressed.
11. Failure to take action at proper times because of faulty instruments.	11. Incorporate means to ensure instruments are working correctly. Provide procedures to test and calibrate instruments periodically.

Figure 10-9. Minimizing operator errors.

Minimizing Operator Errors

CAUSES OF PRIMARY ERRORS	PREVENTIVE MEASURES (TAKEN BY DESIGNER OR METHODS ENGINEER)
12. Fatigue.	12. Avoid placing on operator severe and tiring physical and and mental requirements such as heavy loads, long concentration times, vibration, environmental stresses, or awkward positions.
13. Irritation and loss of effectiveness due to high temperature and humidity.	13. Provide environmental controls. Prevent entrance or generation of heat or moisture in a restricted space in which personnel must operate.
14. Loss of effectiveness due to lack of oxygen, or to the presence of toxic gas, airborne particulate matter, or odors.	14. Prevent generation or entrance of contaminants into the occupied space. Provide suitable life support equipment. Avoid presence in occupied area of lines or equipment containing hazardous gases or liquids. Avoid use in occupied areas or materials which outgas noxious or odorous gases.
15. Degradation of capabilities due to extremely low temperatures.	15. Design for adequate heating or insulation, protective shelter, equipment, or clothing.
16. Fixation or hypnosis.	16. Avoid designs or procedures that require long visual concentrations. Avoid equipment which hums. Provide alternate reference points. Provide procedures to relieve the monotony.
17. Disorientation or vertigo.	17. Provide adequate reference points or means to maintain orientation.
18. Slipping and falling.	18. Incorporate friction surfaces or devices, guard and hand rails, access holes covers on floor openings, or protective harness.
19. Inattention.	19. Provide bright, colorful, and pleasant work areas. Avoid long or monotonous intervals between procedural steps. Use attention-getting devices at critical points.
20. Errors of judgement, especially during periods of stress.	20. Minimize requirements for making hurried judgements, especially at critical times, through programmed contingency measures. Provide references for making judgements: mark meters with safe or unsafe limits.
21. Lack of awareness of hazards.	21. Provide alerting devices; warnings and cautions on the equipment and in instructions. Provide explanations in operating manuals.
22. Lack or understanding of procedures.	22. Ensure that instructions are not ambiguous and are easy to understand. Don't use language that is too technical in instructions to operators.
23. Following prescribed but incorrect procedures.	23. Ensure procedures are correct by run-through tests.
24. Improvising procedures that are lacking.	24. Provide adequate instructions.
25. Failure to follow prescribed procedures.	25. Ensure that procedures are not too lengthy, not too fast, too slow or inconvenient, and are not hazardous or awkward.
26. Misunderstanding of instructions due to noise interference.	26. Reduce noise at source or noise-insulate operator.
27. Lack of data on which to base correct decisions.	27. Provide indicators or other readout instruments for critical parameters and functions.
28. Lack of suitable tools or equipment.	28. Minimize need for special tools or equipment; develop and provide those that are necessary; stress their need in instructions.
29. Hampered activities because of interference between personnel.	29. Ensure that space is adequate to perform required activites simultaneously. Test on a mockup.

Figure 10-9 (cont'd). Minimizing operator errors.

Human Factors Checklist

1. Have instructions been provided on how such equipment should be used?
2. Does the design minimize the necessity for the operator to be constantly on the alert against dangers?
3. Is information provided on operating limits to be observed to avoid a danger or emergency?
4. Are equipment clearances adequate to avoid injury to fingers, arms, legs, and head?
5. Is space adequate to perform required operations without interference from other equipment?
6. Is there a possibility of interference between personnel?
7. Are prescribed procedures complete, correct and adequate for the operations to be performed?
8. Are the procedures hazardous in any way?
9. Are the procedures badly written or hard to understand?
10. Are the instruments easy to see and understand without error or misinterpretation?
11. Are reading instruments and motions for actuating devices in accordance with normal habits?
12. Are safety-critical controls provided with guards or interlocks against inadvertent activation?
13. Would the operator or maintenance man be under stress because of proximity to a hazard such as a hot surface or sharp edge?
14. Have machine guards and interlocks been provided where necessary?
15. Is there similarity between controls located close to each other whose inadvertent activation could cause an accident?
16. Are errors or delays in safety-critical readings possible because of instrument location?
17. Are errors or delays in use of controls possible because of their close proximity, interference, inaccessibility, or awkward location?
18. Must an operator turn his head or his body unduly or otherwise strain to read a critical instrument?
19. Are openings in guards or protective covers small enough to prevent fingers from being inserted into hazardous locations?
20. Is the environment suitably controlled to reduce irritability and loss of effectiveness due to high or low temperature, humidity, smoke, odors, toxic gas or lack of oxygen?
21. Is personal protective equipment required? Can it be eliminated by improved design?
22. Have humming noises which might induce fatigue, drowsiness, or annoyance been eliminated?
23. Have excessively loud, distracting, and impact noises been eliminated? What is the noise level?
24. Have sharp points and edges and rough projections and surfaces been eliminated unless required?
25. Are there pinch-points which should be guarded or are not guarded adequately?
26. Are warnings provided on the consequences of exceeding prescribed limits and for potential dangers?
27. Are monitoring and warning devices available and adequate to indicate a hazard or loss of control?
28. Is it possible to abort an operation rapidly without damaging the product or going through a dangerous procedure?
29. Have instructions been provided on backout or emergency procedures?
30. Is an emergency switch required to shut down the equipment rapidly? Has it been provided on a readily accessible locations?
31. What constitutes an emergency? Can the condition or its effect be eliminated or controlled? Do the instructions inform the operator on what constitutes an emergency and what to do in case one occurs?
32. Are warnings and cautions adequate and contain all necessary information? Has the condition for which the warning was included been examined to see if it could be eliminated or controlled so the warning is not needed? Do the warnings on the equipment correlate with those in the instructions?
34. Does each warning label contain: (1) an alerting word, (2) the hazard, (3) the potential effect, (4) actions to be taken, and (5) other necessary information?
35. Is there a method for ensuring that each safety-critical monitoring or warning device is operable, in operation, and operating correctly?
36. Will the response time after a warning is given be adequate for a person to take action or should automatic corrective devices be used?
37. Have aural or other attention-attracting devices been incorporated to make an operator aware of a highly critical situation if his attention could be distracted?

Figure 10-10. Human factors checklist.

as possible to the point of danger, but it should not put the person reading the warning in a position of danger.

The warning should attempt to convey all the necessary information in as few words as possible. If lengthy explanations are required, it might be possible to provide them along with the operating or maintenance instructions. In such cases, it is necessary that provision be made so that the operators or maintenance personnel have ready access to the instructions. If a label indicates that a manual should be consulted by an operator but the manual is retained in a distant office, the information would be unavailable. A manufacturer could be held liable if such conditions resulted in injury. Therefore, some manufacturers have provided receptacles on their equipment in which operating instructions are to be kept or they have attached the manuals to the equipment. The instructions on the labels on the equipment should correspond to the procedural instructions in any manuals or other pertinent documents.

More and more symbols are being used to warn of hazards or of actions to be avoided. In some instances, these symbols have been standardized. (See American National Standard ANSI 2535.3-1991, "Criteria for Safety Symbols.") Road signs and markings on containers of hazardous materials now use symbols which have been adopted and are understood internationally. If governments have not prescribed designs to be used, technical associations have started developing them for their members' use. In some cases, companies have developed their own symbols for specific hazards involved in the use of their products. Figure 10-11 shows some of those developed by FMC Corporation and by Clark Equipment Company. The FMC manual also provides instructions for designers on how to prepare entire warning labels, including an alerting word, the pertinent symbol to indicate the nature of the hazard, the consequence that can result, and how to avoid the hazard. The manual includes alerting colors to be used. Bilingual label formats are also presented. A collection of symbols for many purposes and types of equipment is presented in Dreyfuss' *Symbol Sourcebook.*[7]

Labels should be affixed as permanently as the normal life expectancy of the equipment on which they are to be placed. If a part that holds a warning label is to be replaced for any reason, the manufacturer should ensure that the replacement part also has the warning.

A warning label should not be used as a substitute for good design. The fact that a warning label has been placed on a piece of equipment is *prima facie* evidence that the manufacturer knew that a safety problem existed. Whether or not the manufacturer would be held liable might depend on whether or not he could show that he had attempted to eliminate or minimize the hazard, the hazard could not be eliminated, design could provide no or only a limited safeguard, and the warning was the only safeguard that could reasonably be provided.

Quantitative Error Prediction

Human engineers have formulated ways by which they may attempt to predict the number of errors that might occur in any operation. In risk assessments, quantitative evaluations must be made not only of potential failures of equipment but also of potential accidents and losses that could be generated by human error. Two of the principal error prediction methods include Data Store and THERP.

Data Store

This was developed by the American Institute for Research in 1962 to predict operator performance involving use of equipment controls and displays and the probabilities of successful operation. In addition, the data indicate the times required to operate instruments and they attempt to identify features that degrade performance. Data Store has tabulated performance information to this end. In analyzing an operation the tasks are listed and the probabilities are obtained from the tabulated data. Individual task reliabilities are then multiplied in order to determine the overall reliability of the operation. Data Store can be used for individual tasks for which probability information is available.

THERP (Technique for Human Error Rate Prediction)

This method was developed at the Sandia Laboratories in an attempt to deal with continuous personnel operations as compared to discrete tasks in the Data Store method. In addition, THERP also attempts to account for dependent operations whereas Data Store's discrete tasks are considered independent.

Warning Symbols

Ear protection
required

Hot surface

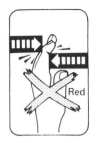

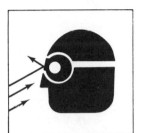

Projectiles-eye
projection required

Falling objects

Electrical shock

Keep hands out
sharp objects

Slippery

Keep hands out (gears)

Symbols in the two left columns are from
FMC Corporation's Safety Monograph 2 and
are reprinted with the company's permission.

The symbols above are used with the permission
of Clark Equipment Company.

Figure 10-11. Warning symbols.

Notes

[1] During World War II there were stories of crewmen in aircraft urinating into hydraulic control or brake fluid reservoirs in order to provide emergency supplies, a feat beyond the capability of a machine.

[2] Some NASA Contributions to Human Factors Engineering, NASA SP-5117 (Washington, D.C.: National Aeronautics and Space Administration, 1973).

[3] If the manufacturer, who is supposed to be highly knowledgeable of his product, cannot recognize a hazard exists, how can the user be expected to recognize it?

[4] Court decisions were made based on accidents which had occurred, but now the requirements of regulatory agencies require these actions even before an accident occurs.

[5] A.D. Swain, Safety as a Design Feature in Systems, SC-R-65-991 (Albuquerque, New Mexico: Sandia Laboratories, September 1965), p. 2.

[6] One of the basic Murphy's laws.

[7] Henry Dreyfuss, *Symbol Sourcebook* (New York: McGraw-Hill Book Company, 1972).

Questions

1. List the six principal ways in which errors are made.

2. List eight factors that will induce an operator to make errors.

3. Discuss six ways in which a designer can minimize operator errors that could lead to accidents.

4. When must a warning be provided to meet common law requirements? List the four pieces of information that should be on a warning.

5. Why was there such a protest over the interlock in 1975 automobiles which made it necessary to buckle the seat belt in order to start the engine?

6. Will the public accept an interlock in automobiles which requires they punch a sequence of numbers to prove they are not drunk before they can start the engine? Why or why not?

7. What are the advantages of "passive restraints" in automobiles? Give an example.

8. The following represent meter faces. Draw arrows to indicate the directions in which numbers get higher. (Assume that the number increase is in one direction only.)

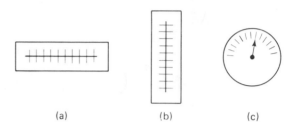

(a)   (b)   (c)

9. From a human engineering standpoint, which of the following arrangements is the best design? Explain why.

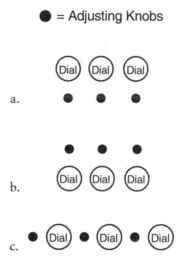

10. Severe damage occurred to an Atlas F missile because of an error. Due to the rapid evaporation of liquid oxygen (LOX) when it first comes into contact with comparatively warm metal, an escape valve had to be opened before pumping began. The operator failed to do so and, as a result, the pressure of the vaporized oxygen caused severe distortion damage to the thin-skinned missile. This error could have been negated by the incorporation of an interlock, or by the even better method of more complete computer programming to ensure that pumping could not begin until after the valve opened when it was supposed to. Discuss whether this accident was solely due to the operator's error, or whether there was also an error on the part of the supervisors, designers, and managers.

11. What type of error could this be considered?

12. Could it be considered to be a design defect, because no interlock was incorporated to prevent operator error?

Minimizing Accidents and Their Effects

General Conditions of Acceptability

Over the years system safety engineers have developed general rules, principles, and priorities in accident prevention whose observance tends to make products safer. For example, a safety engineer would be highly reluctant to accept a design in which a simple malfunction would result in injury or damage. The following conditions have been developed and are considered generally acceptable[1] and indicative of good design. Analyses to determine a product's level of safety should take these into consideration. The acceptable conditions include:

1. Any design that requires at least two independent malfunctions, two independent errors, or a malfunction and an error which are independent of each other to result in an accident.

   The term *independent* must be stressed, and that independence exists between two such events must be ensured by analysis. In addition, for extremely safety critical[2] products that could cause a highly catastrophic accident, more than two malfunctions or errors to have an accident are desirable.

2. Any design that positively prevents an error in assembly, installation, connection, or operation which analysis has indicated an error would be safety critical. For examples, polarized connectors so that different circuits cannot be cross-connected, assymetrical fittings that cannot be assembled incorrectly, or check valves that cannot be reversed.

3. Any design that positively prevents a malfunction of one component or assembly from propagating other failures which could cause other injury or damage. Such designs may be considered *fail-safe*. (See page 102 for additional information on fail-safe designs.) For example, a fuse in a motor circuit will prevent damage to the motor if there is excessive current in the circuit because of a short or other failure.

4. Any design that limits and controls the operation, interaction, or sequencing of a product's subassemblies or components when an error or malfunction could cause an accident. For example, an error in pushing button B before pushing button A might result in damage. An interlock which would negate the action of pushing button B first would safely limit the operation.

5. Any design that will withstand safely an advertent release of energy higher than that normally required. For example, a regulating valve reduces the pressure of a gas from that in a supply cylinder to a lower level. The regulating valve might fail so that the full pressure in the supply cylinder is imposed on what is normally a low-pressure line. To be acceptable, the low-pressure line should be able to withstand the inadvertent release of the high pressure gas either by the strength of the piping itself or by a relieving device.

6. Any design that positively controls buildup of energy to a point where it can potentially cause an accident, for example, through the use of relief valves, burst diaphragms, or fusible links.

Undesirable Conditions

The following conditions should be considered undesirable in any product:

1. No hazardous characteristic(s) that can be eliminated or controlled by good design will be permitted, unless necessitated by functional requirements of the product and unless procedural safeguards are stipulated.

2. No single occurrence, personal error, failure, or component malfunction that will cause personnel injury or major damage to equipment, property, or material will be permitted.

Safety Achievement Methods

A review of engineering literature, specifications, and standards reveals language which indicates that designers do not have a knowledge of safety principles and methods. Such words as "foolproof," "fail-safe," and "perfectly safe" are requirements frequently seen. It is said that a product can't be made foolproof because fools are so smart. Many designers feel that to make a product fail-safe is the ultimate in accident-preventive design. Not only do many of the designers not understand exactly what a fail-safe design is, but they also do not know that there are accident-preventive measures that are far superior. And since safety is a relative condition, a perfectly safe product is probably unachievable, and there are varying levels of safety.

Certain safeguards are more effective than others; for example, a barrier, such as a guard, over a piece of rotating equipment is much safer than a warning sign to be careful. Figure 11-1 is a list of priorities of generalized methods to minimize and control the possibilities of accidents and to reduce injury or damage if an accident does occur. These priorities are discussed in detail below. It might be noted that the design safeguards have the highest priorities on the lists and that the procedural safeguards have the lowest priorities.

Elimination of the Hazard

Hazards can sometimes be eliminated by careful design selection or by good operating procedures. A most common technique is to eliminate cuts, scratches, or punctures of the skin by eliminating rough edges, sharp corners, and points and the possibilities of jagged, broken surfaces. Numerous other examples can be cited, some of which include the following:

1. Using nonflammable materials instead of combustible materials, in products such as sleepwear materials, hydraulic fluids, solvents, and electrical insulation.

2. Using pneumatic or hydraulic systems instead of electric systems when there is a possibility of fire or excessive heating. Fluidic control systems have been applied for such reasons. Using hydraulic systems instead of pneumatic systems to avoid violent ruptures of pressure vessels which could generate shock waves.

3. Using continuous one-piece lines instead of lines having many connectors to eliminate leaks.

4. Using overpasses and underpasses at intersections and railway crossings to avoid collision accidents.

5. Eliminating protuberances, such as handles, ornaments, and similar devices in vehicles, which could cause injury during sudden stops.

Hazard Level Limitation

In certain instances the hazard itself cannot be eliminated or it may not be practicable to eliminate it. But the level of the hazard that could be present can be limited so that no injury and no damage would result. If electric power must be used, it may be possible to use low-voltage, low-amperage power that would not be injurious or damaging. The cordless battery drill is safe, convenient, and effective. The battery provides low-voltage and limited amperage power which eliminates the possibility of a fatality from electric shock.

Hazard elimination and hazard level limitation designs are said to be "intrinsically safe." They are the closest thing to being "perfectly" safe. In certain aspects they will be perfectly safe; for example, a low-voltage, low-amperage system will be perfectly safe against shock, but against other hazards it might not be: for example, there is the possibility that a battery supplying the low-voltage, low-amperage power might blow up.

Intrinsically safe designs require that designers determine which hazards could be present, the level at which each hazard would constitute a danger, and the limitations which should be prescribed. A fuel gas, such as methane, is dangerous and will burn when its concentration in air is within flammable limits. It is common practice to ensure that such a fuel gas outside its usual container never exceeds 20% of the lower flammability limit. If the 20% point is exceeded, a blower could be activated to reduce the flammable gas concentration, an inert gas could be introduced, or a fire suppressant could be injected.

Other methods by which hazard levels are limited include:

1. Using sprays and other conducive coatings to limit the amount of static electricity that can build up.

2. Using grounds on capacitors or capacitive circuits to reduce accumulations of charges to acceptable levels after the power is shut off.

3. Using overflow arrangements that will prevent liquid levels from getting too high.

4. Using solid-state electrical devices whenever flammable or explosive gases might be present. The power requirements of such devices are far below the levels required for ignition of combustible mixtures.

Safety Measures Priorities

Accident Prevention

Intrinsically safe {
1. Eliminating hazards
2. Limiting hazard levels
3. Isolation, barriers, and interlocks
4. Fail-safe designs
5. Minimizing failures
6. Safe procedures
7. Backout and recovery

Minimizing and Controlling Damage

1. Isolation and barriers
2. Minor loss acceptance
3. Personal protective equipment
4. Escape and survival equipment and procedures
5. Rescue equipment and procedures

Although using the option for accident prevention with the lowest number is highly desirable, other considerations may make another option more practical. For example, personnel have been killed when using metal-cased electric drills. Tool manufacturers contend that this was due to improper repairs which resulted in a live conductor touching the metal case when the drill was used. Other potentially fatal conditions could exist when a metal-cased tool is drilled into a live conductor, or when an energized tool using 110 v power is dropped into a container of water or other conductive liquid and someone tries to retrieve it while still energized. The following table indicates why and how trade-offs must sometimes be made.

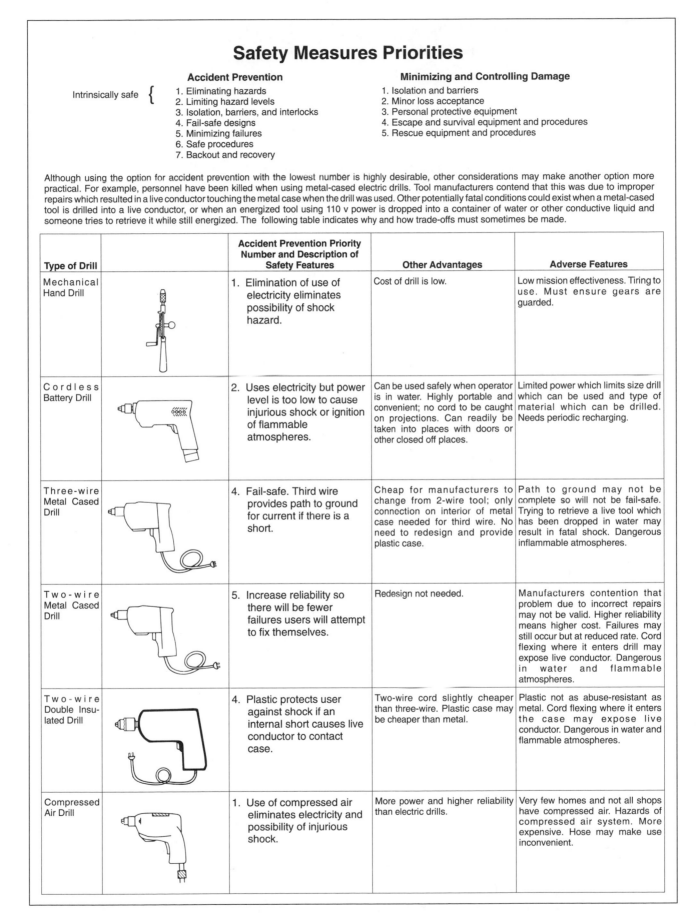

Type of Drill		Accident Prevention Priority Number and Description of Safety Features	Other Advantages	Adverse Features
Mechanical Hand Drill		1. Elimination of use of electricity eliminates possibility of shock hazard.	Cost of drill is low.	Low mission effectiveness. Tiring to use. Must ensure gears are guarded.
Cordless Battery Drill		2. Uses electricity but power level is too low to cause injurious shock or ignition of flammable atmospheres.	Can be used safely when operator is in water. Highly portable and convenient; no cord to be caught on projections. Can readily be taken into places with doors or other closed off places.	Limited power which limits size drill which can be used and type of material which can be drilled. Needs periodic recharging.
Three-wire Metal Cased Drill		4. Fail-safe. Third wire provides path to ground for current if there is a short.	Cheap for manufacturers to change from 2-wire tool; only connection on interior of metal case needed for third wire. No need to redesign and provide plastic case.	Path to ground may not be complete so will not be fail-safe. Trying to retrieve a live tool which has been dropped in water may result in fatal shock. Dangerous inflammable atmospheres.
Two-wire Metal Cased Drill		5. Increase reliability so there will be fewer failures users will attempt to fix themselves.	Redesign not needed.	Manufacturers contention that problem due to incorrect repairs may not be valid. Higher reliability means higher cost. Failures may still occur but at reduced rate. Cord flexing where it enters drill may expose live conductor. Dangerous in water and flammable atmospheres.
Two-wire Double Insulated Drill		4. Plastic protects user against shock if an internal short causes live conductor to contact case.	Two-wire cord slightly cheaper than three-wire. Plastic case may be cheaper than metal.	Plastic not as abuse-resistant as metal. Cord flexing where it enters the case may expose live conductor. Dangerous in water and flammable atmospheres.
Compressed Air Drill		1. Use of compressed air eliminates electricity and possibility of injurious shock.	More power and higher reliability than electric drills.	Very few homes and not all shops have compressed air. Hazards of compressed air system. More expensive. Hose may make use inconvenient.

Figure 11-1. Safety measures priorities.

Isolation, Barriers, and Interlocks

These methods and devices include some of the most common safety measures in use. They are predicated on two basic principles, or a combination of the two: (1) isolating a hazard once it has been recognized and (2) preventing incompatible events from occurring, from occurring at the wrong time, or from occurring in the wrong sequence.

Isolation can be used to prevent an accident or to minimize the damage that could result from an accident. In this section, uses of isolation for accident prevention are discussed. Many of these means of isolation involve the use of barriers. Barriers are a more positive means of isolation than merely separating a hazardous device or operation from personnel who could be injured or equipment that could be damaged.

Isolation can separate incompatible materials that together would constitute a hazard. Fire requires the presence of a fuel, an oxidizer, and an ignition source. If any one of these is isolated from the others, the possibility of fire will be eliminated. Some highly flammable liquids are "blanketed" in their containers with nitrogen or other inert gas so that they are isolated from contact with the oxygen in air.

Isolation is also used to limit the effects of controlled energy release. Tests may require device activation to determine the limits beyond which a flammable or explosive material will activate. A small amount of the material to be tested can be placed in a suitable container that absorbs or can withstand the energy of the reaction. Sensitive explosive devices are generally transported and handled in small quantities in containers. The containers isolate the devices from outside sources of energy which could cause the devices' activation and the containers are able to withstand explosion if it should occur.

Some materials are harmful to humans at all times and must be isolated. Radioactive materials are in this category. If they are to constitute part of a normal process, protection must be provided. Other examples of such isolation protection required during scheduled operations include shielding persons from light generated by a welding arc, isolating workers in paint spray booths, or having sand-blasters wear totally enclosing suits. An engine or machine that produces high levels of vibration and noise can be isolated by using vibration mounts or shields or noise suppressors or by locating the engines or machines in sound-isolated rooms and enclosures.

Machine guards and enclosures are widely used to isolate hazardous industrial equipment. These guards and enclosures are fixed over rotating parts, hot surfaces, pinch points, and electrical devices to prevent a person from coming in contact with the hazard. Other common examples of isolation include:

1. Putting extremely high-voltage components and circuits of a television set in a cage.

2. Using thermal insulation between a heat source and materials or components that could be damaged or adversely affected.

3. Potting of electrical connectors to prevent effects of moisture and other deleterious materials.

4. Using limit stops to restrict travel of mechanical parts.

5. Using shields and screens to keep out foreign objects and contaminants that might jam critical controls, orifices, or valves.

6. Using shields on microwave ovens, on x-ray equipment and in x-ray rooms, and on reactors and similar nuclear devices to contain emissions of harmful radiation.

7. Using metal containers for oily rags to keep air from them until they can be disposed of.

8. Using doors and panels to restrict access to the internal working parts of the moving machinery.

Many of the safeguards listed have interlocks that deactivate the equipment when the safeguard is bypassed. Other interlocks are used to prevent a product, assembly, or system from erroneously being put into an unsafe condition. Interlocks may be used to ensure that critical or hazardous operations are not started until required prior tasks are accomplished. For example, before a person works on an electrical system, the power should be shut off. If the person fails to shut off the power, the interlock on an access panel will shut off the power when it is opened. Figure 11-2 lists many of the devices used as interlocks. Interlocks can be of a type which can be bypassed or which cannot be bypassed when the safeguard is breached.

Any interlocking device that can be bypassed should be one that returns the safeguard to its operating position. For example, closing an access door will automatically reset the interlock. If the hazard may be imminent once the interlock is bypassed, it is advisable to provide an indicator, such as an illuminated light, to warn that the bypass has been activated.

Fail-Safe Designs

Fail-safe design tries to ensure that a failure will leave the product unaffected or will convert it to a state in which no injury or damage will occur. In most applications this will cause inactivation of the product. In any case, the fundamental principle is that a fail-safe design will give first priority to the protection of personnel, second priority to the protection of the environment, third priority to the prevention of damage to equipment, and fourth priority to prevention of loss of function or to degraded operation. There are three fail-safe designs:

1. *Fail-passive arrangements* reduce the system to its lowest energy level. The product will not operate until corrective action is taken, but no further damage will result from the hazard that is causing the

Interlocks

Interlocks are one of the most commonly used safety devices, especially with electrically operated equipment. They take many forms. The following list indicates the principles of the types more frequently used. In some cases, two or more of these principles are involved in the design of one interlocking device. Some interlocks themselves prevent action or motion; others send signals to other devices which prevent initiating the source of the action or motion.

TYPE	MODE OF OPERATION
Limit switches, including: · Snap-acting switches · Positive-drive switches · Proximity switches	A wide variety of limit switches can be used for interlock purposes. They are generally operated by moving an external part of the switch in, out, or sideways to open or close the switch, depending on circuit design. In some cases the limit switch itself will open or close the circuit of which it forms a part; in others, a signal or lack of one from the limit switch will open or close a relay which, in turn, will open or close a power circuit.
Tripping devices	Action releases a mechanical block or triggering device which either permits or stops motion.
Key interlock	Inserting and turning a key in a mechanical lock permits action.
Signal coding	Specifically coded sequences of pulses emitted by a transmitter must match the sequence in a suitable receiver. When the sequences match, the receiver initiates or permits action.
Motion interlock	Motion of the mechanism being guarded against prevents a guard or other access from being opened.
Parameter sensing	Presence, absence, excess, or inadequacy of pressure, temperature, flow or other parameters permits or stops action.
Position interlock	Nonalignment of two or more parts prevents further action.
Two-hand controls	Two simultaneous physical actions by a person are required, sometimes within a specific length of time.
Sequential controls	Actions must be performed in the proper sequence or operation is inhibited.
Timers and time delays	Operation of the equipment can take place only after a specific length of time has passed.
Path separation	Removal of a piece of the circuit or of the mechanical path physically prevents operation.
Photoelectric devices	Interruption or presence of light on a photoelectrical cell generates a signal which can stop or initiate action.
Magnetic or electromagnetic sensing	Presence of a magnetic material stops or initiates operation of the equipment.
Radio-frequency inductive	Sensing of any conductive material, especially steel or aluminium, causes it to operate.
Ultrasonics	Senses the presence of nonporous materials.
Mercury switches	Mercury provides the path between two metal contacts through which current passes. The path can be broken by tilting the switch in which the mercury and contacts are sealed so that the mercury flows away from one contact and breaks the path for the current.

Figure 11-2. Interlocks.

inactivation. Circuit breakers and fuses for protection of electrical circuits and equipment are fail-passive devices. The circuit breaker or fuse opens when the system reaches a dangerous level or a short circuit occurs; the system is de-energized and safe.

2. *Fail-active* design maintains an energized condition that keeps the system in a safe mode until corrective or overriding action occurs or an alternate system is activated to eliminate the possibility of an accident. Redundancy created by use of standby equipment as described on page 68 generally constitutes a "fail-active" design. A fail-active design was a so-called Lifeguard tire which was manufactured and sold years ago when tires were less reliable and before safety rims were invented. This tire had an inner casing and an outer casing, each filled through the same valve but otherwise containing separate air. If the outer casing was damaged or received a puncture so that it was flat, the car rode on the remaining casing, keeping the tire from coming off the wheel and giving the driver an opportunity to stop safely.

3. *Fail-operational* arrangements allow functions to continue safely until corrective action is possible. This type of design is the most preferable. Figure 11-3 shows such a fail-operational orientation of feedwater valves for boilers.

Each design to be made fail-safe must be analyzed for its own specific characteristics. In Figure 11-3 the valve should be open in order to be fail-safe; in other applications the closed position might be fail-safe (Figure 11-4). In an electronic circuit that controls a vehicle's speed, a break in a wire may make the equipment inoperative and safe. A bias signal may control a transistor's output. If the break is in the bias circuit, the transistor's output may increase to a maximum with loss of speed control. In order to be fail-safe, the circuit would have to be designed so that a break in the bias circuit would stop the vehicle.

Much railway equipment is designed on fail-safe principles predicated on the idea that only gravity can be depended on in an emergency. Semaphores, switch signals, and the lights to which they are connected are weight-operated devices. If there is a failure, a heavy arm drops and activates a warning. In the design of retractable landing gear for aircraft the wheels will drop and lock in the landing position if the pressure system that raises and lowers the gear fails.

Other examples of fail-safe devices include:

1. Air brakes on railroad trains and large trailer trucks.

2. Deadman throttles on locomotives and other vehicles and equipment.

3. Control rods on nuclear reactors which drop automatically into place in order to reduce the reaction rate if the rate exceeds a preset limit.

4. Automobile headlight covers that open and expose the lights if there is a malfunction.

Fail-safe systems are not given the highest priority since their operation generally depends on actions which might or might not occur as they should. Snow and ice might jam the weighted devices used by the railroads so that the devices do not work. An electrical fuse might not work fast enough so that a motor is damaged before the fuse blows. (Note: Fuses and circuit breakers are not designed to protect people against shock. The levels at which they operate are far too high for that.)

The term fail-safe is sometimes erroneously applied to redundant arrangements (see Chapter 8). If one item in a redundant arrangement fails, a second and perhaps third are available to keep the product functioning. However, if all of these items fail and if operation of the product fails, the result will be an accident. Redundant arrangements reduce the possibility and probability of a complete operational failure. With a fail-safe product that operates properly, no accident will occur as a result of operational failure.

On January 18, 1969 a three-engine airliner crashed into the ocean off Los Angeles, killing everyone aboard. The Federal Aviation Agency indicated that the accident may have been caused by a complete loss of electrical power. Although each engine drove a generator, one generator had been inoperative before takeoff. The pilot reported a fire in a second engine just before the crash and probably shut that engine and its generator down. As a result, the third and last generator may have been overloaded and failed, cutting off all power.

Failure Minimization

The fact that failures are one of the principal causes of accidents has already been pointed out (Chapter 8). For some of these, fail-safe designs can be provided so that failures will not result in accidents. However, such fail-safe designs may shut down an operation or process which is so critical that the fail-safe arrangement is less preferable than a system, product, process, or operation that will fail only very rarely. To minimize failures, either material or human, which cause accidents four principal methods are used: monitoring, warnings, safety factors and safety margins, and failure rate reductions. All of these but monitoring have been discussed.

Monitoring involves keeping a selected parameter, such as temperature or pressure, under surveillance. Monitoring involves checking operating conditions to ensure that they do not reach dangerous levels and to ensure that no contingency exists or is imminent. Greater benefits will result if contingencies are avoided instead of having to be overcome.

Monitors can be used to indicate:

1. Whether or not a specific condition exists.

2. Whether or not the product or one of its subassemblies is ready for operation or is operating satisfactorily as programmed.

Fail-Safe (Operational)

If the disk of a boiler water throttling valve separates from the stem on which it is mounted, flow of water *over* the disk will force it closed. A boiler may then be starved of water. If the heat is still applied pressure will increase rapidly, and the boiler may rupture violently. When water flow is *under* the disk, the pressure will force the disk away from its seat and flow will continue. The valve in this case will be fail-safe in an operational mode. In other usages closing the valve may be fail-safe. The reliability of the valve will be the same no matter how it is oriented.

The same question arises with the use of solenoid valves in process equipment. If power failure to the valve occurs, which will be the safe configuration, open or closed?

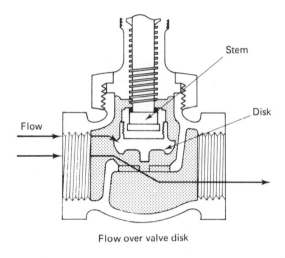
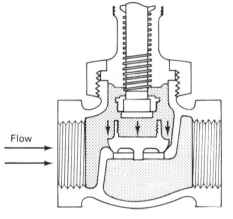
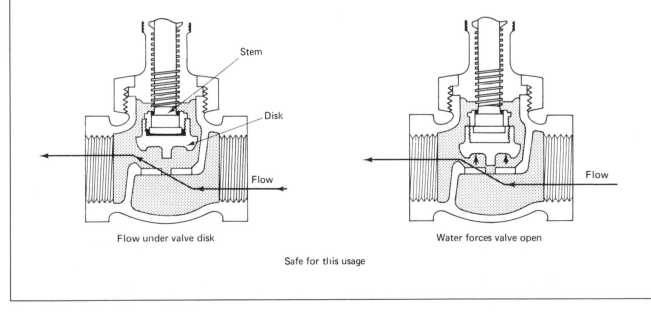

Flow over valve disk

Water forces valve closed

Unsafe for this usage

Flow under valve disk

Water forces valve open

Safe for this usage

Figure 11-3. Fail-safe (operational).

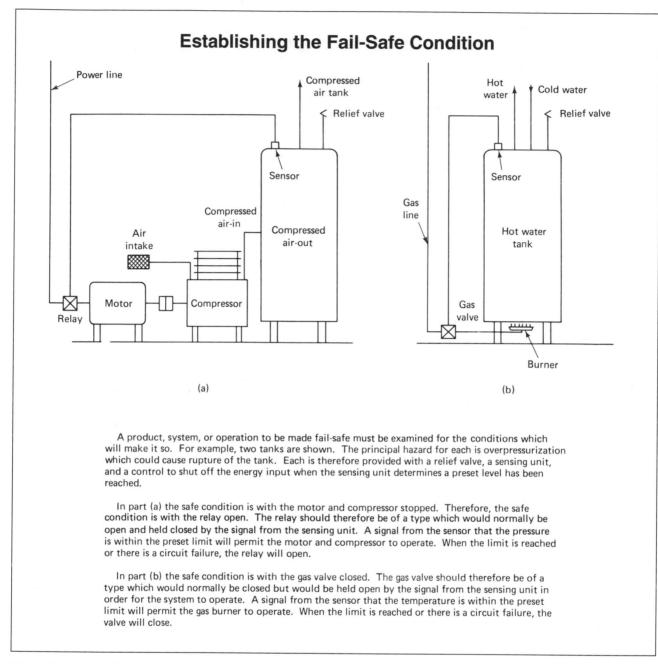

Establishing the Fail-Safe Condition

A product, system, or operation to be made fail-safe must be examined for the conditions which will make it so. For example, two tanks are shown. The principal hazard for each is overpressurization which could cause rupture of the tank. Each is therefore provided with a relief valve, a sensing unit, and a control to shut off the energy input when the sensing unit determines a preset level has been reached.

In part (a) the safe condition is with the motor and compressor stopped. Therefore, the safe condition is with the relay open. The relay should therefore be of a type which would normally be open and held closed by the signal from the sensing unit. A signal from the sensor that the pressure is within the preset limit will permit the motor and compressor to operate. When the limit is reached or there is a circuit failure, the relay will open.

In part (b) the safe condition is with the gas valve closed. The gas valve should therefore be of a type which would normally be closed but would be held open by the signal from the sensing unit in order for the system to operate. A signal from the sensor that the temperature is within the preset limit will permit the gas burner to operate. When the limit is reached or there is a circuit failure, the valve will close.

Figure 11-4. Establishing the fail-safe condition.

3. Whether or not the required input is being provided.

4. Whether a desired or an undesired output is being generated.

5. Whether or not a specified limit is being exceeded.

6. Whether or not the measured parameter is abnormal.

To be of value, a monitoring system must also include some provision for a tie-in with either a warning system, an interlock, or other means by which corrective action can be taken if necessary. With the warning system, information is conveyed to an operator who then takes corrective action. With an interlock, an out-of-limit sig-

nal may shut down operation of the product. A monitoring system may determine whether or not a fire exists and then the system may initiate a signal to activate a fire suppressant system. The monitoring process itself generally requires four major aspects: detection, measurement, interpretation, and response.

Detection

A monitor must be capable of sensing the specific parameter for which it has been selected in spite of all other environmental stresses that could be expected to exist during product operation, either programmed or emergency. For toxic gases, a detector may be capable of measuring extremely small concentrations of toxicants in a laboratory. In an operating vehicle, vibration, temperature variations, moisture, pressure changes, or other environmental factors may degrade performance or cause complete failure. The sensing function may be accomplished continuously, continually but intermittently, or intermittently at the desire of an operator. It must be able to sense and provide readings for only those parameters for which it has been selected and not affected by extraneous or other similar conditions.

It must be capable of detecting the hazard at a level low enough to permit corrective action before an emergency action is required. The input of the monitoring device should be located where it will sense the parameter for which it has been selected. Frequently, poor locations negate the value of a monitor. Fire detectors in homes are sometimes placed in locations distant from where they could be most effective.

Measurement

The parameter that a monitoring device senses may be one in which only one of two conditions can exist, that is, a device is either on or off. The monitor may also determine additional information, such as the existing level of the parameter being monitored continuously or when a predetermined level is exceeded.

The second type of monitor requires a comparison of existing and predetermined levels. Methods for such monitoring vary from those that are extremely simple to others that are very complex. A simple method is to mark a display, such as a dial, with the predetermined limit; and indicator then points out the existing level. An operator observes and compares the existing level with the limit to determine whether or not there is an abnormality. One style of automobile gauge used to monitor engine oil pressure is of this type. In the second type a light goes on to warn the operator only when the oil pressure is less than a preset level and by then the operator may already be in trouble.

Interpretation

An operator must clearly understand the readings provided by the monitoring devices. Therefore, the parameters selected should be meaningful to the operator. Thus, monitoring and indicating to an automobile operator the viscosity of oil would probably have little significance. The interpretation and use of monitored data are tied very closely to warnings. Displays and signals resulting from monitored data should provide timely and easily recognizable information. Readouts may be displayed continuously, when present limits are exceeded, or on demand. At the same time, the operator must be knowledgeable of the exact meanings of any output generated by a monitoring and warning device so that he or she can make a decision on his or her future course of action.

Response

When a monitor indicates that the situation is normal, no response other than continuation of the operation is necessary. When corrective action is required, the more time available to interpret information, reach a decision, and respond, the more likely that the decision and response will be proper and effective. For this reason, whenever possible, the monitor should indicate as early as possible the approach of an adverse condition. The level at which a monitor will indicate the existence of a problem can sometimes be set far from the actual danger level. This can be established by analyzing the situation to be monitored and the urgency of the situation that could arise. For example, air contains approximately 21% oxygen; the danger level for respiration is 16%. A monitor could indicate when the level of oxygen in an enclosed space drops below 20%. The atmosphere at this point is breathable, but the deficiency indicates the existence of a situation that should be investigated.

When the product is such that any response must be made by a person, analysis of the program should ensure that there will be adequate time to take corrective action under foreseeable circumstances. If a serious, critical, or catastrophic condition could result if corrective action were not taken very rapidly, the monitor should be interlocked to activate automatically hazard suppression or damage containment devices.

Other features to be considered during the design of monitors and their attendant warning or activation devices include:

1. Monitors must perform their functions at the highest practicable reliability levels. In extremely critical applications, they must be designed to indicate any failures of their own circuits or, if advisable, to permit periodic, quick checks of these circuits. Monitoring and warning devices must be analyzed as critically as the product in which they are to be incorporated since in the past false indications have induced personnel to take actions that have proved fatal. Monitor and warning circuits should be analyzed by the same logic analysis methods used for other electrical and electronic networks.

2. Failure of monitoring equipment or circuits must not produce other hazardous conditions or damaging effects on the product itself.

3. Monitoring systems must be easy to maintain, check, and calibrate. Procedures for these operations and for testing monitors must be provided.

4. If product failure could cause the loss of the power that is necessary for monitoring and warning functions, it may be desirable to have independent power sources and circuits.

5. The energy level for monitoring must be lower than that which constitutes or contributes to a hazard to the product being monitored.

6. Circuitry within the monitoring system must not provide a path that could cause degradation or failure of the product during operation. Monitor circuit devices should not generate RF energy or other noise in other circuits.

7. Power for monitoring should not be routed through devices in which it could change a safe condition, remove a blocking element, or cause inadvertent activation.

A few of the many applications of monitoring may be mentioned here:

1. Temperature and pressure monitors for engines.

2. Radiation monitors for nuclear reactors.

3. Odorants to indicate leakage of gases that may be toxic or highly flammable.

4. Gas monitors to determine the presence of toxic or flammable substances.

5. SOAP (Spectrometic Oil Analysis Program) involves determining the presence of minute amounts of aluminum, iron, copper, and other metals in engine oil by which wear can be determined. Where abrasion is taking place, and the rate the metal is abrading can be determined, a recommended maintenance schedule can be established.

6. Signature analysis involves recording a pattern of the vibrations emitted by a new product which is running satisfactorily. Subsequent recordings are made at intervals and the new patterns are examined to determine changes that have occurred, how critical the changes are, and whether or not repairs should be made.

7. Infrared detectors to indicate the presence of hot spots or of flames.

8. Liquid-level indicators that warn or initiate action when the liquid reaches a present level.

Warnings

A mishap can often be avoided by focusing attention on the existence of a hazard and the need for care. In Chapter 10 it was pointed out that warnings are legally required to alert users to a hazard a product might have which is not obvious. Labeling and markings and warnings in operating or maintenance instructions and on the product are the principal methods of doing this. There are, however, other effective means, some far more positive for use in more critical situations.

Every method of notifying a person that a hazard exists requires communication, and each and all of the human senses have been used for the purpose. The examples cited below that point out how each sense has been used for warning constitute only a few of the many current applications.

Visual warnings. Vision is the principal sense by which information on the existence of hazards is transmitted to personnel. There are more variations of visual methods than there are of the other senses.

These visual methods include:

1. *Illumination.* A location where a hazard exists is lighted more brightly than surrounding, less hazardous areas in order to focus attention on where a danger might exist. Sometimes spotlighting equipment might also have an additional benefit: security. A lighted power substation would indicate the presence of danger and it would also permit detection of anyone attempting to steal equipment. Lights at obstacles may reduce the possibility of persons or vehicles running into the obstacles.

2. *Discrimination.* A structure, piece of equipment, or fixed object that could be hit by a moving vehicle could be painted a bright, distinctive color or in alternating light and dark colors. A common example is painting emergency vehicles so that they can be readily seen. Recently the traditional red for fire trucks has given way to yellow and international orange so that the vehicles can be seen and recognized more readily. Metalworking equipment may have the operating areas, where hazards exist, painted so that they can be distinguished from the protected areas. Piping and cylinders for toxic, flammable, or corrosive gases or liquids are color coded to indicate the hazards involved. Color coding is used to identify gasoline containing tetraethyl lead (a red dye is added). Accumulations of the dye at connections and joints in a fuel system containing such gasoline help to show where there are leaks.

3. *Signal lights.* Using colored lights is a very common method of identifying the existence of hazards and of avoiding accidents. Fixed or flashing lights may be used, but the colors and their intended meanings generally are:

   (a) Red—existing danger, emergency, malfunction, error, stop.

   (b) Yellow—impending danger, marginal condition, caution, proceed slowly.

   (c) Green—satisfactory conditions, proceed, ready, function activated properly, parameter within limits.

   (d) White—system available, operation in progress.

   Flashing lights are used to attract attention and to indicate urgency. When locomotive headlights were made to oscillate, they became much more effective as warning devices than fixed lights. For this same reason, swinging or flashing red lights at railroad crossings are also more effective than fixed lights. Flashing lights are very often used in conjunction with aural devices (see paragraphs below on auditory warnings).

Fixed lights also attract attention, but to a lesser degree. Long-distance bus operators found that their accident rates decreased when bus headlights were left on during daylight. Another effective fixed-light signal is the reflector used on barriers and road shoulders and as a lane marker. When put on a bicycle wheel, the reflector is especially effective when the bicycle is in motion because it reflects the lights of approaching cars.

4. *Flags and streamers.* These have a long history, especially as signaling devices used by ships to indicate hazards such as operations with explosives or the presence of sickness aboard. A red streamer marking the end of a long load protruding from the back of a vehicle attracts attention. Flags are also attached to wires, ropes, or cables to attract the attention of personnel who might otherwise run into them. A tag on a switch or circuit breaker indicates that the system has been inactivated for repairs or other reason and should not be changed. On one type of smoke detector a metal flag pops out to warn that the battery has been removed and that the device is inoperative. Tags are attached to components to indicate that they require repair, that they should not be used unless special precautions are taken, or that they have malfunctioned.

5. *Labels.* These were discussed in Chapter 10. They may be attached to or painted on equipment where a hazard exists. They may point out high voltage, phase, and power limitations in electrical or electronic equipment; give load, speed, or temperature limitations; warn against pressure hazards and the need to wear protective equipment when servicing pressurized equipment; or indicate low headroom. Lift points and "No Step" markings may be painted on structural elements. Color-coded lines mentioned under 2 above could also be labeled to indicate the contents of the lines.

6. *Signs.* The most common signs are fixed signs, such as road signs to point out curves, intersections, narrow bridges, slippery roads, and other hazards. Signs may be distinctively shaped and colored. Many countries now use symbols that can be understood by persons unfamiliar with the language of the country through which they are traveling.

Consoles for electrical equipment sometimes have electrically activated signs that indicate when a critical malfunction or hazard exists or when a specific action should be taken. Some of the more expensive cars have dashboard devices that warn drivers when there has been a brake failure or the brake has not been released, when less than one-quarter of a tank of fuel remains, or when the driver's or passenger's seat belt is not fastened.

7. *Procedural notes.* These also have been described in Chapter 10. They include warnings and cautions inserted in operations and maintenance procedures, instructions, manuals, and checklists to alert personnel to hazards, possibilities and the effects of errors, special care or actions that must be taken, or protective devices, clothing, or tools that must be used. Those steps in any procedure in which an error or malfunction could result in injury or damage should be preceded by a precautionary note. The warning or caution in the instruction manual, handbook, or list should correspond to the warning or caution labels on the equipment, and any hazard that calls for a label should be mentioned in the instructions.

Auditory warnings. In some situations, visual warnings are inadequate. Personnel are sometimes so occupied that they fail to note visual signals even when they are close to them. Persons may move about, often into positions from which they cannot see a visual warning. A bright, visual signal can be seen over a greater distance than an auditory signal can be heard, but an auditory signal might be more effective within its range. A siren is an excellent example.

Auditory signals can also be used merely to bring attention to a visual display that will provide additional and more detailed information on the condition constituting a problem. Auditory signals can be coded to indicate the type of emergency that exists and the emergency procedure to be followed.

MIL-STD-1472[3] offers guidance on auditory displays and warnings which applies equally well to civilian products. It recommends that auditory signals be used when:

1. The information that is to be disseminated is short, simple, and transitory and requires immediate response.

2. The usual mode of warning by a visual display is restricted by heavy loads on the operator, by variable or limited light, operator movement, other environmental considerations, or anticipated operator inattention.

3. The criticality to respond makes a supplementary or redundant alerting signal desirable.

4. It is desirable to warn, alert, or cue the operator to subsequent additional information or response.

5. Custom or usage has created anticipation of auditory signals.

6. Voice communication is necessary or desirable.

Commonly used auditory warnings are sirens, buzzers, bells, or other alarms on timing devices which indicate when a specific period has passed or that the time has arrived to take the next step in a sequence. Some compressed air packs that provide respiratory protection for limited periods contain alarms that sound when the pressure level in the pack decreases to a predetermined level or after a preset time has passed.

Olfactory warnings. Odors can be detected only when certain gas molecules affect a small area (approximately 1 in.^{2} (6.5 cm.^{2}) in the nasal cavity. Some gases have no odor; others are so strong that even small amounts may sicken the person affected. The body has the ability to desensitize itself against odors fairly rapidly. This ability is an advantage in one way: Odors generally constitute little problem after a person has become desensitized to their presence. In addition, the ability to detect odors varies considerably with individuals and their habits (smoking degrades the capability). These factors reduce the advantages that odorants have for warning purposes, except for short periods and when desensitization has not already occurred. Nevertheless, odorants are used successfully as a warning medium.

1. Addition of an odorant to highly flammable and explosive gases that have no odor of their own. Natural gas from which sulfur compounds have been removed has no odor. To reduce the possibilities of fires and explosions with natural gas, a small amount of odorant gas (Mercaptan) that has a strong odor is added to supplies distributed to homes and shops. The amount of odorant added is such that any leak would be readily detectable while the concentration of flammable gas is still far less than that at which it will ignite.

2. Overheated equipment can sometimes be detected by the odors produced. A lubricating oil having a fairly low vaporization temperature could be used if overheating from friction would volatilize it and make it readily detectable. This method was once used with bearing boxes on railroad car wheels. A material was added that vaporized if a bearing overheated, thus pinpointing the problem for any crewman making an inspection during a stop.

3. The presence of fires can be detected by the odors of gas produced from combustion. Different materials, such as wood and rubber, have characteristic odors that indicate what substance is burning. This method would probably have little use in product design.

Tactile warnings. Vibration is the chief tactile means of providing warnings. Vibration warns that an operation is not as smooth as it should be and is degrading to a failure. A rotating shaft or bearing that is beginning to wear and the rough running of an engine are examples. The roughness may be caused by a worn part, poor timing, low-grade fuel, or a lubrication failure. The magnitude of the vibrations could indicate the severity of the problem.

Vibration provides warnings on streets and highways in a number of ways. Raised lane markers (rumble strips) cause a car passing over them to vibrate. Such markers may indicate that the car is too close to a shoulder or to a center divider or that the car is crossing into another lane. A driver who dozes off may be awakened and alerted to the danger. Pedals on aircraft with electric or hydraulic flight controls are generally equipped with "feel" systems or pedal shakers which apprise the pilot of aerodynamic conditions.

Temperature sensing is another method of providing warning through feeling. Maintenance personnel can determine whether or not a piece of equipment is operating improperly by feeling it with the palm of the hand. An increase in temperature in an air-conditioned space may warn of problems with the equipment, undercapacity for normal requirements, or abnormal loads.

Gustatory warnings. The sense of taste is probably the least important as a warning mechanism. It has been used to determine whether a food, drink, or other material taken into the mouth is dangerous or contains a dangerous contaminant. Medicines that might be dangerous to children may have an additive to give the medicine a bitter taste. A child who sampled the medicine might be deterred from taking more than one swallow. If a food or drug could deteriorate, instructions might be provided to discard if it tastes bitter, salty, acid, or unusual.

Reduce Failure Rates

Failure rates and how to reduce them were discussed in Chapter 8. Incorporating safety factors into equipment and structures was one of the first methods used to reduce failure rates, that is, to make a product three, four, or five times strong as required in order to withstand calculated loads and stresses. Derating is similar, but it is applied to electronic equipment: Operating a component at a stress level far below that which it is capable of sustaining will increase the component's reliability. Using redundancies, screening to remove failure-prone components, and making replacements before the components wear out will all reduce the overall failure rate of the product. If failures are safety-critical and would result in accidents, such improvements would also decrease the number of accidents.

Prescribing Safe Procedures

Reliance on safe procedures should be a last resort and when there is no other practicable means of making the product intrinsically safe. Since most of the time this is not possible, safe procedures are generally necessary. The causes of errors and some of the means by which designers can minimize the possibilities of error are described in Chapter 10. It can be seen that common causes of accidents are the inadequacies of the procedures and the failure to follow the procedures. Chapter 17 describes the making of procedures analyses and how to review them for adequacy. Development, analysis, and publication of procedures for the users of any product are a must. Unfortunately, so many people do not read operating procedures until they have run into difficulty ("when all else fails, read the instructions") that it gives this method a low priority in rating means of preventing accidents.

Backout and Recovery

A malfunction, error, or other adverse condition may eventually develop into a contingency in which the situation is abnormal and extremely dangerous but has not yet generated any injury or damage. It is a critical point: With suitable corrective action an accident can be avoided; failure to act or action which is incorrect or inadequate can permit the situation to deteriorate into a mishap. This interim period extends from the time the abnormality begins to the time that either normality is recovered or a full-scale mishap develops. If recovery takes place, the incident can be considered a near-miss. Actions that should be taken in such a situation must be established by a contingency analysis (see Chapter 17) for each particular operation. In general, these actions can be divided into the following:

1. *Restoring normal sequence.* Conduct of certain operations in wrong sequences can subsequently lead to a failure and mishap. However, there may be an interval during which the situation can be corrected without damage simply by going directly to the correct step in the procedure which may have been bypassed or to another predetermined step from which a new start can be made.

2. *Aborting the entire operation.* Each operation has points at which it can be halted without injury. Sometimes a halt can also be made without damage to equipment, but this is secondary to safeguarding personnel. A missing bolt, leaking oil line, or an inoperative device detected before the operation begins might cause an abort whose only adverse effect might be delay. Abort after the operation begins could have effects of varying magnitudes.

3. *Inactivating only malfunctioning equipment.* This step can be accomplished when the problem occurs with the following items:

   (a) Those that are nonessential to the overall operation at any time.

   (b) Those that can be spared because of redundancy.

   (c) Those that have already fulfilled their function in the overall operation and are no longer required.

   (d) Those for which temporary substitution can be made.

4. *Suppressing the hazard.* When a hazard becomes apparent or exceeds a specific limit, the hazard can sometimes be removed or suppressed. Spillage of a large amount of gasoline could produce a flammable mixture and a fire. The possibility of a fire accident is eliminated by flushing away the gasoline and recreating a normal atmosphere. Such actions may be either automatic or manual, depending on the monitoring and control equipment available.

5. *Accident effect aborting.* A major example of aborting the effects of an accident is by inhibiting the spread of fire in a carbonaceous material is through the use of:

   (a) Halogenated hydrocarbon which changes the process of combustion.

   (b) Smothering the fire by preventing the entrance of oxygen or fuel.

   (c) Cooling the fuel below its ignition temperature.

Damage Minimization and Containment

As long as a hazard exists, there is the possibility, no matter how improbable, that an accident will occur. There is no way of knowing when the accident will take place. Therefore, it is necessary that designers explore to the fullest all means to minimize injury and contain damage. Unfortunately, considerations of cost or functional requirements may make it impractical to incorporate safeguards for complete protection. Some of the protective methods that can be applied are explained in the following paragraphs.

Isolation

Isolation has already been discussed as an accident prevention measure. It is also frequently used as a method of reducing damage that can be generated by violent release of energy as a result of an accident.

Energy-absorbing mechanisms isolate personnel and sensitive equipment from the effects of impact. Bumpers and padded interiors reduce injuries to occupants of automobiles involved in accidents. Foams, excelsior, and similar materials in containers protect items that would otherwise be damaged if the container were dropped or jarred in any way. Pertinent facts on energy absorption processes are illustrated in Figure 11-5.

Almost all of the protective features involved in the term crash worthiness are actually predicated on the principle of absorption of energy. Shoulder straps, seat belts, and other harnesses restrain and isolate an occupant of a vehicle so that he or she will not impact near objects or surfaces or be thrown about and injured.

Another common method is locating the site of a possible accident far from personnel, material, or structures. Explosives' safety quantity-distance criteria are predicated on this principle. Standards are set for the amounts of explosive that can be located or stored at specific distances from other critical items or inhabited areas or structures. As a result, explosives that detonate accidentally will not initiate explosions of other explosives, cause damage to buildings or other structures, or cause personnel injury.

Isolation may be provided by deflectors. Barricades between explosives and inhabited or other critical buildings are doubly effective since they absorb the energy of an explosion and deflect the remainder upward where it will do no harm.

Containment processes are other common means of isolation for damage control:

1. Hazards generated by a mishap can be contained; for example, limiting the spread of fire resulting from an accident, using firebreaks to restrict a forest fire, and spraying water around a magnesium fire to prevent

ignition of nearby flammables or damage from the intense heat.

2. An operation may become uncontrolled as the result of an accident, but damage and injury can be avoided by limiting the effects. A tire may blow on a racing car so that the car spins out of control in the vicinity of spectators. Suitable barriers could confine the vehicle to the limits of the track so that no spectator is injured.

3. Personnel themselves can be provided protection. This point has been made before under crashworthiness and under control of operations. In some systems, certain areas or structures can be designated as "safety zones" where personnel will be safe from the hazards generated by an accident.

4. Materials can be protected by methods similar to those for personnel. Containers of metal, plastic, or other impermeable or impenetrable substances are effective in minimizing damage to materials if a mishap occurs. Waterproof boxes or containers will prevent the contents from damage by water present as the result of an accidental leak or a flood.

5. Critical equipment can be protected in the same way. An electrical motor whose operation may be required in an emergency, such as a flood, can be hermetically sealed so that it will run even when under water.

Personal Protective Equipment

Use of personal protective equipment is another means by which protection from hazards can be achieved through isolation. The user is provided with a limited, controlled environment different in at least one respect from the ambient environment. The difference is the isolation from the hazard.

Personal protective equipment here connotes those garments or devices that a person would wear for protection against a hazard. They may vary from a simple set of earplugs to a complete spacesuit with oxygen equipment for an astronaut. The astronaut is isolated from all space hazards; the earplug user is isolated from noise and the adverse effects that noise generates.

Personal protective equipment may be required to safeguard personnel against harmful environments that cannot be eliminated during necessary operations or that result from mishaps. The equipment must be adequate to protect its user under the worst possible foreseeable conditions. Since conditions may change, equipment that is suitable for one set of circumstances may not be suitable for another. For example, a gas mask usable against chlorine and similar gases would not provide protection against the absence of air. In these cases, an air pack or oxygen generator is necessary.

Needs for personal protective equipment can be divided into the three following categories:

1. *Scheduled hazardous operation.* Operations may have to be conducted in environments that could be as damaging as if an accident had occurred, because the hazard cannot be eliminated. Spray painting in an enclosed space is an example. Protective equipment is frequently provided for numerous other operations and is to be worn while the operation is being conducted. However, the use of personal protective equipment as a substitute for good design, hazard elimination or control, or safe operating procedures should be avoided. An example is requiring a person to wear respiratory protective equipment for operations conducted in a tank or other closely confined space. This procedure is much less desirable and less safe than ventilating the space so that a normal, breathable atmosphere exists and monitoring it to ensure that it remains breathable.

2. *Investigations and corrections.* Detection equipment may indicate or personnel may suspect that an environment is dangerous. It may then be necessary for someone to enter the area, determine the source of the contamination or other dangerous condition, and take corrective action. In some instances, the hazardous material may be known, such as during

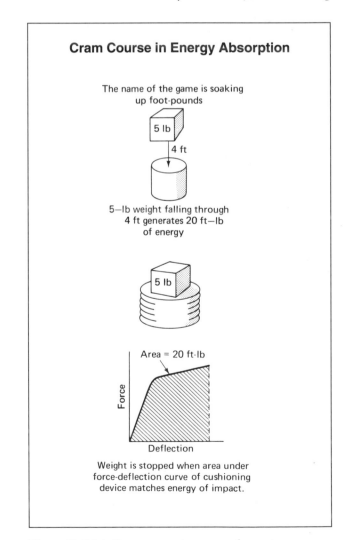

Cram Course in Energy Absorption

The name of the game is soaking up foot-pounds

5 lb

4 ft

5–lb weight falling through 4 ft generates 20 ft–lb of energy

5 lb

Area = 20 ft-lb

Force

Deflection

Weight is stopped when area under force-deflection curve of cushioning device matches energy of impact.

Figure 11-5 (a). Cram course in energy absorption.

neutralization or decontamination of a leak or spill of a toxic, corrosive, or flammable liquid. At other times, the exact natures of the contaminants or their concentrations may be unknown or uncertain. Personal protective equipment for this purpose must be capable of providing protection against a wider range of hazards than for a known hazard.

3. *Emergencies.* An emergency generates the severest conditions and requirements for usage, design, and capabilities of protective equipment. The first few minutes after a contingency becomes imminent or occurs may be critical. Reaction time to suppress or reestablish control of the hazard or to minimize damage or injury is therefore extremely important. Emergency equipment must permit quick response. It must be easy to don and simple to use, especially by personnel under the stress of an emergency. It must be highly reliable and effective against a broad variety of hazards. It must not degrade the mobility or performance of the user unduly and it must not constitute a hazard itself.

Product designers must ensure that equipment designed or selected for personnel protection is suitable for the hazardous conditions that might be encountered. As emergency equipment, it should be considered only as a backup, that is, as a redundant arrangement to be used only if more preferable methods of accident prevention or damage and injury control cannot be used. However, when personal protective equipment is necessary, it must work as intended or the user will be exposed to a second mishap having a much higher probability of being fatal. Analyses of designs, hazards involved, procedures for use, and safeguards to prevent impairment of their performance must be even more stringent than for products and equipment for normal mission purposes. The designs must be extraordinarily errorproof, since the possibilities of ever-present human error are increased because of the stress to which all personnel are subjected during emergencies.

Designs and tests of protective equipment should ensure to the greatest degree practicable that:

1. It will not deteriorate rapidly in storage or in the presence of the hazard against which it is supposed to provide protection.

2. Protective coverings will not become brittle or crack because of the flexing action in normal movement, deleterious materials, temperature extremes, sunlight, or other radiation.

3. It is easy to clean and decontaminate.

4. Clothing to protect against toxic or corrosive gases or liquids is impermeable.

5. Coverings that might be exposed to fire are noncombustible or self-extinguishing.

6. Facilities for storage of emergency equipment are located as close as practicable to the point where its use might be required. The facility must not be so close that the condition generating the emergency

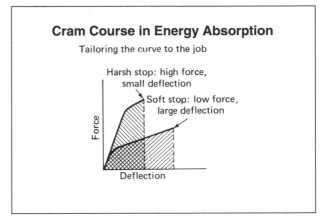

Figure 11-5 (b). Cram course in energy absorption.

will affect the equipment or prevent reaching it for use. Storage units should be easily accessible and marked for quick identification, and their locations should be identified in operating procedures.

7. Instructions are provided on proper methods of fitting, testing, and maintaining protective equipment.

Minor Loss Acceptance

This technique involves following the basic principle on which insurance is predicated: acceptance of a small loss to ensure that a large loss does not occur. A few examples of how this principle has been applied to the design of equipment include:

1. The freeze plug in the cooling system of an automobile engine. If the water in the cylinder block freezes

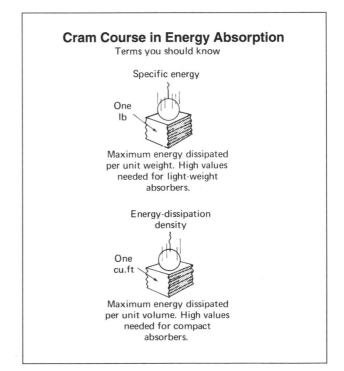

Figure 11-5(c). Cram course in energy absorption.

completely, its expansion will force the plug out rather than crack the block.

2. The fusible plug in a boiler. The plug will not be kept cool if it is exposed because the water level drops below a predetermined level. The heat will not be conducted away; the temperature of the plug will rise; and the plug will melt. The opening created permits the steam to escape, reduces the pressure in the boiler, and eliminates the possibility of a boiler explosion.

3. Providing oil and gas furnaces with blowout panels that give way if overpressurization should result from delayed ignition of accumulations of fuel vapors and gases. This feature prevents or reduces damage to furnace walls, boiler tubes, and other critical parts of the equipment and structure. Similar use of blowout panels or frangible walls is made in explosives-processing plants, where an explosion would otherwise destroy a structure completely.

4. Collapsible steering columns on automobiles. Formerly, drivers were killed or severely injured in collisions when their chests hit the steering columns. With the new designs, the columns collapse under a load so that only slight injury results from that contact.

5. Frangible signposts on highways. If directional control of an automobile is lost and the post is hit, the possibility of injury to people and damage to the automobile is minimized.

6. Shear pins on couplings of motor-driven equipment. If there is an overload, the torque causes shearing of the pin, thus preventing damage to the driving or driven shaft or burnout of the motor.

7. Impact lessening and restraint devices such as bumpers, seat belts, shoulder harnesses, airbags, padding, safety glass, and recessed handle knobs.

Escape and Survival

Deterioration of a contingency may continue until a point is reached after which it is necessary to abandon or sacrifice equipment, vehicles, hardware, or structures in order to avoid injury to personnel. This is the point of no return. Effort has been made to recover from the emergency, to suppress the hazard and any damage that could result, to restore normal conditions, or to isolate adverse effects. If these efforts are unsuccessful, it may be necessary to abandon ship, bail out, eject, or, in some other way leave the danger area. For such situations, escape and survival equipment are literally vital: Lives depend on them.

A distinction would be made here between equipment for escape and equipment for survival. An example is a jet pilot's emergency equipment. The ejection seat helps the pilot escape from the aircraft; other devices safeguard the pilot in and against the new environment. A shield or capsule protects the pilot against air blast, since the pressure of the air through which the pilot will be traveling

initially at extremely high velocity would be similar to that of a high-explosive shock wave. A parachute is then required so the pilot can survive falling so far. In some instances, a temporary supply of oxygen and insulation against the cold may be required. If the flight is over the ocean or other very large body of water, an inflatable life raft is necessary. This raft would have to include rations and water to permit survival for an extended period until the pilot is found. Similar provisions would have to be made if flights were over arctic or jungle areas.

The importance of escape and survival equipment cannot be overstressed for those situations in which they are

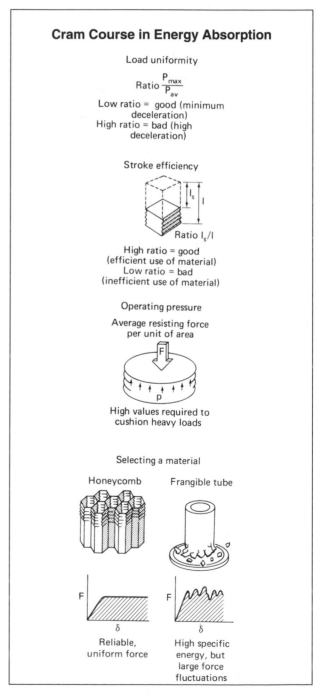

Figure 11-5 (d). Cram course in energy absorption.

necessary. In many instances, however, undue reliance is placed on their possible use, resulting in lack of suitable emphasis on controlling accident causes. Escape and survival equipment should be considered and used only in cases of last resort. To avoid last-resort situations, engineers must do their utmost to eliminate or minimize those conditions that could result in loss of control hazards and in accidents. Equipment design should maximize the use of safety devices and procedures to avoid the necessity of using escape and survival equipment. It is recognized, however, that there are numerous cases in which hazards cannot be eliminated entirely, that accidents will occur, and that escape and survival equipment must be provided.

In some cases, escape may be a fairly easy process; under only slightly different conditions, escape may be impossible. It used to be that, in most large helicopter accidents, the helicopter had a tendency to flip onto its right side. If the right side was the only one in which there was a door through which passengers could leave the vehicle, escape would generally be impossible. A similar problem that existed (until it was corrected by using a more secure latching device) was slamming of the sliding door. In this case, forward impact caused the door to slide shut, trapping the passengers when it jammed.

The same situation applies to the other vehicles, such as automobiles and passenger aircraft. Collision of an automobile may cause the car doors to jam. The occupant may then have to be rescued. If he or she is badly injured and bleeding or if there is a fire and the means of escape is blocked, the results would be fatal. For this reason, commercial aircraft are generally provided with multiple exits to permit evacuation of passengers within a specified time even when a number of escape routes are blocked.

The designs and devices to permit escape after a collision are another aspect of crashworthiness mentioned under isolation of damage in this chapter. Crashworthiness is a three-part concept:

1. Protect a person by isolating the person, generally against impact and other energy effects and hazards, such as fire.

2. Permit the person to escape from the vehicle and to reach safety from any hazards resulting from the crash.

3. Permit rescue operations if the person cannot escape by his or her own efforts (see following section).

Designs for the crashworthiness escape aspects therefore include such items as escape doors and panels, nonjamming doors, knockout windows, and breakaway sections. This last method involves designing a vehicle so that on impact it will break apart at specific locations to provide large openings for the exiting of personnel.

It is evident that escape and survival devices to be incorporated into a product must be considered critical items. They must be analyzed and tested intensively to ensure

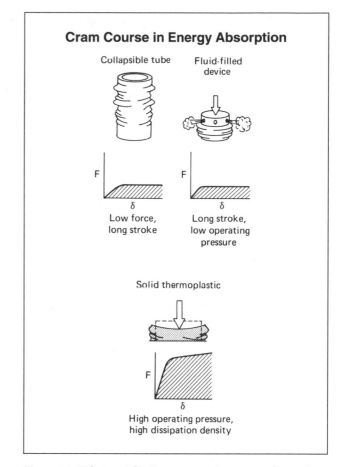

Figure 11-5(d) (cont'd). Cram course in energy absorption.

that they meet their intended purposes with very low probabilities of failure. Such equipment and the environment for which each one is designed are subject to hazards, as was the basis operative system, but there is one major difference: Control of a hazard has been lost and the danger level is much higher.

Failure of a piece of escape or survival equipment may be worse than if no equipment at all had been supplied. In some instances, the items themselves have injured the users because of their poor design or manufacture. Failure or inadequacy when a crisis occurs produces a traumatic shock over and above that which the mishap to the system produced. In addition, the time lost in establishing that the equipment did not work or worked improperly, in determining an alternative course of action, and then taking that action under stress reduce the chances of successful accomplishment. Alternative courses of action may be possible in some instances but not in others. Some actions may be possible up to a specific point in time, after which they are not.

The need for escape and survival equipment and procedures must be established by contingency analyses. Once this task is done, the equipment to be used must be selected carefully. It must be analyzed to ensure that it will fulfill all foreseeable needs and that procedures for its use are available and adequate. The equipment should be studied in detail through Failure Modes and Effects Analysis or other methods. A test program must be developed to ensure that the items will work under expected conditions, that they will satisfy established requirements, and that procedures are adequate. Tests should also be conducted under worst-case conditions to determine whether or not the equipment can be operated and whether or not the procedures can be followed by a partially incapacitated person.

Very often, escape and survival equipment furnished for emergencies is suitable, but failure to maintain the equipment properly allows it to deteriorate so that it will not work as it should. Procedures must therefore be established for both proper use and maintenance and replacements must be made whenever necessary.

Rescue Procedures and Equipment

In any emergency there is the possibility that the person (or persons) involved may not be able to escape under his or her own resources. Provisions must be made for rescue by other personnel if the need should arise. Rescues may be attempted by:

1. Persons familiar with the product and its operation, hazards, and emergency devices.

2. Personnel familiar with the hazards in general but not with the specific equipment. A city fireman may be well-trained in firefighting but may lack training in rescuing personnel from burning aircraft.

3. Untrained personnel who are unfamiliar with the product or the hazards involved but who want to help.

Because these last two categories of personnel can (and do) provide vital assistance, it is advisable to mark any emergency devices so that volunteers can determine how and where to assist the persons to be rescued. Suitable markings and the presence of available devices may mean the difference between a successful and an unsuccessful rescue attempt. Latches on the outside of aircraft to release cockpit canopies are examples. If these latches are marked, all of the above categories of personnel may be able to operate them. If the latches are not marked, only personnel familiar with aircraft or those latches may be able to operate them.

Such devices must be foolproof in an emergency, require little physical effort to operate, and be easy to operate when only a few words of instruction are provided. The instructions should be marked so that they are easy to recognize and easy to understand by a person under stress.

The time to develop suitable rescue devices and procedures and to study the adequacies of those proposed is early in the design stage when contingency analyses should be made. The results of these analyses may determine whether or not changes in equipment or procedures are required or whether or not other protective or rescue devices are needed. The need, discussed in the previous section, for escape and survival equipment to be subjected to rigid analyses because of their criticality is even more applicable to rescue devices. If an escape device fails, the user may be injured or killed. If the rescue equipment fails, both the rescuer and the person the rescuer is attempting to assist may be killed.

Rescue equipment may be specifically designed for a product, may be general-purpose items that can be used for a wide variety of emergencies, or may be improvised from items built for other purposes. An example of the first category is the emergency canopy release for an aircraft. The crash truck on an airfield is an example of the second category. The use of helicopters for the rescue of people from burning aircraft is an example of the third category. The helicopter was not made specifically for the purpose, but it was found that the downdraft from its rotor blades would blow flames in a direction that would permit the escape of persons in the aircraft. The downdraft also provides a path along which rescuers may pass.

Organizations that involve operations in which rescue devices and equipment are used should develop preaccident plans. These plans are necessary even though they may never be put into actual practice. Training must be undertaken to ensure that operators and rescue personnel understand and are proficient in carrying out rescue procedures. Simulated emergencies also help increase proficiency. Investigations of many serious accidents have revealed that personnel died because of the lack of proficiency in the use of rescue equipment and devices or because they failed to follow established procedures. Manufacturers of such equipment would do well to ensure that users are provided with adequate instructions and to conduct training courses in how to use the equipment.

Notes

[1] "Acceptable" to safety engineers.

[2] The term *safety critical* is used for any condition, part, or action which affects or could be affected by any safety aspect of a product.

[3] *Human Engineering Design Criteria for Military Systems, Equipment and Facilities*, MIL-STD-1472 (Washington, D.C.: Department of Defense, May 15, 1970), p. 43.

Questions

1. Discuss whether or not a product can be made "perfectly safe."

2. List four design conditions that are generally acceptable from a safety standpoint if they are incorporated into a product.

3. What are the two general types of safeguards that can be provided against hazards? Which one is preferable? Why?

4. What is "intrinsic safety"?

5. What is an interlock? Give two examples of products on which interlocks are used.

6. Give the order of priorities for a fail-safe design. Why is a fail-safe design less desirable than intrinsic safety or isolating hazards?

7. Does a redundant arrangement make it a fail-safe arrangement? Why or why not?

8. Give five examples of monitoring devices or systems. List the four steps in monitoring hazardous conditions.

9. Explain why a two-wire double insulated electrical tool is preferable, from a safety standpoint, to a three-wire metal cased tool.

10. List the five categories of means by which warnings can be transmitted to an operator or other person. Which category is used most?

11. Give an example in which a minor loss is an acceptable method of minimizing damage. How does this differ from a fail-safe design? In which of these two categories would a fuse be?

12. Discuss why the design of protective, escape, and rescue equipment must be analyzed more critically and be more reliable than the operating equipment with which it will be used.

13. If a product is designed to be intrinsically "fail-safe," can it cause an accident even through an error such as misuse?

14. Discuss where defective designs of emergency equipment can become especially life threatening in use.

15. Discuss whether, and why, you believe the following should be provided in all cases because of possible accident: (a) parachutes on all aircraft; (b) restraint devices and escape chutes on the medium-sized aircraft; (c) automobile air bags for the back seat; (d) motorcycle helmets and restraints; and (e) skateboard rider personal protective equipment.

16. Which of these post-accident devices would you say is least necessary? Why? Name some which are legally required and some which are only advisable.

12

Product Safety Programs

The courts and safety agencies expect manufacturers to take reasonable care in the design and manufacture of their products. Most regulatory agencies are following policies of deterring accidents by having manufacturers anticipate and resolve safety problems before products are released to the market. To satisfy the safety agencies and to lessen their legal problems, manufacturers must produce "reasonably" safe products. Since the term "reasonable" is open to interpretation by others, manufacturers should exceed what *they* consider "reasonable" and produce the safest product possible within cost limitations. To do this requires sustained, systematic, and coordinated programs involving management and technical expertise in all aspects of the development, production, distribution, and operational support of their products. For the safety program to be effective at minimal cost, it must begin as soon as possible after the idea for a new product or a modification is generated.

Management Responsibilities

All tasks in an effective safety program can be separated into the life-cycle phases through which any product must pass. The phases into which the product life cycle can be divided are described below, but through all the phases and over all the tasks there are two factors that must be emphasized: management responsibility and management control. The top manager in any managerial hierarchy involved with a product is responsible for ensuring that the product is reasonably safe. The manager can delegate tasks to be accomplished but cannot delegate the responsibility for ensuring that those tasks have been done.

This principle was brought out in the case of *United States v Park*. The FDA charged Acme Markets and its presi-

dent, Park, with violating the Federal Food, Drug, and Cosmetic Act by permitting food held in a warehouse to be contaminated by rodents. Acme pleaded guilty but Park did not. Park admitted that he was responsible for seeing that sanitary conditions were maintained, but he argued that the responsibility was one he had assigned to "dependable subordinates." The case was tried in a federal court where Park was found guilty. The decision was reversed in a court of appeals and then it was reversed again in the Supreme Court. In 1975 the Court indicated that although company officials may delegate responsibilities, they continue to have the responsibility to follow up such assignments. Although this precedent was set in a case involving food, it would probably result in similar decisions by other courts in similar situations relating to mechanical or electrical products.

Another managerial function related to product safety is in resolving conflicts between the product safety organization and other organizations within the company. To eliminate or positively control a hazard by design may increase the product's cost so much that marketing personnel object. They also object if the product contains too many warning labels. Resolving these problems is a management responsibility. The manager concerned must consider all factors and decide the course of action to be taken.

Other tasks of the various managerial levels include:

1. Preparing directives indicating company or departmental policy on product safety.

2. Assigning responsibilities for implementing and coordinating the safety program.

3. Establishing or designating an organization or personnel personally to prepare the product safety program, coordinate safety activities, monitor progress of the program, and keep the manager informed.

4. Ensuring that programs are initiated and maintained to train personnel in their duties in safety programs and to inform personnel of safety aims, principles, and methods.

5. Undertaking audits periodically to ensure that all responsible organizations are accomplishing their assigned safety tasks within prescribed time limits.

6. Ensuring that there is adequate budgeting and funding for product safety activities.

Audits and Reviews

Managers must continually review safety program activities in order to ensure that they are performed adequately, completely, effectively, efficiently, and on time. These reviews are in addition to the day-to-day control of program tasks carried out by the product safety organization. The review process would include audits and program reviews.

Audits

Audits are undertaken to observe the conduct and progress of the product safety program. They assess:

1. Whether or not company safety policies are being observed.

2. The status of safety activities within each area of responsibility.

3. Whether or not activities for achievement of a safe product are well-coordinated and integrated.

4. Whether or not trade-offs are adversely affecting safety of the product.

5. Adequacy of in-plant and subcontractor safety tasks.

6. Whether or not actions are being taken to determine the existence of hazards in the product, to eliminate them, or to provide suitable safeguards.

Findings reveal where problems exist in the program; the causes of the problems and recommended solutions; where management can make program improvements most effectively and economically; and where additional guidance, redirection, assistance, manpower, or training is required. Audits may be made by managers, members of their staffs, or members of the safety organization.

To ensure that audits are effective, findings should be reported in writing. If a need for improvement is found, a request or direction for corrective action by a certain time should be made. What the corrective action should be and the date by which the action should be completed should also be required. If the corrective action is a lengthy requirement, periodic progress reports should be made until the deficiency has been corrected. Subsequent audits should then determine whether the corrective action is being or has actually been accomplished and is satisfactory.

Program Reviews

Program reviews may be accomplished by managers, committees, or boards. A review should be a critique or evaluation of a problem, analysis, design, or proposed action studied or prepared by others. In this way, the matter under study is subjected to the scrutiny of persons oriented differently from those who made the original effort. Some reviews are interdisciplinary activities in which safety constitutes only one aspect. Other reviews evaluate specific aspects of the product development program.

Interdisciplinary reviews could be like those discussed in Figure 12-1. Interdisciplinary reviews involve the total program in which safety is only one aspect of the overall effort. These reviews are generally conducted by design or systems engineering personnel, but everyone else who is concerned participates. Their inputs indicate how their tasks and results satisfy their program responsibilities. Subjects of interest to safety personnel include review of safety provisions in design criteria, any hazard that may be present, methods of hazard control and other safeguards, and the results of analyses and trade-offs. Reviews are generally held at least at major milestones in a program, such as at the completion of one phase and before the beginning of the next phase. It is generally at such times and from such reviews that changes in design, further analyses, additional verification tests, justifications for specific selections, or more detailed information may be found more desirable. Each review is made at such time to permit incorporating changes before major commitments are made.

Safety reviews are for safety purposes only. Product design is evaluated each time, and whether safety standards, good engineering practices and statutory requirements have been observed is checked. At a safety review personnel may present information on the results of analyses, hazardous conditions, critical components, and product safeguards and protection. Designs of critical components and assemblies, test results, and potential problem areas may be discussed. Operational procedures may be reviewed for adequacy. Here again, the reviewing personnel should be persons other than the design or safety personnel so that new ideas on the material presented may be obtained.

Product Safety Engineer

The product safety engineer may be part of the risk management organization or may be a separate entity. For a simple product, a single person might fulfill all the necessary functions; for a complex product, a large staff might be required. If product design covers a number of disciplines, a number of safety engineers knowledgeable enough to cover all disciplines may be needed. The product safety engineer must be a generalist who is knowledgeable principally in safety program management, safety criteria, and in safety analysis techniques. He or

Reviews

TYPE	WHEN HELD	PURPOSE	DESCRIPTION
Concept	Early in Concept Phase	Establish baseline for product	Requirements concerning functions, performance, cost, and other related factors are reviewed. Proposals for meeting these requirements, and advantages and disadvantages of each proposal are discussed. A preferred approach is tentatively selected. Expected problems for the preferred approach are pointed out, with methods for their control.
Preliminary Design	End of Concept Phase	Review initial design based on proposal selected at Concept Review	Review details of the design. Background material derived from trade-off studies, design analyses, feasibility studies, and laboratory investigations are discussed. Safety personnel provide an initial analysis of hazards involved, methods of control, safeguards to be incorporated, features to be avoided, and other significant information currently available.
Development "Go-Ahead" Evaluation	Development "Go-Ahead" Phase	Evaluate technical, financial, marketing, risk, and other factors.	Review includes analysis of all pertinent aspects of product development, production, sales, financing, potential sales and profits, and risks involved. Results of the PDR are reviewed.
Critical Design Review (CDR)	During Development Phase (There may be separate reviews for subassemblies and more than one review for a complex product.)	Evaluate detailed designs and analysis.	Reviews are made of detailed designs, analyses, and problem areas similar to those at the PDR, but in greater depth. Safety analyses, results of component and assembly tests (especially of failures), progress in hazard elimination, and provision of safeguards developed since the earlier review are covered. Items discussed at the PDR or previous CDRs that resulted in requests for additional studies are generally brought up. Reports on progress are presented if the study is still under way, or reports on findings if it has been completed.
Prototype Review	Towards end of Development Phase	Evaluate prototype design before it is actually built	The latest proposed design is reviewed. Updated or newly completed analyses, tests, and trade-off studies are presented. Items left open for determination at the CDR are discussed. Tests to be conducted and by whom are covered. Procedures are reviewed that have been developed for prototype testing, that test objectives and test sites are adequate, and that no outstanding problems remain uncorrected. Similar reviews are held for subsequent changes and tests.
Production "Go-Ahead" Evaluation	Production "Go-Ahead" Phase	Evaluate advisability of proceeding with full-scale production.	Results of prototype tests are reviewed. Problems determined or encountered in any aspect of the program are evaluated. Where changes are required, the best solutions to be incorporated into production models are determined. This is the last complete review of the product prior to acceptance of the design. Possible manufacturing problems are evaluated. Design for production is frozen.

Figure 12-1. Reviews.

she should know the technical principles of the various engineering disciplines involved in the development of the new product. He or she need not be so experienced or qualified that he or she would have a tendency to undertake tasks which are the duties of the designers. As a program manager, the product safety engineer must rely on the designers to accomplish the duties which are the designers' and not attempt to redesign the product according to his or her beliefs or to criticize design aspects that do not have safety connotations. Because product safety engineers are now often appointed to their positions from other engineering disciplines, they too often concentrate on the areas in which they are knowledgeable to the detriment of other tasks. The scope of their activities is indicated by the tasks listed below in the following section.

Product Safety Organization Tasks

In a big company the product safety staff may be large; in a small company only one person may have this responsibility. In either case, there are specific tasks that must be performed. The product safety staff must:

1. Prepare the product safety directive for the top manager and when requested, assist lower-echelon managers prepare any directives they may wish to issue.

2. Prepare the product safety program. The program must include the necessary tasks and a list of those to whom the top manager should assign responsibility for each task.

3. Prepare the means by which the safety program can be monitored. Later use this means to monitor the significant problems and accomplishments, deficiencies, and required improvements.

4. Review governmental agency requirements, legal decisions, accident reports involving other companies, technical reports, and other documents and information to determine whether or not they affect or relate to the company's products.

5. Prepare safety criteria to be observed by company, subcontractor, and vendor designers based on applicable governmental and voluntary standards; ensure that the criteria are incorporated into specifications and other requiring documents; and ensure that the criteria are observed.

6. Be cognizant of new processes, methods, equipment, and information that might benefit the safety program. Be alert for information on materials that are prohibited, have deficiencies, or have adverse characteristics. Keep pertinent organizations informed of such developments.

7. Review histories of hazards, failures, and mishaps in existing similar products to ensure that design or manufacturing deficiencies are not repeated in the new product.

8. Assist designers in selecting courses of action or alternative solutions to eliminate or contain hazards or to control other safety problems in initial designs, trade-off studies, or equipment modification studies. Participate in design reviews to determine that incompatible or unsafe components, arrangements, systems, or procedures are not incorporated in the product.

9. Analyze the product and its subassemblies to determine whether or not potential hazards have been eliminated or controlled.

10. Determine whether or not monitoring and warning devices, protective equipment, or emergency equipment are required for the product. Ensure that the equipment selected is suitable for the specific hazards which might be encountered.

11. Review proposed operations and maintenance instructions and documents to ensure that critical operations are clearly and properly described and that no hazardous operations are involved. Arrange for safety warnings to be incorporated in instructions, procedures, and manuals.

12. Review warning labels that are to be placed on equipment to ensure that they are adequate, meet all legal requirements, and correspond to warnings in the instruction manuals. Coordinate wording on the labels with the legal department. During production ensure that the labels are adequately prepared, are placed on the equipment, and are in the most effective locations possible.

13. Monitor test reports to determine deficiencies, discrepancies, or trends which might affect safety. Recommend corrective actions to prevent recurrences.

14. Review field problem reports and customer complaints that involve safety. If necessary, ensure that organizations responsible take corrective action.

15. Participate in reviewing accident claims or recall actions by government agencies. Recommend remedial actions if claims or recalls are justified.

Design Engineering Tasks

After the management responsibilities, the responsibilities of the designers are probably the most important in producing a safe product. At the present time the product safety engineer may present the safety guidelines to be observed and review and analyze the product to see that hazards are eliminated and controlled. Most engineers have never received formal training in accident prevention. Their efforts in this area may be based only on their own opinions on whether or not a hazard exists, on apparent and obvious conditions, or on information passed on to them by supervisors, fellow workers or such sources as magazines or technical papers. Therefore, the results may be diverse. To minimize this hit-or-miss diversity in design, which could result in unsafe products, the design engineer, in close coordination with the product safety engineer, should carry out the following design engineering tasks:

1. Review and observe safety criteria prepared by the product safety engineer.

2. Evaluate the product and its components for hazards and establish design or procedural safeguards for their elimination or control.

3. Ensure that safety is given due consideration in trade-off studies.

4. Ensure that information essential to safety, such as test or finishing requirements, is included in manufacturing drawings and specifications, especially for items to be obtained from subcontractors and vendors.

5. Identify required safety devices and equipment that should be incorporated into or used with the product.

6. Identify the means of verifying that safety-critical features of the product and safety devices will operate as intended.

Safety Functions of Other Technical Organizations

Other technical organizations, depending on the organizational structure which may or may not be in design engineering, also have functions that contribute to product safety.

1. *Reliability engineering.* Failure Mode and Effects Analyses (FMEAs) (Chapter 14) should be correlated with safety analyses. Information on failure modes of components used for quality control and maintainability purposes can be highly significant for the reduction of malfunctions which could be safety critical.

2. *Test engineering.* Some of the product safety functions of test engineering are described in Chapter 13. Test engineering here is divorced from routine production and quality control verification; it consists of testing prototypes and complete and thorough testing of random production samples. Test engineering can be highly significant in determining whether or not controls of existing hazards are adequate and whether or not there are hazards of which the designers were not aware.

3. *Field service engineers.* Contributions from field service engineers regarding operating conditions and problems can be very important in the safe design of the product. Designers would therefore do well to consult with field service engineers before initiating designs. They should also have field service engineers review any prototype before mass production of the product is begun.

4. *Production engineers.* Production engineers must ensure that manufacturing defects or changes do not degrade the safety of the product. Examples include leaving unneeded sharp points or edges or rough surfaces on which persons could be cut or cutting or damaging insulation on wires so that a person later could get a shock. Additional information on production engineers' participation in accident prevention programs is included in Chapter 19.

5. *Quality assurance engineering.* Quality assurance personnel must ensure that not only the company's personnel have eliminated or minimized safety-critical manufacturing defects but also that subcontractors and vendors have complied with safe design criteria and practices. Therefore, quality assurance personnel must be knowledgeable of both general hazards, such as sharp edges, which could exist in any product, and hazards and problems that could specifically exist in the company's product for which they are providing quality control.

6. *Technical publication writers.* These writers must ensure that instructions are clear, concise, and complete. If warnings and other notes are needed, they should be conspicuously indicated. The wording on these warnings should coincide with the wording on the warning labels on the equipment. Technical publication writers should ensure that the product safety engineer is aware of the warning and has agreed that the hazard cannot be eliminated or controlled to a point where the warning is not needed. The adequacy of each warning should be approved by both the product safety engineer and the legal staff.

Other Participants

Nontechnical participants and organizations also have functions that are essential in producing the safest product possible. These include:

1. *Purchasing.* Materials, parts, components, and assemblies should be purchased to specifications which include criteria such as those in Figure 5-4. Coordination with product safety and design engineering would indicate which items are safety-critical and for which high reliability and quality control must be stressed.

2. *Advertising.* Advertising copy should be reviewed by legal and product safety personnel to ensure that there is no "puffing" or advertising claim that would inadvertently provide a warranty. If the company is subjected to a recall action, it may be necessary for the advertising department to provide the news media with copy that instructs persons who have purchased the product how to return it or have it repaired.

3. *Legal department.* This department informs product safety engineers and designers of any legal actions that have been taken against any other company that

produces a similar product. This information can be used to determine whether or not the company has a similar problem. Information on settlements and awards can be provided to the risk manager to permit him or her to evaluate the needs for insurance coverage. Both legal personnel and safety engineers should settle on the wording to be included on warning labels. The legal department should be the focal point for actions to be taken in case of a recall or suit, and it should coordinate its actions with those of safety and design engineering, manufacturing and quality control, and other involved organizations (see Figure 20-2).

4. *Risk management.* In some companies product safety engineers may be included in the risk management organization; in others they may be separated because of their separate functions. The risk manager provides for insurance coverage if he or she believes it advisable. If an outside insurance organization is used, the risk manager may be able to obtain from the insurer information on design defects, inadequate warnings, and other problems that should be avoided.

5. *Sales department.* This department can indicate if there are any safety features whose presence would attract customers or whose absence would detract from sales of the product. Conversely, the product safety and design engineers can indicate to the sales department any added safety features in the product which might increase its attractiveness to customers and thus enhance sales. Often safety and legal personnel and sales personnel must compromise on warning labels which sales might feel could prejudice the customer against the product. Similarly, sales personnel would be reluctant to have anything in the product that would raise its price so that a problem of competition arises. Safety devices, especially optional ones, are in this category. Mandatory safety devices are sometimes opposed less because competitors must also provide them. This frequently leads to a cooperative effort to provide a safe product at minimal added cost for accident-preventive design and manufacture.

6. *Customer and field relations.* Customers, either directly or through retailers and distributors, may have complaints about the safety of the product. These complaints may or may not be valid, but they must be reviewed by competent personnel and action must be taken if the complaint is justified. Distributors and retailers must be instructed to recognize what could constitute a safety problem, the action required to correct it for the customer, and how to notify the manufacturer so that the manufacturer can investigate the problem and take corrective action. Failure to take corrective action on a customer's complaint proves highly embarrassing in court if that customer or any other customer subsequently suffers an injury from that same cause and it is revealed that no action was taken. Some companies are very sensitive about this situation. They also feel that much useful information can be derived from the customers and that prompt corrective service ensures customer satisfaction, results in good person-to-person advertising, and helps future sales. To further these programs, companies have initiated systems by which customers who have complaints can call the manufacturer by using a toll-free number.

Product Safety Working Committee

There must be a way to coordinate interorganizational tasks and to assign new tasks that may arise. These are the duties of the product safety working committee. The committee is established by a directive issued by the top manager who directs the participation by each organization, the appointment of a representative who can speak for his or her organization, the frequency of meetings, appointment of the product safety engineer as chairman, and responsibilities of the committee, its chairman, and its members. The product safety engineer notifies committee members when and where the meetings will be held, prepares and furnishes each member with an agenda before the meetings, and prepares the minutes of the meetings, noting especially action item assignments.

Programming the Safety Tasks

A new product does not come into existence fully developed; the process of creation is a complex and lengthy one whose accomplishment can be eased by good programming. All of the tasks already indicated are not accomplished simultaneously; they must be programmed over the life cycle of the product.

The life cycle of a product can be divided roughly into phases. The safety tasks appropriate to each phase are then listed. The most important tasks are listed in Figure 12-2. Details for some are described in various chapters of this book; others are obvious or can be developed with comparatively little effort. In any case, responsibilities for the accomplishment of these tasks must be adapted to the organizational structure and responsibilities of the company (or its subdivision) involved. Figure 12-3 is a checklist which will assist an auditor in determining the adequacy of management's role in a product safety program.

Concept Phase

The concept phase covers the period beginning with the initiation of the abstract idea for the new or modified product. The phase ends when an estimate is completed of whether or not the idea is feasible, commercially acceptable, and economically advantageous. All aspects of the product's development, production, distribution, support, cost, potential sales, production capabilities,

Product Safety Program Tasks

Concept Phase

1. Review previous similar products for safety connotations.
2. Determine past problems with similar own products or those produced by others.
3. Determine potential hazards in proposed product:
   - Injuries to users and maintenance persons.
   - Damage to other equipment and facilities.
   - Damage to company product by its own operation.
   - Damage to company product from outside sources.
   - Company product involved in accident because of failure of outside equipment or environmental factor.
4. Assist designers in preliminary planning.
5. Assist and participate In trade studies.
6. Prepare a preliminary hazard analysis on the accepted concept.
7. Prepare safe design criteria:
   - Review and incorporate existing standards and certification requirements.
   - Determine additional needs where existing requirements are inadequate or nonexistent or safety-related state-of-the-art advancements are lacking.
8. Determine safety tests which may be required for materials, components, safety devices, or operations.
9. Make preliminary determination of safety devices which may be required.
10. Establish safety and reliability requirements to be imposed on subcontractors and vendors.
11. Estimate cost impact of safety program.
12. Make a risk assessment.

Development Go-ahead Evaluation

1. Continue to gather information on hazards, performance, and safeguards.
2. Evaluate safety aspects of proposed changes.
3. Continue to conduct safety tests on candidate materials, components, and devices.
4. Evaluate results of tests to determine feasibility of designs, hardware characteristics, and material properties.
5. Prepare "Get-Ready" plan for Product Development Phase.
6. Prepare budget for costs of safety programs and equipment.
7. Determine interfaces which will exist and information required to coordinate activities between various assembly designers, and manufacturer/subcontractor/vendor safety activities.
8. Prepare directive which will initiate the product safety program; identify the product safety engineer or other person responsible for safety; responsibilities and functions; and responsibilities of other activities.
9. Instruct company personnel in objectives and methodologies of product safety engineering.
10. Initiate means to monitor safety program during following phases.
11. Update safe design criteria as necessary to incorporate changes and additional findings.
12. Establish intracompany liaisons, and with subcontractors, and other interested parties.

Product Development

1. Conduct meetings of Product Safety Committee.
2. Ensure that all organizations are familiar with the program product safety directive and the responsibilities of all organizations for its observance.
3. Continue to assist designers and others in safety matters.
4. Participate in trade-off studies and proposals for detailed design and engineering changes.
5. Prepare safety analyses.
6. Keep appropriate managers informed and alerted to any significant safety problems, potential or existing, and to any safety accomplishments.
7. Determine whether designers are observing safe design criteria. Notify responsible personnel of any deficiencies so that corrective action can be taken.
8. Determine which products assemblies, components, materials, or procedures are safety-critical so that special precautions can be taken during manufacture, test, assembly, handling, shipping and operation.
9. Conduct formal safety design reviews.
10. Establish or review prototype and test plans to ensure: (a) suitable precautions are taken during test to avoid injury or damage; (b) the goals for safety aspects will be achieved.
11. Review procedures to ensure man-machine relationships are optimal to provide the safest product.
12. Review operations and maintenance procedures before publication to ensure they are clear, do not involve any tasks, and contain necessary warnings.
13. Establish means by which design problems can be reported. Ensure that corrective action is taken on each deficiency. Make a record.
14. Document analyses, studies, test results, and other safety related information.
15. Ensure all tasks and tests required by government agencies, standards, codes or regulations are done.
16. Identify safety and protective devices and equipment and warnings to be provided.
17. With legal staff ensure warnings are adequate.

Figure 12-2. Product safety program tasks.

safety, financing, and other factors have been considered. The purpose and magnitude of the proposed product are considered and established. This generally involves the initiation, consideration, adoption, adaptation, and rejection of ideas. The feasibilities of various design, production, and marketing approaches are considered. Many of the factors involved, especially technical factors, may be supported initially by little experience data.

Technical, cost, and other limitations are established. Efforts at this time are significant to minimize later costs of changes. In the final portions of this phase, exploratory tests, preliminary investigations, and initial analyses are made. The characteristics and performance of new materials and processes whose use might be considered have to be investigated and tested. Tests of new materials, processes, and components are made to determine whether or not they meet requirements established earlier in the phase. The safety tasks listed in Figure 12-2 for this phase are accomplished.

It is at this point that much benefit can be derived from initiation of an effective product safety program. The old idea held by some that it is too soon to start a product safety program because there is no product to analyze must be abandoned. Changes, substitutions, improvements and explorations of alternatives can be made at comparatively minor costs.

The results of these deliberations, investigations, tests, analyses, and decisions are recorded in a document which forms a baseline for future actions.

Development "Go-Ahead" Evaluation

After the initial feasibility analyses are completed, the final proposal for a new (or modified) product must be reviewed in order to determine the risks involved in development and production. This time can be used to continue any safety efforts initiated during the concept phase and to prepare for the tasks which must be accomplished during the development phase. Once development is started, designers must have safety guidelines to follow. Preparing these guidelines after the designers have spent time and effort without them can prove costly both in money and in strained relations if changes must be made.

The "go-ahead" plan is prepared on the assumption that management will approve development of the product, possibly with changes. Plans will have to be made for assignment or procurement of product safety personnel and for initiation by the top manager of a product safety program with delegation of responsibilities, means of monitoring the safety efforts, and the myriad other tasks which are necessary for smooth and effective operations.

Development Phase

The development phase formally begins when the "go-ahead" is directed, although there may have been certain preliminary tasks and investigations already completed.

Completion of the phase is sometimes a less definite point. In some programs, tests and evaluations of prototypes may continue into the next phase and changes may be made until the design is frozen for production. Even later, development activities may continue for minor improvements and corrections to be made as warranted. Other developments of a major nature may be withheld if the product must be modified substantially. Major modifications should be programmed for review and consideration as though the product were an entirely new one, and they should be subjected to the tasks indicated under the concept and development "go-ahead" evaluation phases.

Technically, the development phase is the most important phase in the life cycle of a product. It is in this phase that the existence of potential hazards is established and measures are taken for their elimination or control. When the development phase begins, information on which safety analyses is based is often unavailable; analyses at this time are cursory, with more and more details being added as designs are completed and as materials and components are selected. The safety analyses to be made may also be governed by the product and its intended operation and may be selected from Chapters 13, 14, 15, 16, and 17 or modified by the product safety engineer to meet his or her specific requirements.

Elimination and control of hazards early in development, before funds are expended for production and for hardware that might have to be changed, will prove remunerative. Not only are changes in the prototypes costly, but modifications also require retesting to verify safety aspects.

Production "Go-Ahead" Evaluation

This interval may or may not be separated from the end of the development phase. As with the development "go-ahead" evaluation, it is a time for the review of accomplishments, for the assessment of future risks as they affect successful marketing and acceptance of the product, for making final changes prior to mass production of the product and, if the decision is to proceed, for preparing for production, distribution, and field support.

Production personnel should review the design at this time in order to determine whether or not changes are required or desirable to minimize production's costs. After review and acceptance of such changes as have been made the design is frozen. Determinations are made on whether specific components or assemblies will be made in-house or purchased from subcontractors and vendors. Information and criteria for safety-critical items must be transmitted to production managers, to contracts personnel for inclusion in subcontractor and vendor orders, and to product assurance personnel for quality control of in-house and contracted inspections.

Distributors, dealers, and field service personnel should be asked to review the prototype (with final changes) for familiarization and comment. Personnel who may have to maintain or repair the product must be instructed in

Product Safety Program Tasks

Production Go-ahead Evaluation

1. Update analyses of prototype as designed and built.
2. Evaluate prototype performance for safety connotations. Recommend improvements.
3. Evaluate changes recommended by others.
4. Prepare "Get-Ready" plan for Production and Operation Phases.
5. Institute means to:
   - Inform production and quality control managers which items are considered safety-critical and which parameters are especially significant.
   - Ensure that production personnel are instructed to make no design or materials changes of safety critical items without evaluation by product safety personnel.

- Ensure that inspection or test failures of safety- critical items are reported to product safety engineer.
6. Train field service and dealer personnel who will operate the equipment in safety related subjects.
7. Complete the safety analysis of the design as it is frozen.
8. Institute procedures for safety reviews of engineering change requests.
9. Review advertising for the new product, and institute controls over dealers and distributors for same.
10. Provide inputs and review training courses for dealers and distributors on safety aspects.

11. Institute procedures for receiving and processing complaints, claims, failure and trouble reports.
12. Institute procedure for product warranty registration.
13. Institute procedure for ensuring safety-critical service parts are inspected and that they include warnings which are also on the original parts.
14. Ensure that information on items which are safety- critical has been given to production and quality control departments.

Production

1. Ensure that production and quality control managers and personnel are giving special consideration to those items which are safety critical.
2. Ensure that production personnel are making no design changes of safety-critical items without evaluation by safety personnel.
3. Ensure that inspection and test failures of safety critical items are being reported to safety personnel.
4. Ensure that warning labels which should be on equipment and parts are actually there and in proper locations.

5. Analyze customer complaints and field problem reports for safety connotations. Recommend modifications where safety can be improved. Ensure corrective action is taken where a deficiency exists. Ensure records of actions taken are maintained.
6. Ensure that lot number and quality control records are being maintained.
7. Ensure that subcontractors and vendors are meeting safety criteria for parts and assemblies.

8. Keep Field Service Personnel (and customers where advisable) supplied with bulletins which:
   - Remind them of potential hazards and precautions to be taken.
   - Make them aware of newly determined potential problems and corrective measures.
   - Advise them of availability of new or improved safety devices.

Operations And Support

1. Ensure that copies of field problem reports and of customer complaints are supplied safety personnel for evaluation.

2. Provide assistance to company field service and customer personnel on potential safety problems, failures of safety-critical items, or accident investigations.
3. Make field visits to customers or representatives to ensure operations are being conducted as stipulated in procedures and manuals.

4. Visit customer to determine whether he has modified the product or is using it in any unintended way.

Figure 12-2 (cont'd). Product safety program tasks.

Management Checklist

1. Has the chief executive issued a directive which indicates his or her policy towards product safety?
2. Does the directive designate a top-level manager to be responsible for product safety and loss control activities?
3. Is the authority of this manager adequate to carry out the functions effectively?
4. Is the person in charge of product safety and loss control activities experienced and knowledgeable in these matters or is there someone who can be relied on who is?
5. Is the Product Safety staff large enough and diversely experienced enough to handle any problems which might arise?
6. Does the chief executive's policy directive indicate the functions and responsibilities of each organization as they relate to product safety?
7. Is there a means by which progress of product safety program tasks can be monitored?
8. Has a procedure been initiated by which each organization involved with product safety activities routinely keeps all others informed of pertinent matters?
9. Is there a good routing method by which documents relating to product safety will be circulated to all concerned?
10. Have budgets for product safety activities been prepared as part of normal operating functions and adequately funded?
11. Has a company Product Safety Committee been established on which all organizations will be represented by a management level representative, does it meet periodically, and are its efforts effective?
12. Is there a Product Safety Committee for each product line?
13. Does the Product Safety Committee for the product line hold design reviews; review, closeout, or direct action on Potential Hazard Reports; and assign action items to its members?
14. Has a procedure been initiated for generating Potential Hazard Reports and obtaining corrective action?
15. Is the chief executive informed of the progress of safety programs and of any deficiencies?
16. Has a procedure been established by which field deficiency reports and customer complaints concerning safety will be handled?
17. Has a procedure been established by which action will be taken if a recall action is imposed against a specific product of the company?
18. Have training courses been established for all personnel to teach them the functions they must carry out in an integrated and coordinated product safety program?
19. Does control of product safety activities extend to purchases of supplies, components, and assemblies from subcontractors and vendors?
20. Do contracts or purchase agreements require subcontractors and vendors to inform purchasers of any potential hazards involved in use of the purchased product?
21. Have warranties been reviewed and approved by legal counsel?

Figure 12-3. Management checklist.

any potential hazards, safeguards, and precautionary measures. Service manuals and replacement parts, test measurement parameters, and special test equipment must be made available.

Here again, all of these and other activities for successful production, distribution, and field support should be indicated in a "go-ahead" plan that will spell out the responsibilities and tasks for downstream efforts. The product safety engineer should list all of the activities in which his or her organization will be involved and all of the safety aspects of the tasks in which other organizations will participate.

Production Phase

Activities of manufacturing and quality control personnel during the production phase are described in Chapter 19. Although the principal stress on safety now moves from design into manufacturing, the task of monitoring the safety program is as important as ever. Poor manufacturing practices can ruin the best design, and unauthorized changes can negate safeguards or introduce new hazards.

Operation Phase

The old concept that once a product is sold and delivered it is no longer the responsibility of the manufacturer can prove disastrous. Field visits by product safety personnel should be made in order to determine the effectiveness of hazard control methods, whether or not there are unforeseen hazards in the product, whether or not the product is being used in unauthorized ways, and whether or not customer facilities for use of the product are adequate. Many of the items to be monitored are more suitable for large pieces of equipment, but small products can be covered by random surveys. A manufacturer of large industrial equipment should ensure that none of the safety devices supplied has been altered, removed, or bypassed; that operating personnel have been instructed in correct operating procedures and are following these procedures exactly, that no unauthorized changes to the equipment have been made; and that the equipment is not being used for a purpose for which it was not intended and for which it is unsafe.

Even if nothing wrong is found, a visit by a manufacturer's representative, especially one not involved in direct marketing, will indicate to a product buyer the manufacturer's interest in safety. The manufacturer's interest may help customer relations. Assisting the customer with instructions for safe use of the product will help reduce third-party liability suits.

Questions

1. When should a product safety program begin?

2. What is the principal factor in achieving a successful product safety program?

3. List seven managerial tasks in a product safety program.

4. Give six reasons for conducting audits and reviews.

5. List ten tasks product safety engineers should accomplish.

6. List five technical organizations that should participate in product safety programs and describe their accident prevention functions.

7. What are some of the safety functions of other company organizations?

8. From what other organizations might there be opposition to certain aspects of the safety program? To what might they object?

9. Describe how you would set up a product safety program working committee, and describe the functions of the committee.

10. List the phases through which each product passes and list four safety tasks to be accomplished in each phase.

11. Why is it necessary to extend controls of product safety activities to suppliers? How can such controls be imposed?

12. Describe some of the functions of the company's legal staff in a product safety program.

13. Describe a means you might initiate to monitor a company's product safety program to ensure that all required tasks are accomplished.

14. Cases are common where product managers and associates have been demoted, or have lost their jobs, because of accidents resulting from defects in design, manufacture, or construction. Discuss whether this is justified when the accident is caused by a designer's error.

15. Do you believe it was justified when the Chief Executive Officer (CEO) of the Union Carbide Company was jailed (until bailed out) because of the accident at Bhopal which resulted in the deaths of more than 2000 persons, and serious injuries to thousands more?

16. How far down in a company's hierarchy should the managers and supervisors be responsible for the safety aspects of products and their operation?

17. Are the safety aspects of a product no longer the concern of managers once the product leaves the manufacturer's plant? For how long should the safety of a product be a manager's concern?

13

Safety Analyses Programs

Although major disasters and catastrophes have long been analyzed for causes, as a means to avoid and prevent such recurrences, organized efforts to provide a viable methodology of identifying hazards to make possible accidents foreseeable, in order to avoid or control such undesired events, was first established with the concept known as System Safety. One major requirement of this concept is for technical methods of analysis that constitute attempts at foreseeability.

The problem of foreseeability has become an increasingly important factor in determining accident potentiality, on the part of product manufacturers, in cases of legal liability. This is due either to inadequacy of design, or to failure of the manufacturer to properly warn the consumer of a potential product hazard. Foreseeability has been defined as the analysis for evaluating the possibility of an accident *before* it happens, rather than by postmortem.

Foreseeability as a legal matter is a recent concept, although the idea of being able to foretell future occurrences and adverse events is an ancient custom, and many claim to have the ability. Tribal shaman and medicine men threw pieces of bone, oddly shaped knots of wood, or peculiarly colored pebbles on the ground, and analyzed the arrangements in which they fell to foretell the future. The Romans used the entrails of pigeons, doves, sheep, goats, and bulls, a method that went out of style, possibly because of the rising cost of the number of animals sacrificed. A cheaper method of event foreseeability that then came into vogue was astrology, which is still in style today. The claim by an astrologist friend of the wife of a recent President, to be able to foretell the future, may have indirectly been used to influence and guide the actions of the President himself.

A few years ago, a new method for predicting the future, biorhythm, was introduced, based on birth date and three rhythmic cycles. Because birth date is also a basis for astrology, in effect, these two claims of foreseeability are related. Biorhythm was used in Japan a few years ago to determine when bus drivers might become involved in accidents. On days when the concept indicated the driver would be likely to have an unfortunate experience, and was possibly accident prone, he was instructed to be especially careful. The number of accidents is said to have decreased, but it is not known whether this is because of the accuracy of foreseeability due to the method, simply because of the increase in the frequency of warnings, or the result of other unknown reasons.

Another attempt to foresee accident possibilities was tried by safety personnel at the Sandia Corporation in Albuquerque, where an attempt was made to find out whether there is a relationship between accidents and phases of the moon, eclipses, days of the week, and other natural phenomena. The final report on this study indicated only that more study is needed.

These days we have progressed in our methods of foreseeability. No more slaughtered doves or sheep, astrology, or phases of the moon. Safety engineers now use probabilities (which many believe to be an advancement over the entrails and slaughtered doves, and at least not as bloody) but which most courts still have not accepted. Accepted analysis methods of foreseeability used by safety engineers include Preliminary, Failure Modes and Effects, Fault Hazard, Fault-Tree Analysis, or similar modes of hazard identification to provide for accident avoidance or control. Such analyses have been accepted by the courts as foreseeable efforts to eliminate or control the possibility of accidents. Details on the methods of analyses in use, or proposed, are presented in the remainder of this chapter and in the chapters following.

No single method of analysis is entirely adequate to completely evaluate a product in a safety program. As indicated previously, the first hazard analysis must be made almost as soon as the new product is conceived. At that time, design features of the product, materials of which it is to be made, inherent hazards, and operational and maintenance procedures to be used are unknown or have been only tentatively selected. As the development program proceeds, more and more becomes known of the product and the analyses can become more and more detailed. Analyses must be made on a continuing basis, sometimes being made before a design is selected to alert designers to potential hazards; concurrently with design selection to eliminate unsafe ideas before they become firmly fixed into the product; and after design is tentatively completed to eliminate potential problems that arise from the integration of assemblies and that become apparent only after the completion of prototype, component, and assembly tests or after receiving formerly unavailable information.

Predesign and Postdesign Analyses

A *predesign* analysis determines those hazards that might be present in a product to be developed. It may be the basis for the preparation of specifications and criteria to be followed in design; it may indicate undesirable product characteristics, materials, and design practices to be avoided; it may determine safeguards to be provided; and it may tentatively establish tests to be undertaken to verify safety devices and safety-critical aspects of the product.

Studies in the predesign stage may determine specific precautions that must be observed and incorporated into the system and the suitability of specific components and items of hardware, materials, or proposed procedures. It is in the predesign period that discovery and resolution or problems can be accomplished most effectively and economically.

A *postdesign* analysis determines whether or not selected designs, equipment, and procedures meet the standards and criteria established as a result of the predesign analysis. Even when good standards are available, the scope of design selection they generally provide designers sometimes permits choices of designs that are hazardous. The analyses must therefore be undertaken to determine whether or not the selected designs are potentially hazardous. Evaluations must be made to determine whether or not designs that do not provide the best in safety should be modified or redone.

Generally, analyses made concurrently with designs can be made only when requested by the designer. The safety engineer does not keep looking over the shoulder of the designer, nudging the designer's hand if he or she feels that something is being done incorrectly. The safety engineer should have already provided the criteria to be observed; later the safety engineer reviews what the designer has done. Thus, he or she is making a postdesign analysis.

The postdesign analysis may confirm that the designer has done a good job in producing a safe design. If not, the time elapsed after a design is completed and an analysis is made, generally governs the ease with which changes can be agreed to and made. A postdesign analysis soon after the design is tentatively completed can generally be easily changed while the design is still on paper. When portions of the design have been translated into hardware, agreements to make changes and the changes to the designs themselves are more difficult to achieve. Analysis soon after the design is completed also means less lost time and a lesser effect on the completion schedule if changes have to be made. Changes are most troublesome and costly if they have to be made after production of the finished product has started.

Therefore, analyses should start as soon as possible after the product is conceived and should be supplemented continually. Numerous types of analysis are available for use in each phase of product development. The first, but one of the most important, is dealt with in the remainder of this chapter: *the preliminary hazard analysis.* Other types are described in the following chapters. There are still others that are not included in this book because they are used for special situations and are not used frequently enough to warrant inclusion here. Generally, a safety analyst may also adapt methods from other disciplines, modify some of the methods and tables shown here, or combine some of these methods to create a method the safety analyst feels would be most effective for reviewing the product with which he or she is concerned.

Verification

In *Escola* v *Coca Cola Bottling Company of Fresno*, Justice Traynor pointed out in 1944 that "the manufacturer must know the product is fit, or take the consequences, if it proves destructive." He also said, "The only way a manufacturer can know his product is fit is by analysis and test." The analyses that follow are methods for uncovering the existence of potential hazards, for determining whether or not proposed controls will be adequate, and in some instances, for determining the probability that an accident might occur. To actually determine whether or not the safeguards that have been provided are adequate, the safeguards must be verified. This can be done in four principal ways by the manufacturer before the product is released: (1) analysis, (2) examination, (3) demonstration, and (4) test.

Analysis

Analysis is a theoretical evaluation technique which experience has shown can be substituted for other means of verification which may be too difficult or costly to accomplish. For example, there may be a requirement that a pressure vessel be designed with a safety factor of 4. Testing enough vessels by subjecting them to pressures 4 times the maximum operating pressure to provide any degree of confidence in the results would be prohibitive in cost. In most cases, it is acceptable if it can be shown that the design analysis was conducted in accordance with a code such as the A.S.M.E. Code for Unfired Pressure Vessels and that it met all prescribed requirements.

Examination

Most hazardous characteristics of products can be uncovered by examination. The examination may be an investigation by visual or other senses of workmanship or material or whether or not a specific condition exists, by gauging or measurement, or by simple physical manipulation. For example, examination will permit a person to determine whether or not the product has sharp edges or points or, if the product is electrically powered, whether or not there are any places where an uninsulated conductor might be touched accidentally.

Demonstration

The demonstration may be a trial conducted to show that a specific operation can be accomplished, that a piece of equipment will operate, or that a material has or lacks a certain property. For example, a product may have an emergency switch. To demonstrate that the switch works, the product is put into operation and then the switch is used.

Test

Tests are considered demonstrations during which specific measurable parameters must be met. A test may verify that values for a stipulated operational parameter fall (or do not fall) within specified limits, and that application of a stipulated operational parameter will not cause a failure, damage, or hazardous condition. For example, proof pressure tests may require that a container be pressurized to a specific level without causing permanent distortion, leakage, or rupture. A relief valve can be tested to ensure that it works at a set pressure. A rotating device's speed can be measured to determine whether or not it exceeds a specified number of revolutions per minute. A spring may be tested with a measured weight to show that it will sustain a designated load.

A less frequently used means of verification is by simulation. Simulation is used when actual conditions cannot be achieved practically. In a simulation the known characteristics of the product are either extrapolated or compared in a computer against simulated conditions and stresses and outcomes are predicted.

Test Safety Requirements

Safety in test operations is directed at five major requirements:

1. To ensure the safety of test personnel, equipment, and facilities; the safety of items being tested; and of other personnel, equipment, and facilities.

2. To ensure that procedures and equipment for customer use are safe, or that problems encountered during tests are reported so they can be eliminated.

3. To determine whether the product or system has any hazardous characteristics during normal operations.

4. To ensure that information derived from test operations containing safety connotations is suitably documented and supplied to all organizations concerned.

5. To ensure that contractual requirements for safety during operations will be met.

System safety/product safety engineering will:

1. Advise the test manager and other test personnel on any safety matters which may arise.

2. Prepare safety checklists to be completed by test supervisors or safety engineers prior to start of tests.

3. Review test procedures to determine the hazards involved in testing of the system or its components.

4. Review those aspects of safety which are outside the usual scope of industrial safety. For example: loading of missiles or other explosive-actuated devices on aircraft; ensuring the adequacy of procedures in making electrical system connections; testing or reviewing of interfaces between subsystems.

5. Review possible means by which procedures could be carried out incorrectly, and the effects that such mishandling could generate.

6. Recommend changes to reduce the possibility of customer misinterpretation of instructions or of product misuse, and verify all procedures that are to be incorporated into operations handbooks.

7. Participate in analysis of the cause and effect of test failures, discrepancies, or unsatisfactory conditions, in order to establish their effect on safety, and the need for changes in procedures, equipment, or other safeguards.

8. Establish and report those environmental, procedural, design, or other conditions that caused, or contributed to a hazard, so that corrective action will be taken.

9. Conduct, or help to conduct, investigations of near-misses or of mishaps in order to establish causes and corrective actions to prevent recurrences. Prepare reports so that suitable corrective action will be taken.

10. Train field test personnel in System/Product Safety aims, requirements, methods, and input to the overall safety program.

11. Provide input on safety aspects of test reports.

12. Present information, during reviews, on safety aspects of test results, on the need for changes or additional safeguards, on failures and mishaps, and the recommended corrective actions.

Since demonstrations and tests are too often inadequate in number, those that are conducted must be carefully planned in order to obtain significant results. The planning

Confidence Level (Percent)

Reliability	50	60	70	75	80	85	90	95	97.5	99	99.5	99.9
0.999999	693150	916290	1203970	1386290	1609440	1897120	2302590	2995730	3688889	4605170	5298320	6907760
0.99999	69315	91629	120397	138629	160944	189712	230259	299573	368889	460517	529832	690776
0.9999	6932	9163	12040	13863	16094	18971	23025	29957	36888	46051	52983	69077
0.999	693	916	1204	1386	1609	1897	2302	2995	3688	4605	5298	6907
0.998	347	458	602	694	805	949	1152	1498	1845	2303	2650	3454
0.997	231	305	401	462	537	632	768	999	1230	1535	1766	2303
0.996	173	229	301	346	401	473	575	747	920	1149	1322	1723
0.995	138	183	241	277	321	379	460	598	737	920	1058	1379
0.994	115	152	201	230	267	315	383	498	613	765	880	1148
0.993	99	130	174	198	229	270	328	427	526	657	755	985
0.992	86	114	150	173	200	236	287	373	460	574	660	860
0.991	77	101	134	153	178	210	255	332	408	510	586	764
0.99	69	92	120	138	160	188	229	298	367	459	527	688
0.98	34	45	60	69	80	94	114	149	183	228	263	342
0.97	23	30	40	45	53	62	76	99	121	151	174	227
0.96	17	23	30	34	39	46	57	74	91	113	130	170
0.95	14	18	24	27	31	37	45	58	72	90	103	135
0.94	11	15	20	22	26	31	37	49	60	75	86	112
0.93	10	13	17	19	22	26	32	42	51	64	74	96
0.92	9	11	15	17	19	23	28	36	45	55	64	83
0.91	8	10	13	15	17	20	25	32	39	49	57	74
0.9	7	9	12	13	15	18	22	29	35	44	51	66
0.8	3	4	6	6	7	9	11	14	17	21	24	31
0.7	2	3	4	4	5	6	7	9	11	13	15	20
0.6	2	2	3	3	4	4	5	6	8	9	11	14
0.5	1	1	2	2	3	3	4	5	6	7	8	10

Figure 13-1. Number of tests without failure vs reliability and confidence.

must use the results of analyses. Conversely, analyses require tests to verify their adequacy; therefore, the two must go hand in hand.

Demonstrations and tests are costly. This is especially so for safety purposes since a safety problem resulting from a potential failure may not become apparent in one or a few tests. Figure 13-1 indicates that to show that a component or product has a reliability of at least 90% with a 90% confidence level requires 22 tests without a failure. For a simple component, this might not require much effort; for a large or complex product, it might be very expensive. If failures of safety-critical items had to be held to 1 in 10,000 operations (reliability of 0.9999), 23,026 operations would have to be conducted without a failure if the same degree (90%) of confidence were to be maintained.

Using the Results of Analyses

In a properly conducted safety program, hazard analyses have multiple uses:

1. To determine where and what hazards may be present before the product is designed so that they can be avoided, eliminated, or controlled.

2. To show that hazards of a specific character are not present and safeguards for them are not needed.

3. To show that a design has been well done and that safeguards are adequate.

4. To show that mandatory requirements have been met.

5. To determine whether or not the product has any serious defects that must be rectified before it is put into production.

6. To determine whether or not adverse reports or complaints about hazards from the field have any validity, and if they do, the cause of the problem.

If analysis indicates that a product is safe, no further action is needed. When hazards are found that are not properly controlled, corrective action should be taken. If it is not taken, the entire analysis effort is wasted. Also, failure to take action may leave a company more vulnerable legally if an accident occurs and a suit is instituted than if no analysis was made at all. Ensuring that corrective action is taken is known as *closing the loop*. Numerous safety programs have failed because of failures to close the loop.

The worst course of action is to disregard a discovered or reported hazard. Legal procedures are such that failure to take action would probably be discovered if a legal suit were brought against a manufacturer in which someone was severely injured or killed because a hazard had been ignored. It is far better to acknowledge the hazard report and to document the reason any specific action or no action was taken. If a company is aware of a problem, especially a recurring problem, failure to take corrective action can lead to awards for punitive damages that are far greater than the compensatory damages which might be involved. For some products, laws now require that any safety problem be reported to the appropriate regulatory agency of the government. Failure to report the problem may result in the company being fined and possibly a company official being sent to jail.

Suitable procedures should be set up to ensure that each report of a problem is evaluated and that action is taken when required. These procedures usually vary from company to company, but almost all involve the means by which hazard reports are directed to technical personnel for evaluation and recommendations and are then directed to the responsible manager for action. In some companies forms such as the one in Figure 13-2 are used as part of the procedure. These forms differ from company to company, but they always include two items: a place to describe the problem and a place to record the action taken. Other pertinent information the company finds desirable for its records is also included, depending on the company's organization and internal procedures.

Below are comments on the form in Figure 13-2:

1. TO: The addressee might be the product safety organization, the engineering department, or any other person or units concerned with the problem cited. A letter from a customer received by the customer relations office could be attached to such a form and forwarded to the product safety organization by stamping that department's address in the space allotted.

2. REPORT NO.: The product safety organization should maintain a list of all reports generated, the actions being taken, and the actions completed.

3. CLOSEOUT DATE: When corrective action has been taken, or it has been found there is no problem, or no action should be taken, the date of this decision should be entered. This report can then be removed from the active file. The last entry under COMMENTS/ACTION STATUS should show that the organization, such as the product safety committee, which has the authority to close out reports, has closed out the report and that the action is effective on the date shown.

4. SUBJECT: This should be a title or other entry that permits easy and quick identification of the problem.

5. DESCRIPTION OF PROBLEM: If the source of information is a customer's letter or phone call, the product safety office can provide the description from the information in the letter or phone call. If the information is from a source within the company, the initiator of the report or the safety office fills in this block. The safety office should also fill out this block if the problem was generated as the result of a design review or analysis made by the safety organization. The description should also indicate the potential severity of the problem.

6. CURRENT PROBABILITY OF ACCIDENT: The product safety organization can prepare an estimate, either qualitative or quantitative, which will indicate the probability that an accident would occur if no corrective action were taken. If accidents have occurred, information on the frequencies could be included. Later, it would be desirable to indicate under COMMENTS the probability estimate of an accident if the recommended safeguard were incorporated.

7. COMMENTS/ACTION STATUS: Any additional information not carried in other blocks can be carried here. In addition, the organization to which the report is sent provides comments on actions that have been taken or are to be taken. The product safety organization maintains a master file to which all of these comments and status reports are transferred. If the actions required extend over a long period, the safety office should maintain a list of all reports currently open. The organization responsible for taking action should periodically be queried about further progress. All reports still open are brought to the attention of the product safety review committee. The committee indicates which reports are to be closed and any further actions to be taken on active items. The last entry on each report the report is closed out is the CLOSEOUT DATE, which has been discussed above.

In addition to their use in closing the loop for correction of deficiencies, outputs of analyses can also be used for other activities, some of which will be touched on here and discussed further where appropriate. Information derived from analyses which should be transmitted to other responsible organizations include such items as:

1. Warning, caution, and other notes to instruction writers.

2. Requirements for safety-critical items to be procured from subcontractors and vendors to the purchasing department.

3. Requirements for special care in the production and handling of safety-critical components and assemblies to the manufacturing department.

4. Requirements for close monitoring of safety-critical items to quality-control personnel.

Problem Report

SUBMITTED BY: _____J. W. Smart_____

ADDRESS: _____Product Safety Engrg._____

_____ PHONE: ___X 7230___ PRODUCT ___Coffee mill___

TO: Engineering Department Mail Station 6 E254	HAZARD REPORT No. ___80-4___ DATE REPTD. ___2/12/80___ CLOSEOUT DATE ___7/14/80___	SOURCE: DESIGN REVIEW ☐ FIELD REPORT ☐ ANALYSIS ☒ TEST ☐ CUSTOMER ☐ OTHER ☐

SUBJECT:

Inadvertent Start of Mill and Rotor

DESCRIPTION OF PROBLEM:

Mill motor and rotor may start inadvertently when connected to power source if switch (No. 398764-1) has failed closed since mill was shut off and disconnected. If lid of mill is off and cup filled, coffee may be thrown about and into user's eyes. If his finger is in path of rotor, it will be cut.

(Continue on reverse side, if necessary)

CURRENT PROBABILITY OF ACCIDENT:

Pr(accident) = Pr(Switch Failing Closed $\times$ [Pr(Coffee Thrown in Eyes) + Pr(Finger in Path of Rotor)] . The probability of the switch failing closed is estimated at 0.1×10^{-6}; the others are unknown

(Continue on reverse side, if necessary)

COMMENTS/ACTION STATUS:

2/26/80 Engineering Dept. has reviewed this hazard and confirms it is a possibility, even though the probability of malfunction of the switch in the mode required to be a hazard is low, and the probability of an accident even lower. Two safeguards can be employed:

1. Use a double switch, with the same motion activating both switching actions. If one switch fails closed, the other will still be open. Probability of a double failure which will result in advertent activation would be about 1×10^{-12}

2. Provide a warning to the customer to hold cap in place when connecting mill to the power source. Since this is a procedural safeguard it is less desirable than use of the double switch, but with the low probability of occurrence should be an acceptable reasonable risk.

(Continue on reverse side, if necessary)

Figure 13-2. Problem report.

Although the Wright brothers manufactured and repaired bicycles, their interest in heavier-than-air flight had increased for years until they finally accomplished it successfully in 1904. Much guidance was obtained from Octave Chanute, an old, retired engineer who was interested in aviation. Chanute had theorized, and written much on gliding and aviation, from which he prepared an analysis on the characteristics of a successful airplane. Ten years before the Wright brothers first flew at Kitty Hawk, Octave Chanute wrote[1] that the whole subject of aerial navigation could be resolved into ten problems and conditions:

1. The resistance and supporting power of the air.

2. The motor, its character and activity.

3. Selection of the instrument to obtain propulsion.

4. The form and kind of apparatus for sustaining the weight—whether flapping wings, screws, or aeroplanes.

5. The amount of sustaining surface required.

6. The best materials to be employed for the framing and for the moving parts.

7. The maintenance of the equilibrium that is the most important, and perhaps, the most difficult, solution to all the problems.

8. The guidance in any desired direction.

9. The starting up into the air under all conditions.

10. The alighting safely anywhere. Safety in starting, sailing, and alighting is essential.

Failure to satisfy these problems and conditions could result in a catastrophe in almost every case, especially the last. Failure to maintain equilibrium can be equated to loss of control; the materials problem relates to structural failures; resistance and supporting power of air involves problems of excessive drag or inadequate lift; vehicle motor problems can relate to possibilities of lossed propulsion.

Chanute's analysis was done years before the Wright brothers made their first flight in a heavier-than-air craft. Since the first aircraft was flown successfully, technology and dreams have changed dramatically, so that today they include the building of products greatly advanced, and operating in a far more hazardous environment. Such dreams now include the building of artificial satellites and transportation systems that will involve not only space stations, but life support, and emergency systems as well, so personnel can exist comfortably and safely in space. However, because the natural environment has an absence of oxygen, many accidents due to leakage, holing, or other causes for loss of air, could tend to be catastrophic, possibly resulting in injury or death to personnel, as well as major damage, destruction, or degradation of equipment. The entire satellite system, or series of systems will depend on a multitude of products whose reliability will govern the lives, fates, and fortunes

of everyone involved. Like Chanute's analysis of aircraft, an analysis can also be prepared regarding a satellite space station and transportation system.

Foreseeable accidents that might occur, and for which preventive measures can be taken, or adverse effects controlled, include:

1. Loss of the vehicle during launch or boost into orbit. (This has already happened in the case of the "Challenger.")

2. Inability of personnel to return safely to Earth from orbit. (This has happened to Russian cosmonauts.)

3. Loss or injury of a person in the space station itself.

4. Loss or injury to a person during extravehicular activities (EVA).

5. Loss of the vehicle during descent to the Earth's atmosphere.

6. Loss of ability of the station, or its personnel, to accomplish its required mission. Principal hazards which might cause such losses are:

   • Loss of internal pressure in the space station

   • Fire (has already caused the death of three astronauts)

   • Explosion

   • Loss of station power

   • Loss of life-support system

   • Highly contaminated atmosphere

   • Unbearable conditions such as excessive temperature, radiation, vibration, or rotation (spinning)

   • Loss of control of station attitude, especially tumbling

   • Inability to rendezvous with supporting vehicles

   • Inability of personnel to transfer from-and-to ferrying or rescue craft

In effect, both Chanute's analysis and this brief one constitute limited, and not deeply detailed Preliminary Hazards Analyses, and following are more details on this method.

Preliminary Hazard Analysis (PHA)

The preliminary hazard analysis is generally the first analysis made of a new product or a product to be modified. As pointed out under the program tasks indicated in Chapter 12, the analysis should be made during the concept phase of a new product. At the latest it should be made early in the development phase.

Probably the earliest example of a preliminary hazard analysis is contained in the instructions the mythological Daedalus gave to his son Icarus. In Greek mythology Daedalus was a "skilful artificer" who, because of his skills, was refused permission to leave Crete by King Minos. Daedalus made wings of feathers, flax, and beeswax by which he and his son, Icarus, would escape to Greece. Before they flew off, Daedalus advised his son:

> My boy, take care
> To wing your course
> Along the middle air:
> If low, the surges
> Wet your flagging plumes;
> If high, the sun
> The melting wax consumes.

Icarus was so delighted with his wings and the joys of flying he flew higher and higher until the heat of the sun melted the beeswax, the wings came apart, and he fell to his death in the sea below.

Figure 13-3 indicates how the wings created by Daedalus might now be presented in a preliminary hazard analysis. The chart shows that Daedalus could have taken steps to ensure that Icarus did not fly too high. Daedalus failed in his design to provide a safeguard such as a flaxen leash by which he could have restrained his son. (Nowadays an accident investigator would also charge Daedalus with supervisory error. Daedalus knew that Icarus was a headstrong youth, should have monitored Icarus' activities more closely, and should have called him back when he started to fly higher and higher.)

The information in a preliminary hazard analysis can include more than that shown in Figure 13-3. What is included depends on the desires of the analyst. For example, it might be desirable to have a column in which can be listed a rough estimate of probability of an accident from the hazard shown unless a safeguard is provided. It might be desirable to have a column for the estimate of accident probability if a recommended safeguard is provided. Another optional column is one in which could be listed applicable standards.

Figure 13-4 presents a preliminary hazard analysis for a proposed product: an electrically-powered mill to grind coffee beans in small amounts for drip coffee makers. The design concept is that the mill will be approximately 10 in. high; the upper portion will be a cup in which from 5 oz. to 10 oz. of coffee beans will be placed. At the bottom of the cup will be a rotating blade which will cut up the beans when the mill is energized with 115 V electric power. A cover will cap the mill to prevent the beans from being thrown out when the cutting action takes place.

Experience has shown that the most hazardous aspects of any product are generally those in which transformations or expenditures of massive amounts of energy take place. For this reason, when a preliminary hazard analysis is made, the first consideration is given to high-energy

items such as explosives, other materials that could explode, flammable materials, high-pressure fluids, electrical systems, masses in motion or with the potential of being set into motion with high kinetic energy, and so on.

Electrical power at 115 V or more must be considered a high-energy source. In the preliminary hazard analysis for the coffee mill it is therefore considered first. Even the possibility of skin injury is an energy phenomenon in this case: the injury that could result will depend on the force of contact between the skin and a sharp edge, a point, or a rough surface.

The depth to which the preliminary hazard analysis can reach depends on the information available at the time the analyses is undertaken and on whether or not the product is one which is entirely or radically new, similar to one previously made, or is a modification of an existing one. In any case, much information is available or can be derived even in the very earliest stages of product development.

Generic Hazards

It was indicated in Chapter 7 that specific phenomena of any product may constitute hazardous characteristics. For example, if a product uses electrical power, the electricity could have a specific but limited number of potential hazards: possibility of shock, high temperatures that could produce burns and ignition of flammables, arcing or sparking that could ignite combustibles, inadvertent activation resulting in motion injury, loss of power at a crucial instant, or an explosion. The analyst would review each of these and determine whether or not any such cause-and-effect relationship is possible in the product being considered. The analyst can do the same for other aspects of the product: pressure, motion, thermal, toxic, or other hazards.

Mission Considerations

The analyst must review the purpose of the product, its intended functions, and the conditions under which it will be required to carry them out. The review must include detailed examinations not only of the overall product but of each subsystem, individually and as interrelated to other subsystems. The analysis of the mission must include considerations of the environment in which the product (and its subsystems) is to operate. The environmental hazards pointed out in Chapter 9 should be reviewed for life cycle of the product in operation. He or she must also consider its handling, transportation, maintenance, repair, and even final disposal. The usual intended purpose of the product must also be extended to include unintended abuses.

Accident Investigations

For a long time accident investigation was the principal means of ascertaining the hazards in products. It is an inefficient and costly method which cannot be justified

Preliminary Hazard Analysis—Wings

IDENTIFICATION: _____MARK I FLIGHT SYSTEM_____

SUBSYSTEM: _____WINGS_____   DESIGNER: _____DAEDALUS_____

HAZARD	CAUSE	EFFECT	CORRECTIVE OR PREVENTIVE MEASURES
Thermal radiation from sun	Flying too high in presence of strong solar radiation	Heat may melt beeswax holding feathers together. Separation and loss of feathers will cause loss of aerodynamic lift. Aeronaut may then plunge to his death in the sea.	Provide warning against flying too high and too close to sun Maintain close supervision over aeronauts. Use buddy system. Provide leash of flax between the two aeronauts to prevent young, impetuous one from flying too high. Restrict area of aerodynamic surface to prevent flying too high.
Moisture	Flying close to water surface	Feathers may absorb moisture, causing them to increase in weight and to flag. Limited propulsive power may not be adequate to compensate for increased weight and drag so that aeronaut will gradually sink into the sea. Result: loss of function and flight system. Possible drowning of aeronaut if survival gear is not provided.	Caution aeronaut to fly through middle air where sun will keep wings dry or where accumulation rate of moisture is acceptable for time of mission.

Figure 13-3. Preliminary hazard analysis—wings.

as the sole means of hazard analysis. No organization responsible for producing and marketing a product can long sustain a series of accidents as the means of determining potential problems. The consequences of some accidents can be so devastating that analyses must be made before the product is put into operation to preclude even a single mishap. Analyses therefore must be undertaken to determine the presence of hazards that could exist and the safeguards to be taken if they are present.

Accidents, however, do occur and the results of investigations could provide insights into hazards that could be present in similar products, adverse effects that could be generated, practices to be avoided, statistical data on frequencies of occurrences, safeguards that should be provided, and numerous other pertinent facts. Accident data can be derived from a company's own experiences, from files of the industry with which it is concerned, from insurance companies and associations, from government agencies, and from numerous other sources. Information on accidents can generate beneficial inputs to a preliminary hazard analysis.

Critical Incident Technique

Much knowledge of problems with products can be derived from interviews with persons who have had experience with similar products or who are knowledgeable of the experiences of others. One of the means by which this knowledge can be solicited is through using the critical incident technique. This technique consists of interviewing personnel about their involvements of those of their fellow workers or friends in accidents or near-accidents (near-misses) and about hazardous conditions that could result in mishaps. Then a survey is made of a group having had previous experiences. The range of experiences should be as wide as possible. (Maintenance and repair personnel are excellent participants, but operators and supervisors should also be included.) The participants are informed of the study and its objectives. Then they are asked to describe all near-misses or mishaps they can recall which happened to them or their acquaintances. Their recall is stimulated by giving each participant a list of similar incidents. It has been found that people are generally willing to talk about near-misses and about accidents in which others were involved rather than about serious mishaps in which they themselves

Preliminary Hazard Analysis — Coffee Mill

Product: Electrically operated rotary coffee mill for household use.

Hazard	Occurrence (Cause) Description	Effect	Probability (With No Safeguard)	Possible Safeguard	Remarks and References
Electricity	115 Vac power will be used (1) If a metal case is used without double insulation, a person could be shocked by a short to the case. (2) Immersion in water could also be fatal.	Electrical shock to personnel which may be fatal.	(1) No double insulation: Reasonably Probable (2) Immersion in water: Reasonably probable	(1) Double insulation (2) (a) Make waterproof (b) Provide warnings on mill and in instructions	U.L. Standard 73, Motor Operated Appliances, is inadequate to provide reasonably safe product.
Motion injury	(1) Rotating blade used to grind beans will have power adequate to cause severe injury.	(1) Amputation of finger(s) if finger(s) are in dangerous location when blade rotates.	(1) Reasonably Probable	(1) Provide cover with interlock or of design which prevents person from contacting blade when mill can be started. (2) Provide warning about disconnecting mill.	(1) Make analyses of proposed designs to determine if this requirement has been met for normal usage and for inadvertent activation.
Skin injury	Sharp edges, or rough surfaces either from poor manufacture or from breakage.	Sharp edges and points could cause cuts and scratches to skin.	Reasonably Probable	(1) (a) Require that all sharp edges, points, and rough surfaces be rounded. (b) Make mill of material which will not break easily to create sharp edges and points.	(1) (a) Most liable to be a production defect. Monitor production and quality control.

Flying object injury	(1) Rotating blade assembly is a device which could come apart at high operating speeds, especially if a hard object is put in mill by mistake.
	
	(2) Operating mill without cover could permit beans or ground coffee to be thrown out by centrifugal force.
		Parts or fragments of mill thrown out at high speed could injure user. Coffee beans or ground coffee thrown out at high velocity and hitting eye could cause severe damage.	Reasonably Probable	(1) (a) Design to positively secure blade so it will not come off during operation.
				    (b) Ensure that stresses due to rotational speeds will not be greater than strength.
				    (c) Make case and cover strong enough to hold any parts or fragments thrown off.
					Normally, the person operating the mill will be holding it and therefore, in close proximity. Flying fragments and parts will therefore have a good probability of hitting someone.

High temperature	Electrical power loss or mechanical motion can create high temperatures.	Burns to personnel who contact a hot surface.	(1) Metal surfaces: Reasonably Probable
			
			(2) Plastic material: Remote
				(1) (a) Keep power and friction losses as low as possible.
				    (b) Cool mill if there is still a high source of heat.
				    (c) Provide insulation to keep outer surfaces at safe temperature.	

Figure 13-4. Preliminary hazard analysis—coffee mill.

were involved. When the interviewees who knew of near-misses or mishaps but were not participants are added to those who were participants, a considerable amount of information on problem causes, unsafe conditions, and other pertinent facts becomes available. Questioning is carried on as long as the participant can recall any human error or its cause, unsafe condition, or incident. Even isolated items reported by only one participant can be used advantageously by the analyst to alert the analyst to a potential problem that might exist with his or her proposed product. When a larger number of persons interviewed report similar problems and accidents, they can be accepted as indicators of deficiencies that require preventive or corrective action in the designing or manufacture of a product. The method is therefore beneficial in avoiding the common complaint that the failings of one product are often carried over into new designs. Use of the critical incident technique has indicated that for approximately every 400 near-misses there is one accident.

Procedure

Dr. William Tarrants in his doctoral thesis at NYUS described the critical incident technique as carried out at one plant of the Westinghouse Company. The steps may be summarized as follows:

1. A group of employees with previous experience and involvement in manufacturing processes and equipment were selected. Each person included was listed according to various factors, so as to produce as wide a range of experience as possible. Representatives were selected randomly from each factor group.

2. The participants were interviewed and informed of the study and its objectives. They were given an opportunity to withdraw from participation.

3. At the end of the interview, each participant was given a copy of the statement on the study and its objectives, plus a list of typical incidents gathered at other plants. This was to stimulate the recall process.

4. The participants were interviewed again, one by one, approximately 24 hours later, and queried regarding their observations or participation in unsafe operations, errors, or hazardous conditions.

5. Participants were asked to describe any incidents they could recall, whether or not they had resulted in injury or property damage. They were asked whether they recalled any incidents similar to those that had occurred at other plants, as described on the list they had been given.

6. The questioning was carried on until all human errors or unsafe conditions in any recalled incident could be described.

The 20 participants related 389 incidents of 117 different types. Over 50% more potential accident causes were found by this method then had been identified from accident records. One participant estimated that almost 70% of the problems reported occurred every day, indicating an almost constant exposure to danger.

Attempts have also been made to produce equally effective results in obtaining information by the use of questionnaires to be filled in by selected personnel. This has proven to be unsatisfactory for a number of reasons. One fundamental problem was the need for extreme care in selecting and phrasing the questions. Too often, the person completing the questionnaire would give the questions interpretations neither considered nor intended by the person preparing them. Any question should be avoided when the answer depends on an individual's interpretation of why it was actually stated in that specific manner, unless the reason is also explained.

Much information is also submitted to control and action agencies in the form of trouble reports. However, trouble reporting itself generates discrepancies that may be avoided through use of the Critical Incident Technique. Reports may require entries as narratives, checkoff of listed items, or both. Personnel find it time consuming and difficult to prepare a narrative. Even conscientious report writers tend to select the easiest and most rapid means for completing a report. Checkoffs can be done much more rapidly, but these too, often result in omission of information that may be critical. In both types of reports, entries may include information on the immediate or principal cause of an accident, but other contributory causes and factors may be neglected.

Review of Standards and Criteria

Many safety standards and criteria were written to require designs to prevent recurrences of accidents or to avoid occurrences whose possibilities could be foreseen. Understanding a criterion provides insight into the hazard against which it is intended to be used as a safeguard. The analyst can then determine whether or not such a hazard will exist in the product with which he or she is concerned.

Mathematical Models

A mathematical model might indicate interrelationships between physical and phenomenological conditions and processes. The use of computers to create such models permits outcomes to be predicted on which optimal courses of action can be predicated. Accident experience, knowledge of hazardous characteristics of products, possibilities of human error, component failure data, environmental effects, and other pertinent, widely diverse data can be integrated into simple relationships by which product behavior and failings can be explored. Applied to safety problems, mathematical models can be beneficial in a preliminary hazard analysis.

Scale Models

Scale models may vary from those bearing little resemblance to the final product except in the aspect for which they are to be tested to highly sophisticated models that reflect the proposed product in everything but size. Thus, a scale model of an automobile, aircraft, boat, or ship can be used to learn of their aerodynamic or hydrodynamic

Using Mockups

The procedure for using mockups generally will follow the steps listed below, with suitable adjustments for special purposes:

· Establish the purpose for which the mockup is to be made.

· Prepare a detailed checklist of items to be reviewed, relationships to be established, dimensions to be measured or verified, demonstrations to be undertaken, equipment in the mockup which will have to be sturdily built to bear loads, such as seats to be used by persons taking part in the activities, and determine if the mockup will be full-sized or smaller, and if it will represent the entire product or just one portion of it.

· Construct the mockup with the most economical materials suitable for the purpose, such as cardboard or thin plywood. Construction and material need not duplicate the proposed product but should be of similar configuration and arrangement. Where the exact locations of units are not already fixed definitely, they should be made so that they can be easily changed and relocated. Displays such as dials, controls, or access openings can be shown by pin-on representations, painted outlines, or cutouts.

· Run through the tentative procedures that might be expected to be undertaken by the users of the product. Make the study for man-machine interference, potential difficulties in use of equipment and controls or in viewing displays because of physical dimensions or locations. The initial run-through may be made in informal attire, performing the procedures slowly to evaluate each step for possibilities of error, difficulty, or misuse. Have persons of different sizes and operational experience make the run-throughs. Subsequent trials should be made at the expected rate of operation while the operator is wearing the different types of clothing in which he might be expected to be dressed under various weather conditions. Note all difficulties.

· If emergency procedures have been established, repeat the run-throughs as rapidly as possible to determine whether there might be a cause for delay in action, such as an evacuation, use of emergency equipment, or rescue. Time to accomplish the procedure should be determined to ensure it is within the expected limits permissible by the type of emergency which could be encountered. Run through the emergency procedures again but with an adverse condition built-in which might be encountered in a real emergency, such as a blocked exit.

· Repeat all the foregoing trials with updated mockups as changes are made in the expected design of the proposed product.

Mockups involve a form of play-acting whose success depends on the imagination of the analyst as he visualizes the various man-machine interrelationships.

Figure 13-5. Using mockups.

characteristics, stability, impact tendencies, or resistance. Scale models can be used to determine the stresses that might result from high winds and the effects or causes of turbulence, earthquakes, atmospheric dispersion of pollutants, spread of fire, high-speed impacts, or other results which might be too complex to determine by use of mathematical models and too costly when prototypes or production models are used.

Mock-Ups

A mock-up is a nonoperational three-dimensional replica of a proposed item of equipment, hardware, vehicle, or structure. Its configuration represents that of the real-world product which permits analyses to be made of human-machine relationships, especially those which might endanger personnel; possibilities of physical interference between pieces of equipment, personnel, or both; optimal placements of operating instruments and controls; location and accessibility of entrances and exits for normal and emergency use and of emergency equipment; separation or isolation of incompatible materials, operations, and equipment.

A mock-up is generally built early in the development of a product and in accordance with initial concepts of form, structure, size, and arrangements. The mock-up is updated as improvements or new arrangements are tried. A proposed change can be evaluated in a mock-up before a final selection is made in hardware design to ensure that there are no physical problems. Figure 13-5 indicates the procedure for using mock-ups. Figure 13-6 indicates some of the uses and problems with which mock-ups are concerned.

Breadboard Models

A mock-up has the physical appearance of the proposed product, but it does not function. The breadboard model functions, but it may bear little resemblance to the final product. Depending on how soon the breadboard model can be developed governs whether or not it can be useful in a preliminary hazard analysis. One that can be assembled early would be helpful in determining whether or not any functional hazards might exist in the final product. If such an assembly requires much time and effort, it would be too late for the preliminary hazard analysis but

Examples of Uses of Mockups

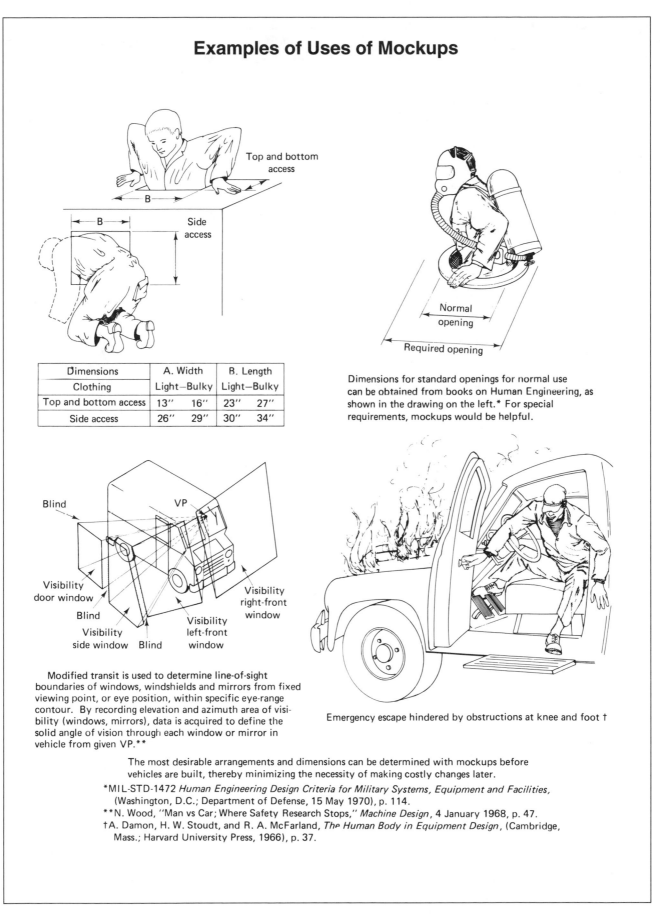

Dimensions	A. Width		B. Length	
Clothing	Light—Bulky		Light—Bulky	
Top and bottom access	13″	16″	23″	27″
Side access	26″	29″	30″	34″

Dimensions for standard openings for normal use can be obtained from books on Human Engineering, as shown in the drawing on the left.* For special requirements, mockups would be helpful.

Modified transit is used to determine line-of-sight boundaries of windows, windshields and mirrors from fixed viewing point, or eye position, within specific eye-range contour. By recording elevation and azimuth area of visibility (windows, mirrors), data is acquired to define the solid angle of vision through each window or mirror in vehicle from given VP.**

Emergency escape hindered by obstructions at knee and foot †

The most desirable arrangements and dimensions can be determined with mockups before vehicles are built, thereby minimizing the necessity of making costly changes later.

*MIL-STD-1472 *Human Engineering Design Criteria for Military Systems, Equipment and Facilities,* (Washington, D.C.; Department of Defense, 15 May 1970), p. 114.

**N. Wood, "Man vs Car; Where Safety Research Stops," *Machine Design*, 4 January 1968, p. 47.

†A. Damon, H. W. Stoudt, and R. A. McFarland, *The Human Body in Equipment Design*, (Cambridge, Mass.; Harvard University Press, 1966), p. 37.

Figure 13-6. Examples of uses of mockups.

it could become a means of reviewing the workings before they are built into a prototype.

Fault Trees

Fault-tree analyses and the method used to make fault trees are described in Chapter 15. The top levels of a fault tree can be used to advantage in a preliminary hazard analysis since the events and conditions at the top of the tree are generally applicable to all versions of a specific product. It is only at the lower, more detailed levels that differences appear. Figure 15-16 is an example of a fault tree used to investigate a hazard that is generic to all types of electric drills that use a grounded, three-wire system to prevent shock. In more complex products, development of a fault tree will lead to considerations of potential problems that can be included in the preliminary hazard analysis.

Extending the Uses of the Preliminary Hazard Analysis

For a simple product, the preliminary hazard analysis may require little change or additional effort to make the final analysis of the product. Figure 13-7 is a proposed product, a child's building block, as drawn in a conceptual sketch. Below it is the hazard analysis which contains the foreseeable potential hazards, the possible safeguard for each hazard, and any other pertinent remarks. Once the prototype is built, the column for "Possible Safeguard" could be revised to eliminate the word "Possible" since choices will have been made. Instead of noting "Round Corners and Edges," an entry "Corners and Edges Rounded to $\frac{1}{8}$ in. Radius" would be made if this actually had been done. Instead of "Ensure That Paint Is of Noninjurious Type," an entry could be made to the effect "Paint Selected Is Nontoxic and Otherwise Noninjurious According to a Written Declaration by the Paint Manufacturer." Information on type, date, and location of the declaration could be recorded under Remarks.

Trade-Off Studies

Trade-off studies are analyses made to enable making a decision on the most advantageous course of action to be taken. Trade-off studies are most commonly made during the concept phase of a product, but they are also made at later points when there are multiple courses of action which could be taken and a management decision is required. Inputs to trade-off studies may be made by designers, safety engineers, reliability engineers, production personnel, marketing representatives, and anyone else concerned with the development, manufacture, sales, service, or operation of the product.

Making trade-off studies is sometimes an iterative process. A designer may come up with an idea for a product; the safety engineer provides his or her first comments as part of the initial trade-off study. A tentative decision is then made, and the safety engineer prepares a preliminary

hazard analysis. This analysis may establish that the hazards involved could be controlled by any one of a number of safeguards. Another trade-off study would then be made to determine which safeguard would be most desirable from the standpoints of effectiveness, cost, government criteria, producibility, reliability, weight, size, and any other factors.

Figure 13-8 shows five coffee mills as they might be conceived by five difference designers. (In actuality, these are simplified drawings of mills that have already been manufactured[2] and were purchased on the open market.) Figure 13-9 is a trade-off study comparing these five mills. It can be seen that the relative safety of these mills varies from the one (No. 2) considered most safe to the one considered least safe (No. 4). The fact that No. 2 is considered most safe does not mean that there will be more accidents with the others; it means that the potentialities for accidents vary slightly. Figure 13-10 presents some possible redesigns that might be considered in a trade-off study to make the mills safer.

An analysis such as this also permits the prospective merchandisers or purchasers an opportunity to evaluate similar products from which they will select one. The Consumer Product Safety Act and the possibility that a legal suit can involve anyone in the chain of commerce require that merchandisers, especially large ones who have wide markets and extensive exposure, be capable of making such analyses.

Child's Building Block

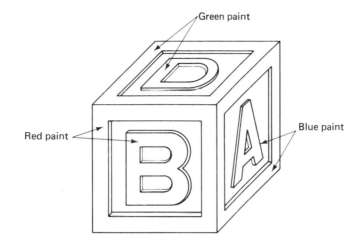

CHILD'S BUILDING BLOCK
Made of hardwood with painted letters and edges

The Block—Hazard Analysis

Hazard	Possible Safeguards	Remarks
Sharp edges and corners Child might cut himself Child might scratch the furniture	Round corners and edges	Round to at least 1/8'' diameter
Weight If block is thrown, could hurt another child or himself. If thrown, could break mirrors, windows, or other frangible objects.	Make block of light plastic	Plastic must be of a type from which child cannot chew a piece.
Child might chew off a piece of wood which scratches his mouth, lodges in his throat, or which he swallows with injurious results.	Select wood of type from which pieces cannot be chewed	If plastic is substituted make certain same precautionary measure is observed
Paint might be toxic	Ensure that paint is of noninjurious type	
Child might break a tooth biting block	Make of soft plastic	Plastic must be of a type from which child cannot chew a piece
Child might try to swallow the block and choke on it	Make of size child cannot swallow	Determine size too large for child to swallow
Child might get it in his mouth from where it might be difficult to remove	Make of size too large to get in mouth or small enough so it won't get stuck	Determine size which would eliminate this possibility
Block might break and child scratch himself or get a splinter under skin	Select wood of type which will not break or splinter	If plastic is substituted ensure it will not fracture to expose rough surfaces

Figure 13-7. Child's building block.

Coffee Mills

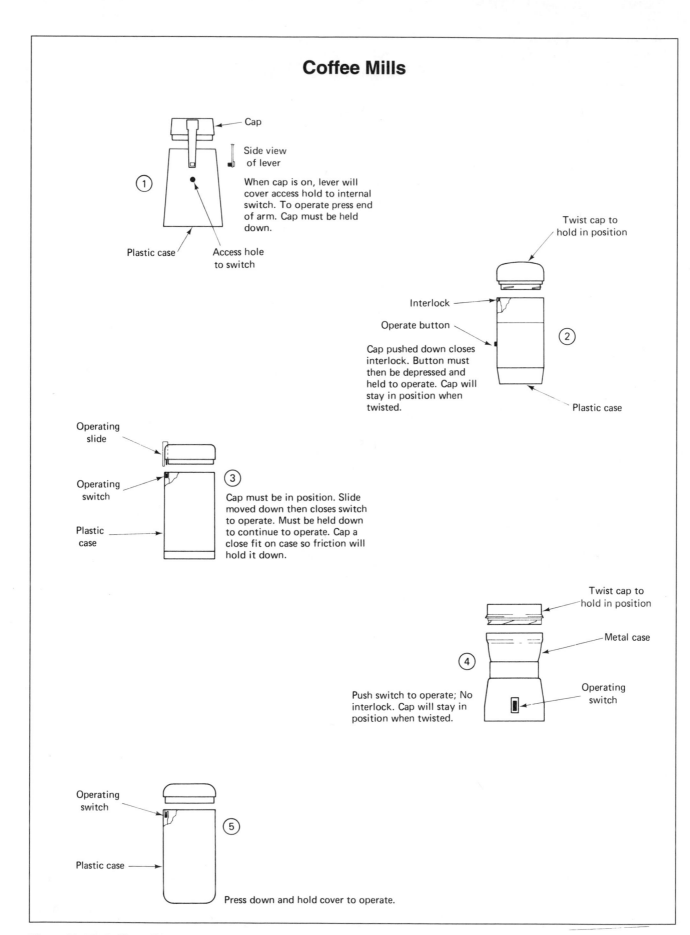

① Plastic case / Cap / Access hole to switch

Side view of lever

When cap is on, lever will cover access hold to internal switch. To operate press end of arm. Cap must be held down.

② Twist cap to hold in position / Interlock / Operate button / Plastic case

Cap pushed down closes interlock. Button must then be depressed and held to operate. Cap will stay in position when twisted.

③ Operating slide / Operating switch / Plastic case

Cap must be in position. Slide moved down then closes switch to operate. Must be held down to continue to operate. Cap a close fit on case so friction will hold it down.

④ Twist cap to hold in position / Metal case / Operating switch

Push switch to operate; No interlock. Cap will stay in position when twisted.

⑤ Operating switch / Plastic case

Press down and hold cover to operate.

Figure 13-8. Coffee mills.

Trade-Off Study — Coffee Mills

Make	Cost	Reliability Comparison	Materials		Capacity (GMS)	Safety	Probability of Occurrence	Remarks
			CASE	CAP		Activation with Cover Off		
1. Norelco I	Cost of one switch plus lever arm and projection on arm.	Only one switch to fail.	Plastic	Transparent plastic	60	(1) Failure of switch in closed position. (2) User turns cover and arm at right angles and closes internal switch.	Remote Remote	(1) Use high reliability switch. Provide warning. (2) Redesign to use slot instead of round access hole. (Call this design Norelco II.)
Norelco II	Less than Norelco I.	Same as Norelco I.	Same	Same	Same	(1) Failure of switch in closed position.	Remote	(1) Use high reliability switch. Provide warning.
2. Braun I	Cost of two switches.	Less than Norelco since either of two switches can fail.	Plastic	Transparent plastic	60	(1) Both switches must fail closed.	Extremely remote	(1) Cost factor could be reduced by using one switch with activating projection as part of cover
Braun II	Cost of one switch cheaper than 1, 2, or 3.	Only one switch to fail.	Same	Same	Same	(1) Failure of switch in closed position.	Remote	(1) Use high reliability switch. Provide warning.
3. Waring	Cost of one switch and side mechanism.	One switch and slide mechanism.	Plastic	Dark-brown plastic	60	(1) Failure of switch in closed position.	Remote	(1) Use high reliability switch. Provide warning.
4. SEB	Cost of one switch. Metal case more expensive for high volume production.	Only one switch to fail.	Metal	Dark-brown plastic	120	(1) Can be operated any time with cover off. (2) Failure of switch in closed position.	Reasonably probable	(1) Still may meet U.L. Standard 73 (Motor Operated Appliances) for this feature. Failure where live wire is grounded to case could result in shock to user. Bottom plate can be removed without tools, or might fall off, exposing electrical conductors. This feature will not meet U.L. Standards.
5. Farberware	Cost of one switch. Cap cheaper than any other.	Only one switch to fail.	Plastic	Smoky-gray plastic	60	(1) Failure of switch in closed position.	Remote	(1) Use high reliability switch. Provide warning.
6. Composite	Slightly higher than regular single switch; cheaper than 2 switches.	Slightly higher than regular single switch; cheaper than 2 switches.	Plastic	Transparent plastic	60	Both parts of switch must fail closed.	Extremely remote	Switch more complicated than normal single switch.

Figure 13-9. Trade-off study—coffee mills.

Redesigns for Improvement of Safety

Although most of the coffee mills in Figure 13-8 are relatively safe, their safety levels can be increased even more, sometimes at little or no added cost. The first two mills will be taken as examples:

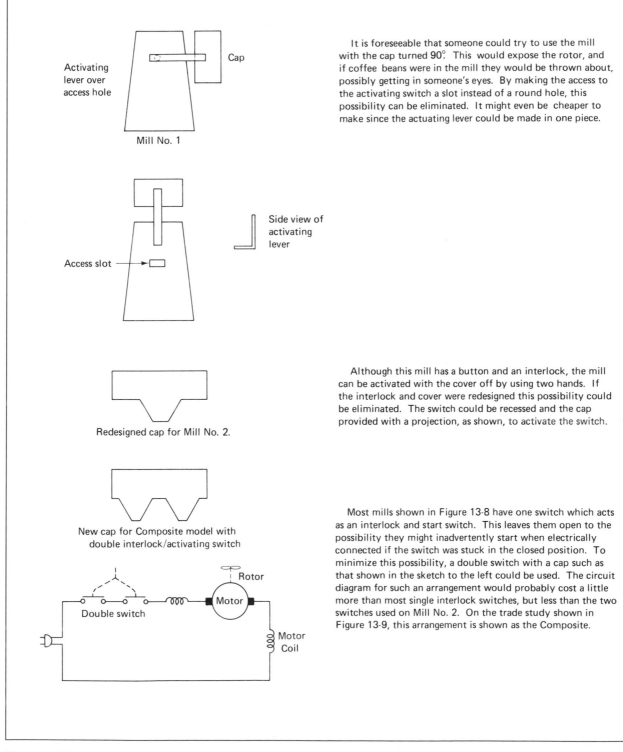

It is foreseeable that someone could try to use the mill with the cap turned 90°. This would expose the rotor, and if coffee beans were in the mill they would be thrown about, possibly getting in someone's eyes. By making the access to the activating switch a slot instead of a round hole, this possibility can be eliminated. It might even be cheaper to make since the actuating lever could be made in one piece.

Although this mill has a button and an interlock, the mill can be activated with the cover off by using two hands. If the interlock and cover were redesigned this possibility could be eliminated. The switch could be recessed and the cap provided with a projection, as shown, to activate the switch.

Most mills shown in Figure 13-8 have one switch which acts as an interlock and start switch. This leaves them open to the possibility they might inadvertently start when electrically connected if the switch was stuck in the closed position. To minimize this possibility, a double switch with a cap such as that shown in the sketch to the left could be used. The circuit diagram for such an arrangement would probably cost a little more than most single interlock switches, but less than the two switches used on Mill No. 2. On the trade study shown in Figure 13-9, this arrangement is shown as the Composite.

Figure 13-10. Redesigns for improvement of safety.

Notes

[1] Valentine, E.S. and F.L. Tomlinson, *Travels in Space*, Frederick A. Stokes Company; 1902.

[2] No. 1 was made by Norelco; No. 2, Braun; No. 3, Waring; No. 4, SEB; and No. 5, Farberware. The numbers are the order in which they were found and purchased.

Questions

1. For what purposes are safety analyses used?

2. What is meant by "closing the loop" in a safety analysis program?

3. If there was a failure to take corrective action when analysis indicated a safety problem existed and an accident occurs in which a person is injured, to what penalties can a manufacturer be subjected?

4. If analysis or testing of a consumer product reveals that the product's use involves a substantial risk, what does the law require the manufacturer to do?

5. Even if designers design to the standards for a specific product, why is it still necessary to make a hazard analysis?

6. How is it possible to determine the potential hazards in a product of a type which has never been built before?

7. What are the advantages of having a good predesign safety analysis?

8. What are the fundamental differences between predesign and postdesign analyses?

9. What is a preliminary hazard analysis? When should it be undertaken? What benefits can be derived from its use?

10. In analyzing a product for potential safety problems, which hazards could be most injurious or damaging and should be investigated first?

11. Give the six types of potential hazards that can exist in electrically powered products and might result in injury or damage.

12. A new product is to use compressed air. List the hazards that might be present.

13. What are the properties that should be investigated in a liquid that might leak from a product?

14. What other types of analyses can contribute to a preliminary hazard analysis?

15. What is the critical incident technique? What are the benefits of its use?

16. Describe the difference between mock-ups and breadboard models.

17. What is a "trade-off study"? What considerations might a trade-off study involve?

18. Describe a procedure for using hazard reports.

19. Discuss the relationship between safety analyses, accidents, and foreseeability.

20. What would be the impression and impact on a court if it could be shown there had been no safety analyses conducted prior to the occurrence of an accident? What would be the potential effect on a claim for liability?

21. Is the fact that a detailed safety analysis had been performed by a manufacturer good for the defendant? Indicate some of the most common methods of safety analysis in use.

22. Which type of safety analysis do you believe is most common for products? Which method of analysis would be good for reduction of errors during product operation by users?

14

Detailed Analyses

As design proceeds, it is possible to make analyses in progressively greater detail. The analyses reflect how the final product will operate, the problems that might be encountered in operation, the malfunctions and failures that might occur, and the hazardous characteristics that might exist. There are numerous methods of analysis which can be used; some can be used in various situations and some are used for specific purposes. There is no one analysis that will satisfy all analysis requirements.

The first method to be described, failure modes and effects analysis, is oriented toward investigating the results that malfunctions of components can generate. Other methods analyze circuits, assemblies, relations between assemblies, specific potentially adverse occurrences, or procedures.

Failure Modes and Effects Analysis (FMEA)

Reliability is defined as the probability of successful accomplishment of a mission within a specific time and under specified conditions. Failure modes and effects analysis was developed by reliability engineers to permit them to predict the reliability of complex products. To do this it was necessary to establish how and how often components of a product could fail. FMEA was then extended to evaluate the effects of such failures.

In this method of analysis, the product to be analyzed is listed by its constituent major assemblies and then by its subassemblies and components. Each component is then studied to determine how it could malfunction, what could cause it to malfunction, and the effect on other components or on higher-level subassemblies, assemblies, and the entire product. Failure rates may then be determined and listed in order to establish the overall probability that the product will operate without a failure for a specific length of time and that the product will operate a certain length of time between failures. It is the best and principal means of determining where components and

designs must be improved in order to increase the operational life of a product and how often it must be serviced. Figure 14-1 is an FMEA of coffee mill No. 1 shown in Figure 13-8.

Since the end effects of failures are frequently established, FMEAs are often used for safety purposes. But since not all failures result in accidents (failure of a transistor in a radio will cause a radio to malfunction but there will probably be no damage or injury), analyzing all the parts, the multiple ways each part can fail, and the resultant effects is generally a time-consuming, inefficient process for safety purposes except in certain instances. In addition, FMEAs don't usually take into account human error and hazardous conditions. They take into consideration, to a limited extent, the effects of environment. They usually do not consider the effects that result from multiple failures. Used with fault-tree analysis (FTA) (Chapter 15), the two can be powerful analytical tools: The FTA is used to pinpoint where an FMEA should be carried out and it provides the additional data the FMEA lacks.

The FMEA can provide the following functions:

1. Systematic review of component failure modes to ensure that any failure produces minimal damage to the product.

2. Determining the effects that such failures will have on other items in the product and their functions.

3. Determining those parts whose failures would have critical effects on product operation, thus producing the greatest damage, and which failure modes will generate these damaging effects.

4. Calculating the probabilities of failures in assemblies, subassemblies, and products from the individual failure probabilities of their components and the arrangements in which they have been designed. Since components have more than one failure mode, the probability that one will fail at all is the total probability of all failure modes. One or more of these modes may be one that can generate an accident,

Failure Mode and Effects Analysis

Component Name and Number	Function	Failure Mode and Cause	Failure Effect On		Probability of Failure $(\lambda \times 10^{-6})$	Corrective Action Available or Recommended
			Next Higher Item	End Item Product		
Cover Cap	Keeps coffee from being thrown about; keeps user from getting fingers into cup where they could be cut by rotor.	Plastic fractures and parts separate. Brittle plastic dropped on hard surface; stepped on or subjected to too great a force when being put in place.	None	None	1	Select plastic which is not brittle.
Switch activating arm	User depresses and holds down free end in access hole to switch which operates mill.	Breaks off cap due to rough handling by user, being stepped on or dropped.	May cause cap to weaken and break if arm breaks off at the cap.	May make product unusable.	100	Redesign. Put switch under cap, thereby eliminating arm.
Case plastic	Major structural part which holds other assemblies together; protects against contact with moving and electrical parts.	Could be broken by impact or crushing.		Resultant sharp edges and points; may make it unusable.	0.5	Use impact resistant plastic.
Vibration dampers (2)	Rubber pads in case. Reduction of vibration and noise by separating metal motor frame from plastic case.	Deterioration of rubber. Could be lost since they are not glued in place.	Fatigue to brittle plastic.	Excessive vibration and noise.	0.01	Glue in place.
Switch, momentary	Completes circuit to provide electrical power to motor.	Failure OPEN: Button to be depressed breaks off. External connection separates. Internal electrical path broken.	Motor fails to operate.	Failure to operate.	35	Select high reliability component.
		CLOSED: Welded contacts inside, internal spring broken.	Motor operates at all times.	Will operate with cover off.		Select high reliability component. Two switches in series.
		DEGRADED PERFORMANCE: Intermittent contact due to weak internal spring.	Intermittent operation.	Intermittent operation.		Select high reliability component.

Figure 14-1. Failure modes and effects analysis (FMEA).

whereas the others will not. Each mode must therefore be considered separately.

5. Establishing test program requirements to determine failure mode and rate data not available from other sources.

6. Establishing test program requirements to verify empirical reliability predictions.

7. Providing input data for trade-off studies to establish the effectiveness of changes in a proposed product or to determine the probable effect of modifications on an existing product.

8. Determining how probabilities of failure of components, assemblies, and the product can be reduced by using high reliability components, redundancies in design, or both.

9. Eliminating or minimizing the adverse effects that assembly failures could generate and indicating safeguards to be incorporated if products cannot be made fail-safe or brought within acceptable failure limits.

In its original usages, failure modes and effects analysis determined where improvements in component life or design were necessary; and because failure intervals and probabilities were estimated, maintenance periods and requirements could be established. FMEA has proven effective for both purposes. Deficiencies can be eliminated or minimized through design changes, redundancies, incorporation of fail-safe features, closer control of critical characteristics during manufacture and use, and identification of areas requiring close control and extra care at the facilities of the subcontractors or users.

Effects of human actions on the product are not generally included in failure modes and effects analysis; these effects are considered to be the province of human engineering. Bioenvironmental engineering is another area of investigation considered only from the standpoint of analyzing equipment required for environment control for failure modes and rates.

Procedure

To conduct a failure modes and effects analysis, it is first necessary to know and understand the mission of the equipment, the constraints within which it is to operate, and the limits delineating success and failure. Once these basics are known, analysis of the equipment can begin. Information and data are recorded on forms such as that shown in Figure 14-1. There are numerous variations of this form. Each organization undertaking an FMEA generally prepares its own.

1. The product is divided into assemblies that can be handled effectively.

2. Functional diagrams, schematics, and drawings for the product and each assembly are then reviewed to determine their interrelationships and the interrelationships of their component subassemblies. This review may be done by preparing and using block diagrams. The block diagram can be assigned reference numbers to permit coordination with the items on the functional breakdown tables.

3. A complete component list is prepared for each assembly as it is to be analyzed. The specific function of each component is entered at the same time.

4. Operational and environmental stresses affecting the product are then established. These stresses are viewed in order to determine the adverse effects that they could generate on the system or its constituent assemblies and components.

5. The significant failure mechanisms that could affect components are determined from analysis of the engineering drawings and functional diagrams. Effects of assembly failure are then considered.

6. The failure modes of all components are identified. Basically, it is component failure that produces ultimate failures of entire products. Since a component may have more than one failure mode, each mode must be analyzed for the effect on the assembly and then on the product. All failure modes are tabulated and the effects produced by each are listed.

7. Each condition which affects a component should be listed to indicate whether or not there are special periods of operation, stress, personnel action, or combinations of events that would increase the possibilities of failure or damage.

8. The hazard category as explained on page 156 may be indicated.

9. Preventive or corrective measures to eliminate or control the hazard are then listed. If the analysis reveals that failure can cause injury, a note may be entered on the necessity of having a safeguard.

10. Probabilities of the occurrence of each component failure may be entered. Initially, they may be estimated from generic rates that have been developed from experience and published in documents such as MIL-HDBK-217B.[1] Figure 8-5 is a sample of such generic rates. Data can be obtained from information centers that collect and collate such information. Almost every large manufacturing company, especially in electronic fields, has files of data on reliability and failure rates of the components, assemblies, or devices that it produces. Subcontractors or suppliers can be requested or required to furnish data on the items that they contract to provide.

11. Probabilities of failure of subassemblies, assemblies, and products can then be computed.

12. Some analyses proceed to determine the criticality of components and the effects that failure will have on the mission. This analysis is called an FMECA (failure mode and criticality analysis).

For additional FMEAs see Figure 14-2, the analysis of an electric soldering pencil; and of an electric steam iron, Figure 14-3.

Failure Modes and Criticality Analysis (FMECA)

Certain components or assemblies in any product are especially critical to the product's mission and the well-being of its operators. Therefore, they should be given special attention and should be analyzed more fully than others. Which components are critical can be established through experience or as the products of analyses.

A component or assembly may be critical because it is inherently hazardous by its very nature. Experience or tests may have shown it to be sensitive, damaging, or both. Major effort must also be made to safeguard those items that could produce injury or damage through single-point failures. A single-point failure is one in which an accident could result from one component loss, human error, or other single, untimely, and undesirable event.

There are numerous examples of designs that can produce single-point failures. One source of power may supply electricity for operation of both critical and noncritical equipment, such as for hospital operating rooms

Failure Mode Effects Analysis Table for a Soldering Pencil

Product   Soldering Pencil   Design File   XYZ

Part No.	Part Description	Function	Failure Mode	Effect	Crit.	Prob.	Remarks
1	Cord Set (includes)	Power from outlet to line cord	Short	Blown fuse—no heat	MA	L	
1a	Plug		Open	No heat	MA	L	
			Insulation failure	Shock hazard	C	L	
1b	Cord	Power from line cord to heating element	Short	Blown fuse—no heat	MA	L	
			Open	No heat	MA	L	
			Insulation failure	Shock hazard	C	L	
2	Handle	Holds everything together—handhold	Break	Shock hazard	C	H	
3	Heating element	Converts electrical energy to heat; transfers heat to tip	Short	Blown fuse	MA	M	
			Open	No heat	MA	H	
			Insulation failure	Shock hazard	C	M	
			Drift resistance	Heat Spec. off	L	L	
			Static electricity buildup	Burns soldered components out	MA	H	
4	Soldering tip	Conducts heat from element to work; provides capability for tinning to enhance heat transfer	Corrode	Poor tinnability	MI	H	
			Impure material	Solder contamination	MA	M	
5	Shroud	Protect user from heat	Break	Iron useless	MA	U	
6	Fiber insulator	Keeps line cord from shorting	Break	Blown fuse; short; no heat	MA	U	
7	Solderless crimp connector	Holds line cord to heater element	Open	No heat; short	MA	L	
					C	L	
			Poor connection	Temp. out of spec.	MI	L	
8	Long screws	Heating element to shroud	Strip threads	Tip will be loose or fall out	MI	H	
9	Short screws (3)	Hold shroud to handle	Strip threads	Iron will fall apart; burn hazard	C	H	
10	Washers under long screws (2)	Prevent screw seizure	None	---	--	-	
11	Nameplate	Identify unit	Writing can fade from heat	Electrical ratings will be illegible	MI	M	

Figure 14-2. Failure mode effects analysis table for a soldering pencil.

and also equipment that could be dispensed with temporarily during an emergency. Overloading noncritical circuitry could cause failure of the entire system. To eliminate such a possibility, various means can be used to ensure that power will always be available for critical needs. The critical circuits could be separated from the noncritical circuits, thus eliminating the possibility that the latter could cause failure. A standby source could be provided to supply both critical and noncritical equipment. An emergency source, circuit, or both could be installed for the critical equipment only.

Criticality is rated in more than one way and for more than one purpose. The Society of Automotive Engineers (SAE) in Aerospace Recommended Practice 926 categorizes criticality of failure modes as:

An Example of FMEA

A steam iron is used as an example of how the FMEA can be applied. The steps of the FMEA can be illustrated with this brief example. In the case of much larger systems or equipments, the larger system or equipments can, and often times must, be divided into smaller subsystems for the purposes of analysis.

The first requirement is the descriptive information. Shown here is the Parts List. Additional information for FMEA would be an electrical schematic and assembly drawings.

The Failure Modes and Effects Analysis is shown.

Parts List

ITEM: Steam Iron _____ Date: _____

MODEL: HSSF44-A _____ Prepared: _____

	P/N	Part	Quantity
1	8930	Plug	1
2	270931	Cord	8 ft.
3	9942	Handle	1
4	12877	Upper Cover...........	1
18	25303	Bimetal Strip...........	1
19	74903	Rivet	1
20	60872	Base Plate	1

Failure Mode and Effects Analysis Example for a Steam Iron

PRODUCT __Steam Iron__   DONE BY _____   _____

DRAWING __#HSSF44 REV A__   CKD BY _____   _____

CODE: C - Safety Hazard
                MA - Major Fault – Requires Prompt Service   RELATIVE   H - High
                MN - Minor Fault – May Require Future Service   PROBABILITY   M - Moderate
CRITICALITY: I - Insignificant   OF OCCURRENCE: L - Low
  (CRIT)   (PROB)   U - Unlikely

Item	Line/ Part No.	Description	Function of Part	Mode of Failure	Effect on System	Crit	Prob	Remarks	Action/ Responsibility
1	8930	Plug	2-Wire Electrical Plug	Short	No heat or steam	MA	L		
				Open	No heat or steam	MA	L		
2	270931	Cord	Power from outlet to iron	Short	No heat or steam	MA	L		
				Open	No heat or steam	MA	L		
				Insulation Fail	Presents shock hazard	C	L	Lack info on insulation heat resistance	Check insulation specs vs industry and Fed. Safety standards. R. Jones due next Design Review
3	9942	Handle	Hold iron, support in upright position	Cracked, broken	Operator inconvenience to unusable	MN MA	L L		
4	12877	Upper Cover	Mount handle plate, water indicator; bolt to lower plate	Tarnished finish	None on operation	MN	L		
18	25303	Bimetal Strip	Sense heat, open & close heat element circuit	Fail Open	No heat, no steam	MA	L		
				Fail Closed	Iron too hot: Surface remains at max temp. of 350°F	MA	M		Prepare test plan for running life test on Bimetal Strip. S. Harris due next Design Review
19	74903	Rivet	Carries current for heating element	Loose burned, surface	Low Heat	MA	L		
20	60872	Base Plate	Hot ironing surface mount for components; channels for steam	Tarnish	None on operation	I	H		
				Stripped Threads loose connection	Noise	MN	L		
					Shock Hazard	C	L		Determine cost of adding lock washer. L. Smith due next Design Review
				Clogged	Decreased amount of steam	MA	H		
21	63923	Pressure Plug	Blow out due to overpressure	Not blow out at pressure limit	Burn Hazard	C	L		a) Check field data for past history. R. Jones b) Draft test plan to check pressure plug. S. Harris c) OC establish sampling plan and inspection for plugs. N. Roberts All due next Design Review

Figure 14-3. Failure mode and effects analysis example for a steam iron.

Category 1: Failure resulting in potential loss of life.

Category 2: Failure resulting in potential mission failure.

Category 3: Failure resulting in delay or loss of operational availability.

Category 4: Failure resulting in excessive unscheduled maintenance.

Criticality ranking may be used to determine:

1. Which items should be given more intensive study for elimination of the hazard that could cause the failure and for fail-safe design, failure rate reduction, or damage containment.

2. Which items require special attention during production, which items require tight quality control, and which items require protective handling at all times.

3. Special requirements to be included in specifications for suppliers concerning design, performance, reliability, safety, or quality assurance.

4. Acceptance standards to be established for components received at a plant from subcontractors and for parameters that should be tested most intensively.

5. When special procedures, safeguards, protective equipment, monitoring devices, or warning systems should be provided.

6. Where accident prevention efforts and funds could be applied most effectively. This is especially important since every program is generally limited by the availability of funds.

Criticality ranking can be accomplished in many ways. The method described by the Society of Automotive Engineers in ARP 926 is made an extension of failure modes and effects analysis (FMEA) and the two are then designated failure modes, effects, and criticality analysis (FMECA). In the procedure for criticality determination, the criticality number for any component is indicated by the number of failures of a specific type expected during each one million operations occurring in a critical mode. The criticality number, C, is calculated and entered into the appropriate column in the FMECA table. The lengthy procedure can be obtained from ARP 926.

Unfortunately, this method requires a great deal of effort (the SAE indicates how it can be simplified) and it does not consider one vital aspect of criticality that could be generated by a failure: possible damage. A very simple method of criticality determination that can be used is to multiply the probability of failure by the damage that could be generated. Another method entails ranking by:

$$CR = P_L \bullet Q \bullet F_R$$

where CR = criticality ranking;

P_L = probable damage resulting from a specific failure mode;

Q = probability of component failure ($1 -$ reliability);

F_R = ratio of occurrence of a specific failure mode.

A specific component can have more than one mode of failure, with only certain ones possibly causing damage or injury. F_R is the ratio of those failures that could generate a specific damage level to the total number of possible failures. These failure ratios can be determined for new systems from manufacturer's data on failure modes, network analyses, tests, or combinations of these sources of information.

Criticality rankings are generally expressed as probabilities, but they may also be indicated in other ways. In some instances, they are designated in categories from 1 to 10 to show the principal items that could generate problems or as letters starting with the beginning of the alphabet. These last two methods are often not based on probabilities but reflect experience, especially with subsequent systems.

Ranking does not complete a critical component analysis. Evaluations must also be made to establish the preventive and corrective measures that should be taken and the safeguards to be incorporated if the hazard that could be generated by critical component failure does pass out of control.

Because of the broad variety of components that can be considered critical, no preferred method of analysis can be specified. A number of specific analyses can be used, depending on the system. Fault-tree analysis, circuit analysis, or failure modes and effects analysis can be used to determine items that would be critical or designs in which single-point failures could occur. A container whose function is to hold a highly pressurized gas can be subjected to any number of different analyses to ensure that its design strength is adequate for the purpose.

Limitations

Failure modes and effects analysis (and failure mode and criticality analysis) is extremely effective when it is applied to the analysis of single units or single failures. Its inadequacies have led to the development of other techniques, such as fault-tree analysis, which it complements excellently. An assembly may have failure modes that do not result in accidents; failure rates related to those safe modes must be eliminated from determination of accident probabilities. The problem of identifying exactly which failures contribute to the occurrence of a specific catastrophe can be overcome to a great extent by using logic methods. Fault trees, in their original usages, were diagrams showing how the data developed by failure modes and effects analysis should be interrelated to arrive at a specific event. In many instances, the reverse process is now being used: A logic analysis establishes those events, failures, or successful operations that could contribute to an accident. A failure modes and effects analysis then studies in detail those conditions that could cause failures, the modes in which failures could take place, and the preventive or safety measures to be taken.

The second major deficiency in this method is the inadequate attention generally given to human error problems because of the concentration on hardware failures. Since every product involves the use of personnel to some degree, and since errors constitute a large percentage of all accident causes, this is a significant omission in any safety study.

Until recently, analyses were based almost entirely on components and their modes and rates of failure. Rough estimates of reliability were made from the number of components in the product. However, studies of product failures have shown that a much greater number are the result of connector problems rather than the components themselves.

Although environmental conditions are considered in establishing the stresses that could cause hardware to fail, the probabilities of occurrence of such environment stresses are rarely used. Instead, a usage factor is incorporated for the type of product application. Another factor is applied for the reduction of theoretical reliability that could result from the substandard manufacture of an assembly. This factor is extremely rough even over a large sample because some items may suffer little damage during production and other items may be so badly damaged that they fail soon.

Fault Hazard Analysis (FHA)

The four major categories of hazards (hazardous characteristics, malfunctions, environmental effects, and operator errors) have already been discussed. Failure modes and effects analysis (FMEA) reviews only one category: malfunctions. To compensate for the lack of consideration of the other hazards, safety personnel developed and have used fault hazard analysis.

Fault hazard analysis was developed at approximately the same time as fault-tree analysis (discussed in the next chapter) was developed. Fault hazard analysis does not use the same logic principles that the fault-tree analysis and the quantitative aspects of failure modes and effects analysis do. It was used originally by analysts who had no knowledge of fault-tree analysis and by those who

wanted a tabulated output which the fault trees did not provide. (Some analysts, as shown in the next chapter, have begun using tabulated data to complement the trees.)

The column headings often used in fault hazard analysis are shown below. Headings can be adapted to the personal preferences of the analyst. The fault hazard analysis is a qualitative analysis; it usually does not have a place for entering quantitative probabilities as does the failure modes and effects table shown in Figure 14-1. The major reason is that probability data on hazardous characteristics and environmental effects are difficult or impossible to obtain. The chief use of the fault hazard analysis has therefore been as a more detailed extension of the preliminary hazard analysis.

Circuit Logic Analysis

Circuit analysis using Boolean logic has been used for years for the design and evaluation of complex electric and electronic circuitry. Its use is increasing as products and their electrical systems grow more complex, as the consequences of failures become more severe, as familiarity with the methodology grows, as more and more electronic devices are used, and as new applications are found. (Boolean logic is also being used increasingly for fluidic, pneumatic, and hydraulic circuit design and analysis.) It has been used to determine how a product can be affected by failures of components in a circuit and also whether or not the circuit can generate damaging outputs. With the increased use of electronics in commonly used products, a knowledge of the principles of logic analysis becomes increasingly important. The fundamental principles of Boolean logic and mathematics are shown in Figure 14-4. Boolean logic also provides the means to establish the quantitative safety level of an electrical circuit or system. The principles involved also form the basis for the fault-tree method (Chapter 15) now widely used in safety analysis, although most of the symbology and the methodology differ from that for circuit analysis.

In circuit analysis, operation is described in terms of interacting electronic components and mechanical devices that open or close to permit the flow of electrical current from one point to another. These circuit elements are represented by logic symbols. A logic equation can be developed to express the condition (on or off, open or closed, successful or failed) of each element and the interrelationships required to produce a specific output

Column Headings for Fault Hazard Analysis

Item, Event, or Condition	What Is the Potential problem?	Why Can It Be a Problem?	Will it Cause Downstream Damage?	What Upstream Input or Component Can "Command" the Undesirable Event?	Compensation or Control	Remarks

Boolean Logic and Its Applications

Boolean algebra was developed originally for the study of symbolic logic. Its rules and expressions in mathematical symbols permit complicated propositions to be clarified and simplified. Boolean algebra is especially useful where conditions can be expressed in no more than two values, such as yes or no, true or false, on or off, up or down, go or no-go. It has found wide application in areas other than symbolic logic. For example, it is used extensively in the design of computers and other electromechanical assemblies incorporating large numbers of on-off (switching) circuits. Other uses are in probability analysis, studies involving decision making, and more recently, in safety and fluidics. The chief difference between the various disciplines in their employment of Boolean algebra is in notation and symbology.

A <u>set</u> is a group of objects having at least one characteristic in common. The set may be a collection of objects, conditions, events, symbols, ideas, or mathematical relationships. The unity of a set can be expressed by the number 1, and an empty set, which contains none of these, by 0. The numerals 1 and 0 are not quantitative values: $1 + 1$ does not equal 2. They are merely symbols. There are no values between the two as there are in probability calculations. Set relationships are sometimes illustrated by Venn diagrams. The following rectangle represents a set of elements that have an undefined common characteristic. In addition, a subset has the characteristic A. All other elements in the set do not have the A-characteristic and are considered being "not-A," designated by $\overline{A}$. $\overline{A}$ is the <u>complement</u> of A, and vice versa. It can be seen that the total of A and $\overline{A}$ is the complete set, expressed mathematically by $A + \overline{A} = 1$, where the left side of the equation is the <u>union</u> of A and $\overline{A}$. The + sign is read "OR", and may be designated in mathematical expressions by other symbols, such as U.

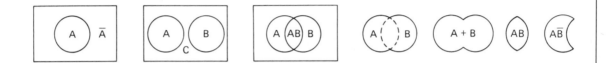

The second diagram illustrates the concept of <u>disjoint</u>, or <u>mutually exclusive</u>, sets. The elements of one subset are not included in the others, and therefore are not interrelated (other than being in the same set). In this case, however, because A, B, and C contain all the elements in the overall set, they are said to be mutually exclusive and <u>exhaustive</u>: $A + B + C = 1$.

The third diagram indicates that some elements of A also have B characteristics. These are indicated by AB, $A \cdot B$ or $A \cap B$, called the <u>intersection</u> of A and B. The intersection contains all the elements with the characteristics of both A <u>and</u> B. When all elements with the characteristic A are counted, those in AB will also be counted. The remaining diagrams in the row illustrate some of the relationships between union, intersection, and complement. Numerous other relationships that can be employed in mathematical expressions have been developed, some of them having been designed as <u>laws</u>. These are listed below, with some explanations on their meaning in Boolean logic.

RELATIONSHIP	LAW	EXPLANATION
$A \cdot 1 = A$	Full and Empty Sets	The only portion within 1 that is both 1 <u>and</u> A is that within A itself.
$A \cdot 0 = 0$		An impossible condition; if it is within the set, it cannot be outside the set.
$A + 0 = A$		The element in a subset plus anything outside the set will have only the characteristics of the subset.
$A + 1 = 1$		The whole, expressed by 1, cannot be exceeded.
$\overline{\overline{A}} = A$	Involution Law	The complement of the complement is the item itself.
$A \cdot \overline{A} = 0$	Complementary Relations	An impossibility; a condition cannot be both A <u>and</u> $\overline{A}$ at the same time.
$A + \overline{A} = 1$		Those elements with a specific characteristic and those without it constitute the total set.
$A \cdot A = A$	Idempotent Laws	An identity.
$A + A = A$		Also an identity.
$A \cdot B = B \cdot A$	Commutative Laws	The elements having both characteristics have them no matter the order in which expressed.

Figure 14-4. Boolean logic and its applications.

Boolean Logic and Its Applications

RELATIONSHIP	LAW	EXPLANATION
A + B = B + A		The total of those elements having the characteristic A or B will be the same no matter the order in which they are expressed.
A(B·C) = (A·B)C	Associative Laws	The elements having all the characteristics A, B and C will have them no matter the order in which expressed.
A + (B + C) = (A + B) + C		The total of all the elements in any subsets will be the same no matter the order in which expressed.
A(B + C) = (A·B) + (A·C)	Distributive Laws	The union of one subset with two others can also be expressed as the union of their intersections.
A + (B·C) = (A + B)·(A + C)		The union of one subset with the intersection of two others can also be expressed by the intersection of the unions of the common subset with the other two.
A(A + B) = A	Absorption Laws	A(A + B) = AA + AB = A + AB since AA = A; A + AB = A(1 + B) = A since B is included in 1.
A + (A·B) = A		A + (A·B) = A + AB = A(1 + B) = A.
$\overline{A·B} = \overline{A} + \overline{B}$	Dualization (de Morgan's) Laws	The complement of an intersection is the union of the individual complements.
$\overline{A + B} = \overline{A}·\overline{B}$		The complement of the union is the intersection of the complements.

Other useful identities are frequently used for simplification of complex Boolean equations. Four of these are:

Identity	Derivation
$A + \overline{A}B = A + B$	Using the Distributive Law: $(A + \overline{A}) · (A + B) = A + B$
$A·(\overline{A} + B) = AB$	Using the Distributive Law: $A · \overline{A} + AB = AB$
$(A + B)(\overline{A} + C) · (A + C) = AC + BC$	Expanding the last two terms: $(A + B)(A\overline{A} + AC + \overline{A}C + CC)$; $CC = C$, $A\overline{A} = 0$, $AC + \overline{A}C = C(A + \overline{A}) = C(1) = C$, and $C + C = C$; ∴ remainder is $(A + B)C$, or $AC + BC$.
$AB + \overline{A}C + BC = AB + \overline{A}C$	This can be simplified by adding a term such as $A + \overline{A}$. The left-hand side then becomes: $AB + \overline{A}C + BC(A + \overline{A}) = AB (1 + C) + \overline{A}C(1 + B) = AB + \overline{A}C$.

BOOLEAN LOGIC APPLIED TO ELECTRONICS DESIGN

With the development of Boolean logic for electronic systems, the concept of gates or connectives was introduced. The symbols for these, a few of which are shown and explained below, are used in logic diagrams to indicate the interrelationships in circuits. These circuits employ numerous bi-stable, or two-state, devices, that can be considered open or closed, off or on. These are known as switching functions, and the mathematics is called switching algebra or network logic.

The truth tables shown on the right are means to indicate when a specific state will exist as an output when any combination of inputs is present. As shown here, the symbol 1 indicates that an input or output is or will be present; the 0 indicates that it is not or will not be present. Each of the truth tables shown is for a two-input gate. Gates with more inputs are more common, differing only in complexity.

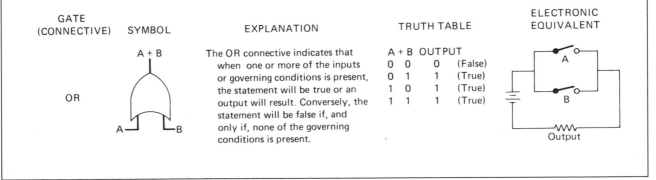

GATE (CONNECTIVE)	SYMBOL	EXPLANATION	TRUTH TABLE	ELECTRONIC EQUIVALENT
OR	A + B (gate symbol) A, B	The OR connective indicates that when one or more of the inputs or governing conditions is present, the statement will be true or an output will result. Conversely, the statement will be false if, and only if, none of the governing conditions is present.	A + B OUTPUT 0 0 0 (False) 0 1 1 (True) 1 0 1 (True) 1 1 1 (True)	(circuit diagram with switches A, B and Output)

Figure 14-4 (cont'd). Boolean logic and its applications.

Boolean Logic and Its Applications

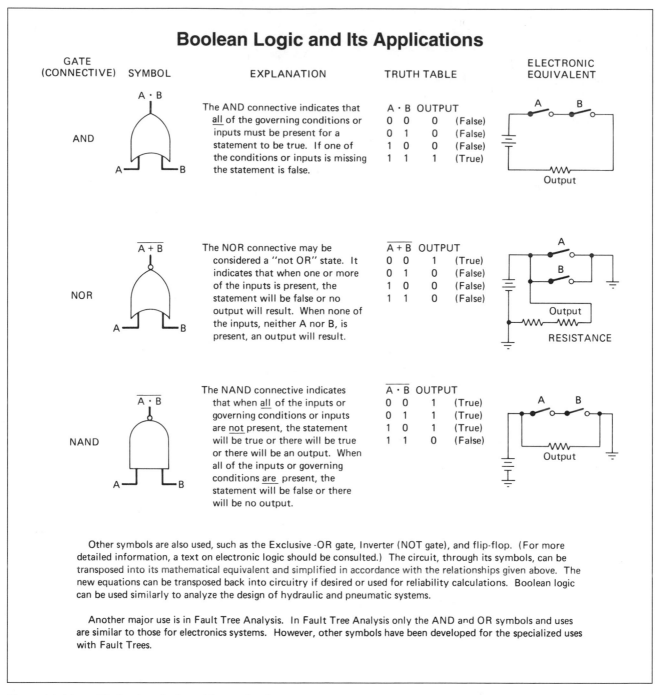

GATE (CONNECTIVE)	SYMBOL	EXPLANATION	TRUTH TABLE	ELECTRONIC EQUIVALENT

AND — $A \cdot B$

The AND connective indicates that all of the governing conditions or inputs must be present for a statement to be true. If one of the conditions or inputs is missing the statement is false.

A	B	OUTPUT	
0	0	0	(False)
0	1	0	(False)
1	0	0	(False)
1	1	1	(True)

NOR — $\overline{A + B}$

The NOR connective may be considered a "not OR" state. It indicates that when one or more of the inputs is present, the statement will be false or no output will result. When none of the inputs, neither A nor B, is present, an output will result.

$\overline{A + B}$		OUTPUT	
0	0	1	(True)
0	1	0	(False)
1	0	0	(False)
1	1	0	(False)

NAND — $\overline{A \cdot B}$

The NAND connective indicates that when all of the inputs or governing conditions or inputs are not present, the statement will be true or there will be true or there will be an output. When all of the inputs or governing conditions are present, the statement will be false or there will be no output.

$\overline{A \cdot B}$		OUTPUT	
0	0	1	(True)
0	1	1	(True)
1	0	1	(True)
1	1	0	(False)

Other symbols are also used, such as the Exclusive -OR gate, Inverter (NOT gate), and flip-flop. (For more detailed information, a text on electronic logic should be consulted.) The circuit, through its symbols, can be transposed into its mathematical equivalent and simplified in accordance with the relationships given above. The new equations can be transposed back into circuitry if desired or used for reliability calculations. Boolean logic can be used similarly to analyze the design of hydraulic and pneumatic systems.

Another major use is in Fault Tree Analysis. In Fault Tree Analysis only the AND and OR symbols and uses are similar to those for electronics systems. However, other symbols have been developed for the specialized uses with Fault Trees.

Figure 14-4 (cont'd). Boolean logic and its applications.

event. The equations can be simplified to eliminate redundant expressions. The final equation and the circuit drawing by which the equation can be depicted are representations of how the original circuit will operate.

A separate equation is written for each connective point or "gate" and these equations are then combined into one equation for the ultimate or end event. These equations for the end events are often initially very complex. However, it is frequently possible to apply reduction techniques to simplify them by eliminating logical redundancies using the Boolean identities and relationships in Figure 14-4. For example, a logic equation might consist of

$$AB \cdot AC \cdot BD(AB + \overline{AB})$$

which can then be expanded to

$$AB \cdot AC \cdot BD \cdot AB + AB \cdot AC \cdot BD \cdot \overline{AC}$$

One AB in the first group can be eliminated, leaving $AB \cdot AC \cdot BD$. Also, since $AC \cdot \overline{AC} = 0$ (AC cannot be both on and off at the same time), the second term can be eliminated entirely. The final expression is therefore $AB \cdot AC \cdot BD$.

Figure 14-5 shows an x-ray safety interlock circuit as a wiring diagram; Figure 14-5 also shows the control circuit portion of it as a logic diagram. Figure 14-6 shows the simplified rearrangement of Figure 14-5. (Figure 15-8 also analyzes the circuit for safety using the fault-tree method.) To conduct a logic analysis, the logic diagram will be used, but the student should also follow each event on the circuit diagram.

The circuit is used to ensure that power to the x-ray generator can be applied to the x-ray cabinet only when the door is closed. When the door is closed, two plungers in the door, which are interconnected by a shorting bar, close two microswitches at the front of the cabinet. These microswitches are in series. Closing the x-ray *ON* switch energizes the circuit initially to provide the x-ray generator with power when the cabinet is connected to a power source. Initial activation also activates a holding circuit which keeps the power on so that the operator need not keep holding in the x-ray *ON* switch. Opening the door to the cabinet or pushing the x-ray *OFF* switch breaks the circuit.

The analysis of the logic diagram begins at A, which represents AC POWER IS ON TO X-RAY TRANSFORMER. A is the output of an AND gate, indicating that inputs B AND C must occur for A to occur. C represents that the machine must be connected to the power line (it is assumed the power source is functioning properly). B is the output of another AND gate with input E, which represents that the shorting bar in the SHORTED PLUNGER ASSEMBLY IN DOOR is properly connected, and input J, which is the output from a logic arrangement known as a *latching circuit*. A latching circuit "remembers" an instruction even after the input is removed, and it is "set" until another "reset" instruction is received. (Without the latching circuit, the x-ray *ON* switch would have to be continually held in the *ON* position.) When the x-ray *ON* switch is activated (high), it (event S) will produce a high output G from the latching circuit. The latching circuit will produce J with two inputs, H and $\overline{K}$. Both H and $\overline{K}$ are dependent on F. F can be assumed to be the fact that the door is closed, since this is the condition that must exist if all prior conditions H, P, R, and L are satisfied. When the x-ray *OFF* switch is not activated, T is considered high. When the *OFF* switch *is* activated, both T and S will be low since the two are presumed to be interlocked.

Examining the possibilities of failures, we can see that nothing can occur unless the door is closed. If the *ON* switch fails closed, the result would be the same as if the switch were intentionally closed, but nothing would operate unless the door were shut.

The Boolean equations are shown in Figure 14-6. The equations and relationships are very simple and need very little simplification. The final equation can be represented by a simplified logic diagram, which is also shown.

Systems that are designed so they will *not* operate until specific events occur involve the concept of *blocking elements*. A blocking element is a device that must be activated or inactivated to change from a safe to an unsafe state. This can be done by a person's action or as the result of an electrical or mechanical process. Electrical interlocks are blocking elements. A blocking element may be connected to a device installed in a circuit to prevent passage of current unless the prescribed condition is satisfied. When the condition is satisfied, the device, such as a relay, will change its state so that the circuit, system, or product (not the relay itself) becomes unsafe. A timer may prevent a device from operating for a set time; the timer acts as a blocking element.

Logic diagrams are well suited to evaluating the effects of blocking elements and when inputs will cause them to change state. In circuits that have interacting elements, it may be found by examination of logic diagrams that certain elements that supposedly act as blocking elements are ineffective. Two or more circuits may exist which create parallel paths. One path may have fewer blocking elements than the other, or the failure probabilities for one path may be far higher than for the parallel path which has fewer blocks.

Logic analysis can be used to determine when a system that has blocking elements that must be removed in order to operate will become unsafe. The input conditions at any AND gate indicate where and how many factors must be satisfied to remove any block. Analysis can show when in the progress of an operation each safety block will be removed. An indicator can show the operator when only one of a specific number of safety blocks remains or when all blocks have been removed, the system is enabled to operate, and extreme care must be exercised.

Thus, applications of logic analysis with safety implications include:

1. Investigations of the possibilities of inadvertent activation of the product or its subassemblies by electrical or electromechanical means.

2. Failure analysis of such devices as fuel quantity indicators, malfunction detection systems, or warning systems.

3. Investigation of interlocks to ensure orderly operation of timers and other devices that must be activated sequentially, deenergization of electrical equipment if access panels or doors are opened, and the interrelationships of blocking elements to prevent occurrences of adverse events.

4. Determination of components and interconnections that must be safeguarded or separated to ensure that blocking elements are not bypassed.

5. Evaluations of occurrences that might make single-point failures possible.

X-Ray Safety Interlock Circuit

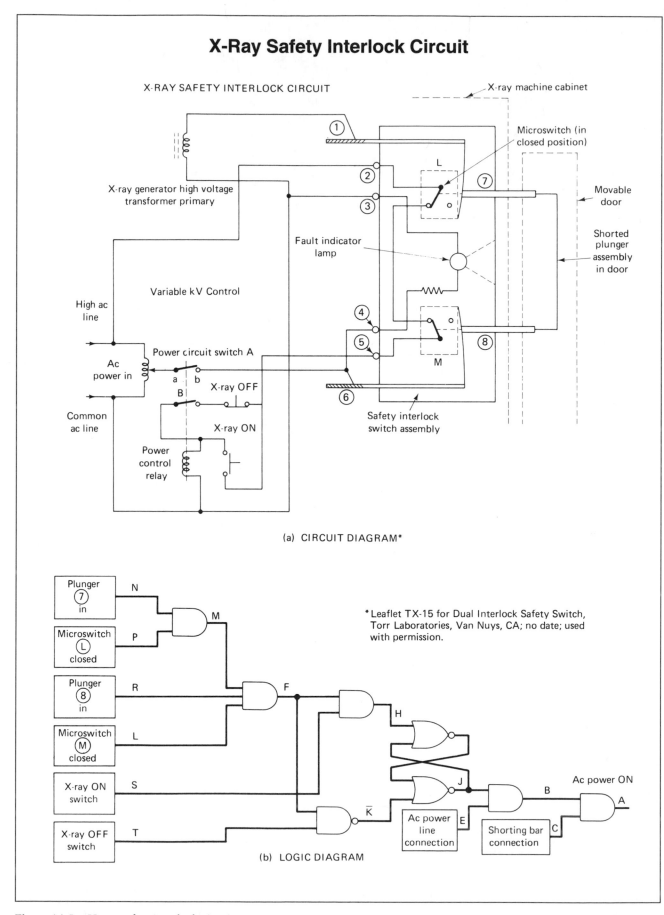

(a) CIRCUIT DIAGRAM*

*Leaflet TX-15 for Dual Interlock Safety Switch, Torr Laboratories, Van Nuys, CA; no date; used with permission.

(b) LOGIC DIAGRAM

Figure 14-5. X-ray safety interlock circuit.

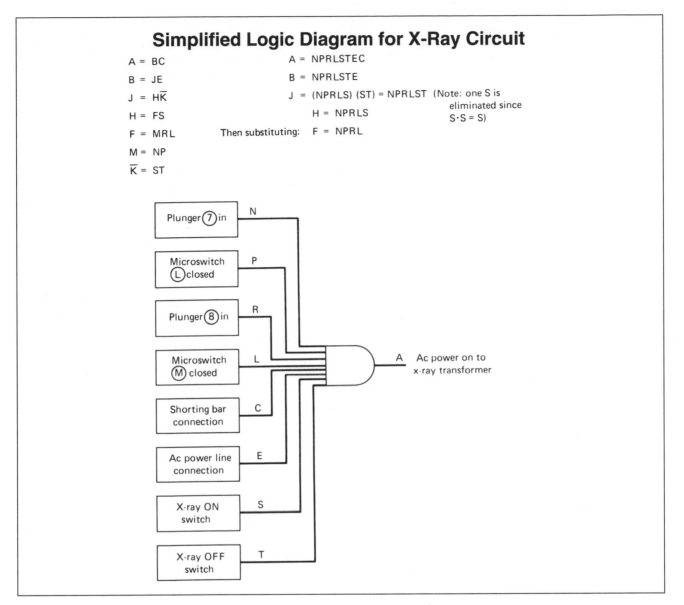

Simplified Logic Diagram for X-Ray Circuit

A = BC

B = JE

J = HK̄

H = FS

F = MRL

M = NP

K̄ = ST

A = NPRLSTEC

B = NPRLSTE

J = (NPRLS) (ST) = NPRLST (Note: one S is eliminated since S·S = S)

H = NPRLS

Then substituting: F = NPRL

Plunger ⑦ in — N

Microswitch ⓛ closed — P

Plunger ⑧ in — R

Microswitch Ⓜ closed — L

Shorting bar connection — C

Ac power line connection — E

X-ray ON switch — S

X-ray OFF switch — T

A — Ac power on to x-ray transformer

Figure 14-6. Simplified logic diagram for x-ray circuit.

Interface Analysis

An interface safety analysis is made to determine the incompatibilities between assemblies and subsystems of a product that could result in accidents. The analysis must establish that separate units can be integrated into a viable system and also that normal operation of one unit will not impair the performance or damage another unit or the entire product. The various relationships that must be considered can be categorized principally as *physical*, *functional*, or *flow*.

Physical Relationships

Two units might each be well designed and built individually and operate properly during separate tests, but they may not fit together because of dimensional differences or they may provide other difficulties which might eventually lead to safety problems. Following are examples.

1. The clearance between units is so small that there is a good possibility that one or more units will be damaged when one unit is being removed or emplaced.

2. Access to or egress from equipment may be impossible or restricted because of dimensions or lack of adequate clearances (Figure 13-6).

3. Inability to tighten, join, or mate parts that should fit closely together can result in structural failures. It may be impossible to join two units because the bolt holes are misaligned. Assemblies must not only mate properly, they must also be easy to separate when required for maintenance. The mating process must also be such that assembly errors will be impossible, have an extremely low probability of occurrence, or will lead to no further problem if a mistake is made.

4. A filter in a tight spot from which it is difficult to be removed will not be cleaned. As a result, the system may clog or the filter may pass matter that should have been removed.

Functional Relationships

Outputs of one unit constitute the inputs to a downstream unit. Unless these outputs and inputs are correct, damage to the downstream unit may result. Conditions that could occur are categorized as follows:

1. *Zero output.* The output unit fails completely. Interconnection failures occur so that the receiving unit does not receive the output of the upstream unit. A connection failure at either end of a line, a break in the line, a short circuit, or loss of hydraulic fluid could cause this.

2. *Degraded output.* A partial failure occurs so that designed or programmed output of the upstream unit is not received by the downstream unit. Partial clogging of hydraulic or cooling unit passages can reduce fluid flow. This can cause decreased cooling effect, delay in activation of brakes or other hydraulically-operated equipment, inadequate lubrication, and similar deficiency effects.

3. *Erratic output.* This condition consists of intermittent or unstable operation. Chattering of relays or valves may cause surges in electric power or fluid flow.

4. *Excessive output.* A unit may overspeed because of a governor failure; the temperature of liquid produced by a heater may be too high because of a thermostat failure; or downstream pressure may be excessive when a pressure regulator fails. Automobile batteries and electrical systems have been damaged because of excessive outputs from faulty voltage regulators.

5. *Unprogrammed output.* Inadvertent operation or erroneous output could cause damage to downstream units. Inadvertent activation or repeats have often caused injuries to machine operators.

6. *Undesirable side effects.* Although its programmed outputs are within prescribed limits, a unit may also generate other outputs that could be damaging. An electrical assembly may perform its function, but it may generate heat that can shorten the lives of nearby units. A television set may generate its picture properly but emit radiation that could injure viewers.

Flow Relationships

Flow between two units may involve a fluid such as water, fuel, lubricating oil, steam, or air or involve energy (electrical, electromagnetic, hydraulic, or thermal) in closed systems, for example, in piping or wiring. Flow may also be unconfined, such as radiation of heat from one body to another. Review of flow relationships constitute part of an interface analysis. The most frequent, severe, and varied problems with any product are generally with the fluids and energy that must flow from one unit to another through confined passages. Some of the potential flow problem causes and effects are indicated below:

1. The connection between two units may be faulty. The lack of adequate bonding can result in electrical assemblies in a product being shock hazards because they are not grounded.

2. The interconnection may fail entirely. High-pressure gas hoses have burst when inadvertently overloaded to pressures greater than those for which they were designed or which they could withstand in a deteriorated condition. Failures have caused hoses to whip violently, injuring persons and damaging equipment within their range.

3. The interconnection can suffer a partial failure. Leakage may occur in the line itself or at the interface between a line and unit. If the line contains a hazardous fluid, even a very small leak may prove highly damaging or dangerous. Analyses must therefore consider the characteristics of the fluids and the effects of any loss. Some characteristics and effects to be considered are:

   (a) *Flammability.* A spray from a high-pressure leak exposes minute particles of liquid to the oxygen in air, creating a highly flammable mixture which requires far less energy to ignite than does a liquid in bulk form.

   (b) *Toxicity.* Some toxic agents are readily detectable by their odor or irritant properties even when the amounts leaked are small. It is sometimes advisable to add an odorant to provide warnings of leaks of a fluid which is odorless or dangerous. Carbon monoxide, nitrogen, or vaporized solvent leaks in enclosed spaces have resulted in the deaths of persons who were unaware that the oxygen level was less than that necessary for respiration.

   (c) *Corrosiveness.* The fluid might be compatible with the material in the line through which it normally flows, but leakage could expose other materials, and possibly endanger personnel. Even so mild a fluid as water will cause corrosion of many ferrous materials.

   (d) *Loss of pressure.* Loss of fluid in a line incorporated in a product to transfer energy hydraulically or pneumatically can degrade the system so that pressure cannot be maintained. If the system is one used for safety purposes, such as an automobile brake system, or one whose operational loss might result in an accident, the loss of the fluid can result in adverse consequences.

   (e) *Lubricity.* Oils and other liquids cause surfaces to become slippery so that personnel can fall and injure themselves. Oil or grease on traction surfaces can cause wheels to slip.

   (f) *Loss of material.* The fluid may be in a line from a storage or pump unit to a second unit where the fluid will perform a function whose failure could result in damage. Loss of oil because of a leak between an oil tank and an engine can cause a lubrication failure that would result in engine damage. An oil leak can cause damage to the environment.

(g) *Contamination.* An oil or solvent on food, insulation, or fabric might ruin the usefulness of the material it contaminates. Other liquids, especially those that leave residues, can coat parts so that they cannot carry out their intended functions.

(h) *Moisture and water.* Moisture and water can cause high humidity, resulting in personnel discomfort and irritation, which increase the tendency to make errors. Water in electrical connectors can cause short-circuiting and product failure.

(i) *Odor.* A foul-smelling gas can irritate or sicken people so that they perform required duties poorly. In some cases, they cannot perform them at all. The amount of gas which is offensive varies and depends on a number of factors, but even a substance that is pleasant at low concentrations is offensive at high concentrations.

Interface analysis illustrates the fact that most products, their subsystems, their operators, and their interrelationships make up a system. Figure 14-7 lists the many subsystems of which products can be constituted, which they constitute, or with which they can interface. Highly complex products with their human operators will incorporate many of these subsystems and their potential hazards. A human may not only be the operator but the control subsystem (guiding a bicycle), propulsion subsystem (pedaling the bicycle), power subsystem (providing power for pedaling), and sensor subsystem (determining if faster pedaling is needed or if a rock must be avoided).

Not only does each subsystem sometimes have inherent hazards but one subsystem may affect another subsystem even while operating normally. One subsystem may generate heat which may affect another subsystem. A malfunction of the lubrication subsystem may cause failure of the power subsystem. To determine whether any interrelationship exists, a checklist should be used. A form such as that in Figure 7-1 can be used in conjunction with the checklists in Appendix A. If an interrelationship involves a potential hazard, the appropriate box in the matrix in Figure 7-1 can be marked. On another sheet notes are made against the row-column address of the box which would indicate the potential hazards that could exist and the reasons the analyst believes that they could exist, the adverse effects that could be generated, and any recommendations for correction or safeguard.

Mapping

Problems that could develop because of the locations or proximities of units, lines, and hazards are frequently revealed by mapping. Mapping involves plotting the problem in question graphically and then determining the existing interrelationships. Below are numerous examples that illustrate the methodology:

1. Distances between fuel lines and ignition sources, such as those on hot engines, can be established. The dangers existing when these are in close proximity are evident. Leakage of fuel from a poor connection or ruptured line onto a hot surface could result in a fire.[2] Many of these dangers can be recognized from drawings that show the locations of connections, lines, engines, spark-producing devices, and similar hazards. In such cases, lines can be designed with a minimal number of connections, connections could be placed where leakage would not hit the hot spot, or a means of isolation could be provided to separate the fuel line and the hot spot.

2. Locations of tanks in storage farms can be reviewed to ensure that there is adequate separation between fuels and oxidizers so that leakage of either one will not result in contact with the other; to determine the necessity for dikes or containment walls to hold liquids if a tank should rupture or leak; and to determine whether or not leakage could endanger personnel or facilities along channels down which the liquid would flow.

3. Mapping of fire zones and fire defense routes has been used extensively for chemical plants where hazardous processes are involved. High-temperature and high-pressure equipment are spotted in relation to other critical equipment that could be damaged if control of a process is lost and a fire or explosion results. Separation distances can be established. Access routes can be plotted for emergency equipment and personnel in case there is a fire or explosion.

4. Emergency evacuation routes, safety zones, and protective structures can also be mapped. These are especially useful when incorporated into contingency analyses and procedures to indicate to personnel the route they should take to safety and the areas and structures considered safe. Engineers who develop or analyze such procedures can use maps to ensure that routes are feasible, are the shortest possible, and involve no obstructions and to ensure that the interval required to move from an area of danger to one of safety is possible under the conditions and time limitations that could exist.

5. Noise level contours and the scopes of their effects can be reviewed through hazard mapping. The uppermost diagram in Figure 14-8 indicates the noise levels at various distances from different types of STOL aircraft. These noise level data are then used to prepare the middle diagram. The dotted portions show the noise levels at various distances from an aircraft that is making an approach and landing. The heavy lines show the noise levels as an aircraft takes off and makes a maximum turn to avoid restricted areas or to proceed on to another destination.[3] The contours established in this way can then be plotted

Product Subsystems

Subsystem	Purpose	Example	Hazards Inherent In This Subsystem
Power	To convert energy from one form to another in which it can be used in the product.	The power unit in an automobile, the engine, converts the chemical energy in gasoline to mechanical energy.	Uncontrolled conversion of energy can cause injury and damage. Loss of control might be fires involving fuels, and explosions, inadvertent activation of the product, or inoperability of the equipment when needed in a hazardous situation.
Fuel	To provide the material containing the energy which the power unit converts to a more usable form.	Gasoline and diesel oil for internal combustion engines, kerosene for heating systems and jet engines, coal for boiler heating.	Leakage or spillage of the fuel could permit fires to be generated; certain types of coal can ignite in spontaneous combustion; lack of fuel will result in lack of power when needed; spilled or leaked fuel can be slippery, contaminate foods and other materials, injure the environment.
Structural	To support, unite, and sometimes protect the other components and assemblies of a product.	Frame of equipment cabinet; truck chassis; skeleton in a body.	Failures can result in collapse of the product, vehicle or structure and loss of support for components and assemblies.
Sensor	Senses the status of operations of the product or its subassemblies or of the environment and informs the operators.	Thermostat or humidistat for an airconditioning system, oil pressure gauge for an engine.	Sensing failures can result in operator not taking proper or corrective action when required.
Operator	Makes decisions based on information from sensors, determines whether situation is normal or requires corrective action. Constitutes the "brain" of the system or product.	Automobile driver; automatic pilot; computer; operator of washer or sewing machine.	Failure to take necessary action when required, loss of control, making error can result in accident.
Control	To provide guidance and direction for operation of a product.	Steering assembly on a vehicle, rudder assembly on a boat, braking system, timer on washing machine.	Loss of directional or braking control of vehicles can result in collisions or upsets. Timing failure can result in cycling failure; failure of energy system to shut off when programmed, with resultant damage, as in a time controlled oven.
Communications	Transmits information between the various personnel, subsystems, and systems.	Nervous system in body, electrical wiring for signals, mechanical linkages, hydraulic and pneumatic lines, electromagnetic waves and pulses.	Lack of communications will make the system or product inoperative; with defective communications, confusion and error, possibly with accidents, will result.
Propulsion	Provides the means by which a mobile unit accomplishes its motion.	Transmission, drive system and wheels on an automobile; jet engines; propellers on aircraft, ships and boats.	Propulsion subsystems generally utilize most of the output of the power subsystems, therefore energy is usually available which can cause injury or damage.
Environmental Control	To protect or ease stresses on personnel or equipment in an adverse or less than optimal environment.	Air conditioning systems in vehicles; life support systems for aircraft, submarines, and space vehicles; cooling systems for electronic equipment.	Failures of environmental control where it is for comfort only may result in loss of operating efficiency which lead to accidents. Environment control loss in life support systems can lead to death of occupants. Loss of cooling reduces reliability of electronic equipment.
Lubrication	To reduce friction of moving parts and thereby lessen motive power required and heat generated.	Oil systems in vehicles; grease lubrication in vehicles, appliances, and construction equipment.	Loss of lubrication can result in damage to moving parts which contact each other. Increase in heat generated may cause parts to expand unduly and to seize.
Safety	To prevent injury or damage in case of failure of one of the other subsystems or of the product.	Lifeboats on a ship; ejection seats in an aircraft; seat belts, shoulder harness, and airbags in automobiles.	Since this subsystem is operable in a hazardous situation, failure will generally result in injury or damage. Analyses of this subsystem should therefore be more critical than for any other subsystem.

Figure 14-7. Product subsystems.

on a map of a proposed landing site. Then the analysis can be evaluated on whether or not a safe route for the aircraft can be established while maintaining an acceptable noise level in inhabited areas. An analysis such as this was prepared to evaluate the patterns of noise levels of the Concorde when landing and takeoff were proposed for New York. Similar analyses can be made to determine and evaluate the noise problems and contours of a piece of equipment to be installed in a location where noise might be a problem. Similar plots have been made to indicate the hazard levels and existence of electromagnetic radiation from microwave equipment.

6. Figure 14-9 shows how mapping was used to analyze accidents involving fires with Army helicopters. Although the mapping was used here in accident analysis, it was undoubtedly an effective way to study whether or not similar hazards exist in new designs. The layouts indicated the susceptibility of fuel tanks to rupture after a hard impact. Study of the seven helicopters in Figure 14-9 showed that in helicopter accidents 90% of the fires were generated by the initial impact of a crash or immediately thereafter. In 80% of the fires, ruptured fuel cells and broken fuel lines caused spillage or leakage of gasoline which ignited when it hit a hot surface, such as the engine exhaust. In major accidents, the helicopter generally rolls over and lies on its side. At least one of the personnel exits is blocked; in some helicopters, it is the only way out of the passenger space. In addition, the fuel tank might come to rest in a position where its remaining fuel would spill onto the hot engine below. Mapping could help determine whether or not there are such problems in new helicopters.

7. Harold R. Willis has suggested a procedure[4] for analyzing the dangers that could be encountered as a bus makes its rounds picking up and delivering children. The purpose of the procedure is to minimize the possibilities of train–bus accidents. The procedure can also be used to evaluate where other types of accidents could occur along bus routes and to provide maps showing routes and potential hazards. Safeguards could then be provided against potential hazards. Public authorities could then approve or disapprove the analysis after review or recommend changes. After the route has been approved and after suitable hazard control measures have been provided, drivers could be given copies of the analysis describing where the remaining hazards exist and instructing how to deal with these hazards.

8. Mapping can be used to determine the extent of potential micrometeorological problems. The maps can illustrate the directions of prevailing winds and areas and facilities that could be affected by contaminants. For example, a liquid oxygen plant was subject to reboiler and compressor explosions. Investigation revealed that acetylene released into the atmosphere from a nearby plant was wind-borne to the compressor intakes. The acetylene accumulated until it reached amounts that reacted explo-

sively. Similar plots can be used to determine the possible effects if a toxic, corrosive, or flammable gas were released by accident or as exhaust from a chemical process in an industrial plant.

Checklist Reviews

Reviews using checklists are a favorite and sometimes effective means of finding hazardous characteristics or other safety problems which could exist in a product or its operation, of determining that controls have been instituted, and of ensuring that a design means has met stipulated requirements. Checklists assist designers in ensuring that they do not incorporate adverse features into the product and that adverse features that cannot be avoided or eliminated are provided with suitable safeguards. Such lists are effective in refreshing a designer's, analyst's, or reviewer's memory. They can guide a person to good engineering practices or specific stipulations in standards, specifications, and codes. Safety engineers and other reviewing personnel also benefit from checklists which help ensure that designers have avoided specifically prohibited or poor practices and that mandatory requirements have been satisfied.

This book has numerous examples of checklists. One method of preparing a checklist is to make a list of questions based on a specific standard. A series can be developed relating to a product, component, or hazard based on a company, industry, or government standard or on good engineering practices. (In many instances a company's own standards may exceed those of industry or the government.) One method of preparing the questions is to rephrase the applicable requirement in question form. In many instances, the checklist is created by listing the requirements of the standard in their existing format.

Frequently the source of the checklist item is included in parentheses at the end of the question or statement. Including the source from which the item was derived is especially helpful if there is a controversy between designers and reviewers about the necessity of incorporating a design feature. When the designer can be shown or can note for himself or herself that the checklist item is based on a firm requirement and not just on the opinion or desire of the reviewer, the designer is more likely to prepare a design or to make changes to conform.

Another indicator frequently shown in parentheses is how the checklist requirement should be verified. As explained in Chapter 13, there are four broad categories of verification usually used: analysis, examination, demonstration, and test. The letters A, E, D, T, or combinations of these letters can be shown at the end of the requirement to indicate which verification should and will be used.

Some checklists provide column spaces for entering remarks on whether or not a provision has been complied with. Other checklists provide column spaces for entering

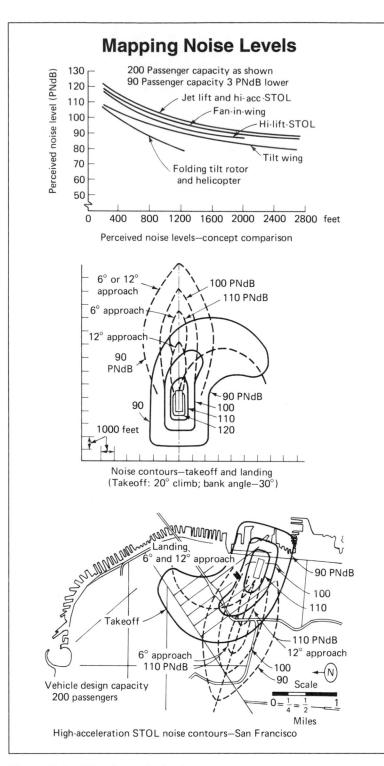

Figure 14-8. Mapping noise levels.

a mark when the item has been satisfied, for answering "Yes" or "No," or for entering comments such as expected completion date, adequacy of a design or procedure to satisfy the checklist items, or similar remarks. In certain cases, checklists may require supplementary lists or tables because an item to be checked may have multiple answers. For example, one answer might be "Yes," another answer might be "No," and so on. In this case, a checklist question might be, "Have electrical connectors been polarized to prevent incorrect connections which could result in equipment malfunctions and damage?" The product may have 20 to 30 connectors. A "Yes" or "No" answer would not be adequate; it would be necessary to review and list each connector and the review results.

Another problem that often arises in the preparation of checklists is applicability. When standard lists are derived

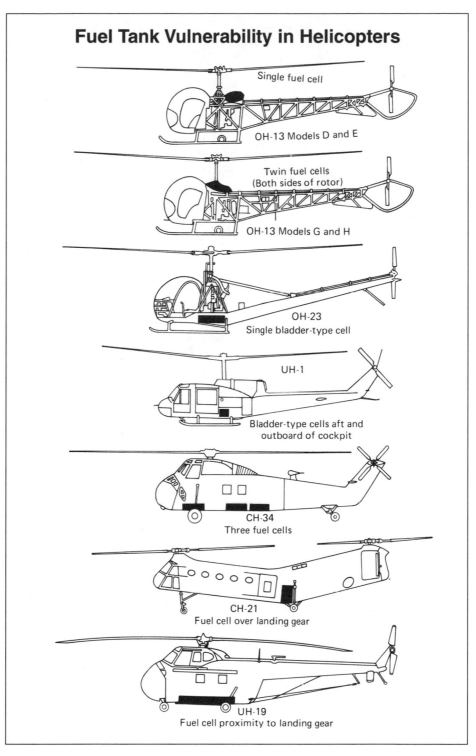

Figure 14-9. Fuel tank vulnerability in helicopters.

from handbooks or similar sources, many of the checklist entries may not be applicable to the product being analyzed. Lists prepared by the method discussed above for a specific product would be more productive.

The checklist format may consist of a series of questions or statements arranged as sequentially as possible within similar areas of review. These sequences may involve dealing with the largest assembly being reviewed first and then with smaller and smaller units. A good practice in preparing a checklist is to first list the items as they come into mind. Usually, one question leads to another. The next step is to eliminate redundancies and then reorder the items into sequences.

To minimize problems *after* a design is completed, it is advisable to provide the designer with a copy of the checklist *before* design is begun. Having to *change* a design in order to eliminate an adverse or inadequate feature or to meet a mandatory or desirable requirement is more costly than designing to avoid or control it in the first place.

Notes

[1] *Department of Defense, Military Standardization Handbook: Reliability Stress and Failure Rate Data for Electronic Equipment*, MIL-HDBK-217B (Washington, D.C., 1965). Other documents on failure rates available from the U.S. Department of Commerce National Technical Information Service include: George Chernowitz, et al., *Electro Mechanical Component Reliability*, American Power Jet Company, AD-422-327; Donald R. Fulton, *Nonelectronic Reliability Notebook*, Rome Air Development Center, January 1975, ADA-005657.

[2] *The Los Angeles Times*, January 19, 1976, had the following item: "Washington (AP)—The fire that destroyed a federally funded prototype mass transit bus near Phoenix last May apparently was caused by leaking oil that ignited on a hot engine exhaust system, the National Transportation Safety Board said Sunday."

[3] D. W. Hayward et al., *Study of Aircraft in Short Haul Transportation Systems* (published by the Boeing Company for NASA, 1967).

[4] Harold R. Willis, "Human Error—Cause and Reduction," paper presented to the Joint Meeting of Midwest Human Factors Society and National Safety Council (Chicago: Martin Company, 1962).

Questions

1. Explain the end results that can be obtained from a failure modes and effects analysis (FMEA).

2. Why won't an FMEA constitute a complete safety analysis of a product?

3. Briefly explain how an FMEA is made.

4. List the column headings commonly used for a FMEA.

5. What is the difference between a failure modes and effects analysis (FMEA) and a failure modes and criticality analysis (FMECA)?

6. What is a "single-point" failure?

7. What advantages does a fault hazard analysis have over a FMEA for evaluating the safety of a product?

8. What are its disadvantages?

9. Explain what is meant by an AND and an OR gate, draw the symbols, give an example, and draw the electronic equivalent to illustrate them.

10. Simplify the following logic equation:

$$E = (\overline{A}BC + A\overline{B}C) + (A\overline{B}C + ABC) + (A\overline{B}\overline{C} + A\overline{B}C).$$

11. What is a "blocking element"? What is its purpose?

12. Explain what an interface analysis is used for.

13. List at least five subsystems of the automobile and the inherent hazards of each subsystem.

14. Describe how a checklist can be prepared to review a product for its safety aspects.

15. Prepare a checklist of at least 20 items to be used to determine whether or not safety requirements for a product have been met.

16. Discuss the need for eliminating the possibilities of a single-point failure.

17. Indicate what you think is a "Common-Cause Failure," "Cascade Failures," and "Domino Effect."

18. How is potential time between failures of a product estimated?

19. What relationship exists between failure rates and warranties for a product?

20. FMEAs can be used to estimate when parts of a product, such as an automobile, should be replaced; unfortunately, this is frequently not done when it should be, so failures, operation breakdowns, and accidents result. Discuss why people don't make these replacements when they should.

15

Fault-Tree Analysis

Background

Most accidents are the result of sequences of events; for example, the sequence of events shown in Figure 15-1. This sequence may have been established after an accident investigation, shows only one sequence that could have resulted in the injury and damage at the right, and is lacking in detail in some of the events which took place.

The use of failure modes and effects analysis may be too time-consuming and costly for safety analyses of complex products and does not include potential problems other than failures, such as personnel error. In many types of products a component failure may result in the product being inoperative but not unsafe.

It is sometimes desirable to have a method of analysis that focuses on the possibility of occurrence of one event, indicates the complex relationships that can cause that event but eliminate extraneous effort, and includes *all* of the contributory factors. Fault-tree analysis was developed for these reasons by Bell Laboratories at the request of the U.S. Air Force. The Air Force wanted to know the possibilities and probabilities of an inadvertent or unauthorized launch of a Minuteman missile and of an inadvertent or unauthorized arming of a nuclear device.

Although it was developed to determine quantitative probabilities, it is more commonly used for its qualitative aspects because of the systematic way the various factors in any situation being investigated can be presented. Quantitative analyses and results still are desirable for many uses, but to make a quantitative analysis a qualitative analysis must first be made and many analysts feel that to obtain the quantitative results is not worth the additional effort.

Analysis Procedure

The method is described in the following paragraphs. The symbols commonly used to draw fault trees are shown in Figure 15-2 but there are variations of these symbols. The examples in this and the next chapter show some of these variations.

Selecting the Top Event

The top event is the event whose possibility (or probability) is to be determined. Its selection is the first step in the process. Figure 15-3 indicates some of these top events and Figure 15-4 illustrates how a series of such events can be selected from a description of a desired set of operations and the design specifications to be used. Top events can be taken from a preliminary hazard analysis. The preliminary hazard analysis for the coffee mill indicates that a person can get a cut if his or her finger is in the path of the rotor blade and the motor starts inadvertently when the mill is plugged into a power outlet. The top event to be explored could be either "Rotor Cuts Finger" or "Motor Starts Inadvertently." In the second case, the dangerous condition is to have the motor start inadvertently. If this does not happen, no harm will be done. The additional factors required to have an accident are therefore included. The tree is shown in Figure 15-5.

Building the Tree

The contributory events that could cause the top event are then drawn below the top event. As the tree is developed downward into "branches," two or more contributory events are separated by "gates." The two principal gates used with fault trees are OR and AND gates. If an OR gate (Figure 15-2) is used, the presence of *any* of the contributory events will cause the event above it to take place. If an AND gate is used, *all* the contributory events connected to that gate must be present to cause the event above it.

Faults, Effects, and Conditions

Each contributory event is now subjected to the same process. Each event is studied to determine the circumstances under which it will occur and the factors that will

Sequence of Events Leading to Rupture of a Pressurized Tank

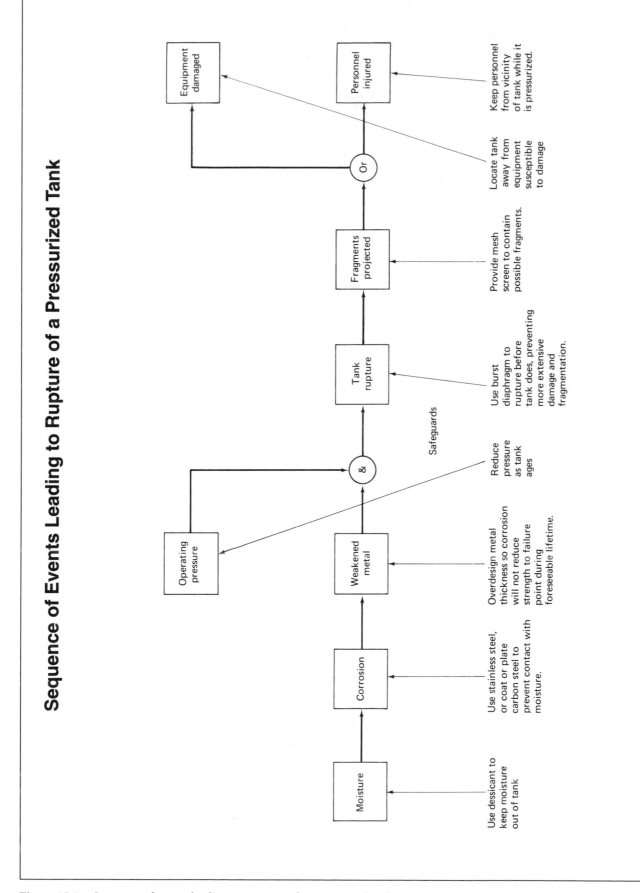

Figure 15-1. Sequence of events leading to rupture of a pressurized tank.

Fault Tree Symbols

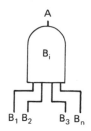

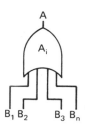

AND gate A logical AND relation. Output A exists if and only if all of B1, B2, ...Bn exist simulttaneously.

OR gate A logical inclusive OR relation. Output A exists if any of B1, B2...Bn, or any combination thereof, exists.

Inhibit gate. Permits applying a condition or restriction to the sequence. The input and condition or restriction must be satisfied for an output to be generated.

Identification of a particular event. When contained in the sequence, usually describes the output or an input of an AND or an OR gate. Applied to a gate, indicates a limiting condition or restriction that must be satisfied.

An event, usually a malfunction, describable in terms of a specific circuit or component.

An event that is normally expected to occu; usually an event that always occurs unless a failure takes place.

An event not developed further because of lask of information or of sufficient investigation is intended when additional information becomes available. Symbol W with a numberical subscript is sometimes used also.

Indicates and stipulates restricitons. With and AND gate, the restriction must be fulfilled before the event can occur. With an OR gate, the stipulation may be that the event will not occur in the presence of both or all inputs simultaneously. When used with an inhibit gate, stipulation is a variable condition.

A connecting symbol to another part of the fault tree within the same major branch. Has the same functions, sequence of events, and numerical values.

A connecting symbol to another part of the fault tree within the same major branch. Has the same functions and sequence of events, but not numerical values.

Figure 15-2. Fault tree symbols.

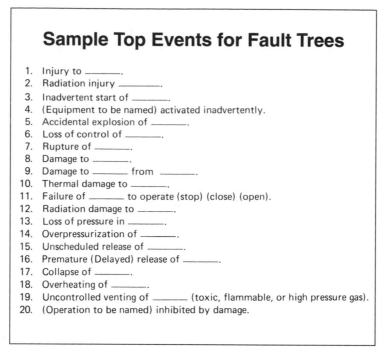

Figure 15-3. Sample top events for fault trees.

Sample Top Events for Fault Trees

1. Injury to _____.
2. Radiation injury _____.
3. Inadvertent start of _____.
4. (Equipment to be named) activated inadvertently.
5. Accidental explosion of _____.
6. Loss of control of _____.
7. Rupture of _____.
8. Damage to _____.
9. Damage to _____ from _____.
10. Thermal damage to _____.
11. Failure of _____ to operate (stop) (close) (open).
12. Radiation damage to _____.
13. Loss of pressure in _____.
14. Overpressurization of _____.
15. Unscheduled release of _____.
16. Premature (Delayed) release of _____.
17. Collapse of _____.
18. Overheating of _____.
19. Uncontrolled venting of _____ (toxic, flammable, or high pressure gas).
20. (Operation to be named) inhibited by damage.

cause it. The product, its purpose, its overall method of operation, and the operations and interrelationships of all its subordinate assemblies and components must be understood. As each event in the tree is listed, the event is then examined to determine whether it could be the result of a *primary fault*, a *secondary effect*, an *input* or *command*, or of multiples or combinations of these. A primary fault is one in which the component itself malfunctions. A secondary effect is one caused by the malfunction of another component or device or outside condition. An input or command event is one caused by an erroneous signal, error, or similar input.

Cause and Effect

Note that as the tree develops, progression *down* its branches indicates *causes* and that moving *up* indicates *effects*. To make the cause-and-effect relationships between more informative, the expression of each event must usually has a subject, verb, and descriptor, for example: "Relay K050 Fails Open." The word "Open" is the descriptor; if it were not present, the entire expression would mean that *any* failure of relay K050 would cause (or contribute to) the event above it. Proper selection of the expression of each event not only is important in qualitative trees in which the sequences can be more easily recognized, but it is also absolutely necessary in quantitative trees so that suitable probabilities and failure rates can be assigned.

Finishing the Tree

The process is continued down each branch until all available information has been used. A tree can be devel-

oped even when details of design or construction are unknown. Thus, Figure 15-6 is a generic tree that can be used for all three-wire power tools. As the design progresses or is completed, additional information can be added.

The bottom level of each completed branch should be a failure, error, or other initiating event. These are generally marked by a circle; a diamond indicates a bottom event that cannot be investigated further, or a bottom event that no one wants to investigate further. For example, the analysis reaches the point where it indicates that the failure of the motor in an appliance would contribute to or cause the event that is being investigated. The appliance manufacturer may not want to investigate the possibilities under which the motor might fail but may want to leave that problem to the motor manufacturer. Bottom events in which significant failures are noted are generally the items for which reliability engineers should be consulted and for which failure modes and effects analysis would be beneficial. If a bottom event is highly critical and the event above is a human error, a human factors engineer could be consulted on ways to minimize such errors.

Using the Tree

At this point the fault tree can begin indicating where corrective measures could be taken. For example, by using the tree for the coffee mill shown in Figure 15-5, one can examine the bottom events one by one. The possibility of a short between *A* and *B*, that connection had been made from *C* to *B* instead of to *A*, that the switch had been manufactured closed, and that the switch had been installed in the closed position could all be

Door Control Considerations in a Rapid Transit System

CONSIDERATION	DESIGN CRITERION	FAULT TREE EVENT
· All doors should remain closed when the train is in motion.	· All doors shall remain closed when the train is in motion.	· Door opens while train is in motion.
· Upon station arrival, the doors should be operable only after the train is stopped and all doors are properly aligned with the station platform.	· Doors shall be capable of opening only after train is stopped and properly aligned in station, or for emergency as noted below.	· Door opens while improperly aligned with station platform.
· The train should stay motionless while the doors are open.	· The train shall not be capable of moving with any door open.	· Train starts with door open.
· Initiation of a door close command should occur only when the door areas are clear.	· Door areas shall be clear before door closing begins.	· Door close initiated when occupied.
· If door closure is prevented by an obstruction, the appropriate door should reopen to allow removal of the obstruction before reclosing.	· An obstructed door shall reopen to permit removal of the obstruction, and then automatically reclose.	· Obstructed door fails to reopen. · Reopened door fails to reclose.
· The train should be allowed to proceed only after all doors are known to be closed, locked, and free of residual obstruction.	· Doors shall be closed and locked before train is allowed to proceed.	· Train enabled to proceed with door open or unlocked.
· It should be possible to open the doors, when the train is stopped anywhere, for safe emergency train evacuation.	· Means shall be provided to permit opening doors anywhere for emergency evacuation.	· Doors cannot be opened for emergency evacuation.

· Considerations in first column taken from a paper by R.J. Pawlak, Task Manager, Mass Transit Safety and System Assurance. U.S. DOT/Transportation Systems Center, entitled: *Automation and New System Design,* presented at the Second International System Safety Conference. San Diego, California; July 1975.

Figure 15-4. Door control considerations in a rapid transit system.

immediately apparent when the circuit is tested. Each mill should therefore be tested by connecting it to a source of power. The employees who conduct the tests must be warned against having their fingers near the rotor blade when the connection is made. That the switch may have failed in the closed position is a reliability problem. A very high reliability switch or a double switch could be used. The possibility of a short between A and B or that the switch might be closed accidentally presents a hazard to the maintenance person who may have removed the operating assembly from it protective case. A warning containing suitable precautions should therefore be included in the repair instructions. The possibility of being able to close the switch accidently should be minimized by the designer, possibly with assistance from the human factors engineer.

Critical Paths

The fault tree as shown indicates *all* the factors, events, and their interrelationships. It is desirable to know which sequence of events is most likely to cause the top event and is therefore more critical than the others. This can be found by breaking the tree down into *cut-sets.* A cut-set is a minimum sequence that can cause the top event (Figures 15-7 and 15-11). The probability of the top events occurring will be the sum of all the cut-sets if all of the sets are statistically independent, that is, that the same event or subevent which is part of another event is not present in two or more cut-sets. If there is any replication of events in any cut-sets, there is no longer independence and the replication must be accounted for in any quantitative analysis. (This point will be stressed again when quantitative methods are discussed.) In Figure 15-7 cut-sets would be H and M, expressed as $H \bullet M$; $H \bullet N$; $J \bullet L \bullet Q$; $J \bullet L \bullet S$; etc. In Figure 15-10 the three cut-sets are $E \bullet F$; $E \bullet H$; and D. Figure 15-11 illustrates a more

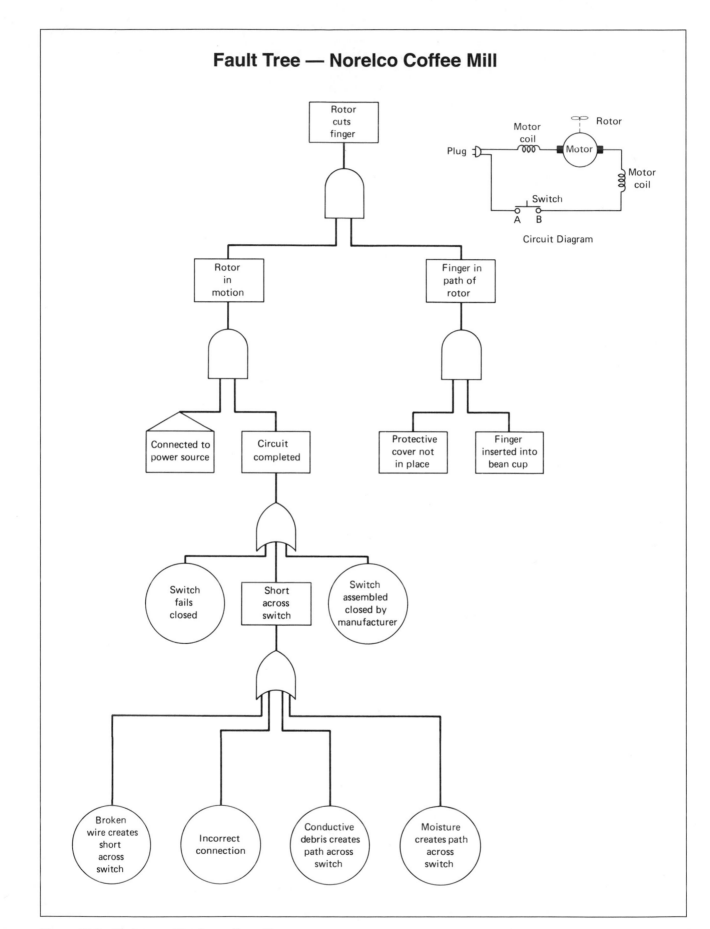

Figure 15-5. Fault tree—Norelco coffee mill.

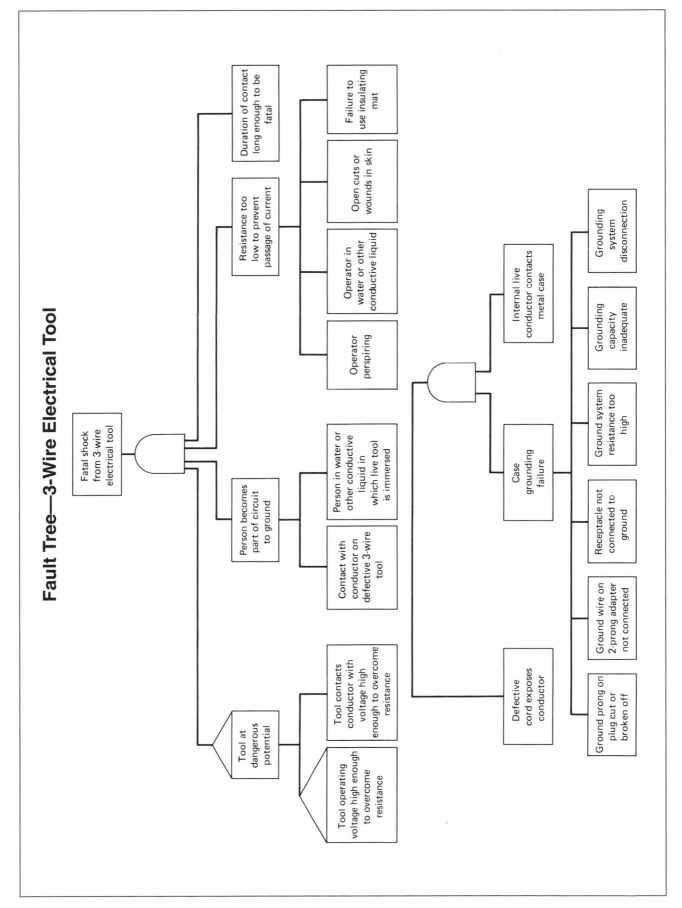

Figure 15-6. Fault tree—3-wire electrical tool.

Fault Tree for EED Circuit

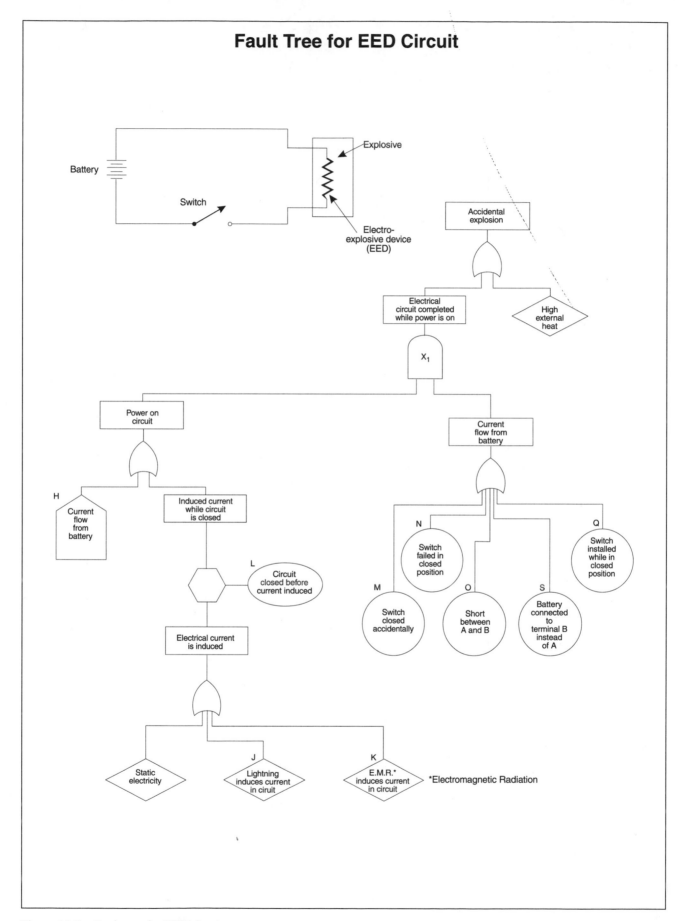

Figure 15-7. Fault tree for EED circuit.

Fault Tree Analysis of an Interlock Safety Circuit

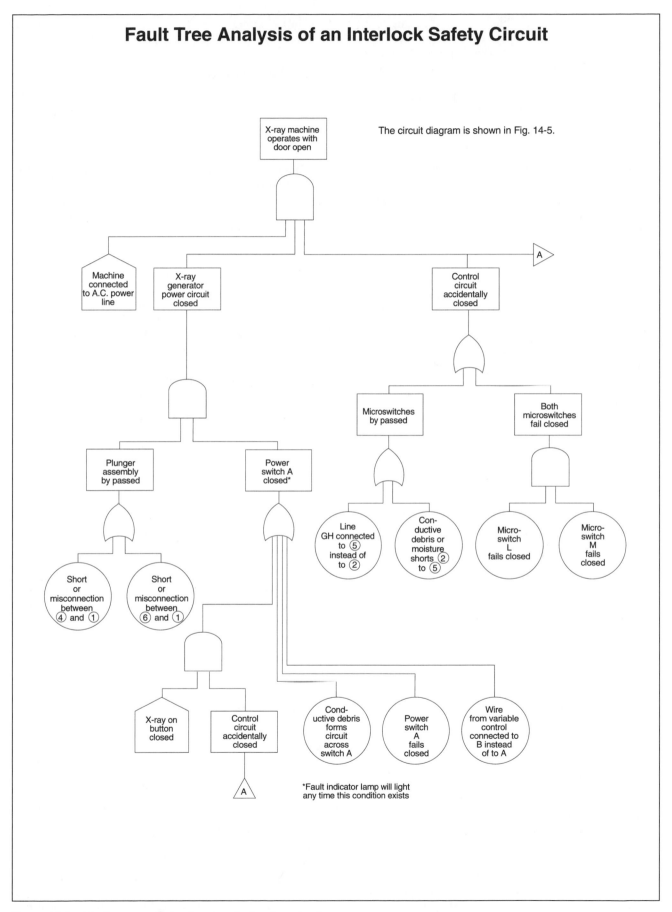

The circuit diagram is shown in Fig. 14-5.

*Fault indicator lamp will light any time this condition exists

Figure 15-8. Fault tree analysis of an interlock safety circuit.

complicated fault tree and the cut-sets that can be derived. Like everything else with fault trees, cut-sets for a simple tree can be prepared manually by the analyst. For a complex product and extensive tree, a computer is used. Computers are sometimes used to draw large fault trees. Once the fault trees are drawn, the computer can also be programmed to prepare the cut-sets.

Relative Determinations of Safety

Generally, a quick determination of relative safety can be made by checking how many AND gates are present. To have an output with an AND gate requires that all necessary inputs be present; therefore the probability of the output occurring is the *product* of all the individual input probabilities. This value is far lower or more remotely probable than an output from an OR gate, given the same input probabilities, which is the *sum* of all the input probabilities. Figure 15-8 presents the fault tree for a design appearing to have a high degree of safety as shown by the fact that there is a multiplicity of AND gates.

Figure 15-7 shows an AND gate relationship which is *not* safe. The symbol at H represents a normal operating condition; it will always be present when the product is in operation. Thus, in the configuration shown, there will always be "Current flow from the battery" (assuming no battery failure) which will put "Power on circuit." This will provide one of the two necessary satisfying inputs into the AND gate at X_1. Any output from Circuit to Firing Device Completed will provide the other input and an accidental explosion will result.

Single-Point Failures

At the beginning of Chapter 11 desirable and undesirable design conditions were discussed. It was pointed out that no design by which a single occurrence could result in an accident was desirable. Such lone occurrences are known as *single-point failures*. The presence of a single-point failure situation can often be uncovered by fault-tree analysis. Figure 15-9 was taken from an actual tree used to analyze a design. It illustrates both the concept of a single-point failure and again how AND gates can be circumvented. The tree shows that an AND gate at MM must be satisfied for the top event to occur. However, event D and its causes are the same as event J. Therefore, if event D occurs, event J will also occur. This will cause both inputs required at gate MM to be satisfied and the top event will occur.

The event at K should also be considered. The house symbol indicates that it is a normal operational event. Therefore, it satisfies one of the two necessary inputs to the AND gate above it. The causes of the other necessary input, L (Relay K312 contacts are closed), are not shown here, but the actual analyses were prepared elsewhere (the triangular transfer symbol indicates that it is shown on another page) and were numerous. If one of those faults occurs, the event "28 Vdc supplied K312 relay contacts" would take place, then "28 Vdc present at thru pin

PC-P18" at both D and J, and eventually the top event. This design is not very safe.

Boolean Equations

Figures 15-9 and 15-10 also show how Boolean equations can be prepared and simplified for fault trees. The fundamental principles of Boolean logic were presented in Figure 14-4. For the top event A to occur requires that two contributory events B AND C both take place. This is shown by $B \bullet C$ where the $\bullet$ indicates AND. B, in turn, can be the result of $D + E$, where the + symbolizes OR (not plus); C can be the result of $F + G \bullet G$, in turn, can be the result of $H + J$. It is also noted that J is the same event as D. Substitutions are made to obtain an equation for A, giving:

$$A = B \bullet C \qquad\qquad G = H + D$$
$$B = D + E \qquad\qquad C = F + H + D$$
$$C = F + G \qquad\qquad \text{and}$$
$$G = H + J \qquad A = B \bullet C = (D + E) \bullet (F + H + D)$$

but $J = D \quad A = D \bullet F + E \bullet F + D \bullet H + E \bullet H + D \bullet D + D \bullet E$

but $D \bullet D = D \quad and \quad D + D \bullet E = D \quad$ *(see Figure 14-4)*

$\therefore A = D \bullet F + E \bullet F + D \bullet H + E \bullet H + D$

but $D \bullet F$ and $D \bullet H$ are included in D *(see Figure 14-4)*

$\therefore A = E \bullet F + E \bullet H + D$

or $A = E(F + H) + D$

The revised fault trees are shown in Figure 15-10. It must be remembered that the symbol + means OR. A lone factor or event, such as D, means that a single-point failure can occur.

Restrictions on Fault Trees

In order to use Boolean logic, the following assumptions and stipulations must be made regarding the entries:

1. An entry can only be in one of two possible modes: on–off, will occur–will not occur, closed–not closed, successful–failed, and so on. There can be no intermediate condition such as being partially successful.

2. Events are independent of each other unless a cause-and-effect relationship, such as a secondary effect, is shown.

Quantitative Analyses

If probabilities are substituted for each factor in the simplified Boolean equation, the probability of the top event can be determined. It is necessary that the equation be simplified first because after the probabilities are inserted there is no way to determine redundancies. The only time that a simplification can be made after a value has been inserted is when the tree contains a house. Since this event is certain to occur, its value of 1 can and should be used. The 1 is not only a numerical value; it is a Boolean symbol in itself. The procedures for simplification have been demonstrated in Figures 15-9 and 15-10.

If the probabilities are inserted in the cut-sets, the probability of the top event occurring along each path can be

Fault Tree—Single-Point Failure

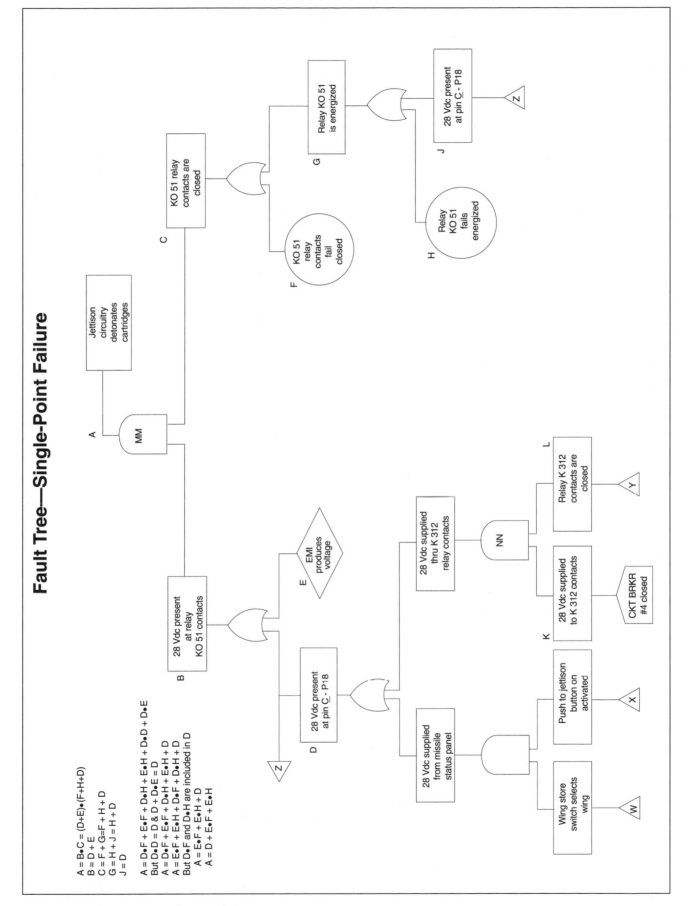

Figure 15-9. Fault tree—single-point failure.

Simplified Trees for Single-Point Failure

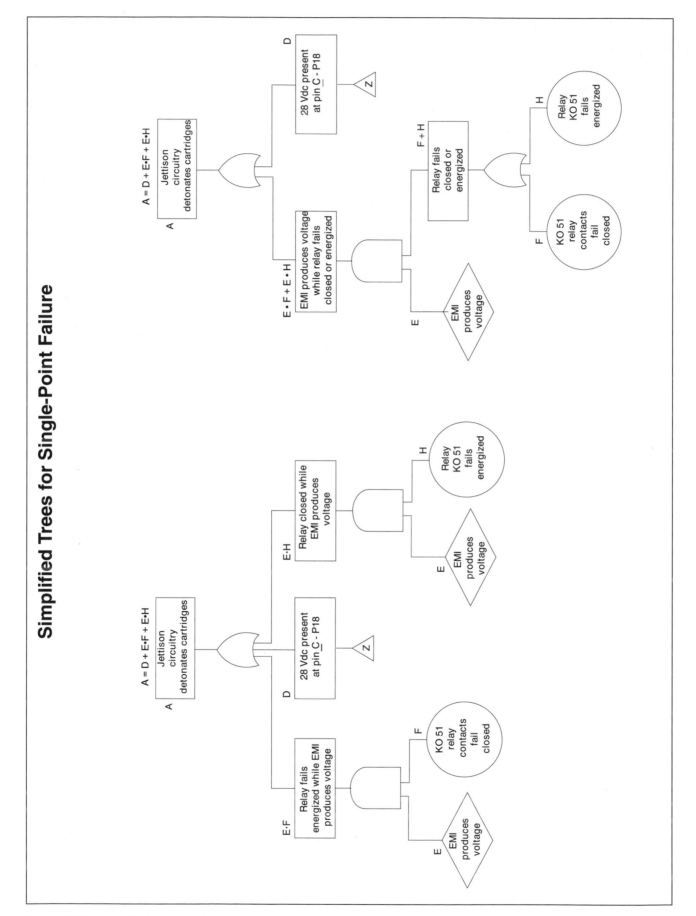

Figure 15-10. Simplified trees for single-point failure.

determined and the critical path, the one with the highest probability, can be established. Figure 15-11 provides a diagrammatic model of a fault tree with representations of events for faults, effects, and conditions described earlier (see page 171).

Using Failure Rates

When the mission time is the same for all the items whose failures are involved in the tree, it is generally easier to use failure rates rather than failure probabilities for each event. The failure rate for the top event is calculated and is then used with the mission time to calculate the probability only of the top event. How this may be done on the tree itself when there are no redundancies is illustrated in Figure 15-12.

Need for Simplification

When the probability of the top event is to be calculated, redundancies must first be removed through Boolean simplification and the simplified equation or tree must be used. Figure 15-13 shows what happens when the failure rate of the top event is calculated without removing the redundancy and how the resultant answer compares with the correct one.

Monte Carlo Simulation

Another problem that sometimes arises in trying to compute the probability of the top event is that failures, errors, and other contributory factors may not occur at the same times, or in some cases, in the sequences which are required to produce it. In many cases, the probabilities of failure or errors are not known and must be estimated. One way of doing this is by a simulation process known as the *Monte Carlo Method*, which is based on chance processes applied to occurrences of events which may be similar in some respects. Further details on the Monte Carlo Method are presented in Figure 15-14. To obtain a fair degree of accuracy and confidence in these simulations requires that results for each factor in the mathematical model be obtained a large number of times. For a complex tree, such simulation processes have become practical only through the use of computers and suitable programming. As mentioned in Chapter 10, Monte Carlo simulations are also being run to determine the probabilities of human errors in complex situations and the effects of such errors.

Other Uses of Fault Trees

Troubleshooting and Maintenance

If the top event selected is that a piece of equipment will not operate, the resulting tree can be used for troubleshooting. The tree will also indicate if there are any components whose operation must be trouble-free if the product is to operate. Maintenance activities should be stressed here. The probabilities of failures of components can be used to determine the number of spare parts that will be needed.

Reliability Calculations

Either the successful accomplishment of a function or the fact that the product will not operate (as in troubleshooting) is taken as the top event. All the events that must contribute to that success or failure are entered, but only material considerations are used with no entries for human error or environmental effects. When the Boolean equation is simplified and a new tree is drawn, a reliability value undistorted by redundancies can be determined.

Accident Investigations

Fault trees can be used for accident investigations in the two following ways:

1. The accident, injury, or damage that occurred is used as the top event, contributing factors are added, and the tree is developed. Events that have a zero probability of occurrence (absolutely could not have happened) are eliminated and the remainder (even if the probability of occurrence is extremely low) are investigated (Figure 15-15).

2. A tree is prepared similar to the one for reliability with the top event the successful operation of the equipment. Each event in the tree is then investigated to determine whether or not a change to a hazardous condition had occurred. When there was a lack of change, the event was eliminated as a causative factor although its occurrence may have been necessary for the accident to have happened. For example, in Figure 15-1 there may have been no change in pressure level, but the fact that the pressure had not been reduced may have contributed to the rupture.

Management Decisions

A method known as MORT (Management Oversight and Risk Tree) now in use in the nuclear industry uses a logic method similar to fault-tree analysis to illustrate the possibilities of wrong or inadequate management actions. The method can also be used to diagram the management actions that may have contributed to an accident which has already occurred. In these trees each event is a management or operator action; no equipment failures and no environmental conditions are used.

Estimating Risks

Risk analysis is discussed in Chapter 18. One method for determining risks that has been developed in the chemical industry uses a variation of fault-tree analysis called the loss analysis diagram (LAD). A LAD is used to compare possible designs and to determine whether or not the potential probability of loss is acceptable to company management.

Typical Fault Tree Configuration and Mathematical Model

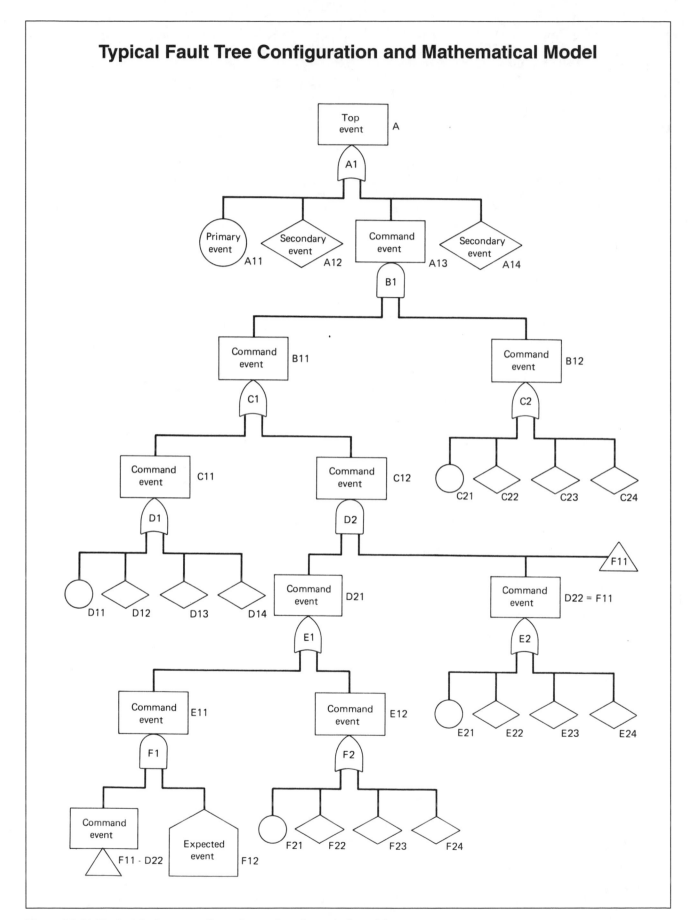

Figure 15-11. Typical fault tree configuration and mathematical model.

Typical Fault Tree Configuration and Mathematical Model

From the Fault Tree, by inspection, $A = A11+A12+A13+A14$
A13 = B11·B12, substituting, $A = A11+A12+A14+(B11·B12)$

B11 = C11+C12, and B12 = C21+C23+C24; hence
$$A = A11+A12+A14+(C11+C12)(C21+C22+C23+C24)$$

C11 = D11+D12+D13+D14, and C12 = D21·D22, substituting,
$$A = A11+A12+A14+(D11+D12+D13+D14+D21·D22)(C21+C22+C23+C24)$$

D21 = E11+E12, and D22 = F11, substituting,
$$A = A11+A12+A14+[D11+D12+D13+D14+(E11·E12+E12)(F11)][C21+C22+C23+C24]$$

E11 = F11·F12, substituting,
$$A = A11+A12+A14+[D11+D12+D13+D14+(F11·F12+E12)(F11)][C21+C22+C23+C24]$$

By idempotent law, (F11)(F11·F12+E12)=F11(F12+E12), hence,
$$A = A11+A12+A14+[D11+D12+D13+D14+(F11)(F12+E12)][C21+C22+C23+C24]$$

Since F11 = E21+E22+E23+E24,
$$A = A11+A12+A14[D11+D12+D13+D14+(E21+E22+E23+E24)(F12+E12)][C21+C22+C23+C24]$$

Also, E12 = F21+F22+F23+F24,
$$\therefore A = A11+A12+A14+[D11+D12+D13+D14+(E21+E22+E23+E24)(F12+F21+F22+F23+F24)]$$
$$[C21+C22+C23+C24]$$

(When and-ing three or more long expressions, it will be found convenient to work from a table similar to the one shown. Starting with E21 and F12, all the third line values have been used in sequence. Next, E21 and F21 have been similarly used. The process is repeated with each entry in the second line before advancing to E22; E22 combinations are likewise exhausted before advancing to E23. This process is continued until all combinations have been formed.)

E21	E22	E23	E24	
F12	F21	F22	F23	F24
C21	C22	C23	C24	

$A = \underline{A11} + \underline{A12} + \underline{A14} + \underline{D11·C21} + \underline{D11·C22} + \underline{D11·C23} + \underline{D11·C24} + \underline{D12·C21} + \underline{D12·C22} + \underline{D12·C23} + \underline{D12·C24} +$

$\underline{D13·C21} + \underline{D13·C22} + \underline{D13·C23} + \underline{D13·C24} + \underline{D14·C21} + \underline{D14·C22} + \underline{D14·C23} + \underline{D14·C24} + \underline{F12·E21·C21} +$

$\underline{F12·E21·C22} + \underline{F12·E21·C23} + \underline{F12·E21·C24} + \underline{F21·E21·C21} + \underline{F21·E21·C22} + \underline{F21·E21·C23} + \underline{F21·E21·C24} +$

$\underline{F22·E21·C21} + \underline{F22·E21·C22} + \underline{F22·E21·C23} + \underline{F22·E21·C24} + \underline{F23·E21·C21} + \underline{F23·E21·C22} + \underline{F23·E21·C24} +$

$\underline{F23·E21·C24} + \underline{F24·E21·C21} + \underline{F24·E21·C22} + \underline{F24·E21·C23} + \underline{F24·E21·C24} + \underline{F12·E22·C21} + \underline{F12·E22·C22} +$

$\underline{F12·E22·C23} + \underline{F12·E22·C24} + \underline{F21·E22·C21} + \underline{F21·E22·C22} + \underline{F21·E22·C23} + \underline{F21·E22·C24} + \underline{F22·E22·C21} +$

$\underline{F22·E22·C22} + \underline{F22·E22·C23} + \underline{F22·E22·C24} + \underline{F23·E22·C21} + \underline{F23·E22·C22} + \underline{F23·E22·C23} + \underline{F23·E22·C24} +$

$\underline{F24·E22·C21} + \underline{F24·E22·C22} + \underline{F24·E22·C23} + \underline{F24·E22·C24} + \underline{F12·E23·C21} + \underline{F12·E23·C22} + \underline{F12·E23·C23} +$

$\underline{F12·E23·C24} + \underline{F21·E23·C21} + \underline{F21·E23·C22} + \underline{F21·E23·C23} + \underline{F21·E23·C24} + \underline{F22·E23·C21} + \underline{F22·E23·C22} +$

$\underline{F22·E23·C23} + \underline{F22·E23·C24} + \underline{F23·E23·C21} + \underline{F23·E23·C22} + \underline{F23·E23·C23} + \underline{F23·E23·C24} + \underline{F24·E23·C21} +$

$\underline{F24·E23·C22} + \underline{F24·E23·C23} + \underline{F24·E23·C24} + \underline{F12·E24·C21} + \underline{F12·E24·C22} + \underline{F12·E24·C23} + \underline{F12·E24·C24} +$

$\underline{F21·E24·C21} + \underline{F21·E24·C22} + \underline{F21·E24·C23} + \underline{F21·E24 ·C24} + \underline{F22·E24·C21} + \underline{F22·E24·C22} + \underline{F22·E24·C23} +$

$\underline{F22·E24·C24} + \underline{F23·E24·C21} + \underline{F23·E24·C22} + \underline{F23·E24·C23} + \underline{F23·E24·C24} + \underline{F24·E24·C21} + \underline{F24·E24·C22} +$

$\underline{F24·E24·C23} + \underline{F24·E24·C24}$

The last equation, consisting of 14 lines, is the mathematical model of the Fault Tree. The quantities underlined are individual paths that can cause the occurrence of the top event (A). There are three single-event paths, 16 two-event combination paths, and 80 three-event combination paths making a total of 99 paths. In the two or more event paths, all events must occur at the same time to have the top event A in an "ON" state.

Figure 15-11 (cont'd). Typical fault tree configuration and mathematical model.

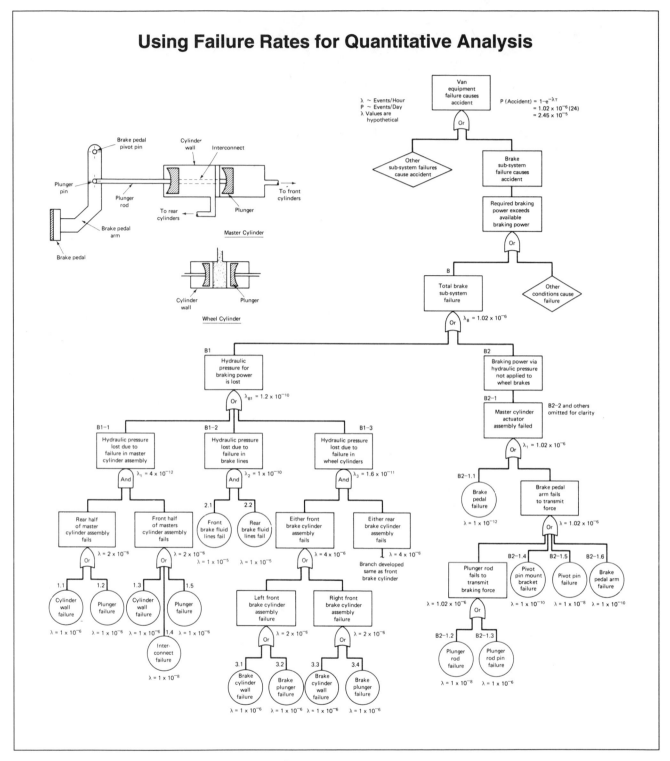

Figure 15-12. Using failure rates for quantitative analysis.

Limitations of Fault-Tree Analysis

A fault-tree analysis is most effective in discovering problems. It ensures that there is no possibility of single-point failure, and can indicate how safe a product is. But many of the good features in a product are designed in because of the standards and criteria designers are given to follow early in any safety program. If the standards and criteria are followed, the need for fault-tree analysis may be reduced substantially. For example, there may be little need for an analyst to prepare a fault tree on the possibility that a person would receive an injury such as a puncture wound. The analyst would better spend his or her time ensuring that the design criteria for eliminating

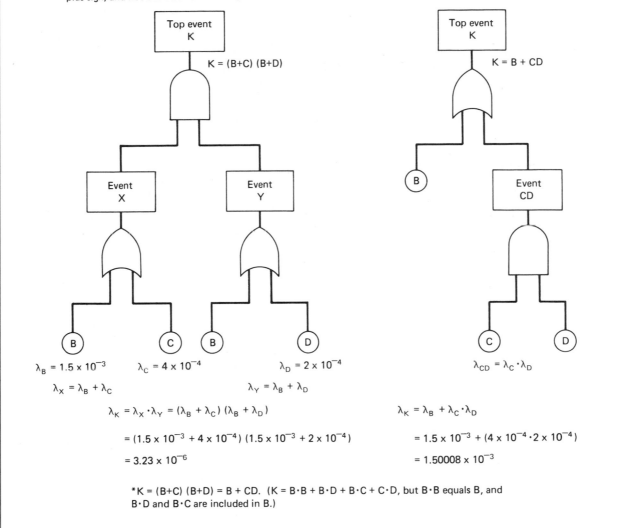

The Need for Boolean Simplification

The tree on the left below represents a fault tree which has been simplified by Boolean logic to the one on the right*. The equations below the trees show that unless the equation is simplified before values are inserted when a redundancy exists, the final answer will be incorrect. (Note that the + sign in the calculations is the arithmetic plus sign, and not the Boolean "OR".)

Top event K

$K = (B+C)(B+D)$

Event X

Event Y

B

Event CD

B

C

B

D

C

D

$\lambda_B = 1.5 \times 10^{-3}$ $\lambda_C = 4 \times 10^{-4}$ $\lambda_D = 2 \times 10^{-4}$ $\lambda_{CD} = \lambda_C \cdot \lambda_D$

$\lambda_X = \lambda_B + \lambda_C$ $\lambda_Y = \lambda_B + \lambda_D$

$\lambda_K = \lambda_X \cdot \lambda_Y = (\lambda_B + \lambda_C)(\lambda_B + \lambda_D)$ $\lambda_K = \lambda_B + \lambda_C \cdot \lambda_D$

$= (1.5 \times 10^{-3} + 4 \times 10^{-4})(1.5 \times 10^{-3} + 2 \times 10^{-4})$ $= 1.5 \times 10^{-3} + (4 \times 10^{-4} \cdot 2 \times 10^{-4})$

$= 3.23 \times 10^{-6}$ $= 1.50008 \times 10^{-3}$

*$K = (B+C)(B+D) = B + CD$. ($K = B \cdot B + B \cdot D + B \cdot C + C \cdot D$, but $B \cdot B$ equals B, and $B \cdot D$ and $B \cdot C$ are included in B.)

Figure 15-13. The need for Boolean simplification.

sharp edges and corners and rough surfaces have been observed.

Effective fault trees can only be made after the product has been designed. A good safety program requires concentration on the designers in the early stages of the program.

Although desirable in some cases, quantitative fault trees to determine probabilities of occurrence of top events are generally costly. Most of the benefits of using fault trees can be derived from qualitative analyses.

Preparation of the tree requires intensive knowledge of the design, construction, and operation of the product so that all of the significant factors will be included. Omission of one factor might affect a qualitative analysis and certainly will affect a quantitative analysis. Lack of understanding may result in the erroneous use of OR and AND gates.

As previously indicated, partial successes and failures are not considered even though they might have effects on performance. However, by careful selection of the terminology by which events are described it is often possible

Monte Carlo Simulation

MONTE CARLO SIMULATIONS

This is the name given to the means of using mathematical simulation, chance processes, and random numbers to determine whether and how frequently the outcome of an event or complex relationship will occur. Equations or problems with uncertain input values which are too complicated to solve by experimental, analytical, or more routine numerical methods are solved by trial. This has been made possible through the use of electronic computers which can accomplish the necessary operations rapidly and within reasonable times.

A simple example of the method is in determining how many heads and tails would result by tossing coins, and from this the occurrence of either one. Instead of actually tossing the coins, a series of numbers can be selected randomly; all odd numbers can be considered heads, all even numbers, tails. With an adequate number of trials by random numbers and by actual coin tossings, the result will be identical or very close. In either case, the number of occurrences of either heads or tails divided by the total number of trials will give the probability of that event occurring.

A more complicated example would be the solution of an equation such as H = A·B + C, where the value of A can be x, y, or z. x has a probability of occurring of 0.20; y, 0.30, and z, 0.50. x is assigned a series of numbers of 01 to 20; y, 21 to 50; and z, 51 to 00 (100). Similar assignments based on their probability distributions are made for B and C. Any method of selecting numbers randomly can then be used: a roulette wheel with 100 numbers, a table of two digit random numbers, or a computer programmed to generate such random numbers. A trial is conducted for A in which the number selected indicates the occurrence of x, y, or z. Similar trials are held for B and C, then all three values are used to calculate a value for H. No great degree of confidence can be placed in the outcome of one set of trials, conducting a large number of trials will result in a distribution of results from which a more accurate mean and range of values can be determined. The accuracy of a Monte Carlo approximation increases as the square root of the number of trials; quadrupling the number of trials doubles the accuracy of the result. To achieve a high degree of accuracy therefore requires a very large number of trials. Thus, a computer must be used since it can simulate in a comparatively short time activities which might normally require hundreds or thousands of man-years if done manually. But in complex situations, even the computer can be overloaded.

In general, the method consists of the following procedure:

a. A cumulative probability distribution function is plotted or tabulated, using the values of data involved along the horizontal axis and frequency or probability of occurrence plotted along the vertical axis. The probability distribution can be one such as in (1) below to illustrate how values for X in the example above would be used, or a continuous distribution such as in (2).

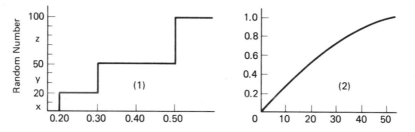

b. A number is selected randomly from a table or random number generator, applied against the vertical axis, and using the curve determining the number on the horizontal axis.

c. The process is repeated for as many operations as desired.

In a simulation program for a fault tree, the various events, their interrelationships, and the probability distributions are entered into a computer. The computer then carries out each step in the process, selecting values and making calculations. Also necessary is information on when specific events might occur; if failures are to be determined, they will only affect the outcome if they occur within the duration of time under consideration. The computer takes all those events which have occurred within that time to determine whether, how often and the probability the top event will result.

Because to obtain a relatively accurate value for the top event for even a moderately complex fault tree a great number of trials is needed, much computer time is required, and the cost of such a simulation may become prohibitive. It has been estimated that a 600 event fault tree will require 300 hours of computer time to estimate a probability of 10^{-5} with a reasonable degree of confidence. To lessen computer time a technique know as Importance Sampling, for which there are a number of methods, was developed. Various computer programs have also been developed to carry out fault tree simulations.

Simulations can be used to determine the effects changes in any of the factors involved will have on the outcome, or in a fault tree, of the top event. Thus, whether an increase in reliability of a component or installation of a safeguard will improve the safety level of a product or operation can be determined by using the Monte Carlo method.

Figure 15-14. Monte Carlo simulation.

Fault Tree for Accident Investigation

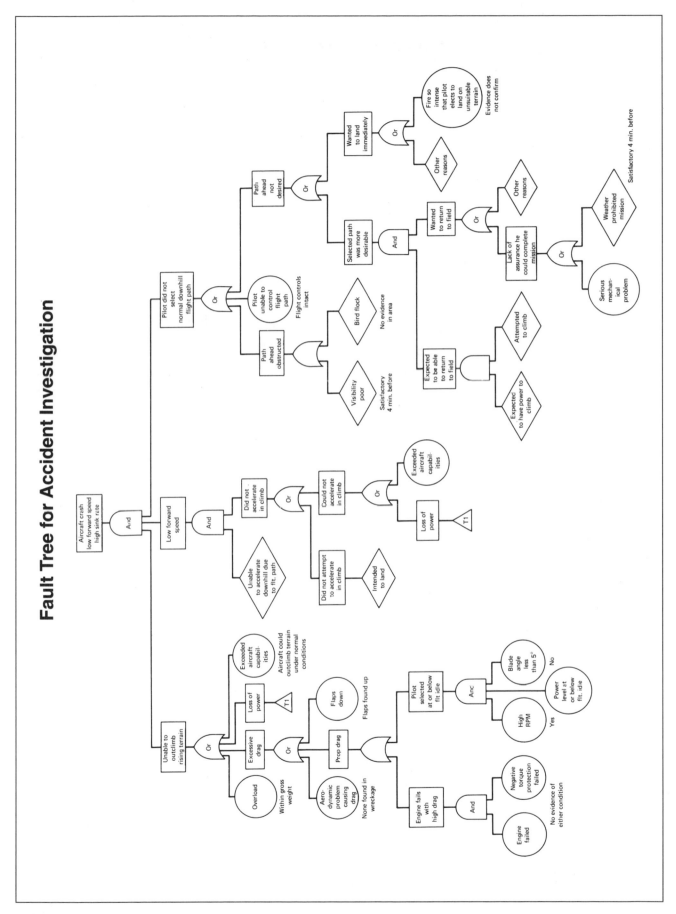

Figure 15-15. Fault tree for accident investigation.

Simplified Type of Fault Tree

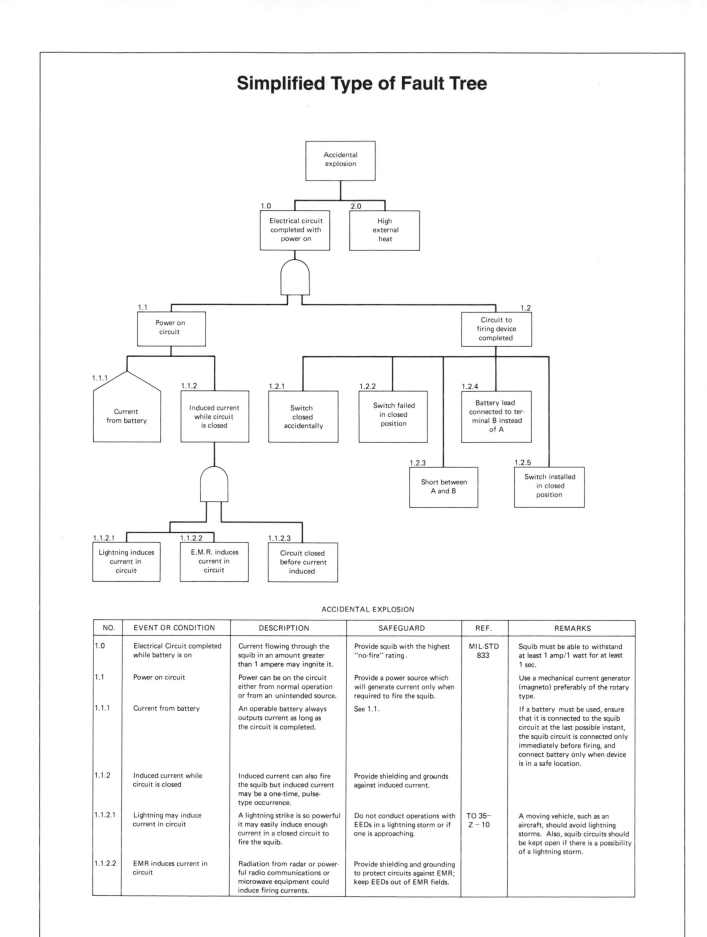

ACCIDENTAL EXPLOSION

NO.	EVENT OR CONDITION	DESCRIPTION	SAFEGUARD	REF.	REMARKS
1.0	Electrical Circuit completed while battery is on	Current flowing through the squib in an amount greater than 1 ampere may ingnite it.	Provide squib with the highest "no-fire" rating.	MIL-STD 833	Squib must be able to withstand at least 1 amp/1 watt for at least 1 sec.
1.1	Power on circuit	Power can be on the circuit either from normal operation or from an unintended source.	Provide a power source which will generate current only when required to fire the squib.		Use a mechanical current generator (magneto) preferably of the rotary type.
1.1.1	Current from battery	An operable battery always outputs current as long as the circuit is completed.	See 1.1.		If a battery must be used, ensure that it is connected to the squib circuit at the last possible instant, the squib circuit is connected only immediately before firing, and connect battery only when device is in a safe location.
1.1.2	Induced current while circuit is closed	Induced current can also fire the squib but induced current may be a one-time, pulse-type occurrence.	Provide shielding and grounds against induced current.		
1.1.2.1	Lightning may induce current in circuit	A lightning strike is so powerful it may easily induce enough current in a closed circuit to fire the squib.	Do not conduct operations with EEDs in a lightning storm or if one is approaching.	TO 35–Z – 10	A moving vehicle, such as an aircraft, should avoid lightning storms. Also, squib circuits should be kept open if there is a possibility of a lightning storm.
1.1.2.2	EMR induces current in circuit	Radiation from radar or powerful radio communications or microwave equipment could induce firing currents.	Provide shielding and grounding to protect circuits against EMR; keep EEDs out of EMR fields.		

Figure 15-16. Simplified type of fault tree.

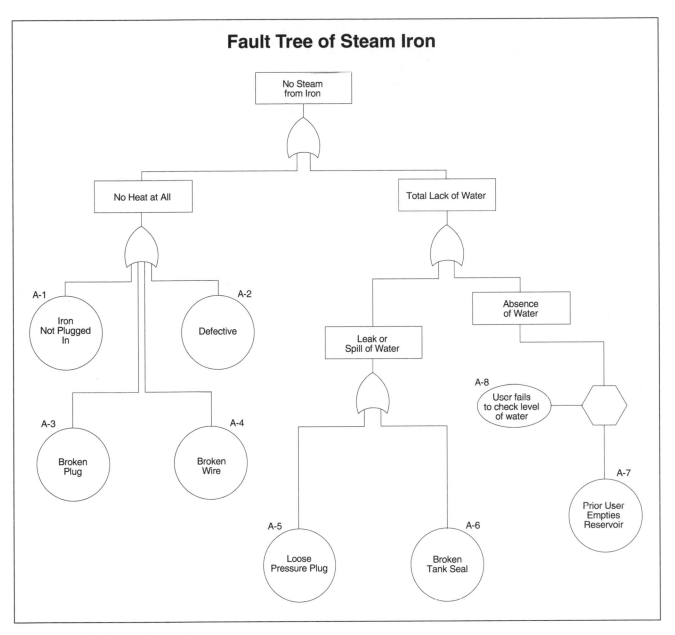

Figure 15-17. Fault tree of steam iron.

to overcome this objection of not including partial successes or partial failures.

Using Boolean logic and making reductions in the equations by which replications are eliminated are often difficult, especially for complex equipment and when done manually. Using computers for such tasks increases the cost. The lack of dependable failure rate data may distort the quantitative results of even a well-developed tree.

When all of the symbols shown in Figure 15-2 are used, they sometimes confuse personnel who have no training in fault-tree analysis, for example, program or product managers. Simplified versions such as that in Figure

15-16 (the same events as in Figure 15-7) may be more desirable.

A fault tree is a logic diagram that shows cause-and-effect relationships but little more. Additional documentation may therefore be required. The tree in Figure 15-16 has had a numerical coding system added which cross-references each event to a table on which such additional information can be provided.

Figure 15-17 (above) is the Fault-Tree Analysis of a common household product, a steam iron. The undesired event in this example, at the top of the figure, is "NO STEAM FROM THE IRON."

Questions

1. List the steps in which a fault-tree analysis is prepared for a qualitative analysis. What additional steps are required for a quantitative analysis?

2. Describe how a fault-tree analysis (FTA) differs from a failure modes and effects analysis (FMEA). How can the two types of analyses be used to complement each other?

3. What is a "cut-set"? For what can cut sets be used?

4. What is a "single-point failure" condition? What would it look like on a fault tree?

5. Following are design requirements. Indicate what the top event might be if a fault tree were prepared for each.

    a. The elevator shall not move while the door is open.

    b. The washing machine shall not operate during its spin cycle unless the top or door to the machine is closed.

    c. Power to the machine will be cut off immediately when the emergency button on its front panel is pushed.

6. For what other purposes than analyzing a product can fault-tree analysis be used?

7. What does an "AND gate" show? An "OR gate"? A "house"?

8. What are some of the limitations of using fault trees? How can these limitations be circumvented?

9. Why could a quantitative result for a fault tree be distorted if the Boolean equation was not written and simplified?

10. Draw the tree for the following Boolean equation:

$$X_1 = AB(CD + EF)$$

11. Write the final Boolean equation for the top event A of the following fault trees in terms of the lowest events.

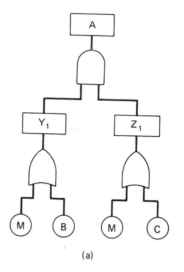

(a)

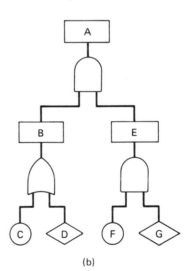

(b)

12. Which of the following trees indicate the possibility of a single-point failure which can cause the top event? Show by a Boolean reduction that a possibility of a single-point failure exists. Draw the simplified diagram for the single-point failure.

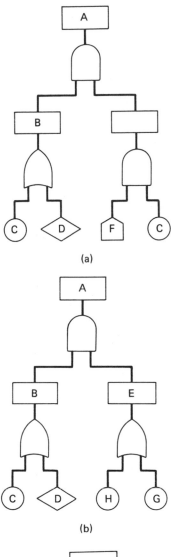

(a)

(b)

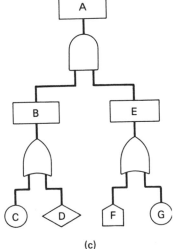

(c)

Data for Figure 15-17 to be used to determine an estimated total probability. Individual probability values to be used include the following: A1-.0008, A2-.0005, A3-.0005, A4-0002, A5-0001, A6-0001, A7-.0008, A9-.0006.

13. What is the calculated probability of *any* mal-occurrence?

14. What is the probability of the cut-set for a complete lack of heat?

15. What is the probability of no steam because of a lack of water?

16. How do you think these two findings would compare with past experience with irons?

Submarines have suffered catastrophes resulting in injury, death, damage, loss of function, or a combination of any or all of these. Causes and effects can be listed as: flooding loss of buoyancy; grounding; collision; fire; explosion; electrical system failure; loss of compressed air; environmental contamination; hull collapse or penetration; seal or weld failure; propeller shaft leakage, damage, or failure; reactor or power transmission failure; and entanglement with cables or nets.

17. Prepare a fault tree which lists as many factors as possible indicating interrelationships.

18. Prepare a fault tree and discuss problems in another totally different environment: a space station.

19. Discuss which of the problems would also exist with another publicized catastrophe: oil tankers running aground.

16

Sneak Circuit Analysis

No one type of safety analysis has been found adequate to study the potential for all accidents and their avoidance. Even failure modes and effects and fault-tree analyses have their shortcomings. Two additional, limited purpose methods of safety analyses described here are "sneak circuit analysis" and "computer safety analysis."

The following description of sneak circuit analysis is taken from an amalgam of information derived from NAVSO P-3634 dated July 1986; papers by John P. Rankin and Tyrone Jackson, and from E. Lloyd and W. Tye's book *Systematic Safety* published in July 1982 by the Civil Aviation Authority in London. Although Lloyd and Tye's book makes no reference to sneak circuit analysis, some of the information in their book appears to apply. The information derived from these cited documents has been used to prepare procedures, and guidance for commercial-type products. As a consequence, the methodology described herein differs from the Navy's because of the desire to use non-military examples. Applicable terms used in sneak circuit analysis are shown in Figure 16-1.

NAVSO P-3634 also observes that one result of the increasingly complex systems is that it becomes extremely difficult to view the detailed interrelationship between components. As a consequence, the design may contain unexpected electrical paths or logic flows, that under certain conditions will produce undesired results or will prevent intended functions from occurring. These situations can be labeled sneak circuits and can be identified in the design phase through use of sneak circuit analysis.

I will start by describing the need for sneak circuit analysis with a bit of personal recollection. During World War II, I flew Marine fighter planes on Okinawa; it was the rainy season. One wet morning our ordnancemen loaded eight 5 in. dia. HVARs (High Velocity Aircraft Rockets) onto my aircraft. I turned on the plane's ignition and the rockets took off, landing and exploding in another squadron's area. A few days later, a friend of mine led a bombing strike on a small island about 40 miles away. Just before he got there, he turned on the ordnance arming switch and the bombs fell into the ocean. We thought that in both cases the ordnancemen had made wrong connections, and didn't realize at the time, we had been victims of what later came to be called "sneak circuits." After the war, similar accidents occurred with more advanced weaponry such as the Sidewinder and Hound Dog missiles.

It was not only the problem of what had occurred with these smaller systems but apprehension that similar problems could be disastrous with larger systems, both military and space, which led to the development by Boeing, and later, General Dynamics and other aerospace companies, of a method of analysis to determine the causes and means of preventing and eliminating sneak circuits and their adverse consequences.

Design Analysis

Sneak circuit analyses are taken to identify:

1. *Design oversights:* The designer did not foresee that sneak paths or other sneak anomalies existed.

2. *Incompatible designs:* Designs prepared by different designers or design organizations that may result in incompatibilities when subsystems or other units are assembled into one product or system.

3. *Changes:* Revisions to designs that may generate paths through which sneak circuits can occur.

4. *System complexity:* In complex systems, design growth as circuits are added may generate sneak

Sneak Circuit Analysis Terms

Network Forest

Two or more network trees such as by interconnected circuits or "black boxes."

Network Tree

One complete topographical representation from power to ground with all components, paths, and modal points in between.

Nodal Set

An individual circuit path showing interconnection points, or nodes, which are part of the same circuit.

Partitioning

Dividing complex interconnected circuits into smaller and less complex circuit portions. Partitioning in this way has a number of advantages: (1) For comparatively small circuits, it permits a manual review of small portions of the circuitry included by an analyst; (2) Permits the effort to be restrained to that called for at the interface with that of another designer such as that supplied by the vendor of a "black box"; and (3) It permits preparation of a table to ease the encoding of data when computer analysis is to be undertaken.

Sneak Clue

Describes an anomalous or erroneous characteristic of topological models of a circuit. Clues are used to uncover design or possible operational conditions. The Navy document provides a large number of clue questions and tabulated checklists that can be used by the analyst, thereby increasing and widening the perspective of the designer. Clues fall into two basic types: those regarding the topological pattern, i.e.: "Can a reverse current inadvertently flow through the crossbar of the 'H' pattern?"; and clues regarding piece parts and circuits configuration. The large number of clues are not necessarily exhaustive, but include the nature of the items the analyst should consider.

Sneak Condition

A latent mode which, independent of component failures within a system, under certain conditions, can initiate an undesired function or inhibit a desired one.

Sneak Indicators

False or ambiguous status display due to improper connection or control of display devices and their sensors that may cause an operator to take undesired action.

Sneak Labels

Lack of precise nomenclature or instructions on controls or operating consoles that can lead to operator errors.

Sneak Paths

Latent path in designed circuitry which permits unwanted functions to occur or that inhibits desired function, even without component failure. Sneak paths are paths along which current, or energy, can flow in an unintended direction. Although this was the original and principal use for which Sneak Circuit Analysis was developed, applications reveal it can be used for other problems.

Sneak Procedures

Ambiguous wording, incomplete or imprecise displays or instructions, lack of caution notes, and similar deficiencies which may result in an operator taking improper actions by applying an incorrect stimulus to the system, especially under contingency conditions.

Sneak Timing

Events occurring in an unexpected or conflicting sequence.

An inappropriate systems response due to hardware or procedural sequences which is incompatible with the design.

Topological Patterns

A means of representing electrical circuitry from points of origin of positive power to any ground points, and including any nodes, electrical paths, and connections, to and from components such as leads, diodes, switches, or disconnects.

Figure 16-1. Definitions for various terms used in sneak circuit analysis.

paths which the person or persons who check the designs may not be able to recognize.

5. *Fixes:* Malfunctions or "glitches" during testing are sometimes corrected by field "fixes" which may solve the immediate problem, but which may also generate other problems which are not recognized immediately.

NAVSO P-3634 provides criteria recommendations for which systems should be submitted to sneak circuit analyses; most notable among these are when:

- System is critical.
- Improper function could endanger life or damage expensive equipment.
- Sneak conditions that occur in operation where correction would be difficult or impossible.

The document lists scores of critical systems for which sneak circuit analysis has been used, ranging from military weapons systems in all three services, to NASA's space systems. With increases in size, commercial aircraft passenger capacities, and potential loss costs in the event of an accident, it is expected that the use of this analysis method will continue to increase.

Although principal use of sneak circuit analysis has been chiefly for electronic systems, another analysis method, which produced some of the terminology still in use for sneak circuits, was originally developed by J. E. Rivas and D. F. Rudd at the University of Wisconsin as an Army study for fluid control systems. The authors indicate how complex some hydraulic systems can become by pointing out that with a system employing 17 valves, each of which can be in either an open or closed position, there can be a total of 131,072 final valve position combinations. "The system is viewed as an assembly of *connectors* which are joined at 'nodes.'" (Lloyd and Tye's book points out many of the hydraulic flow problems on commercial aircraft.)

Similar problems arise with electronic systems such as those in computer circuitry for which an analyst often has difficulty in finding and eliminating errors in computer circuitry, especially since more types of sneaks and anomalies can occur electrically than can energy through more securely confined hydraulic lines.

The Boeing Aerospace Company developed its methodology in 1977 and applied its technique to about 100 projects over the space of ten years. It was stated that in performing the sneak circuit analysis for the U.S. Army's Pershing missile, 20 sneak circuits, 12 design anomalies, and 40 drawing errors were found. NAVSO P-3634 lists a large number of projects for which sneak circuit analysis was used.

Sneak circuit analyses performed by Boeing, General Dynamics, and others are considered proprietary. However, no information is provided in this document on analyses costs, although a rough order-of-magnitude cost estimates are based on quantities of component parts.

A sneak circuit problem involving automobile radios was detected in the late 1960's (see Figure 16-2). Other examples are shown with products of greater complexity: the failure of a train to stop where desired and its doors opening inadvertently, and lastly, a radar monitor control unit that failed to cease operations when the unit was shut off, indicating a sneak condition.

Automobile Radio Anomaly

The components through which the current flowed in the automobile (Figure 16-2) included not only the radio, but also the power source, the generator/battery, the ignition switch, brake switch, tail lights, other flashers, and finally to ground. A latent sneak circuit path was not detectable by usual testing methods because no hardware failure could be found. Recently, a humorous TV commercial for a company named Circuit City showed a potential problem due to the improper installation of an automobile radio by others. After the faulty installation had been completed, the automobile driver turned on the ignition and *all* the electrical systems, including the windshield wipers, electric windows, and blaring radio began operating at once. The problem may have appeared humorous, but to the driver it would probably be so annoying he would make certain it was repaired immediately and properly, or have the installer hauled into court.

General Analysis Procedure

A sneak circuit analysis involves the following steps:

1. Identify the adverse events that might arise because of a sneak circuit in a product. The possibility is identified by a previous undesired occurrence, or the desire to forestall the occurrence of all possible sneak circuit problems. Where such an anomaly might be safety-critical and a highly undesirable possibility might have been identified by prior use of previous reviews such as a preliminary, failure modes and effects, or fault-tree analysis.

A fault tree is not adequate for detecting a sneak anomaly, but is useful in zeroing in on where a failure, caused by a sneak circuit, could lead to an adverse event such as the failure of a train or elevator door opening inadvertently at an improper point.

Figure 16-3 indicates why in a network where a circuit is to be analyzed whether certain trees (circuit segments) are critical to the analysis and should be subjected to a failure modes and effects analysis or whether the segment can be omitted from any further analysis; therefore providing an analysis saving consideration.

2. Further information that will be required for a complete analysis includes block diagrams such as from

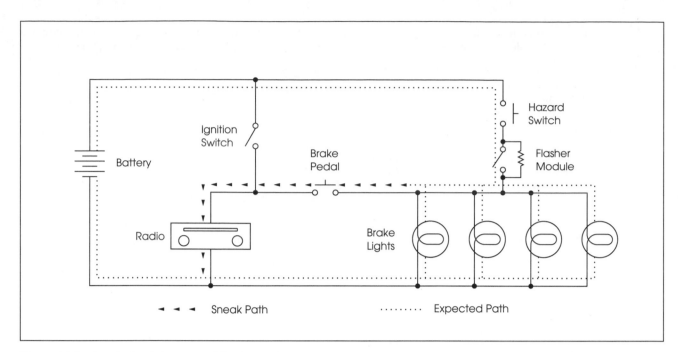

Figure 16-2. Sneak circuit in automobile electronics.

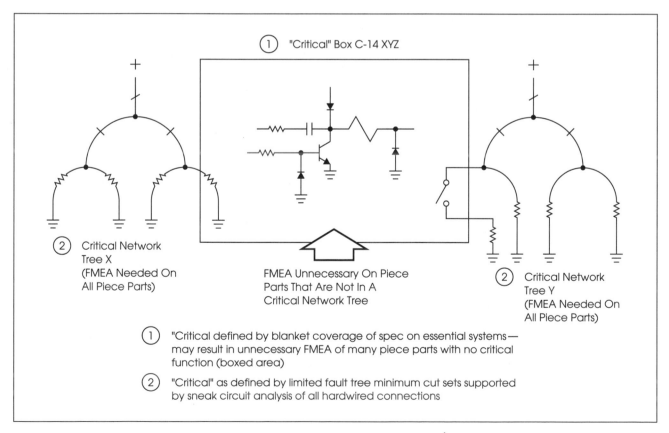

Figure 16-3. Using sneak circuit analysis to determine the need for FMEA analyses.[1]

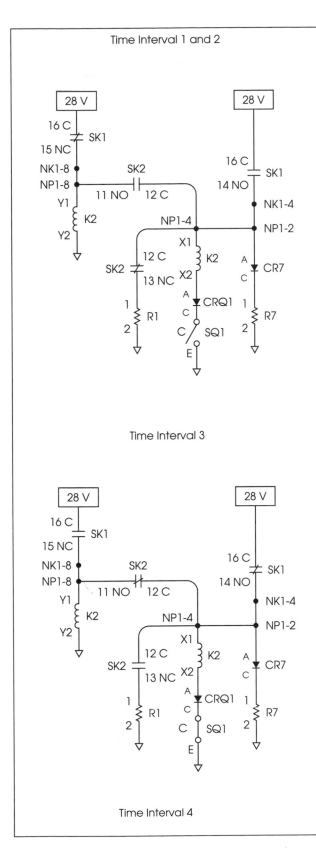

Time Interval 1

- No 28 V power available.
- All relay contacts and switches are in their normally de-energized states.

Time Interval 2

- 28 V power is provided by aircraft generators.
- The Y1/Y2 winding of relay K2 is energized, holding its contacts in their existing positions, i.e., contacts 11-12 open, contacts 13-12 closed.

Time Interval 3

- Aircraft in flight.
- Main radar switch is closed.
- Relay K1 is energized.
  Its normally open contacts (16-14) close, and its normally closed contacts (16-15) open.
- Power is removed from relay coil Y1/Y2.
- Voltage is applied to CR7, causing transistor Q1 to conduct.
- The X1/X2 winding of relay K2 is energized.
  It normally open contacts (11-12) close, and its normally closed contacts (12-13) open.
- Power is restored to the Y1/Y2 coil; however, since power was never removed from the X1/X2 coil, the relay does not change state.

Time Interval 4

- Aircraft lands, internal power maintained.
- Main Radar switch is opened.
- Relay K1 is de-energized.
  Its contents return to their normal de-energized positions.
- As SK1 contacts switch to energized state, power is removed from CRQ1 base which opens the X1/X2 coils.
- Power is also removed from Y1/Y2 simultaneously. Therefore SK2 does not change state.
- Since SK2 contacts 11-12 remain closed, power is supplied to the Y1/Y2 coils and the base of CRQ1 simultaneously.
- CRQ1 switches X1/X2 to ground before the Y1/Y2 coils can switch SK2 off due to the long time constant in the coil and mechanical inertia. The X1/X2 coil dominates.

Figure 16-4. Description of aircraft radar sneak path.

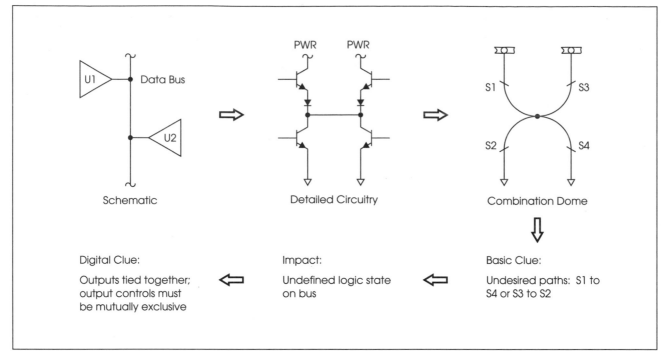

Figure 16-5. Additional example of clues applied to typical topographs.

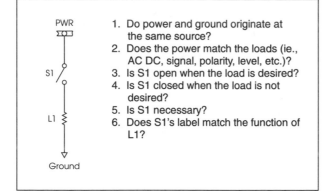

1. Do power and ground originate at the same source?
2. Does the power match the loads (ie., AC DC, signal, polarity, level, etc.)?
3. Is S1 open when the load is desired?
4. Is S1 closed when the load is not desired?
5. Is S1 necessary?
6. Does S1's label match the function of L1?

Figure 16-6. Sneak clue examples for straight line topograph.[2]

a Fault Tree or similar study; schematic drawings; complete listings of interfaces; time intervals as usages of the product, its components, and circuits in use change (see Figure 16-4); and detailed lists of all components with their functions and operations. These detailed lists can be taken from those previously prepared for a FMEA.

3. The circuitry is marked with partition points so the overall analysis can be divided into more easily manageable proportions. In some systems, these different subsystems are allotted for accomplishment by different designers, contractors, or vendors. Partitioning (Figure 16-5) permits preparation and drawing of nodal trees in accordance with topological patterns, of which there are five. Trees are topological representations of the actual circuit components and their interconnections within the system. In general, the topology requires that higher voltage potentials be placed at the top of the tree, the lower voltage at the bottom, and functional flow is shown from left to right.

Figure 16-5 indicates representations as a schematic diagram, detailed circuitry, and topograph as well as clues which are recommended as investigatory questions that might be used in such an analysis. Additional clues are prepared because of a straight line topograph.

4. Figure 16-6 represents a small electrical segment, shown as a schematic drawing from power to ground, and with circuitry details comprises a straight line topograph, the simplest of all. The same figure indicates clues that might be posed regarding that simple circuit segment.

5. Figure 16-7 indicates how a path report in a complex system for wire segments might be completed and identified for coding purposes. Additional information on the portion of a black box with a simpler detail schematic to be analyzed is shown in Figure 16-8, with information to be encoded.

Coding information would have been developed from topological representations with each tree of a size to permit preparation of a computer coding table, listing "From–To" identification of components, and circuit segments.

6. Although small systems using up to 20 nodes can be analyzed manually, for a complex system, the data is encoded for computer processing, using either keypunch cards or a computer terminal. The information entered must include every component and signal-path segment.

Path Report, Automated Sneak Program

Power-to-Ground Thru Switch and Node

Wire Bay	Termination Item	Pin	Area Harness	Box Reference Designator	Box Drawing Number	DIO	IMP	Remarks
HAC	PWR	028V		9473		0	.0	
HAC	SK1	NC16		9473		0	.0	
HAC	SK1	0015		9473		0	.0	
HAC	J5	0008		9473		0	.0	
HAC	J434	0008		245		0	.0	
HAC	NY1K2			245		0	.0	
HAC	SAK2	NOA1		245		0	.0	
HAC	SAK2	NOA2		245		0	.0	
HAC	NX1K2			245		0	.0	
HAC	J434	0004		245		0	.0	
HAC	E434	0001		245		0	.0	
HAC	J434	0002		245		0	.0	
HAC	J87624	0012		245		0	.0	
HAC	J240	0005		9007		0	.0	
HAC	CR7	000A		9007		0	.0	
HAC	CR7	000C		9007		0	.0	
HAC	R7	A3K3		9007		0	.0	
HAC	R7	B3K3		9007		0	.0	
HAC	KQ1	BASE		9007		0	.0	
HAC	KQ1	EMIT		9007		0	.0	
HAC	GND	0900		9007		0	.0	

Figure 16-7. Path report, automated sneak program.

Black Box Detail Schematic

Input Form

Box Ref Des	Module	Subsystem	Dwg. No.	Rev	Part No.	Box Title
702A2	A48	EPS	7623551	A	7623551 -1	MOT CONT

	FROM		TO		DIODE	IMP	REMARKS
	ITEM	PIN	ITEM	PIN			
702A2	J1	A	SF10	1			
	SF10	1	SF10	2			15 AMP
	SF10	2	SH105	3			
	SK105	3	SK105	1			MOT CONT
	SK105	1	J1	B			
	J1	B	SK104	6			
	SK104	6	SK104	4			MOT CONT
	SK104	4	J1	C			

Figure 16-8. Computer coding table prepared from topological representations of a black-box tree.

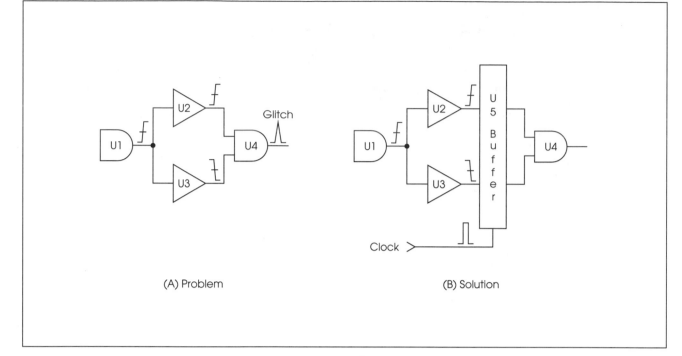

Figure 16-9. Recombining digital signals (sneak timing) example.[2]

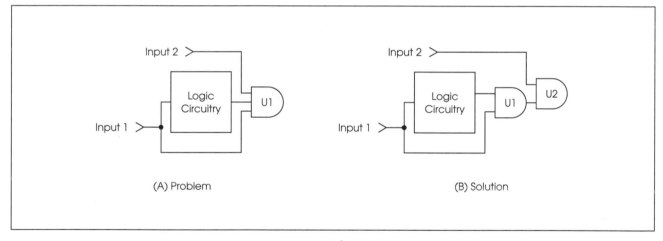

Figure 16-10. Recombining digital signals (sneak state) example.[2]

7. The data is then processed to establish all point-to-point continuity paths for the system using an appropriate software program. Very large programs use 15 individual COBOL routines run serially on a computer. Programs are proprietary but may be available for sale. The output will indicate all possible paths that can exist.

8. Sneak "clues" are then used to identify and analyze sneak problems by posing questions to the analyst similar to those in Figure 16-6, which provides the simplest example, of a topograph, a straight-line circuit which extends from a positive power source through a switch, and load, to ground.

Clues for Detecting Sneak Conditions

In addition to the clues provided as examples in Figure 16-6, clues used for detecting sneak conditions may be categorized as those associated with piece parts and configurations or as topographic pattern clues used in analyzing network trees.

Appendix C to NAVSO P-3634 consists entirely of clues which range from topograph trees, circuit configurations, component piece parts and design concerns; the number and type of clues available will continue to increase with experience of analysts, new systems, rectification of previous errors and the desire for greater coverage.

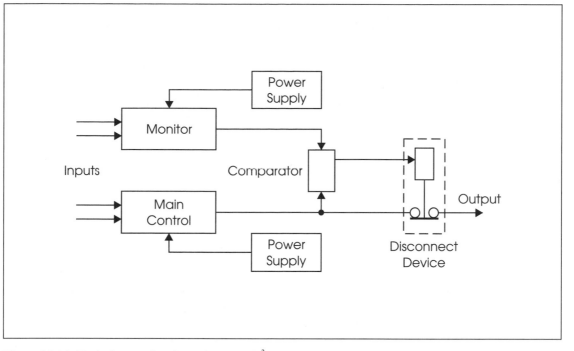

Figure 16-11. Typical control and monitor system.[3]

Tyrone Jackson also provided two examples (Figures 16-9 and 16-10) that show sneak problem causes and their solutions. He also pointed out the major benefits of sneak circuit analyses:

1. Improves confidence in system usage reliability, availability, and safety prior to usage.

2. Reduces testing, drawing changes, and life cycle costs.

3. Complements, but does not replace or supersede, fault/failure analyses.

4. Provides an overall view of system hardware.

5. Provides some sneak problems that might arise because of common cause failure.

In their book on commercial aviation, Lloyd and Tye pointed out a typical control and monitor system (Figure 16-11). The cause of an anomaly is shown with an example of a potential problem in a typical aircraft monitor and control system, "an autopilot" in which the output of a monitor, a replica of the main control channel, is compared with that of the main channel. The description also pointed out the possibility of a fault which not only causes the malfunction, but also inhibits the device which monitors the system and disconnects it or gives warning of its failure, "In addition to causing failures or malfunctions of redundant channels there is also the possibility of a fault in an aircraft control and monitor system."

One of the sneak topographic clue questions in sneak circuit analysis is, "Can a reverse current inadvertently flow through the cross member of the 'H pattern'?" Lloyd and Tye's book shows diagrammatically (Figure 16-12) the cause of a problem with grounding (earthing). A joint in the earth connection might cause an A.C. component to be injected into the D.C. equipment and D.C. component into A.C. equipment, with possible malfunctions, particularly where sensing and amplifying circuits are involved.

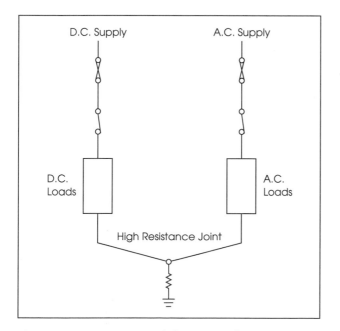

Figure 16-12. Common earth for D.C. and A.C. equipment.[3]

(Project) Common Cause Failure Analysis					
Critical Function Set	Commonality	Critical Event	Potential Cause	Effect	Remarks
Door & Speed Control 2-A)T38–Left side door	Connector DJ2	Electrical shorts:	1) Conductive contaminant	Left side doors driven open and emergency brakes inhibited.	Violation of design criteria—redesign recommended.
2-B)T102–Emergency brakes		Pins H–J–K	2) Metallic shearing of wire bundle	Doors 1 & 3 driven open.	Adjacent pins—credible.

Figure 16-13. Documentation format for common cause failure analysis.[1]

A reverse current and inadvertent flow through the cross member of the "H" pattern might be created by a joint in the earth connection, leading to the problem indicated by Lloyd and Tye, with a possible malfunction due to a sneak path.

Lloyd and Tye go on to say:

> Integrity of such a system [the autopilot and monitor] can be undermined in one of the following ways:
>
> 1. Lack of electrical and mechanical segregation between the main control and the monitor.
>
> 2. Lack of adequate segregation within the comparator leading to cross connection.
>
> 3. The use of common power supply or modulation or ripples or pulses can cause malfunction of the main control and at the same time inhibit the monitor.
>
> 4. Electromagnetic interference affecting both the main control and the monitor in the same way.

Lloyd and Tye's excellent book goes on to describe (not discussed here) some potential mechanical problems, especially those due to common causes, the reasons for them, and their solutions. Faults that might occur because of a common cause, leading to failures and resulting in adverse effects, are indicated in Figure 16-13 by Rankin.

Figure 16-14 illustrates a plug map which shows the layout of a multi-pin connector. It can be seen that a sneak might occur not only because of the bending of pins so there is electrical contact, but also because of the possibility of the presence of moisture or a small amount of water that may facilitate a sneak path. It was just such a problem with a multi-pinned plug that led to the opening of train doors that should not have occurred as shown in Figure 16-15. It should also be pointed out that the Hound Dog missile was prone to such sneak problems during testing, because moisture accumulated in the large

multiple-plug connector that parted when the missile separated from the aircraft on launch.

Figure 16-15 indicates how an anomaly existed because of the D-2 multi-pin plug connector so that a train door opened when it should not have. This figure details not only the items involved and the sneak path, but also how two trees (inserts 38 and 102 in Figure 16-15) comprised the anomaly. The result was the unintended operation and opening of the door on the left side of a train, that should have led to its automatic emergency stopping, but did not.

The sneak path occurred between the pins of connector DJ2, shorting pin H to J. Under normal circumstances, limit switches on the door edges would sense the opening and cause removal of the fail-safe emergency relay in Tree 102.

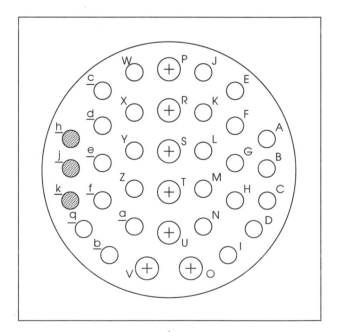

Figure 16-14. DJ2 plug map.[1]

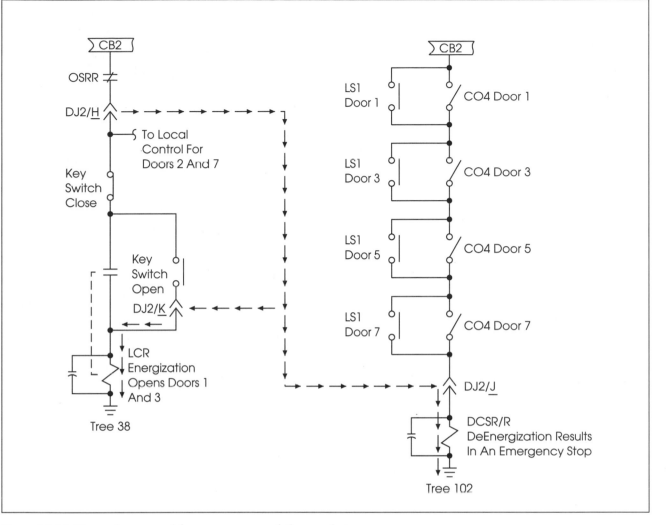

Figure 16-15. Network trees used for common cause failure analysis.

Thus, the train would normally stop upon any unplanned opening. However, as the illustration shows, if pin H is also shorted to pin J of the same connector, power will be maintained on the EMERGENCY STOP relay even after the doors open. Therefore, stopping will be inhibited and the door driven open during shorting of these three pins simultaneously, in violation of safe design criteria. The train could travel at commanded speed while the car doors were open, due to a single failure-type event. Although there had been no violation regarding separation of pins from power and ground as is normally required. It was believed the presence of water, from rain or after washing, may have resulted in a common-cause problem.

It may have been such a sneak problem that occurred soon after the BART (Bay Area Rapid Transit) system began operating, when a train failed to stop when intended, doing so only when it hit a bumper at its terminal end. No one was hurt, but fears of the passengers delayed the use of the system until the necessity for rapid transit overcame the fear of possible future accidents. Opinion at the time was that the mishap was probably due to the existence of a sneak circuit.

Jackson discussed the sneak problem in an aircraft radar unit that would not shut down when so directed. This provided a clue and indication of the existence of a sneak circuit after a monitor lamp from an aircraft monitor circuit failed to de-energize when the main radar switch was opened (see Figure 16-16). The sneak circuit caused battery power that could be aborted only by removing power completely from the aircraft. The topological trees of the sneak path producing the sneak condition was: "When switch is opened, power is supplied to Y1/Y2 coils and base of Q1, simultaneously resulting in Q1 switching X1/X2 to ground, before Y1/Y2 coils can switch S2 off."

Computers and Safety

Related to sneak circuit analysis is a proposed method I have called "Computers and Safety." For this, Figure 16-17 has been provided. Although the use of computers and their terminology has been widely accepted in daily practice, wider usage, especially in conjunction with

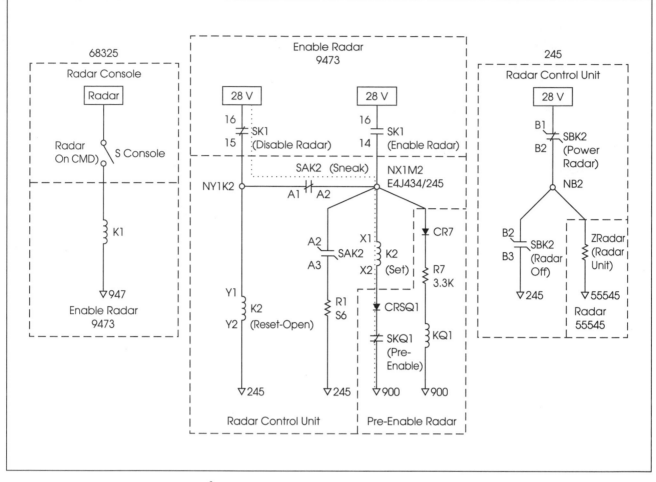

Figure 16-16. Aircraft radar sneak path[2].

sneak circuit analysis presented earlier, is given here. Sneak software conditions and anomalies which might come about in both sneak circuit and computer safety analyses are listed in Figure 16-18.

The reason I believe everyone should be knowledgeable in the subject of computers and safety is that the hazards are so insidious. When some designers in high-tech industry were queried on the subject, they contended that computers might fail, but were entirely safe and free from injurious accident possibilities. However, one reason for the new concern about computer safety is that a maintenance man in a Japanese company was killed because of the failure to program a robot against an actual hazard. The most notable computerized robot systems, other than for military products, are for use in the automobile industry, in hope that they will realize great savings in labor costs.

To ensure that any computerized industrial system will be safe, the following method of analysis is being presented. Just as other analysis methods already discussed in this book, this proposal is oriented towards accident prevention. In this instance, the example will postulate hazards which might arise with a system designed to direct a robotics machine to make electric spot welds in an automobile fabrication plant. Included will be one of the many program routines that would be required in the software. Possible actions, effects, and precautions that have to be taken in automobile body spot welding are: After verifying that the auto body is properly positioned, the robot would have to position any welding electrode properly, then provide suitable electrical power for a good weld, and finally shut it off at the proper instant when the spot weld is completed satisfactorily. The robot would have to position the welding electrode in elevation and then rotate it in azimuth after which the electrode would be extended until it was close enough to the work to operate on it. Electric power would then be supplied and shut off at suitable times, all done through computer software.

Assuming the software program had been adequately tested and all "bugs" eliminated, an analysis might be made of the problems that could occur. With any anomaly that might result, adverse occurrence would probably be due only to multiple hardware failures. Any adverse occurrence would provide a clue to the problem, but safety would be ensured; if there is no firing after a proper signal, there will be no weld. If firing duration is too short, the resulting weld may be weak; too great an amperage, or too long, may cause a burn in the thin metal creating either a hole or an unsatisfactory weld. There should be no power firing unless all required positioning has been

Some Computer Terms Applicable to Safety Analyses

Abort

To stop further activity either because of an error, completion of a program, or failure to proceed further properly.

Address

The location for stored information.

Bug

An error in a program.

Central Processing Unit (CPU)

The unit which acts as the "brain" to govern all actions, computations, and other functions.

Chip

A minute solid-state device which contains all the elements of a processor, including transistors, diodes, capacitors, other necessary components, with interconnecting circuitry, all in a wafer sliced from a silicon crystal.

Code

A representation of data or instructions in symbolic form.

Crash

Complete loss of all memory and programmed instructions.

Flowchart

A set of sequential procedures represented by symbols.

Glitch

A problem or failure in a program so a computer fails to perform properly; usually more severe than a bug.

Hardware

The electromechanical components, with the connecting circuitry of a computer.

Integrated Circuitry

The lines through which the minute amounts of current pass through the processor.

Language

The means of expressing instructions to the computer. Many types of computer languages have been developed and are in use, each depending on the type of desired activity, from highly complex mathematical calculations to word processing.

Logic

The reasoning used in the design of software. Computer logic follows an orderly, step-by-step procedure.

Processor

The electromechanical portion of a computer that does the work.

Program

A set of detailed instructions contained in the software.

Routine

A set of instructions in a planned sequence for a computer program to follow.

Software

The program in a computer on which and when each unit will execute the instructions the software contains.

Specification

A statement which presents a detailed description of the design, aims, capabilities to which the computer must perform, the results it must achieve and the limitations to which it is subject, and other information such as speed of performance, size, or cost.

Subroutine or Sub-Program

A portion of an entire program which can be called up when, and as, necessary; especially where there are repeated uses at different times.

TMTT (Tell Me Three Times)

To ensure a transient has not created a problem, analysts recommend the use of TMTT, 2/3 (two out of three), or other software verification features such as repeating a signal a number of times.

Figure 16-17. Some computer terms applicable to safety analyses.

Sneak Software Conditions and Anomalies

Missing Logic

- Unused logic
- Invalid wait loops
- Bypassed logic
- Open-ended logic
- Logic Loops
- Conflicting tests
- Invalid outputs

Software Design Concern Conditions

- Improper sequence of instructions
- Unnecessary logic
- Unreferenced labels or variables
- Redundant logic
- Difficulties with future maintainability due to inconsistencies between software specifications and code
- Module structure/length
- Software Document Errors
- Discrepancies found in any two specification documents

Figure 16-18. Sneak software conditions and anomalies.

confirmed. Any possible injury or unsatisfactory weld due to unforseen safety problems should be denied by the software.

Any computer anomaly capable of producing an adverse effect can be the result of either an electromechanical failure in or to the central processing unit, or an error in the computer's software. Because software is written by humans, computers are subject to the same errors to which humans are prone. For this reason, not only must software be prepared according to the rules for software preparation that are generally taught, but after a program has been prepared, it should be tested. Because of the nature of computers, the program can be run, tested, and modified repeatedly, as desired, until all anomalies are eliminated.

Unfortunately, even this positive feature can cause a problem: a software error might cause unending repetition so that the computer might continue to print the same message endlessly or continue to take, without stopping, the same action, much like the one that occurred with the inexperienced sorcerer's apprentice who could not stop the relentless input of salt, once he had started it, so the seas became salty. Computers themselves have no capacity for originality of thought, and any capability, including that of making an error, must either have been implanted in its software or must have been made by a human computer operator. In any case, to lessen the potential problem of errors by operators, computer programmers incorporate methods of verification

such as the one known as TMTT, before computer operation can proceed further.

Aside from software problems, computers may fail because of problems in hardware or their interconnections. More annoying than any outright failure is an intermittent malfunction in any part. The result of a problem might be manifested by a:

- Zero output
- Degraded output
- Erratic output
- Unprogrammed output
- Undesirable side effect

Figure 16-19 shows how some types of problems, causes, and numbers (numbers of alerts), are obtained through conventional screening methods; failure avoidance would be to provide corrective action to the problem shown in the remarks column. This figure, prepared by Lockheed Missiles and Space Co. for NASA's Ames Research Center under contract NASA-6060, indicates experience with various components and shows some, but not all, of the experience figures to indicate problems that were found.

Testing of even a trivial program is an exhaustive task; witness the example in Figure 16-20, which is one of comparatively minor complexity. The question has been posed as to whether there is some method for finding all, or a high percentage, of computer software errors. The answer not only has been "No," but also that it is unlikely that this will change in the foreseeable future.

This unfavorable prognosis requires that a radically new approach be employed for a usable method of analysis for potential safety problems that can lead to minimization of software problems, and incorporation of safeguards through software measures. This had led to the method suggested here. The example to be provided is a program designated for the XW-91-100, a laserwelder used to safely make spot welds on automobile turrets.

The first safeguard is a metal eyelid that must be raised out of the way before any attempt is made to fire the laser. In addition to having suitable software for ensuring that there is no attempt to fire the laser, either against the closed lid or outside a desired area, an electrical limit switch and a hard stop can be designed. This can provide additional safeguards in the event that there is a failure in either the software or hardware. Resolvers also will provide information to the computer so with any detected anomaly, all further action will be aborted.

Software control of the computer will be programmed to inhibit firing into any prescribed area or before the eyelid is moved out of the way. Both of these controls will lessen any unnecessary expenditure of energy.

Further information regarding the XW-91-100 laserwelder, adverse events, potential effects, causative signals that could

Software Problems Identified Through Conventional Screening Methods

Problem	No. of Alerts/ Items	Problem Causes	Conventional Screens	Remarks
Lifted beads	7	Poor bonding processes. Excessive bonding pressure causing bond distortion and cracking at the heel.	High temperature storage, thermal shock, acceleration, burn-in, electrical testing.	Power cycling will induce fatigue and accelerate cracked and packed wire failures. Marginal bonds could be degraded by conventional screens and still pass.
Metalization	3	Moisture contamination or residual TCE from cleaning process.	Thermal shock, acceleration, hermetic seal, burn-in, electrical testing.	Hermetic seal will prevent contamination from using environment. Process-induced contaminants may cause degradation of parts during conventional screens without precipitating failure.
Parameter Deviation	3	Moisture contamination in encapsulated gas ambient. Moisture in package due to defective hermetic seals.	Dew point test, hermetic seal.	Dew point test could be ineffective with well-passivated devices. Moisture contamination could cause corrosion.
Conductive Contamination	9	Loose solder, weld splatter, slack leads, or poor lead dress.	Acceleration, electrical testing, radiographic inspection.	Radiographic inspection limitations are generally particles of .001 in. size or larger. Acceleration may be ineffective for particulates.
Parameter Deviation	6	Channeling due to lack of channel stop protection.	High temperature reverse bias, burn-in, electrical testing.	Conventional screens are adequate.
Mechanical Anomalies	3	Corroded leads, notched leads. plating pin-holes, and bare spots on leads.	Visual inspection.	Conventional screen is adequate.
Microcracks on Window Cutout	2	Steep oxide steps cause thin metalization at contact windows and metalization tends to separate.	Minimum of 30 cycles temperature cycling. 100% electric tests. Scanning electron microscope scan on sample	Marginal devices may not be screened.
Lifted Chips and Cracked Die	4	Pyroceram bonding of silicon chip to package provided poor adhesive. Proper pyroceram may not have been used. Cracked die resulted from temperature coefficient mismatch between silicon die and pyroceram.	100% precap visual, temperature cycling, variable frequency vibration, consistent acceleration. 100% electrical testing, radiographic inspection.	Conventional screens are adequate.
Wire Corrosion	3	Glass splatter from sealing hardglass flatpack to hover lid deposited on aluminum lead, possibly reacting with contaminants and moisture in the package and corroding the wire to an open condition.	100% recap visual, gross leak test	Conventional screens are adequate.
Voids and overetched metalisation	1	Holes in photoresist permitted etchant to penetrate masked area	100% electrical tests.	Conventional screens are adequate.
Open Beads	3	Improper alloying schedule causing poor aluminum adhesion to silicon; formation of gali-aluminum intermetallic, overbonding with excessive temp/pressure, improperly placed beads, rebonding after silicon is exposed.	100% precap visual stabilization bake, mechanical shock, thermal shock, constant acceleration random vibration, sample bond pull tests.	Conventional screens are adequate, however tight process controls and high quality standards are important.
Open Metalization	3	Corrosion of aluminum in presence of moisture (Hydrated alumina), scratches during handling and assembly, thinning over oxide steps, aluminum pulling toward alloyed contact, faulty oxide removal.	Precap visual, stabilization bake prior to seal, hermetic seal tests, temperature cycling, power burn-in at elevated temperature. Sample scanning electron microscope scans.	Tight process controls and handling procedures required. Processes and designs should be reviewed for adequate metalization thickness and grain size. Devices prone to migration failure may not be screened.

Figure 16-19. Software problems identified through conventional screening methods.

Software Problems Identified Through Conventional Screening Methods

Problem	No. of Alerts/ Items	Problem Causes	Conventional Screens	Remarks
Lifted beads	7	Poor bonding processes. Excessive bonding pressure causing bond distortion and cracking at the heel.	High temperature storage, thermal shock, acceleration, burn-in, electrical testing.	Power cycling will induce fatigue and accelerate cracked and packed wire failures. Marginal bonds could be degraded by conventional screens and still pass.
Bulk shorts	3	Dopant spikes during diffusion, dendritic growths caused by silica crystal imperfections and pinholes, diffusion anomalies resulting in isolation junction breakdown.	Precap visual, thermal bakes, operating life tests	Process controls required in addition to conventional screens.
Metalization Shorts	9	Unetched metalization and smears, extraneous conductive material from leads, bonds, eutectics, or solders from bonding die attach, or package sealing procedures, carbonized material on die surface.	Precap visual, radiographic electrical tests.	Conventional screen may not detect all shorts. Improved process controls and cleaning procedures required. Die passivation should be required.
Metalisation or bond to silicon shots	4	Oxide pinholes, metalization mask misalignment, lead bond at edge of die, bond made over oxide step, poor scribbing and dicing, stress cracks in oxide.	Precap visual, temperature cycling, over voltage tests, electrical tests.	Conventional screens are adequate. Most problems of the type can be eliminated by better processing standards and controls.
Lead Shorts	7	Leads too long, improper chip orientation, sagging leads, leads touch edge of die, loops shorting to package, glass seal precipitating lead between leads.	Precap visual, vibration tests, shock tests, radiographic inspection, electrical tests.	Conventional screens are adequate.
Operational Degradation	9	Design deficiencies, inversions caused by phosphorous glass passivation, reaction of output transistor with plastic case material, missing diffusier.	Electrical tests at ambient and extreme temperatures.	Conventional screens are adequate. Avoid use of plastic devices.
Operational Degradation	2	Overfritting of glass during die bonding causing glass to extend up the side and onto chip surface, cracked die, photoresist residue, pyroceram voids.	Precap visual, radiographic electrical tests, environmentals per MIL-STD-863-Method 5004.	Conventional screens are adequate. Avoid glass frit bonding approach.
External Anomaly	3	Package identification obliterated by solvents, chip bond eutectic overflowed to aluminum bond on substrate forming intermetallics.	Precap visual, radiographic, high temperature storage, thermal cycling, shock acceleration, variable frequency vibration.	Conventional screens are adequate.

Figure 16-19 (cont'd). Software problems identified through conventional screening methods.

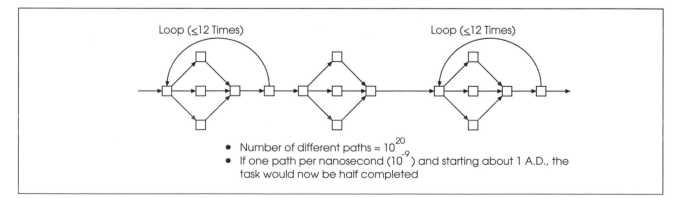

Figure 16-20. Testing computer software paths.

Computer Software Analysis

1 Computer Controlled Units of System	2 Adverse Event That Could Be Initiated by Computer Output Error	3 Potential Effects of Adverse Event	4 Input Signal to Computer Controlled Unit That Would Generate Each Adverse (Unsafe) Event	5 Proposed Safeguards	6 List Program Steps Which Could Produce Products or Permit the Unsafe Event	7 Alterative Internal Progress Actions Which Could Adversely Affect this Step	8 Means of Avoiding Alternative Action
1. Turret							
2. Laser/ Welder	2a. Laser/ Welder fires inadvertently.	2a. (1) Hit an intended target (2) Hit protective cover which is not fullyopen (3) Waste of ammunition	2a. Failure to inhibit welder firing signal	2a. (1) Software program to inhibit firing unless all safety conditions are satisfied. (2) Software program to inhibit firing unless protective cover is fully open. (3) Not a safety problem.	2a. (2). Current program permits laser/welder to fire when only "Cover Fully Open" signal is received, even if cover is actually closed. Noise or electromagnetic effect could erase a critical instruction.	2a (2). Failure in software program to include provision to inhibit firing when a short circuit results in "Cover Fully Open" and "Cover Closed" signals are both inputted to controller. (Controller acts only on "open" signal.)	2a. (2). Modify software program so that firing will be inhibited unless both "Cover Fully Open" AND no "Cover Closed" are received (CFO CC). Check subroutines toensure they will satisfy all foreseeable requirements and inputs.
	2b. Welder fires in proscribed area.	2b. (1) Damage to own equipment (2) Injury or damage to nearby personnel or equipment	2b. Failure to interrupt firing signal.	2b. (1) Software program will interrupt firing if a command would direct the laser into the proscribed area, or if line of sight of the weapon approaches the limit to that area. Also, mechanical stops to prevent firing into proscribed area. (2) Same.			

Figure 16-21. Computer software analysis.

generate each adverse (unsafe) event, and proposed safeguard software controls are provided in Figure 16-21.

Possible abnormal conditions or anomalies with the unit that could receive an erroneous input are considered. Possible defective software is identified here. Information on controller hardware interfaces that affect the software program should be provided. A transient voltage change because of poor regulation might wipe out a computer program, data, an address, or other information. This evaluation can be done through the use of "clues" similar to the methodology described previously for sneak circuit analysis. Also, similar information on possible common-failure-mode causes and effects can be provided.

Other considerations found to be significant are durations of intervals of safety processes that are especially safety critical; for example the time period when firing of the laserwelder begins and when it is interrupted.

The failure of a software routine should be described if safety related.

Additional program items of interest that might be considered have been added to this figure in columns number:

6. Any foreseeable, undesirable action that might generate an unsafe event.

Computer Software Analysis, cont'd

9 Control to Limit Alternative Action Which Cannot Be Eliminated	10 Means of Identifying Erroneous Output	11 Means of Inhibiting Erroneous Output	12 Inputs to Computer Which Can Cause Unsafe Output Signal(s)	13 Program Step to Avoid or Identify Erroneous Input	14 Program Step to Inhibit Processing Erroneous Input	15 Operator Capability to Change Program, or Words, or to Provide Erroneous Inputs	16 Remarks
2a. (2).Only remaining possibility not covered by software program is that cover might be partially open AND there might be an erroneous "Cover Fully Open input signal. Probability of these occurring simultaneously is so remote it can be disregarded.	2a. (2). Provide an additional input signal (photoelectric cell or interlock at cover) and comparison routine in software program.	2a. (2). Provide redundant routines and compare after completion. If they do not correspond, inhibit firing. Repeat routine three times (TMTT–Tell Me Three Times) to ensure it is not a one-time processing error.	2a. (2). "Cover Fully Open" switch fails in position which erroneously indicates "Open." Short circuit within wiring to computer occurs so erroneous "Open" signal is inputted.	2a. (2) Include subroutine in program which will indicate that both "Cover Fully Open" and "Cover Closed" have been received will indicate there is an erroneous input. Separate the connector pins for wires used for "Open" and "Closed" circuits. Present design uses redundant "Open" switches, but both switches are tied to same circuit to controller. Provide separate circuits to controller and incorporate routine to compare inputs. If hey differ, compare to similar arrangements and utput of routine for "Closed" circuits; or automatically inhibit firing.	2a. (2). Routine to abort firing if computer receives both "Cover Fully Open" AND "Cover Closed" signals.	2a (2). Operator cannot affect this action.	2a. (2). Designer may want to analyze time factors for nrew comparison routine to ensure it does not unduly delay system capability. It would be beneficial to classify processing of this roeutine as a critical instruction so a subroutine will be included to ensure avoidance of errors.

Figure 16-21 (cont'd). Computer software analysis.

7. Any possible alternative program which should fail to prevent the unsafe event.

8. Identify any logic change that will correct the condition in column 7.

9. Indicate the software control to limit the alternative action that might be taken by an operator.

10. Describe the software or combination of software and hardware that will identify any erroneous output or lack of output signal from the controller. Included should be check works and check values to recognize an input, computer, or output error. This will ensure that values of signals inputted are identical to stipulated values. Critical values which may be especially significant should be included. This will help in determination of "clues" where anomalies might exist.

11. Means of inhibiting erroneous outputs will include descriptions in other columns of means of preventing and identifying the unwanted event; here the software change is described that results in inhibition of the erroneous output.

12. Any input condition that can cause an erroneous or unsafe output signal to the controller is described here.

13. The software routine or other technique that will indicate an erroneous signal being inputted into the controller is described here; also noted here are any possible corrections to prevent the erroneous signals from being generated.

14. Software program that will refuse to process an erroneous signal, or inhibit outputting of one is indicated here.

15. Note here whether the operator has any capability to change or modify any program, and whether an operator can bypass, in any manner, any of the logic in the software.

16. Note under "Remarks" any software error, hardware failure, or action that might affect the proper outcome of the events described.

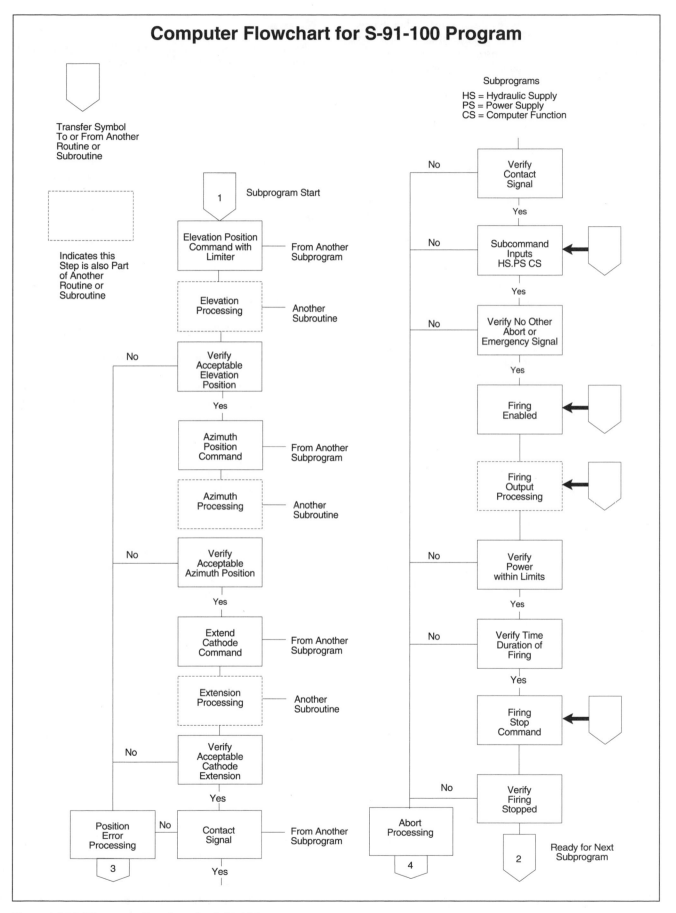

Figure 16-22. Computer flowchart for S-91-100 program.

The analyst may also find it desirable to list, either in new columns or under "Remarks," any specific test for safety to verify the adequacy of the program. This can include the proposed test and when it is accomplished.

It is believed advisable to point out a few terms used with the XW-91-100 laserwelder, including the term "target" that indicates the point where a spot weld is to be made. "Target not within TD" signifies the absence of the chassis because it has moved out of position but another one has not moved into a proper location. The term "electrode," normally applied to a welding rod, is used to indicate the path of the laser. A flowchart for the computer controlled S-91-100 program is shown in Figure 16-22.

It is important to note that the logic is oriented to ensure utmost safety in computer operation of the laserwelder. Conditions that all must be satisfied to safely fire the laser are contained in the following logic expression:

PA = Laserwelder P̲o̲i̲n̲t̲i̲n̲g̲ to a Safe Area.
PA = Laserwelder N̅o̅t̅ Pointing to a Safe Area. [The bar over the symbol indicates "Not" is in accordance with accepted logic notation.]
PZ = Satisfactory Azimuth Position.
PE = Satisfactory Elevation Position.
PA = PZ•PE
Also

TT = Laserwelder on Target.
HS = Hydraulic System Operating Properly.
PS = Power System Operating Properly.
CS = Computer System Operating Properly.
CF = Protective Cover Fully Open.
CC = Protective Cover Closed Signal.
TD = Target Within Range

Successful accomplishment which will permit firing of the laser is shown by the logic equation—

$$:Fire\ Approval = :PA•CF•CC•TT•CS•TD$$

With all logic signals satisfied there should be no inhibition against firing, but if an anomaly does occur, there should be an interruption in firing of the laser.

The need for operation of industrial equipment and processes of even grater complexity than that of the laserwelder will require the use of computers. When computer-controlled equipment are called for, and used, where people cannot exist safely (such as places where high levels of radiation or toxicity exist, unbreathable atmospheres, or ocean depths), special critical software will also be needed.

Notes

[1] From a paper presented by John P. Rankin at the IEEE Symposium on Nuclear Power Systems, San Francisco, Calif., October 23, 1981.

[2] From a paper presented by Tyrone Jackson at the 5th RAMCAD Technical Interchange Meeting, April 12, 1989.

[3] E. Lloyd and W. Tye, *Systematic Safety* (London: Civil Aviation Authority, 1982)

Questions

1. Discuss the differences, depths, advantages, and limitations of the following: Failure Modes and Effects, Fault-Tree and Sneak Circuit Analyses.

2. List four causes of sneak circuits.

3. Give some benefits of sneak circuit analyses.

4. What is a common cause failure? Describe how, and because of what, it most often takes place. What is a cascade of failures? Describe in fault tree terms, such as a single-point failure, and how one might occur or be prevented.

5. What sneak conditions are dependent on component failure? Are hardware failures the chief reason for sneak circuits? How does this differ from failures in computers?

6. What are sneak indicators and sneak clues?

7. How can the environment contribute to a sneak circuit? Could the event shown in Figure 15-5 (Moisture erects a path across a switch) generate a sneak circuit condition?

8. What is partitioning and how is it used?

9. How many kinds of topographs are there? What are they used for? Describe the simplest.

10. What is a network of trees—a forest? What is their relationship with partitioning?

11. How can a multiplicity of pins in a large multi-pin connector lead to a sneak condition?

12. Describe how a Fault-Tree Analysis can be used in the initial stages of a Computer Safety Analysis.

13. What is the difference between hardware and software? What is a routine, bug, or glitch? What does TMTT mean and how is it used?

14. Describe some of the problems that can result and be manifested in computer outputs.

15. Indicate some causes of computer hardware problems.

16. List some of the anomalies with computers similar to those with sneak circuits.

17. List five concerns regarding software.

18. Because computer programmers and operators may make errors, what kind of safeguards can be incorporated to protect against them?

19. List and discuss what you believe are five advantages of computers over performance of typical humans.

20. What are at least five capabilities where humans are superior to computers.

21. It has been said that directions and commands to persons would be better for safety if expressed in the manner in which computers must be commanded; express your opinion.

17

Operating Hazards Analysis

So far in this book safety analyses have been oriented chiefly toward uncovering problems which might exist with hardware. They did, however, include consideration of human-machine-operations relationships. Operating hazards analyses intensively study the actions of operators as they are involved in specific situations such as product operation, test, maintenance, repair, transportation, handling, emplacement, or removal. In such analyses, the orientation is chiefly on the personnel who are to perform the tasks and secondarily on equipment. The end result may include items required for support of the worker, such as identification of tools and equipment to perform required functions; safety devices and emergency equipment for the worker's protection; and warnings and contingency procedures to guide the worker. The results may be recommendations for design or procedural changes to eliminate or better control hazards. Operating hazards analyses should be initiated early enough to allow time to recommend changes that should be considered and undertaken prior to final acceptance of a product for production.

Procedure Analysis

A procedure is a set of sequenced actions for operating, assembling, maintaining, repairing, calibrating, testing, transporting, handling, installing, or removing a product, assembly, or component. Procedure analysis reviews these actions and any instructions for their accomplishment to ensure that:

1. The required tasks, human–machine–environment and person-to-person interrelationships, and the sequences of operational steps will not lead to an accident.

2. The accomplishment of the tasks does not expose personnel to any hazards.

3. The instructions are clear and effective and do not induce errors that could lead to accidents.

4. Alternative actions a person could take which could result in mishaps are precluded or the effects of such actions are minimized.

5. Safety-critical steps are highlighted with warnings and cautions.

6. No extraordinary mental or physical demands are made for programmed operations.

7. Times for accomplishment of safety-critical tasks are realistic.

In carrying out this analysis, the analyst must:

1. Examine the procedure and each step within the procedure for effect, necessity, and clarity. Personnel tend to take shortcuts in order to avoid arduous, lengthy, uncomfortable, or ambiguous procedures. The shortcuts sometimes can lead to errors and accidents.

2. Examine each procedure and each step, no matter how simple it appears, for possibilities of error, alternative actions, and adverse results.

3. Determine whether or not special training, knowledge, or capability is required which the prospective operator might not have.

4. Review the causes of error tabulated in Figure 10-9 and attempt to eliminate or minimize the possibilities of as many of them as possible.

5. Verify the proposed, tentative procedures by examining, demonstrating, and testing (Chapter 13).

The outputs that can be generated from a proper procedures analysis of a product include the following:

1. Corrective or preventive measures that should be taken in order to minimize the possibilities of an error resulting in a mishap.

2. Recommendations for changes or improvements in hardware or procedures to improve efficiency and safety.

3. Development of warning and caution notes to be included in the most effective places in the procedures and on the equipment.

4. Requirements for special information or training of personnel who will carry out the procedures.

5. Recommendations for special equipment, such as personnel protective clothing or devices, which would be required for the operations to be undertaken.

Conducting the Analysis

Figure 17-1 shows one of the earliest and most basic methods of conducting a hazard analysis for a task which is still widely used. A known task is selected and subjected to an analysis similar to that of a Preliminary Hazard Analysis. The method shown is simple and informative regarding hazards due to equipment failures which could occur when a task is being accomplished. However, this method's shortcomings include lack of information on

where in a sequence the task is to be accomplished, the programmed procedure to be followed, possible alternative actions by the person using the procedure, the effects of such alternative actions, and potential safeguards for those actions. This method can, however, and should be used with the more detailed analyses discussed later.

Figure 17-2 presents one method of programming the steps in a sequence of operations in which bubbles (or ellipses) represent events arranged in the orders and relationships in which they are to occur. The numbers between the bubbles are the expected times between two events. (In one method the time for accomplishment of a task is noted in the bubble. In another method the bubbles are plotted on a time scale.) Tasks for investigation by analyses such as those in Figure 17-1 can be selected from a bubble diagram. Figure 17-3 presents a table of reliability estimates which indicates probabilities of correct accomplishment of an operational task element.

Figures 17-4(a) and (b) show an improved method of sequencing which can be used for procedural analysis, in this case for coffee mill No. ① shown in Figure 13-8, which indicates how the other analysis requirements can be satisfied. The events are arranged so that the columns are assigned letters and the rows are numbered for identification. Each programmed event is then listed in a table by its column and row identity. (It should be noted that the column of events under PROGRAMMED ACTION DESCRIPTION makes up the complete procedural list for the prospective user.) Alternative actions foreseeable

Procedures Analysis

TASK	DANGER	EFFECT	CAUSE	CORRECTIVE OR PREVENTIVE MEASURES
Charge nitrogen pressure vessel	1. A loose hose may whip.	Personnel could be injured or equipment damaged.	Hose failure; connection failure; failure to tighten connection adequately	Tie down, chain or sandbag hose at close intervals. Personnel wear hard hats and face shields. Establish torque values for tightening connections. Warning and caution notes in procedures.
	2. Vessel bursts.	Fragmentation. Fragments may injure personnel or damage near by equipment.	Inadequate strength	Use high safety factor design. Provide warning against over-pressurizing system. Do not expose pressure vessel to heat. Incorporate relief and safety valves. Test vessel to ensure that it will carry required pressure.
	3. High-velocity gas escapes.	Gas may blow solid particles into eyes or against skin. Loss of gas may cause system to become inoperative due to lack of pressure.	Leak; hose failure; loosening fitting on pressurized system; crack	Procedures to provide warnings to depressurize system before attempting to disassemble connectors. Personnel to wear face shields.

Figure 17-1. Procedures analysis.

Technique For Evaluation and Analysis of Maintainability (TEAM)

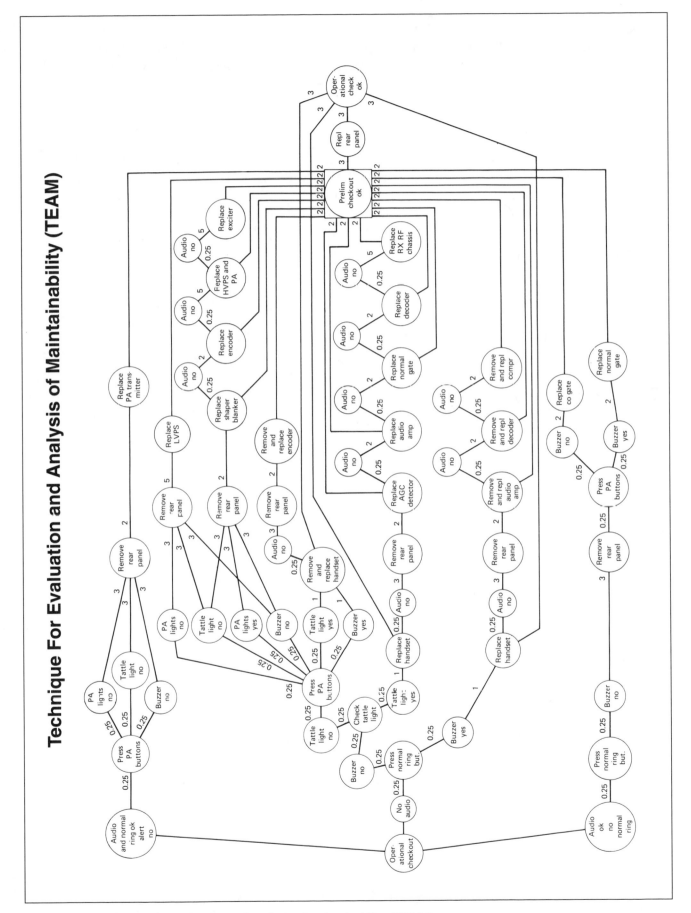

Figure 17-2. Technique for evaluation and analysis of maintainability (TEAM).

Mean and Standard Deviations of Ratings and Reliability Estimates for the Task Elements

TASK ELEMENT	RATING MEAN	S.D.	RELIABILITY ESTIMATE	TASK ELEMENT	RATING MEAN	S.D.	RELIABILITY ESTIMATE
Read technical instructions	8.3	2.2	0.9918	Remove initiator simulator	4.1	1.9	0.9983
Read time (Brush Recorder)	8.2	2.1	0.9921	Install protective cover (friction fit)	4.1	2.2	0.9983
Read electrical or flow meter	7.0	2.8	0.9945	Read time (watch)	4.1	2.1	0.9983
Inspect for loose bolts and clamps	6.4	1.9	0.9955	Verify switch position	4.1	1.9	0.9983
Position multiple position electrical switch	6.3	2.4	0.9957	Inspect for lock wire	4.1	2.1	0.9983
Mark position of component	6.2	2.1	0.9958	Close hand valves	4.0	2.6	0.9983
Install lockwire	6.0	2.3	0.9961	Install drain tube	4.0	2.1	0.9983
Inspect for bellows distortion	6.0	2.7	0.9961	Install torque wrench adapter	3.9	1.7	0.9984
Install Marman clamp	6.0	1.8	0.9961	Open hand valves	3.8	2.6	0.9985
Install gasket	6.0	2.1	0.9962	Position two position electrical switch	3.8	1.5	0.9985
Inspect for rust and corrosion	5.9	2.1	0.9963	Spray leak detector	3.7	2.0	0.9986
Install "O" ring	5.7	2.2	0.9965	Verify component removed or installed	3.5	2.4	0.9988
Record reading	5.7	2.3	0.9966	Remove nuts, plugs, and bolts	3.5	1.7	0.9988
Inspect for dents, cracks, and scratches	5.6	2.4	0.9967	Install pressure cap	3.4	1.6	0.9988
Read pressure gauge	5.4	2.2	0.9969	Remove protective closure (friction fit)	3.2	1.6	0.9990
Inspect for frayed shielding	5.4	2.3	0.9969	Remove torque wrench adapter	3.0	1.6	0.9991
Inspect for QC seals	5.3	2.6	0.9970	Remove reducing adapter	3.0	1.7	0.9991
Tighten nuts, bolts, and plugs	5.3	2.6	0.9970	Remove Marman clamp	3.0	1.7	0.9991
Apply gasket cement	5.3	2.3	0.9971	Remove pressure cap	2.8	1.8	0.9992
Connect electrical cable (threaded)	5.2	2.2	0.9972	Loosen nuts, bolts, and plugs	2.8	1.3	0.9992
Inspect for air bubbles (leak check)	5.0	2.2	0.9974	Remove union	2.7	1.4	0.9993
Install reducing adapter	4.9	1.6	0.9975	Remove lockwire	2.7	1.5	0.9993
Install initiator simulator	4.9	2.5	0.9975	Remove drain tube	2.6	1.4	0.9993
Connect flexible hose	4.9	2.4	0.9975	Verify light illuminated or extinguished	2.2	1.6	0.9996
Position "zero in" knob	4.8	1.6	0.9976	Install funnel or hose in can	2.0	0.8	0.9997
Lubricate bolt or plug	4.7	1.6	0.9979	Remove funnel from oil can	1.9	1.4	0.9997
Position hand valves	4.6	1.6	0.9979				
Install nuts, plugs, and bolts	4.6	1.7	0.9979				
Install union	4.5	1.8	0.9979				
Lubricate "O" ring	4.5	2.5	0.9979				
Rotate gearbox train	4.4	2.0	0.9980				
Fill sump with oil	4.3	1.6	0.9981				
Disconnect flexible hose	4.2	2.0	0.9982				
Lubricate torque wrench adapter	4.2	2.2	0.9982				

Figure 17-3. Mean and standard deviations of ratings and reliability estimates for the task elements.

by the analyst are also shown and listed. The hazard that an alternative action might constitute is described and then the possible safeguard. Each step in the procedure and its alternatives should be reviewed to determine whether or not they could trigger any of the problems listed in the preliminary operating analysis.

This type of analysis can be used when the product is still in an early development phase when the designer has in mind how he or she expects the future user to operate his or her product. Or it can be used when the prototype is ready for testing and the procedure must be verified. The difference between the two analyses is illustrated in Figure 17-4(b). In Figure 17-4(b) line B2, the entry under the POTENTIAL HAZARD heading reads "Mill breaks, especially if cap and case are hard, breakable plastic." Under SAFEGUARD the entry is "Make mill of resilient plastic which will not break if dropped." These entries might be made if the materials for the mill still had to be selected. Entries after the prototype has been built might read: "Cap and case are of hard plastic and may break if dropped" or "Mill is made of resilient plastic which will not break even if dropped on a hard surface."

The procedure analysis of the coffee mill has as each event an action by a person. Figure 17-5 provides a diagrammatic procedure analysis of the operation of the x-ray equipment whose safety circuit is shown in Figure 14-6. In Figure 17-5 the events are both personnel and equipment action and the conditional states that result from these actions. Such combinations will result in more complete analyses since they will also indicate the equipment failures and results that might occur even when each programmed action by the operator is accomplished as it should be.

Each event shown by a block can be broken down separately into its own detailed sequence. In Figure 17-4(b) event K4 is described as "Repairs motor or cord." A diagram and table can be prepared separately to describe in sequential form how the repairs should be made.

If a procedural sequence has already been prepared, it is not necessary to prepare the diagram. The list alone can be used. The steps in the programmed sequence can be shown without the column and row references as they are in Figure 17-4(a). The other columns in the table can remain the same, showing any alternative actions, potential hazards in the alternative actions, and the possible safeguards.

Procedures Verification

After the operating procedures are analyzed, using any of the methods described to alert the writer to potential hazards, it is necessary to verify the procedures. This verification should be done by someone who was not involved in writing or analyzing the procedures. His or her familiarity with the instructions could enable the person to follow steps which might be unclear to others. Therefore, a person, or persons, who would represent the potential user should make this verification review.

The person verifying the procedures could use the checklist in Figure 10-10 to assist him or her. In addition, the person should try to perform the procedures as prescribed by the procedures writer and then try to anticipate any alternative actions the user might take. Then the person should determine which actions might be dangerous. The person performing the procedures or the safety engineer should verify that safeguards will work as intended, that emergency stop systems can be reached and will stop an operation when they are supposed to, that a detection and warning device will operate when subjected to potential field stimuli, that personnel protective equipment can be reached and donned within planned lengths of time, and that emergency routes and exists are practical.[1]

A diagram for analysis of a more complex product, an x-ray safety interlock, is shown in Figure 17-5 which, because of the hazard of injurious radiation, necessitates that operation procedures can result in nothing but complete safety.

Quantitative Analyses of Procedures

There are several methods for quantitatively evaluating the probability of procedural errors. Data Store, developed by the American Institute for Research, has tables of human reliability data which indicate the probability that persons will perform tasks successfully. THERP (Technique for Human Error Rate Prediction)[2] is a method used to quantify the probability of successfully accomplishing an entire procedure. The steps used in THERP are as follows:

1. The proposed procedure for an operation is broken down into its constituent tasks.

2. Each task is assigned a probability of success (reliability), such as shown in Figure 17-3. Whenever alternatives of action are possible, suitable assignment of values is necessary.

3. The probability of successful accomplishment of each sequence of tasks is obtained by multiplying the probabilities for each task in the sequence. In certain instances, the tasks must be examined to decide whether they are dependent events or independent events and to establish suitable mathematical relationships.

If this method is combined with that shown in Figure 17-4(b), the following can be accomplished:

1. The probability that the entire sequence under Programmed Action Description will be accomplished successfully can be established. The probability of an accident if the programmed procedure is followed would then depend on the probability of an injurious or damaging malfunction or environmental problem.

2. The probability that each programmed action will be more complete can be estimated.

3. The probabilities of those alternative actions occurring which could result in accidents if no safeguard

Procedure Analysis for Coffee Mill

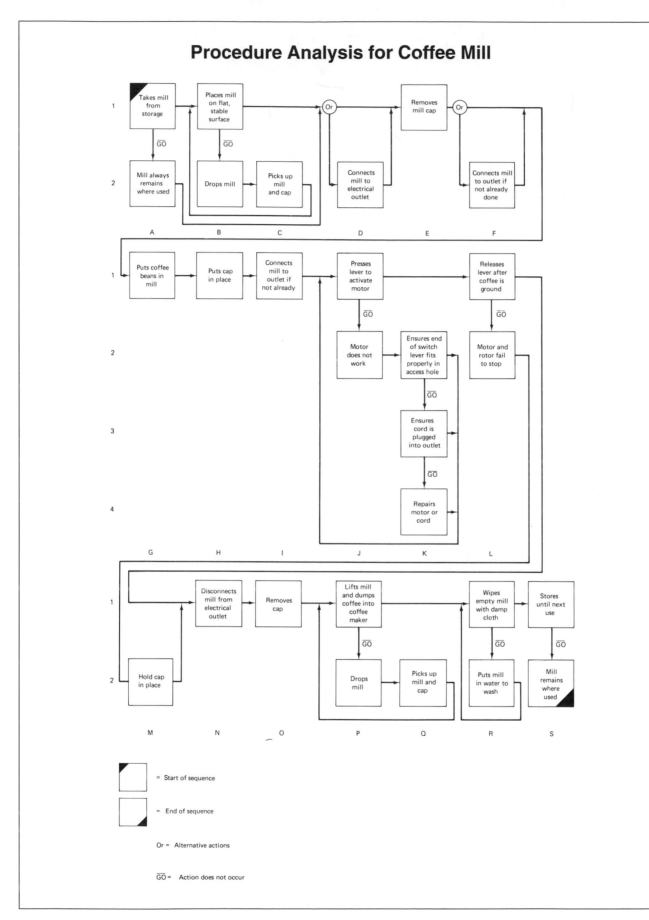

Figure 17-4(a). Procedure analysis for coffee mill.

Procedure Analysis for Coffee Mill

EVENT NO.	PROGRAMMED ACTION DESCRIPTION		ALTERNATIVE ACTION	POTENTIAL HAZARD	SAFEGUARD
A1	Takes mill from storage	A2	User always leaves mill where it is used and connected.	Mill may develop short and burn if left connected.	Unplug and store.
B2	Places mill on flat, stable surface.	B2 C2	Drops mill. Picks up mill and cap	Mill breaks, especially if cap and case are hard, breakable plastic. User may cut himself on ragged fragments.	Make mill of resilient plastic which will not break if dropped.
E1	Removes mill cap.	D2	Connects mill to electrical outlet.	Switch fails closed; motor and rotor start. Finger will be cut if in path of rotor.	Provide instruction not to connect mill when cap is off.
G1	Puts coffee beans in mill.		----------	----------	----------
H1	Puts cap in place.	F2	Connects mill to electrical outlet if not already done.	Switch fails closed; motor and rotor start. If cap is not already in place coffee beans may be thrown about, possibly injuring user.	Provide instruction not to connect mill when cap is off.
I1	Connects mill to electrical outlet.		Mill may already have been connected.	Switch fails closed when first connected; motor and rotor start. If cap not held down, may be thrown off and coffee beans or grounds thrown about.	Provide instruction to hold cap firmly in place.
J1	Presses lever to activate motor.	J2 K2 K3 K4	Motor does not work. Checks end of switch lever to ensure it is fitted properly into access hole. Ensures cord is plugged in. Repairs motor or cord.	Short due to defective wire or plug could permit user to be shocked.	Rubber grommet where cord enters mill to prevent chafing cord. Have repairs made by qualified repairman.
L1	Releases lever to stop motor after coffee beans are ground.	L2 M2	Motor and rotor fail to stop; switch failed closed. Hold cap in place.	Releasing or taking off cap would permit coffee to be scattered.	Provide instruction that if motor fails to stop disconnect mill from electrical outlet.
N1	Disconnects mill from outlet after motor stops.		Leaves mill connected.	See A2.	----------
O1	Removes cap.		----------	----------	----------
P1	Lifts mill and dumps coffee into coffee maker.	P2 Q2	Drops mill. Picks up mill and cap.	Mill breaks, especially if cap and case are of hard, breakable plastic. User may cut himself on ragged fragments.	Make mill of resilient plastic which will not break if mill is dropped.
R1	Wipes empty mill with cloth.	R2	Puts mill in water to wash.	If mill is still connected to electrical supply and put in water, user could be electrocuted.	Provide warning against putting mill in water; make mill waterproof.
S1	Stores mill until next use.	S2	User always leaves mill where it is used and connected.	Same as A2.	----------

Figure 17-4(b). Procedure analysis for coffee mill.

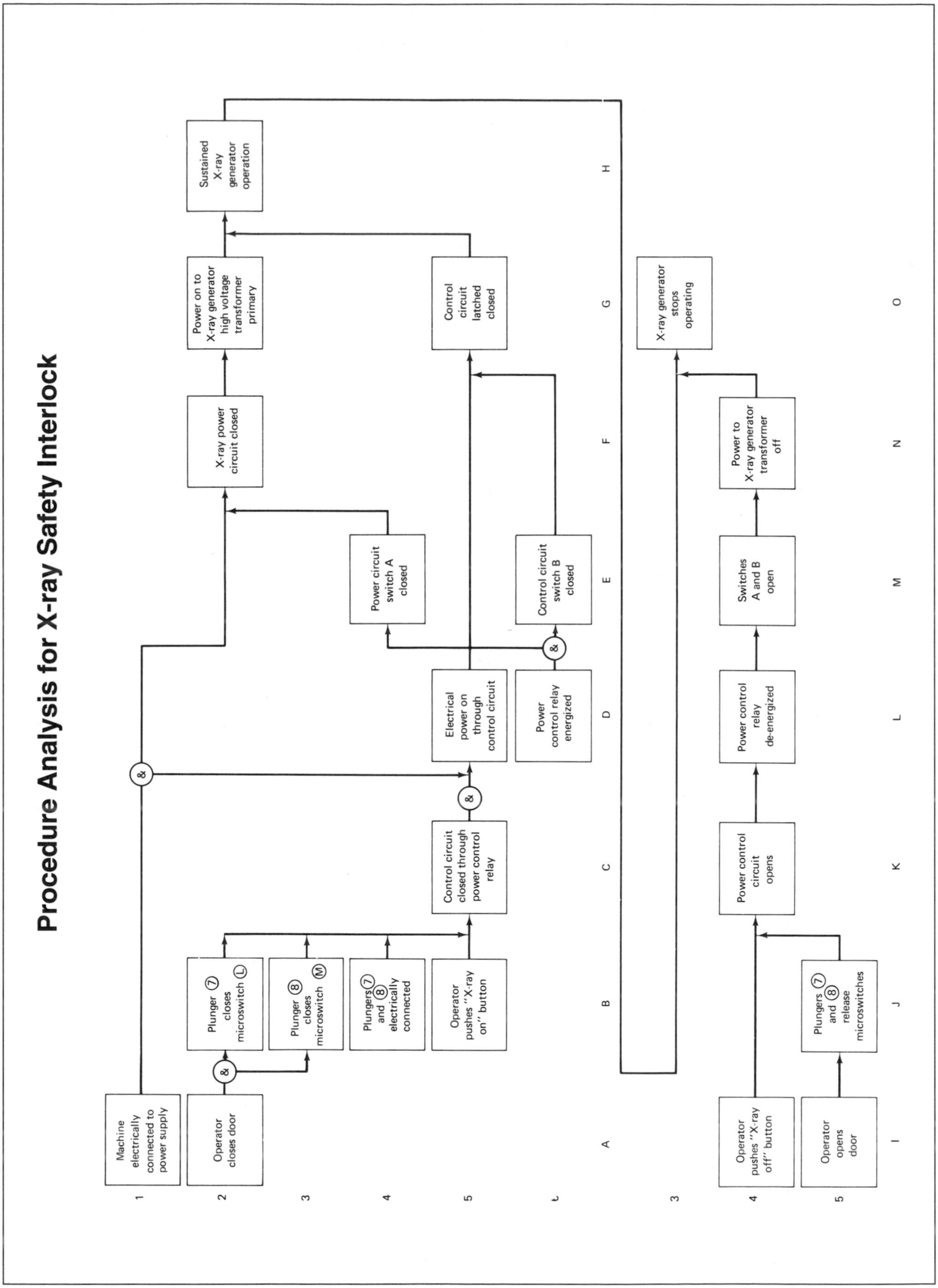

Procedure Analysis for X-ray Safety Interlock

Figure 17-5. Procedure analysis for x-ray safety interlock.

is provided could be approximated from human reliability values.

4. The probability of an alternative action resulting in an accident when the safeguard indicated is provided can be approximated.

The chief drawback in using any quantitative method such as THERP is the lack of accurate human reliability data. Almost all of these probabilities were derived from laboratory tests and may not be valid for field conditions. Personnel who use the product may not have the capabilities of the laboratory workers with whom the data were established. Variations in temperature, vibration, and other environmental factors from laboratory conditions will cause field results to differ from theoretical or laboratory results. For example, a laboratory worker who has to set a dial to a specific value over and over again may tire and make errors, but an operator in the field who has to set the dial only once a day or once a week may be more careful. Gradual accumulation of field experience data may gradually eliminate this objection to quantitative analyses.

Contingency Analysis

Procedures analyses are used to review normal situations involving programmed events. As long as a hazard exists, there is also a possibility that loss of its control will occur. A contingency is an emergency or potential emergency caused by the occurrence of an unprogrammed event which exists as a transitional stage between normal operation and an accident. Actions during the first few seconds or minutes after control over a hazard is lost may determine whether or not control can be reestablished and an accident avoided. If an accident does occur, contingency analysis can determine whether injury or damage must occur or whether they can be avoided or minimized by suitable safeguards. These facts should be established by a contingency analysis.

The severity of any contingency depends on the magnitude of the affecting condition and the ability of the product to withstand it, the configuration at the time of occurrence, the available reaction time, and the capability of the operator or equipment to take corrective action. A contingency analysis must consider all these factors. Actions that can be taken to reassert control of the situation so that a safe condition is achieved must be reviewed at each point in time when adverse factors can arise.

To reassert control of a situation and to minimize the possibilities of an accident occurring, emergency and backout procedures must be prepared, tested, and adopted before the product is released for general use. When an emergency arises, there may not be enough time for a person to react properly if he or she must simultaneously determine what is wrong, the best corrective action, and how to carry out the action decided on. When a critical or emergency situation occurs unexpectedly, even the most controlled individual is under stress and his

or her ability to react calmly and suitably is degraded. (Probably the only time a person will react as fast or faster in an emergency than he or she will normally is when the person is so highly trained and alert for contingencies that he or she acts reflexively.) A person trying to accomplish multiple tasks within the extremely short time available in most contingencies may be overwhelmed and unsuccessful. His or her best chance of successfully rectifying the situation is through previously developed and tested procedures.

These procedures should be the result of a contingency analysis of each critical operation in which control of a hazard could be lost. Tests to supplement the analyses may determine that persons cannot react fast enough to overcome adverse situations within the necessary time limits. The product and its operation may then have to be altered in order to increase the time available to act in an emergency, additional preventive devices may have to be provided, or automatic devices may have to be provided for rapid corrective or suppressive action.

When more time for reaction is available, the analysis should determine whether or not containment can be effected by the operator, the limits within which the operator can attempt to correct the problem, if it is necessary to evacuate the premises, or when the operator's efforts should be directed only to protecting himself or herself. The containment procedures should be simple and easy. If monitoring and warning devices, controls, equipment, or tools are required to make them easy, they should be provided. In any case, these procedures should be written so that they are easy to understand and so that there is no ambiguity, complexity, or lack of clarity that would delay a person under stress in understanding or carrying them out.

The procedure analysis described for consumer products may, in most instances, be entirely adequate. But for more highly energetic and extraordinarily dangerous products, where the extent of injuries and damages might be greater, wider in scope, involve large numbers of persons, and possibly more extensive losses and liabilities, a more introspective and detailed, although lengthier method of procedure analysis is presented. The extraordinarily hazardous products for which the detailed analyses might be used include tasks involving: highly toxic chemicals, radioactive substances, highly-flammable liquids and gases (especially in large amounts as in control methods for inputting or withdrawing combustible materials from storage tanks or farms) deflagrating or high explosives, and where needs for observance of good procedures would be desirable (control of aircraft, vehicles, or other means of transportation).

The procedure analysis methodology and attendant instructions already presented remain the same, but because the operation may be more hazardous and the procedure lengthier, the following is recommended: Figure 17-6 presents the matrix format, which might be used in preparing a procedure analysis, while Figure 17-7 is a completed matrix of the operational procedure. Because

Procedure Analyses Format							
1	2	3	4	5	6	7	8
Manual Ident. No.	Designated Action Description	Possible Alternative Actions	Potential Effects of Alternative Actions	Measure(s) to Avoid Alternative Actions	Measure(s) to Avoid Effects of Alternative Actions	Remarks	Warnings and Cautions

Figure 17-6. Procedure Analyses Format

safety is of prime concern, the table also shows hazards of which all persons must be aware, probability of presence of the hazard, safeguards, and organizational activity designated for any oversight or corrective action.

Although procedures for an operation may have been adequately prepared and written, too often a failure, error, or adverse condition occurs, attributable to no foreseeable or preventable source. For all reasons, foreseeable or not, it is beneficial that safety engineers be aware of methods of preparing a procedure for combatting any possible adverse contingency.

The following three examples of occurrences where prior use of procedure and contingency analyses have been, or would have been, beneficial provide the reasons why contingency analyses are prepared and desirable. Figure 17-8 describes accidents aboard two submarines, one in which the existence of good procedures was of benefit when a contingency arose, while the second, somewhat similar occurrence ended in almost complete disaster. The third example, detailed in Figure 17-9, the disaster aboard the tanker *Mega Borg* describes what happened when there had been a complete lack of planning prior to the onset of any contingency.

A contingency will exist when one or more, but not necessarily all, events in an AND gate (see Figure 15-2) leading to an adverse event in a fault tree are inadvertently present. "Inadvertently" is used to distinguish the situation from one of the conditions or events in which an AND gate of a fault tree is intentionally satisfied until only one restraining condition remains. For a fire to occur, four factors are required: a fuel, an oxidizer, the two in a flammable mixture, and an ignition source. If one or two of these exist, the contingency might be easily controllable, depending on the materials and other factors. For example: with a liquid hydrocarbon spill oxygen is normally present in the air, both constituting a strong contingency for a fire. Thus, if three of the necessary factors are present unintentionally, the contingency would be a grave one for which quick corrective action would be highly desirable in order to prevent the condition from degrading into an accident. For this reason, when there is such a spill on a freeway, or there is a wrecked tank car, the area is generally evacuated until the contingency has been overcome.

Figure 17-10 is the suggested format for use in a contingency hazard analysis while Figure 17-11 provides a completed example for the firing of a large caliber cannon

such as the 155 mm self-propelled howitzer. The procedure to be followed for the operation of this Army weapon is of interest because of its similarity to the procedure that should have been used by the Navy so that the accident which occurred aboard the *U.S.S. Iowa* could have been avoided. Although there were prescribed procedures, there may have been a lack of observance because the procedures were too lengthy, ambiguous, or difficult to follow.

Contingency Analysis Procedure

1. Select the contingency to be investigated. The selection might be made from a preliminary hazard analysis, a procedure analysis, or a top event for a fault tree selected as shown in Figure 15-3 or Figure 15-4. (Note: The fault-tree analysis can be used to determine what could cause the contingency event; the contingency analysis can establish what can be done to contain and limit it should it ever occur.)

2. Sketch the sequence or chain of events which might take place in a contingency situation. The method used in Figures 17-4 and 17-5 might be used for this purpose.

3. Analyze the chain of events to determine whether or not there is a possible action that could forestall each event. (See Figure 15-1 as an example.)

4. Select for adoption for corrective actions which would be most effective in terms of minimizing the adverse effects at minimum cost. Use of one or more corrective actions may be advisable, depending on whether the end effect of the contingency could be minor or catastrophic.

5. Ensure by analysis and test that the corrective actions selected will be effective and reliable.

Designers are usually so engrossed in designing for normal, programmed performance that they often pay little attention to contingencies that might occur. Following are some of the items that should be considered:

1. *Product vulnerability.* The conditions and time when the product is vulnerable to loss of control should be established. Each type of error, malfunction, or outside event that could generate a contingency should be reviewed.

Completed Procedure Analysis

A1/ A2	Moving projectiles from inert area to loading room	4-wheel cart (weight-1800 lbs. loaded) Guards missing on 4 sides of cart beds No adequate braking device	Proximity of cart operator and other workers and equipment to cart while it is being moved Wheels binding or coming off cart	Tilting or bumping 4-wheel cart while it is in motion Maneuvering and stopping moving cart	Projectiles falling over in cart bed and out of cart bed to floor Loss of cart control Cart tilting spilling projectiles on floor Cart striking work station where first increment of explosives is being poured pinching and crushing the explosives	Injury to cart operator and others in close proximity Injury to operator and others in close proximity Detonation	III II	OS-N OS-I AN Z41 OS-N OS-D AN 01.1	a. Compartmentalize cart bed or b. Install guards on 4 sides of cart bed c. Provide steel-tip safety shoes (2500 ft./lb. variety) for cart operator and others in work area d. Provide an adequate braking system for cart e. Reduce the number of projectiles in cart or make the job a two-man operation f. Maintenance of cart	Ind Eng Saf Ind Eng Pro Eng Mai
B1	Bring explosives (Comp A3) into loading room	Tote box (weight-100 lbs. loaded) Inadequate handles for workers to get firm grip	Manner by which tote box is carried by two female workers	Hands of workers slipping off small handles	Dropping tote box Pinching and crushing explosives	Back injury Foot and leg injury Possible detonation of explosives	II		a. Reduce weight of explosives in tote box b. Provide larger handgrips on tote box c. Instruct workers in correct lifting methods	Pro Eng Ind Eng Per
A3	Inspect projectiles and load first increment of explosives	Composition A3 explosives	Airborne particulates	Pouring first increment of explosives into projectiles via funnel	Buildup of static charge Operator inhaling airborne particulates	Fire and possible detonation Respiratory, eye, and skin damage to workers Damage to or loss of operating facility	II	OS-G AN Z9.2 OS-I ANZ1 Z2 C33.8 OS-I AN Z22.1 AN Z88.2 OS-S AN Z41 OS-S AN Z12	a. Installation of local exhaust system with collector. b. Installation of conductive plate under feet of worker or install conductive floor. c. Protective equipment - Eye protection. - Respirator for worker pouring first increment. - Conductive shoes if conductive floor is provided. d. Monthly maintnenance inspection to determine serviceability of conductive plate or floor. e. Static arrestors.	Mai Mai Saf Mai Ind Eng

* OS = OSHA Regulation, AN = American National Standards Institute

Figure 17-7. Completed procedure analysis.

2. *Detection and warning methods.* The means by which the error, malfunction, or outside condition or its effects can be detected should be determined. Whether or not the detection methods will be adequate or the warnings easily understood and whether or not necessary information will continue to be supplied during the emergency should be evaluated.

3. *Corrective actions.* To effect recoveries, minimize or contain damage, and to eliminate or reduce injuries, many decisions must be made long before operation of the product begins. Whenever possible, product design should permit recovery from a contingency without exposing personnel to danger.

The *Squalus* and the *Thetis*

On 23 May 1939 the American submarine *U.S.S. Squalus* sank to the bottom in 240 feet of water off the New Hampshire coast during a trial dive in a series of acceptance tests. A later investigation reported that according to the indicator lights in the submarine, the main air induction valves were closed as it submerged, but the valves were actually open. Twenty-six men of those aboard were drowned when she sank.

The admiral in command had prescribed procedures for all test dive operations, and for any emergencies that might arise. When no surfacing report had been received within the specified time indicating the test dive had been successful, the admiral became concerned. He ordered another sub, about to start a long voyage, to proceed through the area of the missing boat, directing it to look for any signs of the *Squalus*. The *Squalus* was found and its predicament determined within hours.

Although the submarine was equipped with Momsen lungs for escape (which like similar British and German designs these were found to be, and were declared, ineffective after the war), their use was considered inadvisable by the commander because of the water depth and temperature, except as a last resort. The Admiral had rescue operations initiated immediately. Distant highly trained and specialized personnel, suitable rescue ships, and equipment were brought hurriedly to the site and were in action within 24 hours. All of the trapped men who had not drowned immediately were rescued 16 hours later.

Eight days after the *Squalus* accident, a similar acceptance test dive of the British *H.M.S. Thetis* took place. The bow of the *Thetis* flooded when a torpedo tube was inadvertently opened so she sank to the bottom of the Irish Sea. There the water was only 130 feet deep, but because the craft sank at an angle, 18 feet of the 275 foot sub remained above the surface. Unfortunately, although the regular crew normally consisted of 53 men, 103 persons were on-board the sub. The manager of the operation had permitted other supervisors, observers, technicians, and seemingly almost anyone else who had a desire to go to board, including two waiters to feed the horde.

When a small escorting ship failed to discover what happened to the sub, it attempted to get a message to its headquarters. Receipt of the message was delayed when the messenger boy blew a tire he had to repair. Divers on a tug sent to provide assistance proved to be ill-equipped to handle the rescue work. The only other support ships available were a flotilla of destroyers under a commander who knew little about submarines. Each new rescue attempt was developed only after the previous one had failed.

The lack of managerial control and good procedures cost 99 men their lives (seven men tried using the escape apparatus, but only four reach the surface alive). All the others died of suffocation. The overcrowding had reduced the survival time available for a successful rescue. In addition, lack of planning for possible emergencies and the use of hurriedly improvised procedures (that failed), increased the time it took to reach the trapped men.

During World War II, the procedure for use of underwater equipment was found faulty when a contingency necessitated the need for personnel to rise to the surface from a disabled or sunken submarine. As a result, the procedure to reach the surface in any contingency was changed, using no equipment at all, only the bubble of air in which the person attempting to escape was enveloped while rising. This procedure, developed by the British as the result of many losses of submarine personnel, is now taught in all navies.

Figure 17-8. The *Squalus* and the *Thetis*.

4. *Points of no return.* In some cases, the countermeasures for the contingency may be inadequate and the situation will worsen. A point may then be reached at which the attempt to correct the situation should be abandoned and efforts redirected to safeguarding personnel. In certain emergencies, efforts must be diverted from saving the equipment to preventing the adverse condition from affecting other equipment or facilities. When these transfers of effort should be made must be delineated carefully. Persons in an emergency may wait too long attempting to save equipment and thus may endanger their lives unduly; or they may abandon a correctable situation prematurely while they are not endangered. Instructions must be provided on where these abandonment points, or points of no return, lie so that personnel know beforehand exactly when they might be in danger and take escape action.

5. *Emergency equipment.* The types of emergency equipment that might be required should be selected and tested to ensure their adequacy. Locations must be carefully selected so that emergency equipment will be readily available when required. Tests of the emergency equipment's suitability and location should be made under conditions as much like those as the foreseeable emergency as possible.

6. *Safety zones and evacuation routes.* A contingency analysis must also determine locations where personnel will be safe during an emergency. In some cases, personnel must evacuate an unsafe structure or vehicle and move to a safe location. Safe routes should

Lessons of the *Mega Borg*

A prime example of the need for analysis and planning to avoid uncertainty and confusion in the event of a potential disaster, was the fire and loss of oil on June 25, 1990 aboard the tanker *Mega Borg*. This catastrophe indicated the unavailability of the procedures and serious lack of equipment to be used as well as personnel that might be required. This accident demonstrated the fiasco that can arise due to the lack of suitable preplanning long *before* any contingency, emergency, or accident.

Catastrophes involving accidents with oil tankers, resulting in tremendous losses of oil, occurred with the *Torrey Canyon* off Land's End in England on March 18, 1967 with oil loss creating a disaster to the coast of France and again with the *Exxon Valdez* in Alaska in March 1989. However, little was done to prevent another serious contingency by the preparation of procedures for the control of any similar accident.

The news media reported (June 25, 1990) regarding the accident to the *Mega Borg*: "Incredibly, emergency crews were not able to attack the flames with anything more effective than sea water. Nozzles and pumps for firefighting had to be shipped in from the Netherlands and oil containment equipment from London. This took two days. Experts were brought in from Alaska, Seattle, France, Mexico, and from nearby areas of the United States to assist in controlling the fire and the spread of the oil that had been lost."

The comment from the Center for Marine Conservation was: "There was general confusion about where the equipment was and who was in charge." The procedures and equipment necessary for handling any sort of contingency had evidently been lacking.

Figure 17-9. Lessons of the *Mega Borg*

be determined and analyzed beforehand to ensure that they are adequate for the personnel who must be evacuated and to ensure that there is time available for the evacuation.

Additional aspects of contingency situations are discussed in Chapter 11. Figure 17-12 provides a checklist that might be used to help the analyst to determine the adequacy of a product in a contingency.

Another aspect of response time analysis involves study of the interval that may be available for rescue or survival. This interval depends on how long personnel can remain in the existing environment during an emergency. In this case, an emergency is considered to exist from the time a situation arises from which injury can result until the persons are situated where they are safe.

One report postulates that when a large number of emergencies for which survival times, approximate or definite, are charted against probabilities of survival, a family of curves can be developed depending on the specific hazard.[3] These curves will have the general form:

$$F = e^{-f(t)}$$

where

F = *the fraction of cases having survival times exceeding a specified time t*

$f(t)$ = *a function of time*

The form of the curve was derived from data taken from accidents in which submarines were lost. The study was attempting to determine how long crews involved in

space flight emergencies could survive threats to their lives. The results are shown in Figure 17-13 for the seven threats considered. The average curve approximates the general function just described with a Weibull curve of the form:

$$F = e^{-At^{\alpha}}$$

where the constants $A = 0.219$ and $\alpha = 0.5$. The average curve is shown by the dotted line. The authors indicate that a closer fit to empirical data would be:

$$F = 0.3e^{-Bt} = 0.7e^{-Ct}$$

where the first term applies to death by drowning and the second to asphyxia. Due to the lack of data, determination of values for the constants for these curves was not possible. It should also be pointed out that values used in at least one case are questionable. The *Thetis* (discussed earlier in this chapter) carried personnel (103) who numbered almost twice the normal complement (53). The survival time was therefore reduced by at least that ratio. Furthermore, interruption of attention during accomplishment of a critical procedure will reduce available time to respond to any contingency. The response time therefore is unduly increased until the environment reaches a harmful level to the point where the body begins to object physiologically. As conditions worsen they may finally reach a lethal level. Certain causes of death can be calculated by determining how long it would take in an emergency for a specific environmental condition to reach a harmful level.

1 Adverse event to which contingency might lead	2 Description of contingency	3 Possible cause of contingency	4 Indicator that a contingency has occurred	5 Means of verifying that a contingency has occurred	6 Action to prevent contingency from developing into the adverse event	7 Means of verifying that the contingency has been controlled	8 Precautionary measures	9 Remarks

Suggested Format for Contingency Analysis (table title spanning above)

Figure 17-10. Suggested format for contingency analysis.

SYSTEM: 155 mm Self-Propelled Howitzer

1 Adverse event to which contingency might lead	2 Description of contingency	3 Possible cause of contingency	4 Indicator that a contingency has occurred	5 Means of verifying that a contingency has occurred	6 Action to prevent contingency from developing into the adverse event	7 Means of verifying that the contingency has been controlled	8 Precautionary measures	9 Remarks
Injury or death to gun crew because of delayed recoil.	A failure to fire may be due to a hang fire. If a cannoneer moved in to open the breechblock and the propelling charge ignited he might be injured or killed by the recoil.	1. Propelling charge inserted with red bag toward projectile and not toward breech. 2. Faulty primer. 3. Failure to remove igniter protective cap. 4. Wet propelling charge.	Weapon did not fire.	Attempt to fire weapon two additional times. 1. Wait two minutes after each attempt to fire. 2. Remove and examine primer. 3. If primer had fired insert new one and try again. 4. If primer has not fired repair/replace primer or firing mechanism component.	1. Evacuate all personnel but chief of Section and No. 1 cannoneer. 2. Stand clear of recoil path. 3. If round is not fired or removed in six minutes evacuate all personnel from weapon and notify E.O.D. or Ordnance.	1. Weapon fired. 2. Propelling charge and projectile removed from weapon.	All failures to fire should be treated as hang fires with the idea that weapon firing will occur after a time delay.	See Procedure Analysis for situations which could result in failures to fire. Each failure to fire should be treated as a contingency.
Injury or death to gun crew by back blast when breechblock is unlocked or open.	A failure to fire may be due to a hang fire. If the breechblock is unlocked or opened and the propelling charge is ignited the backblast which would occur could kill or severely injure anyone in the immediate vicinity of the rear of the gun.	Same	Same	Same	Same	Same	Same	Same

Figure 17-11. Contingency analysis.

Checklist for Contingency Analysis

1. What type of emergency can arise with this product?
2. Is there an emergency shutoff device on the equipment?
3. For what types of emergencies is the device provided?
4. Are safeguards available which will prevent loss of control of the hazards?
5. What will happen if a second failure occurs and the safeguard also malfunctions?
6. What types of errors can create an emergency?
7. Have interlocks and other devices been incorporated to prevent errors from creating an emergency?
8. If an emergency can occur, are backout instructions provided?
9. Are backout instructions readily available, clear, concise, easily understandable, and easy to accomplish, especially for a person under stress?
10. Will the emergency or backout procedure overwhelm the person who has to carry them out because he has already been working near the limits of his capabilities during normal operations?
11. Are the emergency devices high reliability items or are they liable to fail when needed?
12. Will information an operator needs in an emergency be readily available and easily understood without chance for misinterpretation?
13. If fire is a possibility, is there a means by which it can be detected and suppressed? Will reaction time be adequate for personnel to take corrective action or should the action be automatic? If a person has to take action, are the devices he must use clearly marked?
14. If a fire occurs, will the materials involved generate toxic gases which could be fatal? Is there any means to safeguard personnel against this hazard?
15. In case of fire, is there any means by which the availability of fuel to the fire can be shut off?
16. Are escape routes and exits clearly and permanently marked? Are they of adequate size and number to permit all persons who might be present and persons who might be encumbered to leave within safe exit time?
17. Is there any environmental factor which could degrade possible recovery from the emergency, such as high wind, extreme cold, heat or rain? Can and should provisions be provided to compensate for their possible occurrence?
18. Is there a specific event which indicates when any attempt to control the situation should be abandoned and actions directed towards escape? Has such a "point-of-no-return" been established?
19. Is there a time limit beyond which corrective actions should not be attempted? Has such a "fall-back" time been established?
20. Will the detection and display devices used for normal operations continue to provide information during an emergency if it is needed?
21. Is there a system to provide light if the usual lighting system fails during the emergency?
22. What are the power requirements which might be needed during an emergency? Will they be available or must auxiliary units be provided?
23. Will communications be available during the emergency if needed?
24. What injuries could personnel suffer in the emergency? Will any require immediate assistance or first aid? Will they be available?
25. If rescue might be necessary, are accesses marked and easy to operate so rescue personnel will almost immediately be able to understand and use them?

Figure 17-12. Checklist for contingency analysis.

Notes

[1] Ian Ormes and Ralph Ormes in *Clipped Wings* (London: William Kimber, 1973) mention that in September 1940 the RAF Bomber Command forwarded a list of complaints regarding the Manchester bomber. "Not least in their objections was the point that the emergency exits are too small to carry a parachute. 'If a descent is to be made by parachute, it is useful to take one with you.'"

[2] A. D. Swain, *A Method for Performing Human Factors Reliability Analysis*, Report SCR-685 (Albuquerque, N.M., Sandia Corporation, 1963).

[3] S.H. Dole, *et al.*, *Contingency Planning for Space-Flight Emergencies*, Memorandum RM-5200-NASA (Santa Monica, Calif., RAND Corporation, 1967).

Questions

1. Why is the use of a detailed Procedures Analysis advantageous in the development of new products?

2. A Failure Modes and Effects Analysis involves hardware; what does a Procedure Analysis involve?

3. Can an inadequate Procedures Analysis contribute to problems with products? What kind? Could it contribute to accidents, injuries, and liabilities?

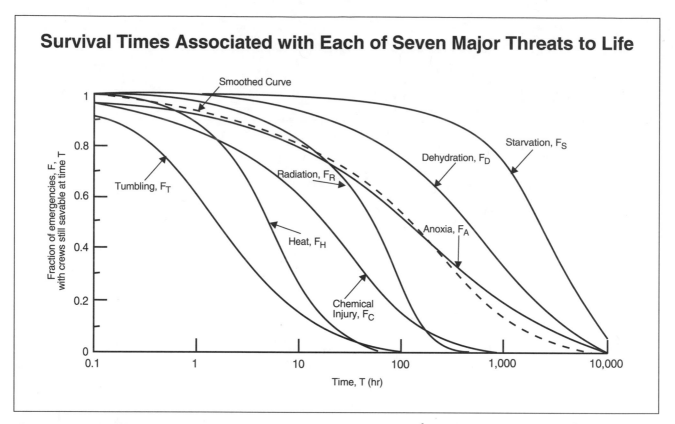

Survival Times Associated with Each of Seven Major Threats to Life

Figure 17-13. Survival times associated with each of seven major threats to life.[3]

4. Explain how an analyst can determine what hazards might be present in an operational procedure.

5. Why is it advantageous to make an analysis of a product what could be hazardous in operation?

6. Explain the difference between a contingency, an emergency, and an accident. How might one degrade into the other? Give an example.

7. Describe the procedure for a contingency analysis.

8. List five products in which a contingency might arise, describe what they might be, and the measures to be taken to either correct them or to prevent them from deteriorating into an emergency or accident.

9. Prepare a table with a contingency analysis of a household product or small appliance.

10. Why is time important in a contingency? Describe a hazard in which there is no element of time in which a contingency can be prevented from degrading further.

11. Why is it necessary to make apparent in a procedure all warnings. Is it necessary for the warnings to be in English?

12. What would happen if there was a failure to warn, an accident occurred, and a person was badly injured? Would the courts hold that there had been negligence? Discuss some of the provisions that have to be provided in a warning.

13. Discuss what might happen if a procedure was faulty; could this lead to a failure or error? In a serious contingency, would users tend to make errors or not?

18

Risk Assessment

In 1905, President Theodore Roosevelt took an underwater cruise in the *Plunger*, one of the first submarines. The *New York Times* promptly gave the old Rough Rider a stern lecture on taking risks. Accidents in submarines, because of the many hazards they contain, make submergence in one a very risky endeavor even now.

On February 8, 1968 President Charles de Gaulle of France attended a memorial service to honor the crew of the French submarine *Minerve* which had been lost, with all hands, on the previous January 27; cause unknown. President de Gaulle then took an underwater cruise in the *Eurydice*, a sister boat to the *Minerve*, to demonstrate that French submarines were not as hazardous and risky as had been reported. It may have been thought that little risk was involved, but a little more than two years after de Gaulle's cruise in *Eurydice*, on March 4, 1970, the *Eurydice* disappeared in the Western Mediterranean with all hands; cause unknown. Evidenced by the losses of the submarines, risks there undoubtedly were, it is doubtful that either Presidents de Gaulle or Roosevelt (over 60 years earlier) even thought of or were deterred by the risks involved.

Risk has been defined in a number of ways, with one consideration common to all: a probability of occurrence of an adverse event. Risk can mean:

1. The probability of an accident.

2. The probability of a person being injured or killed.

3. The loss or losses a manufacturer can suffer from an accident or series of accidents.

4. The chance an operator or other person is willing to take to enjoy the benefits of the activity he or she would undertake.

Knowledge of the risk involved with any product permits the person responsible for its manufacture or operation to decide whether or not the danger is reasonable, can be accepted, must be reduced, requires that protective measures be incorporated, or whether or not the operation must be canceled. The user of a valid risk assessment method may be able to determine whether or not probable losses over a period of time will be bearable, to decide on amounts that can justifiably be spent on accident prevention measures to reduce losses, and be able to make comparisons between accident rates and losses for different but similar products or designs.

Risk of an Accident

Previous chapters have shown how the probability of an accident with a product or for a specific operation can be established by analysis. In addition, if a product has been in use or if an operation has been conducted over a long period of time, it may be possible to obtain probability data from experience.

Insurance companies base their charges on such experience data. Care, however, must be used in the application of past information. For example, a company might be called on some time in the future to insure a nuclear submarine to be used for commercial purposes. Data are available on submarines, but these data apply to military use only. The design, construction, operational capabilities, requirements, and hazards would differ. In addition, a nuclear submarine, either military or commercial, could not use much of the experience data of submarines whose prime power was diesel or gasoline engines, which were not compartmented or which had other differences.

This reasoning is why insurance companies do not base their premium rates for new airliners on experience with older model planes that have been flying for many years. With each new product there is a break-in and learning period during which losses might occur. These losses were formerly accepted as part of introducing a new product, insurance companies charged enough to cover potential losses, and the manufacturer of the new product paid if he wanted insurance.

Now the consequences of some accidents would be so severe that to have even one learning accident cannot be accepted. Many product manufacturers are beginning to find that the volume of any specific product put on the market is so great that an accident-causing defect found in one item means that the defect and potential for an accident exist in other items.

A manager may want to know the risks of exposing the company when a product is put on the market. The manager may also want to use quantitative values to compare the safety levels of two or more designs or procedures so that the safest one can be used. If a safer design or procedure is more costly, the manager would like to know how much the safety level is increased by an expenditure of a specific amount of money. When there are alternatives, the manager will want to spend the available funds where they will provide maximal benefit. (Such analyses are now being used extensively in the nuclear power and chemical industries.) The risk manager must attempt to achieve the best possible compromise between loss potentials due to accidents and accident prevention costs.

Acceptability of Risks

To be "perfectly safe," a product would have to permit no possibility of causing injury or damage under any circumstances. No product meets this ideal of being perfectly safe and free from danger at all times. A user of a product must therefore always expect and accept some risk in its operation. How much of a risk is acceptable depends on the benefits derived from using the product. When the risk is greater than a person finds acceptable, he or she considers the product "unsafe."

In addition to the common usage of the term "acceptable risks," the courts speak of "reasonable risks" and "unreasonable risks," and the Consumer Product Safety Act mentions "substantial risks." All of these terms are so poorly defined that their usages create difficulties when they are to be used as measures. It has been said that a problem really can't be appreciated until it has been quantified. Therefore, there have been attempts to quantify risks and the benefits derived from their acceptance.

Whether or not the risk of participation in a hazardous activity is acceptable to a person depends on the benefits derived from the activity. Starr[1] divided risks into voluntary risks and involuntary risks. A voluntary risk is one in which the individual participates in an activity by freely accepting the risk and based on the individual's own values and experiences. An involuntary risk involves participation in an activity that is governed by some controlling body, such as an airline company, which may be the only one fully aware of the criteria and options in the overall decision process. An individual must accept another's judgment for participating in the activity. The article presents, among other considerations, a graphic relationship between voluntary and involuntary risk-acceptability in terms of probability of a fatality and annual benefit in dollars (Figure 18-1). (How the risks and benefit values were derived is presented in the article.) The conclusions reached by the analyses are:

1. The indications are that the public is willing to accept "voluntary" risks roughly 1000 times greater than "involuntary" risks.[2]

2. The statistical risk of death from disease appears to be a psychological yardstick for establishing the level of acceptability of other risks.

3. The acceptability of risk appears to be crudely proportional to the third power of the benefits (real or imagined).

4. The social acceptance of risk is directly influenced by public awareness of the benefits of an activity, as determined by advertising, usefulness, and the number of people participating.

5. In a sample application of these criteria to atomic power plant safety, it appears that an engineering design objective determined by economic criteria would result in a design-target risk level very much lower than the present socially accepted risk for electric power plants.

A study for the U.S. Atomic Energy Commission in 1974[3] presents statistics on accidental fatalities for the U.S. population (Figure 18-2). In one chapter, comments made include:

Types of accidents with a death risk in the range of 10^{-3} per person per year to the general public are difficult to find. Such high risks are not uncommon in some sports and in some industrial activities, when measured for the limited groups at risk (i.e., exposed to the hazards involved). Evidently this level of risk is generally unacceptable, and when it occurs, immediate action is taken to reduce it.

At an accidental risk level of 10^{-4} deaths per person per year, people are less inclined to concerted action but are willing to spend money to reduce the hazard.

Risks of accidental death at a level of 10^{-5} per person per year are recognized in an active sense.

Accidents with a probability of death of 10^{-6} or less per person per year are evidently not of great concern to the average person.

The values in Figure 18-2 illustrate one problem with the use of quantitative assessments. All the fatality risk values shown are based on total U.S. population in 1969, which may not be valid in some cases. For example, if half the people of the United States do not travel by air, the probability of any one of them being killed (or of having been killed in 1969) in a plane crash is zero. The probability of the average air traveler being killed is increased to 1.8×10^{-5}. The probability of a person who travels more than the average (which isn't specified) is even

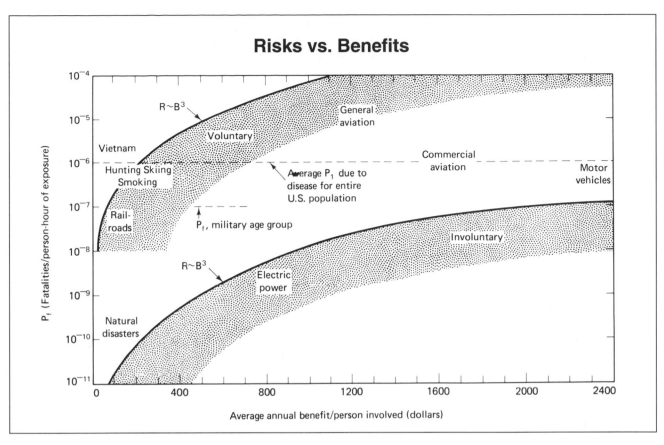

Risks vs. Benefits

Figure 18-1. Risks vs. benefits.

higher. This method of risk assessment becomes even more invalid when the operation considered is one in which few persons participate. Assume that there were 160 persons killed in hang gliding accidents in that year (the same as Figure 18-2 lists as being killed by lightning). When the total U.S. population was used as the base for determining the risk, the probability of a fatality is 5×10^{-5}, as shown; a relatively safe operation. However, if there were only 20,000 enthusiasts who participated in hang gliding and they suffered a 160-person loss each year, the fatality risk is 8×10^{-3}. To make correct and comparable risk assessments it is therefore necessary to base them on correct and acceptable assumptions and data.

Relativistic and Probabilistic Methods

Methods of quantification can be divided into those that are *relativistic* and those that are *probabilistic*. In the relativistic method, which is the easier and more commonly used method, the range of ratings that will be used is divided into a limited number of classes, such as 4, 6, or 10. A group of evaluators then assign a rating that most closely approximates the safety or danger level that the product or operation has as compared to similar products or operations. Figure 18-3 indicates how safety connotations of maintainability tasks may be scored in

this way. The Underwriters Laboratories and Sax's *Dangerous Properties of Industrial Materials* have such relativistic systems (the two differ) for rating toxic chemicals according to degree of hazard.

For a number of years the British Civil Airworthiness Authority (CAA) has required that manufacturers of aircraft which must be certified by the CAA must meet quantitative safety requirement. These requirements are shown in Figure 18-4 to demonstrate the criteria used. In the United Sates a quantitative system for evaluating safety levels of Air Force equipment has been adopted. Use of the "Real Hazard Index" is principally to permit management decisions to be made regarding whether or not action should be taken to improve the safety level of systems or products.

A probability is the expectancy that an event will occur a certain number of times in a specific number of trials. A probabilistic method would therefore express the safety level of a product, event, or operation in such terms. Reliability engineering, statistical quality control, maintainability, and system effectiveness apply probabilities in engineering. The safety level of a product or operation can be indicated by values approximated from experience data from similar products, synthesized results from information on similar subassemblies, preliminary tests, or extensions of these. A mathematical expression for the probability of an accident from the operation of any product is presented below. This expression incorporates

Individual Risk of Acute Fatality by Various Causes

(U.S. Population Average 1969)

Accident Type	Total Number for 1969	Approximate Individual Risk Acute Fatality Probability/yr[1]
Motor Vehicle	55,791	3×10^{-4}
Falls	17,827	9×10^{-5}
Fires and Hot Substance	7,451	4×10^{-5}
Drowning	6,181	3×10^{-5}
Poison	4,516	2×10^{-5}
Firearms	2,309	1×10^{-5}
Machinery (1968)	2,054	1×10^{-5}
Water Transport	1,743	9×10^{-6}
Air Travel	1,778	9×10^{-6}
Falling Objects	1,271	6×10^{-6}
Electrocution	1,148	6×10^{-6}
Railway	884	4×10^{-6}
Lightning	160	5×10^{-7}
Tornadoes	91	4×10^{-7}
Hurricanes	93	4×10^{-7}
All others	8,695	4×10^{-5}
All Accidents		6×10^{-4}

[1] Based on total U.S. population.

Figure 18-2. Individual risk of acute fatality by various causes.

factors for all four categories of hazards: hazardous characteristics, malfunctions or failures, environmental effects, and operator errors.

$$P(accident) =$$

$$\frac{I}{\Sigma H_A (1 + C_H + N_H) + H_M (1 + C_H + N_H) (1 - H_S) +}$$

$$\frac{II}{\Sigma F_A (1 + C_F + N_F) + F_M (1 + C_F + N_F) (1 - H_S) +}$$

$$\frac{III}{\Sigma (C_A + N_A) (1 - H_S)}$$

which can be broken down into:

$$I = \Sigma [H_A + H_M (1 - H_S)] (1 + C_H + N_H)$$

$$II = \Sigma [F_A + F_M (1 - H_S)] (1 + C_F + N_F)$$

$$III = \Sigma (C_A + N_A) (1 - H_S)$$

where each of the following represents the probability:

F = of all material failures occurring under foreseeable conditions;

F_A = of those failures occurring that will result in accidents (no corrective action possible);

F_M = of those failures occurring that will result in accidents unless possible, timely corrective actions are taken;

H_M = of any correctable human failures occurring that could cause or permit an accident: wrong decision, inadequate response, lack of corrective action, wrong action;

H_A = of any irreversible human failure occurring that could cause or permit an accident;

H_S = of proper action taken as required: correct decision, suitable response, proper corrective or preventive action;

C_A = of the product having an adverse characteristic that could cause injury, damage, or loss without material failure or error;

C_F = of the product having an adverse characteristic that could cause material failure;

C_H = of the product having an adverse characteristic that could cause human failure;

N_A = of the product encountering an adverse, extraordinary environmental condition that could cause injury or damage without failure or error;

N_F = of the product encountering an adverse, extraordinary environmental condition that could cause product failure (includes conditions not normally considered under F because they are too improbably or unforeseeable);

N_H = of the product encountering an adverse, extraordinary environmental condition that could cause human failure.

The expressions for I and II indicate the probabilities of accidents that can be caused by operator error and failures (malfunctions), respectively. The expression $(1 - H_S)$ indicates the probability that a preventable accident actually can be avoided by human action. When the hazardous characteristics of a product have been eliminated or controlled, the value for C will be zero. Similarly, if environmental conditions will not affect the product, all expressions for N will become zero. The expressions for I can be estimated or approximated by a quantitative procedures analysis as indicated in Chapter 17; the value of II can be approximated by a failure modes and effects analysis.

This method attempts to quantify the probabilities of accidents through quantification of the various hazards. The results would include all accidents possible from all causes in a product or operation. Fault-tree analysis, currently the principal method of accident quantification, is oriented so that values of specific events are used, all leading to the probability of occurrence of the top event only. Using fault trees to find the overall probability of all accidents could be done in two ways: (1) Evaluate each and all top events, sum them up, and eliminate any redundancies or (2) use as the top event the possibility of any accident.

It has sometimes been proposed that failure rates from reliability analyses be used as measures of quantitative safety levels. The full equation given above indicates very clearly why, in most cases, this cannot be done. Other factors which affect safety are not included in reliability analyses or experience data.[4]

Risk of Injury or Death

The probability of one or more persons being injured or killed depends on the following probabilities: (1) that an accident will occur, (2) that someone will be in a position where the effects of any accident could injure the person, and (3) the specific degree of injury that a person exposed to the effects of an accident will suffer. Thus:

Pr(specific injury) = Pr(accident) • Pr(exposure)•
Pr(specific severity of injury)

Pr(accident) can be established by the quantitative methods indicated in previous chapters. The probability that a person will be exposed can vary all the way from 0, which means that the person is not exposed at all or is completely safeguarded, to 1, which means that if an accident occurs, the person will be injured or killed.

If a person is injured, what is the probability that the injury will be of a specific level or more or less than that level? Accidents could involve situations in which the person may not be injured at all or in situations in which if the person is injured, the person will suffer an effect ranging from a minor injury to death. Two persons may be standing side by side when a pressure vessel ruptures. One person is killed; the other receives only minor injuries.

One possible way to approximate the probabilities of results is by using the Monte Carlo Method. A probability distribution could be simulated by computer analysis as indicated in the preceding chapter.

Manufacturer's Losses

Risk is an expression of probable loss over a specific period of time or over a number of operational cycles. Risk can be indicated by the probability of an accident times the loss in dollars, lives, or operating units that could occur. This concept of risk involves consideration of the frequency at which mishaps could occur and the possible loss levels.

Mathematically, risk can be expressed by:

$$Risk = DM_T = DMN$$

where

D = probable loss per mishap;
M = predicted mishap rate;
N = total length of time, number of periods, or number of operational cycles during which the mishaps occurred or could occur;
M_T = number of mishaps.

For example, a product has a planned life cycle of ten years during which each of 50 vehicles may be operated 1500 hours per year. Operations of similar products indicate that the losses due to accidents average $700 each. Accidents occur 3.5 times per 10,000 hours of operation. If the cost of the new product will be three times that of the old product, what will be the risk (expected loss) due to damage per year?

Risk = $3 \times 700 \times 3.5 \times 10^{-4} \times 50 \times 1500 = \$55,125$ *per year*

Risk determination and prediction have provided the concept on which insurance has been based for hundreds of years. Cases in which complete loss of equipment can result can be evaluated comparatively easily. More complex problems exist in evaluating potential losses when there is a range of possibilities that can occur. For example, the probability of a mishap to a product might be estimated from past experience. However, the possible losses in any accident can vary from zero damage to complete destruction of the product. For any detailed evaluation, it is necessary to use subjective probabilities in which the probability of any specific level of damage occurring is further dependent on the probability that, first, an accident will occur and, second, that the accident will involve a specific level of damage. A company could categorize as follows the probability of each level of damage of a product valued at $100,000 if an accident should occur:

Damage($) (1)	Average ($) (2)	Probabiltiy* (3)	(2) × (3)
1–1000	500	0.100	50
1000-10,000	5,500	0.750	4,125
10,000-20,000	15,000	0.070	1,050
20,000-30,000	25,000	0.030	750
30,000-40,000	35,000	0.020	700
40,000-50,000	45,000	0.015	675
50,000-60,000	55,000	0.005	275
60,000-70,000	65,000	0.004	260
70,000-80,000	75,000	0.003	225
80,000-90,000	85,000	0.002	170
90,000-100,000	95,000	0.001	95
		1.000	$8,375

*Assumed value

The table is predicated on the premise that when a mishap does occur, there will be damage. Mishaps from all causes may occur at a rate equal to 3.0 per 100,000 hours of operating time. The number of losses between $1000 and $10,000 will therefore be:

$$3.0 \times 0.75 = 2.25 \ per \ 100,000 \ hours$$

The total monetary loss for damages between $1000 and $10,000 for 100,000 hours of operating time can be expected to be

$$2.25 \times 5500 = \$12,375$$

The expected average loss for any mishap in a series of mishaps can be approximated by the summation of the average of each loss category times its probability. The result in this case is $8375. Expectations are therefore that 3.0 mishaps may take place every 100,000 hours with an average loss of $8375 per mishap and a total dollar loss of $25,125.

Monte Carlo simulation would probably make it possible to predict, through use of a computer, the probable losses a company could suffer from accidents resulting only in damage. From this, the level of self-insurance and the level of total insurance necessary could be predicted. Unfortunately, the increases in personal injury claims and awards are less predictable.

The various economic factors due to accident prevention and losses which must be considered in marketing a product have been discussed in Chapter 3. The costs involved over a product's life cycle can be expressed by:

| Cost of safety for a product over its life cycle | = | Accident prevention + insurance costs + recall costs + program costs |
| | | + accident and claim losses – reimbursements |

Reimbursements

Reimbursements may be received in a number of ways. A company whose products are covered by insurance may be considered to have received a return on its investment of insurance premiums.[6] When an accident occurs, there may be a claim for injury or property damage. The insurance company investigates the claim (if the company believes the investigation is justified), defends the manufacturer in court, and pays the claim and attendant costs if the case is lost.

There are limits. Manufacturers attempt to reduce their insurance costs as the premiums rise. One way is to reduce the total amount of coverage; another way is to increase the "deductible" or self-insured level. The insurer pays anything over the deductible; the insured party is obligated to pay the deductible. Thus, a manufacturer might carry $10,000,000 worth of insurance with a deductible of $100,000. If a claim for $500,000 must be paid, the manufacturer pays the $100,000 and the insurer pays the balance. For any payments less than $100,000, the manufacturer pays the entire amount. If the manufacturer suffers a series of losses in separate accidents for which he must pay deductibles up to the contracted level, the manufacturer could suffer high losses even if insured. Therefore, a compromise (based on assessments of all the risks involved) must be made between maintaining a high deductible and possibly suffering greater losses if an accident or series of accidents occurs and maintaining a low deductible and paying high premiums. Coverage of "first-dollar" losses having no deductible becomes expensive.

A second form of reimbursement is in the positive effects of having good safety programs. One company expanded its safety program after one of its products was subjected to a recall action. Controls over subcontractors were intensified for safety purposes. As a result, dealers returned fewer products because of deficiencies; thus, the safety program more than paid for itself.

The Insurance Services Office reported that in product liability cases 97% of the bodily injury payments and 89% of property damage payments are covered by insurance. The remainder is paid by the defendants who have no insurance coverage, deductibles, and awards which exceed policy limits.

In addition, a manufacturer who achieves a reputation for producing safe products generally benefits. The public has no way of evaluating the safety of products and will follow the recommendations of those it believes are knowledgeable in the field. Thus, if an adverse report on the safety of a product is written by a consumer organization, either governmental or not, or if a recall action has been an-

Scoring Maintenance Tasks

PROTECTIVE DEVICES

This item encompasses equipment design provisions for self-protection against damage to component or parts after a malfunction has occurred. If a system has protective devices such as fuses, circuit breakers, relief valves, rupture discs, etc, the equipment can then be considered protected from further damage as well as aiding in the isolation of the malfunction. If no provisions have been made for the inclusion of protective devices within a system, further damage and increased repair time could be a direct result.

SCORING CRITERIA

1. To be scored when automatic shutoff devices protect parts or components from further damage after a malfunction occurs in a critical area. A typical example of such malfunction would be if the bias supply fails, and B+ voltage is automatically cut off by circuit breakers, fuses, or relay action;
2. To be scored when automatic shutoff devices do not protect parts or components from further damage, but visual indicators or audible alarms warn personnel of the situation;
3. To be scored when a critical malfunction occurs, and parts or components are not protected by automatic shutoff devices, indicators, or alarms. Involves malfunctions that damage parts or components because automatic shutoff devices or alarms were not provided.

CHECKLIST

Protective Devices:

1. Equipment was automatically kept from operating after malfunction occurred to prevent further damage (this refers to malfunction of such areas as bias supplies, keep-alive voltages, etc) 4;
2. Indicators warned that malfunction has occurred 2;
3. No provision has been made . . . . 0.

SAFETY (PERSONNEL)

This item determines if the maintenance action requires personnel to work under hazardous conditions, such as being in close proximity to high voltage, high pressures, radiation, toxic fumes, high temperatures, etc, or working on elevated structures such as scaffolding.

SCORING CRITERIA

1. To be scored when the maintenance action did not require personnel to work under hazardous conditions. The maintenance action did not require precautions to be taken, since the task was not associated with high pressures, moving parts, etc.
2. Applicable when precautions were taken due to hazardous conditions causing slight delays in maintenance action. A typical example would be when the task required that filters must be cleaned with volatile solvents requiring some degree of caution;
3. To be scored when precautions taken due to hazardous conditions would cause excessive delay to the maintenance action. Such precautions would be the use of SCAPE suits when working in areas that may be contaminated with oxidizer, or when working in areas in close proximity to high voltage, etc.

CHECKLIST

Safety (Personnel):

1. Task did not require work to be performed in close proximity to hazardous condition (high voltage, radiation, moving parts, etc) 4;
2. Some delay encountered due to precautions taken 2;
3. Considerable time consumed due to hazardous conditions . . . . 0.

Figure 18-3. Scoring maintenance tasks.

nounced, sales of that product will probably drop. Conversely, a favorable recommendation may help sales.

Total Safety Costs

The total cost of the product includes development, manufacturing, advertising, overhead, shipping, and numerous other costs, including that of safety. If the cost of all the safety aspects mentioned goes up, the total cost of the product goes up. However, some of the factors in the equation cannot be established until after the product has been marketed and in the hands of the consumer. Accident and claim losses may occur long after[7] a manufacturer has halted production of a product and can no longer recoup those losses by raising the price of the specific product that generated the losses. These factors and their interrelationships demonstrate from an economic standpoint why accident prevention programs are desirable. Evaluation of the factors involved permits making decisions on whether money should be spent for improvements in safety of the product or in increased insurance premiums.

Every manufacturer is subject to accident prevention program costs and usually to insurance costs when the manufacturer puts a product on the market. The manufacturer may or may not be subject to the other factors in the cost equation. Most of the factors indicated interrelate with one another. (These factors are summarized in Figure 18-5.) If the manufacturer has a good accident prevention program and designs the product safely, he may not be subject to recall actions or his product may not be involved in accidents and their attendant losses. Some manufacturers need not worry about recalls be-

Two Methods of Quantitative Risk Assessment

PROBABILITY OF OCCURRENCE	QUALITATIVE PROBABILITY	APPROXIMATE NUMERICAL PROBABILITY (PER FLIGHT OR PER HOUR OF FLIGHT)
Probable	Likely to occur a number of times during the total operational life of each aeroplane of the type	10^{-5}
Improbable	Refers to a range of expected frequencies embracing:	
Remote	Unlikely to occur to each aeroplane during its total operational life but may occur several times when considering the total operational life of a number of aeroplanes of the type.	10^{-5} to 10^{-7}
Extremely Remote	Unlikely to occur when considering the total operational life of a number of aeroplanes of the type, but nevertheless, has to be regarded as being possible.	10^{-7} to 10^{-9}
Extremely Improbable	So unlikely to occur that it does not have to be regarded as possible.	Less than 10^{-9}

The regulation goes on to define the categories of effects which could be generated as: Minor, Major, and Catastrophe. Only certain combinations of probabilities and effects are permitted:

PERMISSIBLE COMBINATIONS

PROBABILITY OF OCCURRENCE	MINOR EFFECT	MAJOR EFFECT	CATASTROPHE
Probable	X		
Improbable			
Remote	X	X	
Extremely Remote	X	X	
Extremely Improbable	X	X	X

*Taken from the third draft of ISSUE 1 PAPER NO. 670, 29th October 1975, British Civil Airworthiness Requirements.

- -

U.S. AIR FORCE METHOD FOR CALCULATING REAL HAZARD INDEX (RHI)*

Category I - Negligible: Hazards will not result in injury, occupational illness, or system damage.
Category II - Marginal: Hazards may cause minor injury, minor occupational illness, or minor system damage.
Category III - Critical: Hazards may cause severe injury, severe occupational illness, or major system damage.
Category IV - Catastrophic: Hazards may cause death or system loss.

QUALITATIVE PROBABILITY	LEVEL	SPECIFIC INDIVIDUAL ITEM	FLEET (OR INVENTORY)
Frequent	6	Likely to occur frequently.	Continuously experienced.
Reasonably Probable	5	Will occur several times in life of individual item.	Will occur frequently
Occasional	4	Unlikely to occur in life of one specific item.	Will occur several times
Remote	3	So improbable that it can be assumed that this item will not experience.	Unlikely to occur but possible.
Extremely Improbable	2	Probability of occurrence cannot be distinguished from zero.	So improbable that it can be assumed that the fleet will never experience
Impossible	1	Physically impossible to occur.	

Qualitative Probability	Category	I	II	III	IV	
		Real Hazard Index				
1		1	2	3	4	
2	Permissible	2	4	6	8	
3	Combinations	3	6	9	12	
4		4	8	12	16	Combinations Not Permitted
5		5	10	15	20	
6		6	12	18	24	

Combinations with a Real Hazard Index of 9 or more not permitted.

*In 1977, the order of the categories was reversed (Category 1 – Catastrophic). The old categories are used to illustrate how the method works.

Figure 18-4. Two methods of quantitative risk assessment.

Interrelationships Between Safety Costs

Effect On: / Increase In:	Accident Prevention Costs	Insurance Premiums	Recall Costs	Accident & Claim Costs	Reimbursements
Accident Prevention Costs	✕	Premiums usually lower than for an unsafe product which has not been subjected to an effective safety program during development.	May eliminate recalls	May eliminate or reduce numbers or severities of accidents	Reduction in numbers of accidents or in accident severities will reduce insurance reimbursements. Benefits received in other ways will increase monetary returns.
Insurance Premiums	Cost of insurance may induce manufacturer to increase expenditures and undertake expanded accident prevention programs.	✕	No interrelation	"Nuisance" claims and sizes of claims may increase if claimants are aware or assume manufacturer is covered by insurance	Increase in premiums may result in choice of higher deductibles and less insurance coverage.
Recall Costs	Increase in recalls and attendant costs will require improvement in safety programs.	Will increase cost of insurance coverage for recalls.	✕	If recall occurred before accident, may reduce accidents and claims and attendant costs.	Public may not buy from company whose products are being recalled.
Accident & Claim Costs	May force improvements in product accident prevention program.	Will increase costs of insurance, possibly to point where they might be unbearable.	Accidents and claims will trigger investigations which might result in recalls and attendant costs.	✕	Insurance reimbursements may pay part of settlements or awards over the deductible. Returns from other benefits negative
Reimbursements	Benefits other than insurance coverage reimbursements may induce manufacturer to increase expenditures on accident prevention programs.	Reimbursements from insurance can only be increased by increasing insurance coverage with attendant higher premiums.	No interrelation	No interrelation	✕

Figure 18-5. Interrelationships between safety costs.

cause their products do not come under laws that call for such actions.

The size of insurance premiums may affect the size of the insurance reimbursements. A company may feel that since the cost of the insurance is so high and that the risk involved is so low, it would be better to use a higher deductible (self-insured) amount. A tradeoff must thus be made between the certainty of having to pay premiums and the uncertainties of having recalls, accidents, or other claims which might be covered.

Assessing the Risks

To minimize costs a product manufacturer will want to keep the safety cost as low as possible. The manufacturer must evaluate each of the factors in the cost of safety equation. The one factor which is under positive control of the manager for product manufacture is the accident prevention program. It is this factor that has the most far-reaching effect, of all those shown, on all the other factors. Even without a numerical assessment it is evident that an effective product accident prevention program is of primary importance in minimizing safety risks to a company.

The Cost of Accident Avoidance

Perhaps one of the earliest, and certainly one of the most meaningful, articulations of the negligence standard was that of Judge Learned Hand, who defined what ordinary and prudent care meant. The standard and liability assignment rule, as articulated by Judge Hand, was that a given party is negligent, and hence liable for damages, if the arithmetic product of the (economic) loss attendant to the accident and the probability of the accident occurrence exceeds the cost of avoiding the accident. *United States v Carroll Towing Company* 159 F.2d 169 (2d Civ. 1974).[8]

Or, a manufacturer could be held liable if:

Cost of accident avoidance < (probability of an accident) × (loss due to the accident)

This legal concept presumes that the knowledge of the loss due to the accident will be known. Most managers would like to know early, long before an accident occurs, how much to spend on an accident prevention program to make the product safe. The equation on page 237 can be used with a slight modification to indicate the factors involved:

Accident prevention program cost	=	Savings in insurance premiums + recall costs which can be avoided + accident and claims costs which can be avoided − reduction in reimbursements

Problems with Quantitative Methods

Although the trend is toward using quantitative methods to set goals and to determine whether or not these goals have been achieved, there are problems and objections to using them, for example:

1. Probabilities are too often used to show that an accident or injury might occur only infrequently so that corrective action need not be taken.

2. If an accident results in legal action, the fact that a product or an operation was dangerous speaks for itself and the probability of its occurrence, past or predicted, is immaterial.

3. Effort is frequently diverted to proving through rationalization that a product meets or exceeds a stipulated level.

4. Lack of dependable probability data for complex products, non-electronic components and equipment, or other factors creates results which are also undependable.

5. Quantitative methods of analysis and data sources are not yet standardized.

6. The costs for quantitative analysis are generally far higher than for qualitative analysis, especially for large or complex products, and do not provide a commensurate return.

7. Quantitative analysis often requires use of personnel highly capable in mathematical techniques, and for complicated analyses, the use of a computer.

No matter the depth or type of safety analysis used to determine risk in the use of any new product, actuaries may avoid technical methods of analyses prepared prior to any actual evaluation from past operational experience with the product. Through records of accidents with similar products that have been used, adjusted for past losses to establish the risk involved with that type of product, and the premiums to be charged, any adverse experience then determines whether premium costs go up or down with accident occurrences. This would also be true with similar products already on the market. Even if the number of accidents remains the same, premium costs will tend to increase because of the ever growing number and size of court awards for liabilities resulting from product accidents, which have caused great apprehension within insurance companies concerned about the risk of losses they might take.

Law of Safety Progress

The *law of safety progress*[9] is based on the economic aspects of safety and may be of interest here. It is based on the idea that a company that produces an unsafe product must either correct it or suffer costly losses. Government agencies may institute recall actions, liability claims may be instituted, or the loss of customers for a product alleged to be unsafe may exert pressure for the correction of deficiencies.

When governmental, legal, or economic pressure is brought against a company, all other companies making the same or similar products will undoubtedly examine their own products to ensure that they do not have those failings. If the products do, they would probably take corrective action. Gradually, because of these improvements, withdrawals of defective products, or because of the failures of their producers and removal from the market of their products, the safety level of the remaining products will improve. This can be stated as a law:

An unsafe product will bring on corrective action or drive its producer out of business, thereby raising the safety level of all such products.

In the July 8, 1991 issue of the *Los Angeles Times*, the article entitled "RISK," which dealt with California Supreme Court rulings on liabilities for accidents, contained much pertinent information. Quoted in the article is the following comment from a member of the California Trial Lawyers Association:

A ruling preventing injured parties from obtaining damages would be a severe handicap. It would allow a wrong-doer to avoid responsibility even though he was partially or totally at fault. The dispute has emerged in the wake of a major shift in California civil liberty law that took place 16 years ago. Before then, under the all-or-nothing doctrine of contributory negligence, injured people who were only partly responsible for the harm they had suffered were barred from suing another party for negligence. In 1975, the State Supreme Court adopted the doctrine of comparative negligence, saying the damage must be apportioned according to the degree of fault of the various parties.

Attorneys for defendants say basic fairness requires that individuals be held accountable for the risks they take knowingly, and voluntarily assume.

A judge of the U.S. Ninth Circuit Court of Appeals said, "the legal system was effectively subsidizing 'irresponsible and self-destructive behavior'."

Notes

[1] Chauncey Starr, "Social Benefit Versus Technological Risk," *Science*, Vol. 165 (September 19, 1969), pp. 1232–1238.

[2] The fact that approximately 50,000 persons per year were killed and 1,800,000 injured (1969) in automobile accidents appears to be a risk which the U.S. public was willing to accept. There was, however, much objection to the fact that 47,000 U.S. men and women were killed and 304,000 were wounded in Southeast Asia, a far lesser number.

[3] WASH-1400-D, *Reactor Safety Study—An Assessment of Risks in U.S. Commercial Nuclear Power Plants*, Atomic Energy Commission, August 1974.

[4] Take the case of Daedalus and Icarus mentioned on page 137. A reliability engineer would say that Icarus had exceeded the limits Daedalus had specified and therefore Icarus' flight should not be counted for reliability determinations (reliability, we repeat, is the probability of successful accomplishment of a mission *within specified limits* and over a specified length of time). Since Daedalus' flight was the only one made within the limits specified, it was the only one that should be counted. Since the flight was completely successful, the achieved reliability was 100%. But from the safety engineer's standpoint, the accident rate was 50%.

[5] This is in accordance with the old cliche that with insurance you win only when you lose.

[6] This is one of the reasons manufacturers and insurance companies have asked for laws limiting the length of time claims can be made after a product has been originally put on the market or sold.

[7] From *Interagency Task Force Report on Product Liability, Legal Study*, Vol. IV, Dept. of Commerce, Washington, D.C., 1977.

[8] This law was first stated in the author's *Handbook of System and Product Safety* (Englewood Cliffs, N.J.: Prentice-Hall, 1972), p. 31.

Questions

1. When people use the word "risk," what are some of the meanings they might have in mind?

2. Explain why someone might want to know what risk there is in using a product.

3. What is meant by voluntary risk and involuntary risk?

4. People will generally take greater voluntary risks than they will take involuntary risks. How much greater risk will a person usually take if it is voluntary?

5. How much greater risk is there in a year for the average automobile traveler as compared to an air traveler as indicated in Figure 18-2? Do you think the probabilities shown in the figure are valid?

6. Explain what analyses can be used for determining quantitative risk.

7. Explain how risks of using different products can be made relativistically.

8. Explain how the "Real Hazard Index" is used. What is its purpose?

9. When can quantitative failure rates be used to indicate or evaluate safety levels?

10. What effects do increasing insurance premiums have on coverage?

11. Although courts indicate that safety costs should be included in the cost of the product, why is this sometimes impossible?

12. Explain how a good accident prevention program will reduce costs.

13. Discuss the Law of Safety Progress. Is it borne out in actual circumstances?

14. Comment on who benefits from doctrines of contributory negligence and on comparative negligence.

15. Comment on an attorneys' belief that individuals should be held accountable for risks they take and voluntarily assume.

16. Is the risk voluntary if a worker believes that he or she must operate a product known to be hazardous, or be fired?

16. Is the risk voluntary if a worker believes that he or she must operate a product known to be hazardous, or be fired?

17. Discuss the comment of the Judge of the U.S. Ninth Circuit Court of Appeals that "the legal system was effectively subsidizing irresponsible and self-destructive behavior."

18. Discuss whether all these comments will tend to stop manufacturers and distributors from producing and marketing products whose use might be considered marginally or reasonably hazardous.

19

Manufacturing the Safe Product

General

Production defects are second only to those product deficiencies created by inadequate design as accident causes. Figure 19-1 indicates a few of the numerous recall actions initiated by the Consumer Product Safety Commission because of production defects. Defects similar to these in critical components or assemblies have caused numerous accidents. Following are some of the principal problems which can be present in a poorly controlled manufacturing program.

Generating Hazardous Characteristics

Improper production techniques can actually create hazardous characteristics in products. Failures to remove metal burrs, points, or sharp edges are common examples. Removing too much insulation from wires will expose so much of the conductor that a person might touch it inadvertently and be shocked.

Unauthorized Changes

A common cause of product safety problems is the changes which production personnel sometimes make in order to reduce production costs, difficulties, or both. For example, a designer may have required the use of two different sized or types of connectors in order to avoid cross-connecting circuits. A value engineer or production manager may not realize the reason for this requirement and may change it to use one size of connector. He or she would undoubtedly believe that he or she had been saving money by eliminating the need for purchasing and stocking more than one size and by minimizing possible errors in the manufacturing process. He or she would also have eliminated an accident prevention feature of the product.

Another reason for unauthorized changes is that a production supervisor will try to minimize any interruption to his or her work schedule. If a design problem arises, the supervisor is reluctant to wait for the change approval process to be completed. Having to consult with designers and waiting for them to review the problem and develop a solution is time-consuming. During that time, either production is halted or deficient items or assemblies are produced which may have to be replaced or redone later. It is at such times the supervisor is impelled to make a decision.

In order to prevent changes from being made indiscriminately, it is advisable that the changes be controlled. Each change should be evaluated by the design engineering department. If further analysis for safety reasons is required, design engineering should ensure that product safety engineering evaluates the impact the change would have. In many cases, each and every change is evaluated for its safety aspects by a safety engineer, who may have a better insight than the designer into whether or not a safety problem is involved.

Figure 19-2 presents a summary chart of an excellent example of controls that one company uses for engineering changes both within its plants and those of its suppliers. Other companies have configuration control boards that are responsible for ensuring that each proposed change is evaluated by all organizations concerned before a change may be made.

Controls on changes must be imposed and carried out not only for operations in the manufacturer's plant but also for all supplies, components, and assemblies received from vendors and subcontractors. It was pointed out in the chapters on analyses that product safety problems are commonly generated by problems with components. Control of both their quality and of changes will mitigate these problems.

Examples of Recall Due to Production Defects

PRODUCT	POSSIBLE DEFECT	UNITS AFFECTED	ACTION
Snowmobile	Defective weld may cause steering handle to break	5,000	Shipments stopped, instruct dealers by mailgram on inspection and repair; certified letter to be sent to all owners
Snowmobile	Ski saddle may have poor weld, may break causing steering loss	538	Notify consumers by certified mail; return to distributor for reweld. All units in production corrected
Luau torch set	Leaking seam causes flammable fluid to run down side of pot	2,352	Stopped sales; returned to warehouse
Circular saw	Lower movable guard may keep up in a partially open position	680	QC improved. Old bearing plates with improper screw are being scrapped. New plates being made
Aluminium electric fry pan	Crack in heating element	8,200	Return to previous method of furnace brazing
Black and white TV receivers	Intermittent or loose connection causes electric arc which could carbonize PC board which can ignite TV cabinet	35,000	Production change
Gas furnace	Cracks in furnace heat exchanger may allow carbon monoxide to enter the heated air stream	100,000	Replaced cracked exchangers as discovered
Color TV receivers	Insulation of line cord shows evidence of damage during manufacturing. Possibility of physical contact with exposed conductors, shock hazard	99,280	Inspect and replace defective cords
Fluorescent under-the-counter light	Poor wiring, rotating base terminals, black electrical tape for insulation may result in electric shock	15,000	Discontinue sale, returned units destroyed
Wringer-washer	Misapplied wire connectors on motor cord; possible line potential on electrically isolated motor frame	255	Dealer notified to inspect and repair subject washers

Figure 19-1. Examples of recall due to production defects.

If development and safety programs are conducted properly, production personnel should have little need for changes. These personnel should have participated in design reviews, trade-off studies, and safety reviews while the product was being developed. Production problems that could be foreseen should have been considered at those times, not later as afterthoughts. Production capabilities, methods, tooling and machine requirements, whether the product should be manufactured in-house or elsewhere, and subcontractor and vendor selections are some of the items that should have been considered long before production began.

Care of Safety-Critical Items

Safety-critical items require more care than items that are not safety-critical. Which items are safety-critical can be determined from the safety analyses. Too often determinations of criticality are left to production or quality control personnel who may have only an incomplete knowledge of which items are safety-critical. In some cases, guidance for quality control personnel consists of giving them a copy of the code, regulation, or standard the product must meet and then letting them decide which product features are critical.

Certain items are always obviously safety-critical. These include materials and components that are dangerous in themselves (explosives, toxic or radioactive substances), materials which in combination are dangerous and must be separated (solvents and alkali metals, hydrocarbons and strong oxidizers), and safety devices. Others are less obviously safety-critical and the fact that they are can sometimes be established only by detailed analyses.

Summary Chart of Section 2 Controls

	Symbol And What It means To Whom → Records, and procedures required ↓	△F* Eng. Spec.		△F N* Eng. Spec. N = 1,2,3...		△N* Eng. Spec. N = 1,2,3...	
		Company site	Vendor site	Company site	Vendor site	Company site	Vendor site
Eng'g Considerations — 1	Chief engineer to be notified of design changes. (Ref. II.A.I.G)		Vendor: inform of design changes		Vendor: inform of design changes		Vendor: inform of design changes
2	Chief engineer or project manager review and approval on drawings or changes to drawings including part number changes. (Ref. II.F.)	Yes		Yes		Yes	
Manufacturing Considerations — 3	Establish and maintain written routings. Review existing routings for adequacy - record changes for histoic reference. (Ref. II.A.I.A.B.D.)	Present routings acceptable		All routings to include designated specs		Required on designated specs only	
4	Include identified detail specifications in routines marked with safety symbol(s). (Ref. II.A.2., II.E.)	No detail specs designated		Include and assure designated specs		Include and assure designated specs	
5	Chief engineer or quality control manager approval required on change in manufacturing method or process. (Ref. II.A.I.E.)	Yes	Related to specs only	Yes	Related to specs only	Related to designated specs only	Related to designated specs only
6	Quality control manager review of changes in routing sequence or "off-routing" procedures--regarding inspection. (Ref. II.A.I.F.)	Yes		Yes		Related to designated specs only	
7	Chief engineer or project manager approval required on blueprint deviation. (Ref. II.B.I.)	Any detail spec.		Any detail spec.		For designated specs only	
Common — 8	Identify safety related "in-process" information by identification symbols (includes detail when identified). (Ref. II.E')	Yes see lines 4 and 10 of chart		Yes see lines 4 and 10 of chart		Yes see lines 4 and 10 of chart	
Inspection Considerations — 9	Establish and maintain incoming inspection procedures. Review existing procedures for adequacy. (Ref. II.A.1.A.B.C.D.)	Present procedures acceptable		All procedures to include designated specs		Required on designated specs only	
10	Include identified detail specifications marked with safety symbol(s) in procedures. (Ref. II.A.2., II.E.)	No detail specs designated		Yes		Yes	
11	Keep inspection records of purchased parts on file by part number. (Ref. II.D.)	Yes		Yes		Yes	
12	On any manufactured lot found to be non-conforming, inspect 100% or obtain deviation (see line 7). (Ref. II.C.2.)	Any detail specs.		Any detail specs.		For designated specs only	
13	On any vendor manufactured lot found to be non-conforming, inspect 100%, return, or obtain deviation (see line 7). (Ref. II.C.1.)	Any detail spec.		Any detail spec.		For designated specs only	

*"F" indicates current or expected manufacturing and inspection procedures are adequate to insure part integrity. Where the letter "N" is shown, a number will indicate the total number of "safety related" details. All other references are to paragraphs in the engineering specification.

Figure 19-2. Summary chart of Section 2 controls.

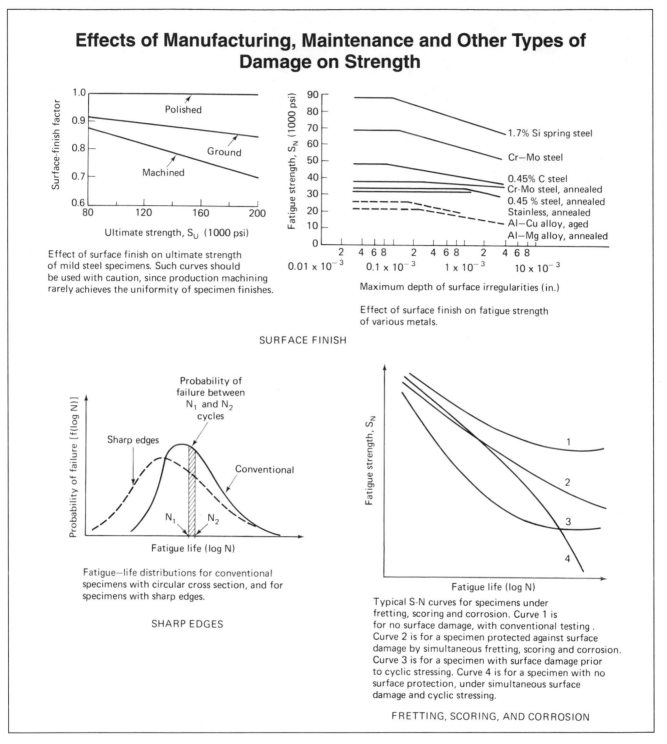

Effects of Manufacturing, Maintenance and Other Types of Damage on Strength

Effect of surface finish on ultimate strength of mild steel specimens. Such curves should be used with caution, since production machining rarely achieves the uniformity of specimen finishes.

Effect of surface finish on fatigue strength of various metals.

SURFACE FINISH

Fatigue–life distributions for conventional specimens with circular cross section, and for specimens with sharp edges.

SHARP EDGES

Typical S-N curves for specimens under fretting, scoring and corrosion. Curve 1 is for no surface damage, with conventional testing. Curve 2 is for a specimen protected against surface damage by simultaneous fretting, scoring and corrosion. Curve 3 is for a specimen with surface damage prior to cyclic stressing. Curve 4 is for a specimen with no surface protection, under simultaneous surface damage and cyclic stressing.

FRETTING, SCORING, AND CORROSION

Figure 19-3. Effects of manufacturing, maintenance and other types of damage on strength.

Generally, the information on criticality is stipulated on drawings accepted for production. The problem, however, is that there is a tendency to minimize the number of critical items. A judicious compromise must be reached between imposing an excessive number of critical items on production and quality control personnel and citing as many of them as possible. When too many items are listed as critical, personnel may tend to ignore them. On the other hand, the workload of quality control personnel might be increased to the point where their capabilities are overloaded and their effectiveness lost.

Inspection and testing of every individual component, subassembly, and assembly in a complex system for each important parameter are prohibitive economically. If testing must be done to verify the quality of production, a test plan must be developed and followed in order to produce the greatest beneficial effect within the limits of available funds. This test plan requires knowledge of the criticality of each item, the best means to indicate whether or not the provisions of specifications or other requirements have been met, and the points in time when tests should be made for maximum effectiveness. It is uneconomical to incorporate a defective unit in a larger assembly and then have to tear down the assembly when the defect is found. Tests must be carried out early enough to permit elimination of defective items before unnecessary work is done but not often enough to impose an unbearable workload and cost. Many defects cannot be detected by visual inspection after the components in which they exist have been incorporated into larger assemblies. Others may be damaged in a subsequent operation. The operation may then be regarded as critical, and tests may be made after the operation is completed.

Manufacturing Defects

Production deficiencies can degrade an excellent design. Poor workmanship can reduce the strengths of products so that they fail at loads far less than those for which they were designed. Figure 19-3 indicates the effects on strength of surface finishes, poor workmanship, or damage. Any of these may create stress concentrators at which fatigue cracking and failure of stressed parts will begin.

Poor welds can lack strength or the heat of welding could degrade the strength of the base metal. Welds performed under contaminated conditions can cause the welds to be porous. Failure to clean welds can leave debris, residues, and other deleterious materials which will lead to corrosion and loss of strength. Excess amounts or loose beads of solder, pieces of cut wire, and other debris can bridge small gaps between unprotected conductors, permitting short circuits to occur when the equipment is turned on.

Excessive heat can also degrade surface finishes so that they fail. Excessive heat from welding, heat treating, or soldering can cause degradation of metals and the proximity to heat sources can cause deformation or melting of plastics.

Other defects can result from failure to tighten assemblies or to include safety wires, cotter pins, or similar holding devices so that critical parts separate in use. Over-torquing of parts creates inherent stresses in the assembly so the assembly may fail when the operational load is applied.

Failure to include warning labels on assemblies may leave manufacturers vulnerable to claims of "failure to warn" if an accident occurs. Warnings should be placed not only on the original assembly but also on the replacement part if the replacement part is the one that held the warning.

At one time, it was believed that failures of complex products were mostly caused by failures of their components. It has now been determined that more failures actually occur because of the weak connections made between or to these components. In electrical systems, a wire or cable may break because of flexing, crimping, or cutting during manufacture or installation. Connections may separate because of poor soldering, failure to remove corrosion products or their causes, failure to provide electrical bonds or grounds, or lack of locking devices. In mechanical systems, fittings on pneumatic or hydraulic lines may not be tightened adequately, lack of cleanliness may cause clogging of orifices and other critical flow passages, welds may fail, or hoses may be damaged so that they fail under pressure or separate from couplings and whip.

Production Errors

Production errors may be similar to those listed in Chapter 10 for operator errors and most of the corrective actions are the same as those shown in Figure 10-9. Errors made by production workers may be the result of the following:

1. Speedups to meet production quotas or to obtain premium pay.
2. Employee fatigue.
3. Inadequate selection or training of workers.
4. Too little, poor, or no supervision.
5. Poor motivation or distraction of workers.
6. Unsatisfactory working environment conditions.
7. Inadequate or poorly designed equipment, tools, or facilities.
8. Lack of instructions, drawings, or specifications.

Quality Control

The quality control organization is responsible for ensuring that a high-quality output is produced by the production organization. Quality control organizations do not have responsibility for the production processes and would not even be necessary if all products were produced without fault. Unfortunately, deficiencies occur in every manufacturer's plant and efforts must be made to uncover them before the product is released into the marketplace. Beau[1] points out:

Three facts of life are with us continually, and are stated as follows:

1. All factory mechanics will certainly make mistakes resulting in poor workmanship some of the time.
2. All inspectors will certainly make mistakes and pass (accept) bad work some of the time.
3. It is a certainty that some material will progress to higher levels of assembly or be delivered to

Relationship of Quality and Share of Market

Relationship of quality and share of market:

Percent of Businesses with	MARKET SHARE		
	Under 12%	12-26%	Over 26%
Inferior Quality	47%	33%	20%
Average Quality	30%	36%	30%
Superior Quality	23%	31%	50%
No. of Businesses	169	176	176

Note almost half of the companies with less than 12% market share have inferior quality and half of the companies with over 26% of the market have superior quality. There is some indication that higher quality and larger market share are related

Relationship of both market share and quality with ROI:

Market Share	PRODUCT QUALITY		
	Inferior	Average	Superior
Under 12%	4.5% ROI	10.4% ROI	17.4% ROI
12%-26%	11.0% ROI	18.1% ROI	18.1% ROI
Over 26%	19.5% ROI	21.9% ROI	28.3% ROI

Interestingly, companies with low share of market and superior quality had greater ROI than companies in the middle range of market share but inferior quality. Thus there is an indication that a small company can improve profit by improving quality even though it may not be feasible to improve market share because of capacity or similar reasons.

Relationship of marketing expenditures and quality with ROI

Product Quality	RATIO OF MARKETING EXPENDITURE TO SALES		
	Low Under 6%	Average 6-11%	High Over 11%
Inferior	15.4% ROI	14,8% ROI	2.7% ROI
Average	17.8% ROI	16.9% ROI	14.2% ROI
Superior	25.2% ROI	25.5% ROI	19.8% ROI

If quality is poor, increasing marketing expenditures has a pronounced inverse effect on ROI. A less pronounced effect, but still inverse, is shown when quality is in the average range or superior. In any given range of marketing expenditure the increase of quality performance appears to have a beneficial effect on ROI. This would seem to indicate that in working to improve ROI a prudent management would analyze its quality position before making commitments for large increases in marketing expenditures.

Figure 19-4. Relationship of quality and share of market.

the customer with unknown and undetected defects which might cause trouble.

Quality control is also concerned with inspecting and testing all materials, parts, and assemblies received from suppliers. A manufacturer is responsible for the product he furnishes a customer; this responsibility includes all the items that the manufacturer obtains from subcontractors and vendors. The need for control over vendor and subcontractor efforts has already been pointed out. The minimum requirements that every supplier should meet are listed in Figure 5-4. Specific requirements may be added for each supplier as the needs warrant. In addition, the purchaser should stipulate a prohibition against changes without the purchaser's approval.

Initial assurance that the items furnished by suppliers meet the prescribed requirements can be undertaken at either the suppliers' plants, the receiving plant, or both. Responsible suppliers make their own inspections and tests to ensure that their products meet the stipulated parameters. For critical items, the purchaser may have his or her own quality assurance personnel conduct or observe inspections and tests in the supplier's plant. The purchaser may also conduct reinspections in the purchaser's plant. Some manufacturers classify suppliers according to the number of defective items they deliver. The products of a highly-rated supplier are given only a minimal inspection. Those of a low-rated supplier are given an intensive inspection, that is, if the products are purchased at all.

Records must be maintained in case there are questions later about the quality of a specific shipment. Data may indicate that a specific lot has an undesirable and possibly dangerous characteristic. These data may assist in establishing the extent of a problem that becomes apparent in the field. In case of a claim, it may prove that an item which failed had been inspected, had passed, and was not defective when it was in the hands of the manufacturer.

Inspections and tests during and immediately after processing and assembly must be carried out at those times and locations where the most effective results can be produced. In addition, it is necessary to establish whether or not inspections and tests should be made by sampling or on all items (100 percent). For some items, such as flashbulbs, a 100 percent test is impossible except for specific parameters; with other items, it is impractical and uneconomical to do so. Sampling programs that are judicious compromises must then be established. Critical items may require 100 percent inspections and tests whenever possible. It has been pointed out that the criticality of an item for safety purposes can be determined from hazard analyses.

Inspections and tests are necessary to reveal those items that fail to meet prescribed limits. That a product or subassembly has not been assembled correctly so that it constitutes a hazard can sometimes be established by test. As shown in Figure 15-5, an incorrectly assembled switch could cause an accident. The third reason was pointed out in the discussion of safety factors and margins (page 61): Inadequate or loose quality control will result in wide dispersion of strength values and greater possibilities of failure than will tight control.

Quality control personnel must know the parameters the product is to meet, the deficiencies that might be present, the criticality of the items to be inspected, and the reports that must be made so that records can be maintained. For reliability purposes, criticality is usually defined as critical, major, or minor. There are slightly different definitions among different manufacturing organizations. One set of definitions is listed below. According to these definitions, almost every safety-related item is "critical."

1. *Critical:* Any fault that is likely to result in serious consequences, e.g., danger of loss of life or serious injury, or the virtual certainty of a major complaint and damage to the supplier's reputation.

2. *Major—serious:* (a) Probability of the product failing to give good performance; (b) likelihood of complaint if the proportion so defective is appreciable.

3. *Major—less serious:* (a) May cause some failure in use; (b) likely to cause the customer some trouble, e.g., in installation or maintenance; (c) major defects in appearance or finish but with no bearing on performance or utility.

4. *Minor:* (a) Minor defects in appearance and finish; (b) technical faults which, while undesirable, are unlikely to cause trouble or poor performance.

The designer can indicate to quality control personnel that a part, dimension, or property is critical by including it on a list of critical items or otherwise designating it appropriately on a drawing. One method uses a broad arrow to point to the item in question. The letter C in the body of the arrow indicates that it is a critical item; the letter M indicates that it is an item of major consideration. Another method uses a heavy solid arrow to show that the item is critical and a hollow arrow for major items.

To standardize quality control methods, the personnel involved should be provided with detailed instructions on the following:

1. The means by which the quality of the products is to be verified; destructive or nondestructive tests; 100 percent inspection or statistical quality control; by examination, demonstration, or test (see page 133).

2. The frequency of sampling and levels of defectiveness by which a lot is to be considered acceptable or unacceptable.

3. Records to be retained of lots inspected, number of items inspected, and number of items found defective.

4. Frequency of calibration of inspection equipment.

5. Action to be taken if it seems that a process has gone out of control.

6. Procedure to be followed if there is a discrepancy between the approved drawings or specifications and the items being inspected.

7. How to identify items that have passed inspection.

8. How to mark nonconforming items and to segregate them so that they will not be assembled into finished products.

Because quality control personnel generally work so closely with production personnel, information on problems that have arisen is usually verbally brought to the attention of production personnel immediately. Any deficiency, whether reported verbally or not, should be reported in writing to the production manager. When the problem uncovered by quality control is one of failure to meet requirements on approved drawings and specifications, the production supervisor can direct that those requirements be met by correcting the production processes. If the problem appears to be one of design, the report should also be sent to design engineering. (It is at this point that the problem of making unauthorized changes may arise.)

To assist the production manager in understanding the magnitude of the problem, the deficiency report should include information on what the deficiency is, where and when it was first encountered, how many items or lots are affected, and by what actions quality control personnel are attempting to limit the effects of the problem (such as segregating defective parts). Quality control personnel may suggest "fixes" by which the products can be reworked to meet the required standards.

Mertz[2] has pointed out the numerous advantages, other than reduction in product liability suits, which accrue from good manufacturing and quality control programs. Among these are reductions in:

1. Costs of scrap and rework.

2. Having to order extra quantities of materials to compensate for possible need to replace defective items.

3. Shipping costs from and to customers on returns.

4. Payment delays because of defective items.

5. Time spent by sales personnel explaining away quality problems to customers.

6. Customer cost of removing and reinstalling a replacement.

7. Losses in sales.

8. Lost income because of defective items.

9. Damage caused by inoperative, failed, or missing items.

Figure 19-4 presents some of the relationships Mertz developed between quality and return on investment (ROI). In each of the comparisons shown the ROI is greatest when product quality is highest.

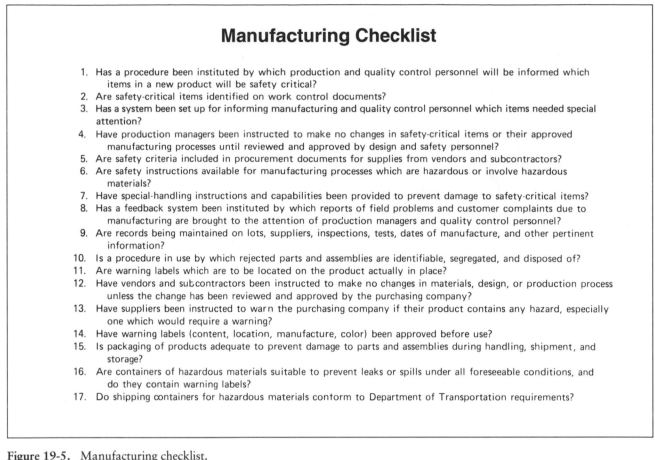

Manufacturing Checklist

1. Has a procedure been instituted by which production and quality control personnel will be informed which items in a new product will be safety critical?
2. Are safety-critical items identified on work control documents?
3. Has a system been set up for informing manufacturing and quality control personnel which items needed special attention?
4. Have production managers been instructed to make no changes in safety-critical items or their approved manufacturing processes until reviewed and approved by design and safety personnel?
5. Are safety criteria included in procurement documents for supplies from vendors and subcontractors?
6. Are safety instructions available for manufacturing processes which are hazardous or involve hazardous materials?
7. Have special-handling instructions and capabilities been provided to prevent damage to safety-critical items?
8. Has a feedback system been instituted by which reports of field problems and customer complaints due to manufacturing are brought to the attention of production managers and quality control personnel?
9. Are records being maintained on lots, suppliers, inspections, tests, dates of manufacture, and other pertinent information?
10. Is a procedure in use by which rejected parts and assemblies are identifiable, segregated, and disposed of?
11. Are warning labels which are to be located on the product actually in place?
12. Have vendors and subcontractors been instructed to make no changes in materials, design, or production process unless the change has been reviewed and approved by the purchasing company?
13. Have suppliers been instructed to warn the purchasing company if their product contains any hazard, especially one which would require a warning?
14. Have warning labels (content, location, manufacture, color) been approved before use?
15. Is packaging of products adequate to prevent damage to parts and assemblies during handling, shipment, and storage?
16. Are containers of hazardous materials suitable to prevent leaks or spills under all foreseeable conditions, and do they contain warning labels?
17. Do shipping containers for hazardous materials conform to Department of Transportation requirements?

Figure 19-5. Manufacturing checklist.

It has been found that programs to improve the quality of manufactured products are often triggered by the potential threats of possible recalls and liability suits. It then develops that corrective measures instituted for safety reasons result in overall savings instead of in increased product costs. To maintain or improve manufacturing programs so that defects which cause accidents are minimized, use of a checklist such as in Figure 19-5 is often helpful.

Other Production Records

In addition to quality control records, it is advisable that a manufacturer maintain other production documents. These include:

1. Copies of purchase orders, advertising literature, test reports, and other available information on suppliers' items.

2. Manufacturers' reports on materials used in production.

3. Lot numbers and the quantities included, components which constituted a lot, serial numbers, and dates of manufacture.

4. Reports of tests prepared by outside laboratories.

Prototype Testing

The last important phase in the production of a new product is testing. In many cases, the prototype to be used may be hazardous, therefore a knowledgeable safety engineer should review the proposed product, test, and facilities to ensure the safety of all personnel during test activities.

Notes

[1]J. F. Beau, "Management of the Human Element in the Physics of Failure," paper presented at the Third Annual Symposium on the Physics of Failure in Electronics, Chicago, Illinois (September 29, 1964), p. 8.

[2]Orville R. Mertz, "Quality's Role in ROI," *Quality Progress* (October 1977), p. 14.

Questions

1. List four manufacturing problems having safety connotations and explain how they could have happened.

2. Give four examples of common defects that result from manufacturing defects and result in recalls.

3. Why might production personnel want to change a design? From a safety standpoint, why must changes be controlled?

4. Explain why knowing which items are safety-critical can save money.

5. List seven causes of production errors.

6. Why is it necessary to maintain production, test, and quality control records?

7. What are the four categories of criticality usually used by quality control personnel?

8. Describe some items that are always safety-critical.

9. What are some of the advantages that accrue from good manufacturing and quality control programs?

10. Explain why tight production controls improve safety margins and improve failures.

11. Explain why careful handling of components, assemblies, and the complete product is necessary during manufacturing, shipping transportation, and storage.

12. Discuss which persons and activities in a manufacturing company might be involved if, because of accidents, there is a recall resulting in a change in design and production.

13. Manufacturers have been sued because of accidents due to both faulty design and/or production. Discuss which of these two might constitute the more serious problem.

14. Discuss whether a manufacturing company's responsibility ends with acceptance of a product and after the product leaves the manufacturer's plant. What are the effects on warranties?

15. If it can be believed, or shown, that parts inspections were inadequate, discuss whether this would adversely affect sales or a court claim for liability because of an accident.

16. Figure 2-4 lists milestones in legal liability. Cite your belief regarding how many of these stemmed from cases that arose because of products considered defective in design, production, or both.

20

Operations Phase Activities

The operations phase begins when the product the manufacturer has developed is first put to use and it lasts until the last product has been disposed of. The operations phase is unique in one respect when compared to other phases. The manufacturer no longer has control of the product because ownership has been transferred. Yet the manufacturer may still be subjected to penalties even when the product has been misused and even for actions the manufacturer performed in good faith during the development and production phases.

Routine tasks to be accomplished before and during the operations phase are listed in Figure 12-2. Some activities are certain to take place during the operations phase for which the manufacturer must make ready, such as requests for repairs of the product or for parts by which others can make the repairs. Other activities are uncertain, unexpected, and all too frequently, unhappy, such as recalls and lawsuits for accidents.

Maintenance

Any product developed for long-term use will involve maintenance, either preventive or corrective (repairs). The designer must ensure that such maintenance is adequate to keep the product in a reliable and safe condition. In addition, the designer must also ensure that when repairs are being made that the person doing the work will not be injured. The results of the designer's efforts during development will become apparent during the operations phase.

Maintenance safety problems can be separated into those that lead to injuries or damage from lack of or improper maintenance and those that occur during the accomplishment of maintenance itself.

If maintenance is not accomplished when required, parts and assemblies may outlive their useful lives, begin to wear out, and fail. Not all failures will result in accidents; some failures will result in the product not functioning. Other failures could generate injury or damage. Each potential failure must therefore be investigated to determine whether or not this is a possibility of injury or damage.

Improper maintenance can have a wider scope of effects. It has happened that connections on electrical tools that have metal cases were connected erroneously during repair. The tool was given a hazardous characteristic which had never existed before and which could lead to accidents in which the user could be electrocuted. The maintenance errors which generate such problems occur less frequently than those which generate failures, but they are still common. Numerous examples have been pointed out by the U.S. armed services in their safety magazines to alert personnel to such problems and the need for care. Frequently cited are cases in which maintenance personnel have left tools, flashlights, and other objects where they interfered with or jammed critical moving parts, such as flight controls. If such occurrences are frequent or highly critical, safeguards have to be provided.

The designer must consider the various kinds of people who would attempt the maintenance work and their skill levels. Their technical competencies and experience may vary widely. For example, they may be people who do their own work as a hobby or to save money, people who are hired to repair products of all companies, customer-service personnel working for the company that manufactures the product, or service personnel for the company that uses the product. Some people who do their own work are enthusiasts who like to keep the products they own in top shape, but even most of these people are less capable than well-trained professionals.

Maintenance Checklist

1. Have human engineering principles been employed to minimize maintenance problems?
2. Can the product be repaired by other than specially trained and equipped personnel?
3. Can a product which has been disassembled for repairs be reassembled incorrectly so it will be dangerous to the user?
4. Could making repairs to the product be dangerous in any way to the person doing the work?
5. Are there instructions available for maintenance and repair?
6. Are the instructions clear and easily understandable?
7. Do the instructions contain warnings to alert the repairman to any hazardous situation? Are the warnings located in easily noticeable places?
8. Are there any safety interlocks which must be bypassed to adjust or repair the product? Will the interlocks reset automatically when the product has been repaired and is ready for operation?
9. Is there any indicator present which would warn that a safety-critical part or assembly needs maintenance?
10. Is the equipment designed to keep it from operating and causing damage after a malfunction has occurred?
11. Do the repair instructions indicate when protective equipment must be worn because of a hazard?
12. Are there warnings present where a repair action might release a device with stored energy that could cause injury (such as removing a cover to a compressed coil spring which might hit a person if freed suddenly).
13. Has the necessity for use of special tools to repair safety-critical items been minimized?
14. Are the items which require most frequent maintenance as accessible as possible?
15. Has an effort been made to minimize the cost of replacement of safety-critical parts which may become defective?
16. Is there any means which make it immediately apparent when one component or subassembly of a redundant safety-critical arrangement has failed and should be replaced?
17. If a fuel or other hazardous fluid must be removed from a product to be repaired, is there a means to drain it completely without danger?
18. Is there a warning against working on a pressurized system or an electrical system which could shock a person?
19. Are test points located where they can be reached easily? Are sight glasses located where they can be read easily?
20. Have the voltages at test points been reduced to levels which will minimize hazards to maintenance personnel?

Figure 20-1. Maintenance checklist.

Generally, most people who do their own work do so to minimize the cost. Designers must remember that in many instances cost is the critical factor that determines whether maintenance is accomplished at all, when it is done, and how it is done. The cost factor also means that many people will not do or have maintenance work done until the need becomes urgent. By that time the useful life of a critical part may have been exceeded and it fails. Failure could then result in damage to other parts. For example, failure of an oil pump could result from the presence of dirt, sludge, or other contaminants because the user neglected to change the oil because of the cost of the oil. Failure of the pump could result in starvation of oil to shafts, bearings, or other devices, thus causing their damage.

Problems which could be generated by maintenance, lack of maintenance, or poor maintenance can be reduced or eliminated by good design. If design cannot eliminate a problem completely, it is necessary to provide suitable procedural safeguards. These are much less effective than preventive designs and should be used only as a secondary means of avoiding errors. The best solution, of course, is to provide components and assemblies that require no maintenance at all, such as greaseless bearings and hermetically-sealed units.

If maintenance-free units cannot be provided, a designer may be able to use such features as:

1. Designs that are as simple as possible since complexity generally increases maintenance problems.

2. Fail-safe designs that will prevent injury or damage if there is a failure.

3. Devices that will permit early detection or prediction of degradation or of potential failures so that maintenance can be performed before the failures actually occur.

4. Easy accessibility so that items that must be maintained are not difficult to check, service, remove, or replace.

5. Elimination of the need for special tools and equipment.

6. Designs that minimize the possibility of maintenance personnel being injured by contact with a hot surface, through electrical shock, or by being hit by rotating or reciprocating equipment or escaping high-pressure gas. Designs should not require that maintenance or adjustments be done near hazardous operating equipment or parts. Guards should be provided against moving parts and interlocks should be provided to deny access to hazardous locations.

Examples of Recalls Due to Design Defects

EXAMPLES OF RECALLS DUE TO DESIGN DEFECTS

PRODUCT	POSSIBLE DEFECT	UNITS AFFECTED	ACTION
Rubber male electric plug	Possible shock hazard	50,140	Production ceased; engineering changes made
Gift rattle	Failed drop test; ingestion of small pellets	64,830	To be destroyed
Rubber softball bat grip	Handle disengages from bat; may cause bodily injury	4,800,000	To be determined
Face mask of youth football helmets	Mask may break upon contact	167,000	Advised to return helmets for test of guard. If found faulty, free replacement. No cost to consumer
Shredder	Possible dismemberment if hand is placed in machine	36,000	Proposed
Infant carrier	An unharnessed infant might slip into position allowing neck to become entrapped in lap belt retainer opening	265,000	Redesign for new units; retrofit kit for existing units
Lawn mower tractors	Gas tank filler spout may swell causing difficulty of engagement of gas cap; fire hazard	30,037	Replacement part was sent to all customers
Electric worm probe	Ground potential and/or direct contact with bare metal exposing user to electrical contact; shock hazard	36	Recall all units sold and refund. Cease further manufacture of item and stop all advertising of product
Crossbows	Defective latch may release arrow (when safety is off without activating trigger) causing injury to user or bystander	23,353	Recall and replace defective latch
Baby pacifiers	Size and design of pacifier permit it to be lodged in baby's throat; possible choking hazard	168,420	Pacifiers are being recalled
Hair dryer	Fan failure; possible fire hazard	25,000	Recall and return units to manufacturer

Figure 20-2. Examples of recalls due to design defects.

Labels should be provided to warn against hazards that cannot be eliminated (the use of warnings should be secondary to good designs which eliminate or protect against the hazard).

7. Protection of sensitive components or assemblies from damage which could result when removing, installing, or adjusting them or nearby parts.

8. Development of procedures that will minimize the possibilities of maintenance errors.

If the manufacturers have not had the foresight to realize the need for simplifying maintenance and repair requirements, the ensuing problems will probably come back to plague them during the operations phase. Manufacturers at one time held to the view that once ownership of a product was transferred to a customer and the express warranty period had ended, the manufacturers bore little responsibility for any further adverse results. This situation has, as indicated in Chapter 2, changed dramatically and drastically in the past few years. Each manufacturer must therefore foresee and plan for problems that may and will arise because of the need for maintenance and repair of the product. Figure 20-1 is a list which can be used to assist a manufacturer in determining whether or not he has taken care of the commonest problems which might be encountered during maintenance, test, or repair of his product.

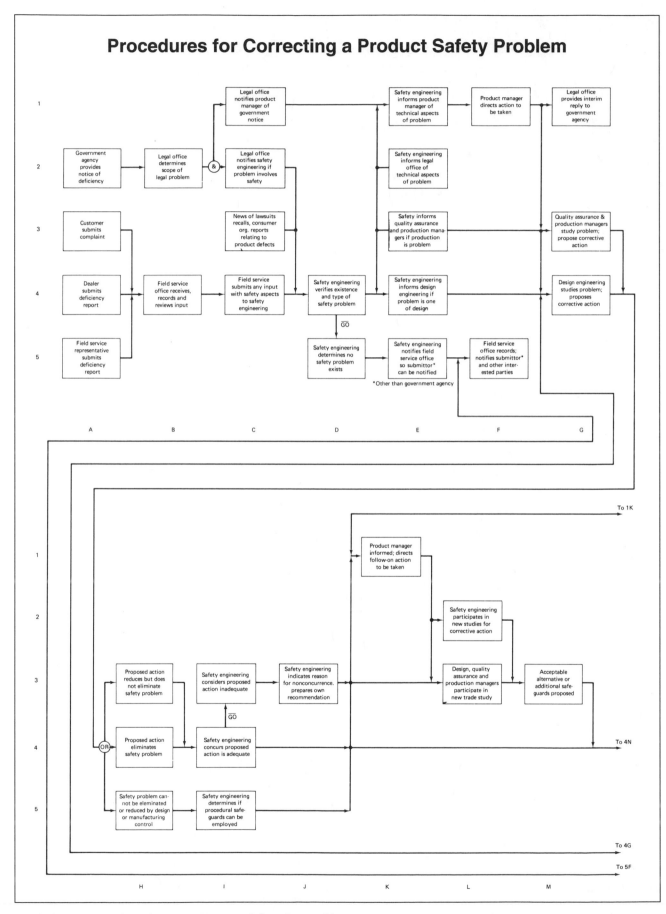

Figure 20-3. Procedures for correcting a product safety problem.

Procedures for Correcting a Product Safety Problem

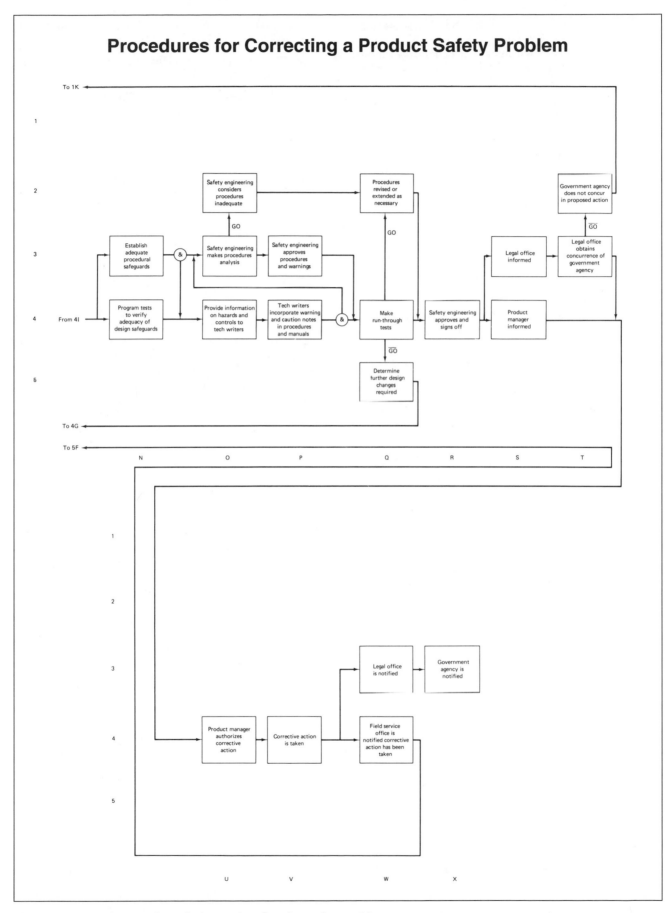

Figure 20-3 (cont'd). Procedures for correcting a product safety problem.

Modifications

It is rare that a product which has reached the operations phase does not undergo modifications. As McAllister has pointed out.

> Safety is no different from all other product attributes (such as performance or durability) in that, as the art progresses, we discover how to do things better or less expensively today than we could do them yesterday. It follows that as time goes on, the optimal safety level of products should continuously rise. This leads to another paradox. If there is to be progress in product safety, it follows that products deemed optimally safe by yesterday's standards will not be deemed optimally safe by today's; similarly, products deemed optimally safe by today's standards will not be deemed optimally safe by tomorrow's.

Some of the modifications will be made to change the style of the product; to make it more powerful, more efficient, or more reliable; to increase its functions; or to make it safer. When the change is to be made for safety reasons, it is sometimes unwise to make the change if there is litigation under way regarding the product. Trial lawyers in some states have used the fact that a manufacturer modified, or intended to modify, a product which was involved in an accident as evidence that the change was an admission that the product was defective. If a change is to be made when such a situation could arise, it is advisable that the reason for the change be well-documented. If possible, changes in the state-of-the-art, availability of new materials, or some of the other non-safety reasons for change mentioned above should be pointed out.

Modifications should proceed through a progressive safety program in the same way that an entirely new product being developed does. Designers of modified products have the benefit of experience with the original products. Even with these benefits, however, the modifications, especially if they are extensive, may contain new safety problems.

Recalls

Preparing for a recall of those products which might be subjected to such an action is similar to preparing for an emergency. The recall may never happen, but it is advisable to know what to do to lessen the impact if it does. Recalls can be instituted for five principal reasons:

1. Analysis indicates the presence of a potential hazard which could lead to an accident.

2. Reports by users, consumers, or other personnel of unsafe conditions, characteristics, or occurrences.

3. An accident, or accidents, revealed an unforeseen deficiency.

4. Violation of a government act, standard, regulation, or other mandatory requirement.

5. The characteristics of the product are incompatible with advertised claims for safety.

When the manufacturer by analysis (or test) determines that a consumer product has a safety defect that has a substantial risk, the Consumer Product Safety Commission must be notified. The initial notification must be made within 24 hours of discovery of the defect. If the notification is made by phone, written confirmation must be forwarded to the Commission within 48 hours by the chief executive of the company. (This responsibility may be delegated to another person, but the delegation must be provided the Commission in writing.)

When the Commission receives information from other sources regarding a possible substantial hazard, the Commission evaluates the risk which might be present. If the Commission concludes that a substantial risk to the public does exist, the manufacturer is sent a "Pre-15(b) Letter" indicating the Commission's awareness of the problem. The Commission asks for an evaluation of the product, the number involved, complaints received, and details of corrective actions taken. Subsequent actions are dependent on whether the Commission considers that a substantial hazard does or does not exist.

Figure 19-1 and 20-2 indicate some of the recall actions initiated by the Consumer Product Safety Commission. The examples have been selected from Appendix J of two of the Annual Reports of the CPSC. In addition to the actions selected which have been segregated in the figures to design and production defects, there are numerous recall actions whose exact causes cannot readily be identified from the information given in the reports. For example, 350,000 lampholder mounts for floodlights had to be recalled for repair or replacement because of "possible shock when internal wiring gets close to housing, causing arcing."

From the description of the defect it is not possible for a reader to determine whether this was a design or production defect.

In any case, receiving a notice from a government agency that a product may be potentially defective and might be subjected to a recall action is a traumatic experience for a manufacturer. Most manufacturers are unprepared for the actions that must be taken. Figure 20-3 presents a procedure which can be used, subject to variation for each individual company, as a basis for evaluating and determining whether or not a safety problem actually exists with a product and, if it does, its severity and scope and the corrective measures to be taken. Figure 20-4 complements the procedure in Figure 20-3.

Checklist for Responses for Recall Actions or Reports of Safety Problems

1. Is there an organization to handle complaints, safety problem reports, and recall actions?
2. Does this organization have the authority to convene a board which can review the problem, determine the cause, and develop the course of action to be taken for correction?
3. Do the company records show any instances of previous customer complaints or other reports on this matter?
4. Does the review of the complaint reveal that a defect actually exists which constitutes a substantial risk of injury?
5. If not, does the company intend to contest the notice of recall action?
6. Has the company's product liability insuror been notified of the problem?
7. Is the reason for the defect readily identifiable?
8. Can the total numbers of defective items and of items produced be determined?
9. Is there any means by which the lots of defective items can be identified by model and serial number?
10. Can the plant, unit and process which have created the defective product be identified?
11. Were the faulty units manufactured only on specific dates?
12. Are quality control records available to determine whether the parameter which caused the defect was one which was monitored?
13. What change(s) will be necessary to correct the deficiency?
14. If it is a production defect, what changes in production will be made to eliminate the problem?
15. What additional quality control measure will be used to ensure that any recurrence of defects will be caught before the defective products leave the plant?
16. Is it necessary to halt shipment of similar products which are in stock?
17. Is it possible to bypass the production step which produced the defect until such time as the corrective action is taken or will the production line have to be shut down?
18. Are records available by which the dealers and purchasers of the defective products can be located and informed?
19. How will dealers and purchasers be made aware the product has a defect?
20. Will it be necessary to have the defective product recalled or can it be repaired by dealers, other company representatives, or by the purchasers themselves?
21. Will it be necessary to refund the purchase price of all defective items?
22. What will the expected cost of correction be?
23. Is there an accounting procedure by which all the costs of recall, refund or replacement can be determined for insurance coverage purposes?

Figure 20-4. Checklist for responses for recall actions or reports of safety problems.

Accident Claims

The fact that a person sues a manufacturer under the strict liability concept does not automatically mean that the manufacturer has lost the case. The Report for the Interagency Task Force on Product Liability states in its Legal Study that in appellate cases the defendant "won" approximately 49 percent of the time. In a survey of jury verdicts in 1970–1975 in Cook County, Illinois, the plaintiff won only 35 percent of the time. The report states that many courts are applying standards of "reasonableness" in regard to products and further goes on with:

> A review of over 650 reported cases by our Legal Study produced some evidence that part of the product liability problem stems from the fact that some manufacturers are producing unreasonably unsafe products. There are the relatively new televisions that catch fire, garments that ignite, hammers that chip, ladders that break, machine tools that confront a worker with higher risks than are reasonable. In that connec-

tion, our legal contractor noted that in 132 of the 655 cases sampled, plaintiff relied solely on the fact that there was a defect in the manufacture of the product that caused the injury. Plaintiff was successful in 58 of those cases, was unsuccessful in 36, and 46 were remanded. Careful product liability prevention technique in the area of quality control might have curbed some of these lawsuits.

Plaintiff was less successful where he alleged it was a defect in design that caused his injury. Here, product liability prevention techniques might also have prevented suits from arising, but it is less certain because some courts do permit a "hindsight" judgment about whether or not the manufacturer designed his product carefully.

The Legal Study also showed that some manufacturers do not provide adequate instruction about the dangers that may spring from their products. On the other hand, some courts have applied principles of hindsight in requiring that "product use" instructions be more specific and detailed.

It appears from the surveys made that accident prevention programs and the application of accident prevention techniques would be more and more successful in combating product liability losses. In 1978 the Supreme Court of California appeared to have adopted a new concept: where there are design alternatives and the one which is chosen is the least dangerous, the company would be absolved of liability if an accident with injury occurred.[2]

Accident Investigations

At one time accident investigations were the principal means by which the existence and causes of safety problems were uncovered. Today, because of the potentially high claims and awards which might result, it is uneconomical (and in some cases, criminally illegal) to find out through bitter experience that a product is unsafe. In most cases, the causes of accidents can be established by analysis and safeguards provided to some degree. Even so, accidents may result and investigations to determine the causes and responsibilities are useful.

A manufacturer may have his/her own personnel make the investigation, or the investigation may be made by the company's insurer, with or without assistance from the manufacturer. In any case, when the product warrants that the company participate in accident investigations, it is advisable that specific personnel be designated to participate in the investigation if there is an accident. The personnel so designated might be engineers from the home plant or representatives in the field from a service agency, but they must be aware that there is specific information they should be looking for in the investigation and that there are specific tasks they must perform and specific actions they must take.

1. The investigator should know how to question and obtain statements from persons who were involved in the accidents, who were eyewitnesses, or who otherwise have direct knowledge of what happened.

2. If it was an industrial accident, the investigator should determine whether or not the employer knew that a dangerous condition existed. In many industrial accident cases, the injured employee is restricted from suing his or her employer and sues the manufacturer of the equipment or product which was involved in the accident. Nevertheless, an employer may be held liable even under the worker's compensation laws if he or she knew about a dangerous condition, knowingly failed to do anything about it, knew that an injury could result, and the condition was the proximate cause of the accident. In California, an employer can be held liable if he or she knowingly violated a Cal-OSHA law and the violation resulted in an accident. The investigator, to protect the product manufacturer, should attempt to find out whether there was anything which indicated serious or willful misconduct on the part of the employer.

3. The investigator should take measurements and make a diagram of where personnel, equipment, and facilities were located immediately prior to the accident and make a diagram of locations of personnel, parts, fragments, and remaining equipment and facilities after the accident. Whenever possible, photographs should be taken of everything and from as many viewpoints as possible.

4. The investigator should take notes about such conditions as housekeeping in an industrial plant, lighting, and warnings. If the accident happened outdoors, the investigator should take notes about the weather conditions, visibility, and other conditions existing at the time of the accident. All statements and notes should, if possible, be recorded, preferably in writing.

5. If personnel were involved, the investigator should find out whether or not any of them were injured and how serious the injuries were, the names and addresses of doctors or other personnel who treated the injured personnel, the hospitals to which the injured personnel were taken, and if they refused treatment, to whom such refusals were made.

6. If the part or assembly whose malfunction caused the accident is readily apparent, the investigator should find out whether it has been taken to have a failure analysis made and where the analysis is to be made and then try to get a copy of the analysis report.

7. If the cause of the accident is not readily apparent, potential causes can be developed by fault-tree analysis. The investigator can then determine which theoretical causes could not have been possible in the case under investigation (see Figure 15-15). The remaining theoretical causes, especially those which appear to constitute a cut-set, should be given more intense investigation. As evidenced by fault-tree analysis, accidents are generally the result of sequences and combinations of events. (Less frequently is an accident the result of only one cause, that is, a single-point failure.) It is up to the investigator to try to establish these sequences and combinations.

The investigator's report should be reviewed by a board made up of personnel knowledgeable of the product. A board collectively can sometimes detect inconsistencies in the circumstances of the accident facts and in the conclusions derived.

Information derived from accident investigations can be used to:

1. Inform the insurer of the circumstances of the accident, if the insurer has not provided its own investigator.

2. Alert design and production personnel to accident causes which they might be concerned.

3. Counter claims and lawsuits.

4. Verify how good safety analyses were in the past and to provide inputs to improve and expand knowledge of causative factors for future analyses.

5. Modify company safety criteria to forestall or minimize the possibilities of similar accidents.

Failure Analysis

In many cases, failures may have occurred which were potential causes of accidents but accidents did not result. It is important that such failures be investigated to determine if the failure was unique or if the failure was characteristic of the component or product.

Many of the aspects of failure analysis are similar to those of accident investigation:

1. As much information as possible about the circumstances under which failure occurred should be collected, especially from those directly involved. Attempts should be made to determine whether or not there was any activity that could have overstressed the part, such as overloading or an impact.

2. It should be determined whether or not there were any indications that a defect existed or that a failure was imminent.

3. Measurements and diagrams should be prepared indicating where the failure occurred, locations of the failed pieces, and any contributing factors.

4. By examination it should be determined whether or not there had been any stress concentrations, metal fatigue, or heat or temperature effects. Very often these can be determined by external visual examination (magnifying glass or microscope), x-rays, dye penetrant methods, and similar techniques.

5. Electrical failure evaluations might be conducted by using resistance measurements (continuity checks, insulation resistance, dielectric strength).

6. Mechanical tests of tensile strength and hardness can be used where applicable.

7. Failures, like accidents, are generally the results of sequences and combinations of events, all of which should be considered.

It is especially advisable if more than one case of failure occurs to a safety-critical component or assembly, and the company knows about it, that either corrective action be taken or the reason for the lack of corrective action be justified. Otherwise, if an accident should occur and no action had been taken on previous similar failures, the manufacturer not only has an excellent chance of losing his/her case but also of being subjected to punitive damages.

On the other hand, the fact that a company can show that it was making efforts to reduce risks can mitigate or avoid serious charges if an accident occurs. After an industrial accident in which six men were killed, four executives of a drug company faced criminal charges for second-degree manslaughter and criminally negligent homicide. The court dismissed the charges after it was shown by memoranda and letters that there was an awareness of the condition and "a strong resolve and determination to minimize the risk to well within safe limits." Such action in a product safety case may not be as similarly effective in winning against claims for compensatory damages, but it should tend to avoid punitive damages or criminal charges.

Customer complaints should be given the same due consideration for the same reasons. Few customers are technical personnel, and it would probably be necessary to contact customers to obtain detailed information on which tests and failure analyses can be based. In some cases, the customer may have the failed or defective component which could be obtained for test and analysis. Quick response to a customer's complaint of a failure is often good for customer relations and it may also forestall litigation.

Notes

[1] John F. McAllister, General Electric Company, "Product Safety—Who's Responsible?" at Union College, Schenectady, N.Y., May 1977.

[2] *Barker* v *Lull Engineering*, S.C., California, 1978.

Questions

1. Explain why a manufacturer would want to ensure that his product is easy to maintain from a safety standpoint.

2. List six desirable features that relate to maintenance which designers should attempt to incorporate into their products.

3. List the five reasons for which products can be recalled.

4. Which federal regulatory agencies can order recalls? What types of products can each agency order to be recalled?

5. Which is generally more severe, a recall for a design or a manufacturing defect? Why?

6. If a manufacturer is sued for damages, what are the chances of the plaintiff's winning an award in court?

7. What do you consider the best defense against accident claims?

8. Why would a manufacturer be interested in participating in an accident investigation?

9. What are some of the methods of safety analysis with which a person making an investigation should be familiar?

10. List some of the items that should be investigated when making a failure analysis.

11. Why is it important that action be taken on results of accident investigations, failure analyses, and customer complaints?

Hazardous Characteristics of Products

The following pages contain information on product characteristics that could cause injury or damage. Each product should be examined to determine whether or not its design, manufacture, or operation could involve such characteristics.

A checklist is presented immediately after the description of each hazard that might be present. The checklist shows not only some effects that could be generated by the hazards but also their causes. This information can be used to prepare a preliminary hazard analysis or other review of a product *before* it is designed so that designers and product safety engineers will be alerted to the need for action to eliminate or control hazards.

The information might also be used in accident investigations in which the effects are known in order to orient the investigator toward potential causes.

Acceleration

General. Objects in motion contain kinetic energy which even in small amounts can cause injury or damage. The injury or damage will result, not from the motion itself, but from the acceleration, deceleration, or other transfers of energy. Acceleration occurs when there is a change in velocity; the word acceleration is used here when velocity increases, deceleration when it decreases.

Acceleration. Acceleration occurs when any vehicle, body, or fluid is being set into motion or its speed increased. It may occur when propulsive power is applied, when an object is dropped or otherwise affected by gravity, impacted by another object or force, or subjected to a centrifugal motion. A common accident resulting from acceleration is "whiplash," in which a person in a stopped car which is hit from the rear by another car suffers injury to his or her neck and shoulder muscles.

Other problems which can result are the sloshing of liquids in or over the tops of containers as they accelerate linearly, because of centrifugal force as the vehicles in which they are contained round a curve or the containers rotate, or because the vehicle hits a bump. Spring-actuated devices may not perform properly if their action is in the direction of the acceleration (or deceleration) and occurs at the same time.

Deceleration. Deceleration can be considered negative acceleration in which speed decreases. Its most acute and most common manifestation is in impact, which is treated in the next paragraph. Another common occurrence of deceleration is in a "water hammer" in which quick closing of a valve in a high-velocity flow system results in a sudden stoppage of the fluid, generally with noise and vibration. As with acceleration, sloshing and loss of liquids, especially in open containers, will occur with sudden decelerations.

Impact. Impacts, especially from falls, are the most frequent type of accident and injury. Persons have been killed striking their head after a fall from a standing position, yet Lt. I. M. Chissov of Russia fell 22,000 ft. without a parachute and survived (from Guinness *Book of World Records*). He struck the edge of a snow-covered ravine and then slid to the bottom. He suffered a fractured pelvis and severe spinal damage.

Impact Experience

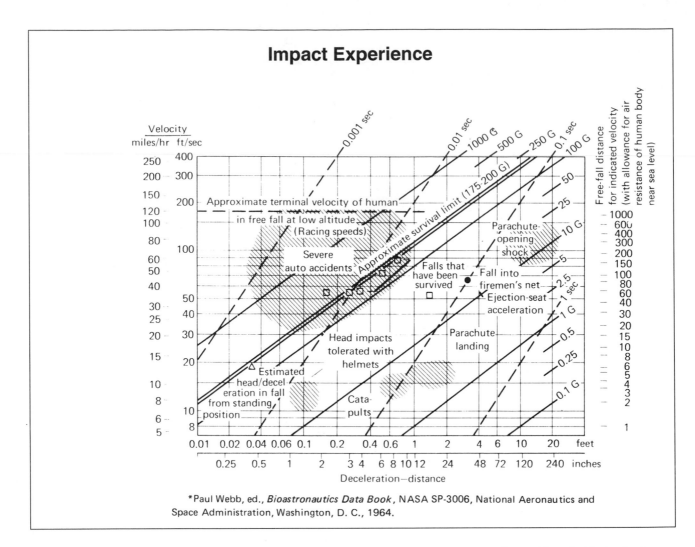

*Paul Webb, ed., *Bioastronautics Data Book*, NASA SP-3006, National Aeronautics and Space Administration, Washington, D. C., 1964.

The effect of any impact is governed by the impacting velocity, rate of deceleration, and orientation of the body. The following figure indicates some of the interrelationships. (Values are plotted on the basis of g's, or multiples of the acceleration of gravity, approximately 32 ft. per sec. per sec.) White and Bowen have indicated that 50% of all persons impacting against a hard surface with a velocity of 18 mph (equivalent to a fall of 11 ft.) will be killed. Assuming the hard surface deflects only ¼ in. when struck by the head, it can be seen from the figure that an impact at 18 mph would probably be fatal.

Another impact problem is that of an object striking the body. Studies have indicated that a skull will fracture when it is impacted by a force of about 50 ft.-lb. (600 in.-lb.). (A 5-lb. hammer or other object dropping 10 ft. would have this energy.) The following table presents experimental results indicating effects of impacting missiles. Lawn mower blades have peripheral speeds of 150–300 ft. per sec.; even a small object thrown off can cause serious damage.

Effect of Missiles on Human Cadavers

Type of Missile	Mass(g)	Velocity (ft./sec.)	Effect on Man
Spherical bullets	8.7	190	Slight skin laceration
	8.7	230	Penetrating wound
	7.4	360	Abrasion and crack of tibia
	7.4	513	Travels through thigh
Bullets	6–10	420–266	Treshold for bone injury
	6–15	751–476	Fractures large bones

Source: C.S. White and I.G. Bowen, Comparative Effects Data of Biological Interest (Albuquerque, N.M.: Lovelace Foundation for Medical Education and Research, 1959), p. 19.

Hazards Checklist—Acceleration

Possible Adverse Effects

Injury to personnel. A person may:
  Be hit by an object set in motion inadvertently
  Hit a hard surface during a sudden start or change in velocity
  Hit a sharp edge or point when startled
  Fall or be thrown backward during sudden forward acceleration
  Lose his or her balance under centrifugal force
  Be thrown against the ceiling of a vehicle in a sudden drop or other falling maneuver
  Fall to the ground or other hard surface
  Be hit by an impacting fragment or missile
Overloading, deformation, and failure of structural members
Deflection of piping
Deflection and bottoming of shock isolated parts and springs
Cracking or breaking of lines or equipment by impact of high-velocity fragments.
Breakage of cables, ropes, chains, and pins by sudden overloads
Fracture of brittle materials
Opening or closing of hinged parts, doors, or panels
Seating or unseating of spring-loaded valves or electrical contacts
Shorting of closely spaced electrical parts
Bending of bimetallic strips, thus changing instrument readings and calibration
Pressure surges in liquid systems (water hammer)
Sloshing and loss of liquids from open containers
Loss of fluid pressure

Possible Causes

Acceleration:
  Vehicle, body, or fluid being set into motion or increasing speed
  Outside force applied against an unrestrained body
  Any falling body or dropped object
  Vehicle on a downgrade
  Uncontrolled loss of altitude or height
  Impact by another body
  Turbulence or motion over rough terrain
  Sudden valve opening in a pressure system
  Centrifugal motion
  Sudden reaction by a surprised person

Deceleration:
  Vehicle, body, or fluid decreasing speed or being stopped
  Impact due to hitting another body, a structure, or the terrain
  A falling body being arrested
  Inadequate shock-absorbing materials or devices
  Sudden closing of a valve in a fluid system with high-velocity flow
  Friction or other resistance to motion

Failure to accelerate or decelerate:
  Inadequate or loss of motive power
  Friction or drag
  Failure of an unlatching or restraining mechanism to release
  Loss, failure, or inadequate braking capacity
  Wet, oily, or other slippery surface

Chemical Reactions

General. Chemical reactions can be so violent that they can cause immediate injury through explosions, dispersion of materials, and emissions of large amounts of heat. They can be so mild that their effects can be ascertained only over a long period of time. These long, gradual effects can result in injury or damage as they contribute to failures of equipment, other materials, and structures. Heat, light, electrical energy, mechanical shock, or any other form of energy can initiate reactions. Rates of reaction generally increase with the original temperature of the reactants.

Disassociation. Disassociation is the breakdown of a chemical compound molecule. High-explosive molecules disassociate after a threshold level of energy is applied to initiate the reaction. The threshold level to cause disassociation varies, depending on the stability of the molecule. Chemicals that will disassociate violently include chlorites and chlorates (a mass of which exploded and leveled two whole blocks of buildings in New York in 1900); nitrites and nitrates (an explosion of a shipload devastated Texas City in 1974); permanganates and chromates; and iodates and bromates. Acetylene at pressures over 15 psi is extremely sensitive, will disassociate if shocked

mechanically, and will explode violently. Liquid ozone is so unstable and sensitive that it will detonate from the shock of being poured from one container to another. Organic materials in contact with liquid oxygen are similarly unstable and sensitive.

Combination. Combination is the chemical reaction that results in reactive particles forming stable molecules. In most cases, the formation of molecules results in the release of energy. Fires occur when fuel and oxidizer molecules break down into reactive particles after initiating energy is applied and then unite in new combinations in a self-sustaining process in which chemical energy is changed to thermal energy and released. Although the chemical equations for a combination generally appear to be rather simple and straightforward, each chemical reaction is a complex process during which numerous intermediate reactions occur. Even in the supposedly simple combination of hydrogen and oxygen, 14 different intermediate steps have been found. After the fairly stable molecules are broken down into reactive particles, the process depends on contacts between the particles. There are numerous particles (especially from a complex molecule) and numerous stable and unstable results which occur as the particles impact each other and combine. Anything which will enhance these reactions, such as a

Hazards Checklist—Chemical Reactions

Possible Effects	Possible Cause

Corrosion:

Material degradation
Reduction in strength
Binding of moving surfaces, nuts, and other parts
Loss of resiliency in springs
Surface roughness
Contamination of the system
Changes in physical and chemical properties
Holing of containers
Failures of load-bearing structures
Failures of electrical connections

Leakage of corrosive or reactive substances
Condensation of atmospheric moisture
Gases released from industrial processes
Acids resulting from combustion
Smog
Incompatibility of materials
Salt atmosphere or salt used for ice melting on roads
Acids created by lightning
Damaged protective surfaces
Electrolytic action (dissimilar metals)
Stray electrical currents
Ground moisture
Moisture from respiration or vegetation
Presence of humidifying equipment
Flooding or immersion

Disassociation, chemical:

Explosions
Nonexplosive exothermic reactions
Hot gases
Material degradation
Swelling of organic materials

Temperature of compound raised to point reaction begins
Presence of suitable catalyst
Ultraviolet radiation
Heavy shock

Fire (see checklist for Flammability and Fires)

Oxidation (other than by air):

Increased reactivity of combustibles
Easier ignition of flammables
Normally low flammable materials may burn easily
May cause violent or explosive reactions
Partner in hypergolic reactions
Corrosion of metals
Deterioration of rubber, plastics, or other organic
materials

Chemical combination involving an oxidant such as:
    Oxygen or ozone
    A halogen or halogen compound
    Oxidizing acids and their salts
    Nitrates, chlorates, perchlorates, hyperchlorites,
      chromates
    Higher valence compounds of mercury, lead,
      selenium, and thallium

Replacement, chemical:

Exothermic reactions
Explosions
Violent spraying of corrosive material

Fluorine and water
Sodium and water
Nitric acid and water

catalyst, will make the overall reaction move faster. Anything which will interfere, such as the presence of nonreactive particles or a reduction in temperature, will slow and perhaps stop the reaction. Too much carbon dioxide interferes with the chain reactions involving hydrocarbons or hydrogen. Nitrogen will usually not interfere chemically but as a diluent will interfere with physical contact between the particles. Therefore, although both are normally inert gases and will stop a fire by dilution, carbon dioxide is also effective because of its interference with the intermediate chemical reactions.

Corrosion. Corrosion is a slow combination process, generally affecting metals, in which the amount of heat released is slow and gradual. Chief causes of corrosion are contact between iron and moisture in air, leakage of a reactive substance (water or other chemical) onto metals, and electrolytic action between two metals in contact. The worst effect of corrosion is in the deterioration and loss of strength and integrity of the metal affected.

Replacement. Replacement is the act of a highly active chemical radical taking the place of a less active one in a molecule. Thus, fluorine is more active than oxygen and will replace oxygen in water to form hydrogen fluoride. In some cases, double replacements may take place when two compounds are mixed. For example, sodium hydroxide will react with ammonium chloride to give the more stable compounds salt and water. In some cases, the resultant reactions have produced toxic gases which have proved fatal. Sodium hypochlorite has been mixed with an acid by housewives and has generated chlorine in restricted spaces in amounts which have overwhelmed the user.

Electrical Hazards

General. There are six basic hazards that must be considered if electrical power is to be used: shock to personnel, ignition of combustible materials, heating and overheating, inadvertent activation, failure to operate when and as required, and electrical explosions. Radiation is treated elsewhere.

Electrical Shock. Electrical shock is the stimulation of the body's nervous system by an electric current or discharge. The effects produced by 60-Hz current might be: 1 ma—perceptible, tingling sensation; 5-20 ma—freezing to the live conductor; 25-75 ma—paralysis of the respiratory muscles causing asphyxiation, collapse and death; 75-300 ma—ventricular fibrillation (self-perpetuating twitching) of the heart; 2.5 or more amperes—heart clamping, respiratory paralysis, and burns. Shock intensity and effects also depend on the current path, frequency, and duration. Sixty hertz is almost the worst frequency possible in this respect since it is about that at which the highest possibility of fibrillation exists. A shock can come from touching a bare conductor, through inadequate insulation or an insulation failure, broken electrical lines or equipment, a lightning strike, or other massive static electricity discharge.

Ignition of Combustibles. Sparks, arcs, or high-temperature metal surfaces can cause ignition of a flammable mixture. A high-temperature metal surface can cause ignition of a liquid or solid combustible material. The National Electric Code cites the types of atmospheres that are hazardous. To prevent ignition problems, electrical systems use explosion-proof equipment; hermetic sealing; encapsulation, embedment, and potting; or liquid filled or pressurized equipment. Even better is to prevent arcing or sparking by keeping the power levels below the point at which these would occur, and to reduce surface temperatures of electrically-heated devices to less than that necessary for ignition.

Heating or Overheating. Use of electrical power results in production of heat, either intentionally or unintentionally. Metal surfaces may become hot enough to burn a person. Anyone who touches a hot surface may suffer a burn, depending on the temperature and length of time of contact. Overheating can cause failures of operating equipment since increasing the operating temperature will almost always degrade electrical equipment reliability. As indicated in the paragraph above, heating or overheating a metal surface may make it hot enough to ignite a combustible mixture.

Inadvertent Activation. Injuries or damage could be caused when a piece of equipment starts up unexpectedly. Persons in positions where they could be injured have been hurt by unexpected starts or repeats so that fingers, hands, feet, or bodies have been caught and crushed.

Failure to Operate. In most cases, failure of an electrical device leaves it in a passive state and safe. There are situations in which the passive state is the unsafe one. For example, a smoke detector, turn indicator, warning light, or heart pacemaker might not operate when it should. Failure of an electrical component in a control might result in loss of control so that the vehicle runs away.

Electrical Explosions. Transformers and circuit breakers have exploded when massive amounts of current have been impressed across them. Batteries in automobiles and in small calculators have exploded when they were shorted. Electrolytic capacitors have exploded when installed with revere polarity and then energized.

Explosives and Explosions

General. Explosions are highly destructive because of the extremely high release of energy which occurs in a short time. Explosives are substances developed and used specifically for this purpose. Explosions, however, can occur with numerous other substances. Generally, an explosion will result in the generation of large amounts of gas, heat, noise, and sometimes light. Damage and injury may result from the rupture and fragmentation of a container, from the shock wave created by a rapidly expanding mass of hot gas, from heat or fire, or from release of toxic gases.

Hazards Checklist—Electrical

Possible Effects	Possible Causes

Shock injury

Accidental contact with live circuit through:
    Touching bare conductor
    Inadequate insulation
    Cutting through insulation
    Deteriorated insulation
    Defective assembly of electrical tool or appliance
    Erroneous connection
    Lightning strike

Thermal effects:

Possible Effects	Possible Causes
Burns	High I^2R losses
Degradation of performance	Inadequate cooling
Overloading and burnout of equipment	Overloads
Ignition of combustibles	Short circuits caused by:
Melting of soldered connections	Inadequate or deteriorated insulation
Degraded reliability	Erroneous connection
Softening and melting of plastics	Bare conductors touching
Circuit breakers, fuses, and cutouts opening	Dirt, contamination, or moisture
deactivating equipment	Corrosion
	Excessive or loose particles of solder or cut wire
	Bent connector pins
	Improper wiring
	Improper mating of connectors
	Lightning strike

Arcing and sparking causes:

Possible Effects	Possible Causes
Ignition of combustibles	Gaseous gap between conductors caused by:
Buildup and welding of contacts	Loose connection
Surface damage to metals	Opening of switches, relays, circuit breakers, and
Interference with electrical equipment operation	similar devices
Electrical noise and cross talk	Electric arc welding
	Lack of bonding or grounding
	Deteriorated or inadequate insulation
	Lightning strike

Inadvertent activation of the product or a device:

Possible Effects	Possible Causes
Untimely equipment starts	Stray current from:
Endangering personnel working on or in equipment	"Sneak" circuit
supposedly inoperative	Cross-connection
	Personnel error
	Misapplied test equipment power
	Static electricity discharge
	Coupling

Electrical system failure, making:

Possible Effects	Possible Causes
System inoperative in hazardous situation	Malfunction caused by:
Safety equipment inoperative	Power source failure
Release of holding devices	Power surge opening fuse or circuit breaker
Detection and warning devices inoperative	Component failure
Interruption of communications	System overloading
	Short circuit
	Operator error
	Lightning strike

Explosion of:

Possible Effects	Possible Causes
Batteries	Short circuiting
Circuit breakers, transformers, and similar	Presence of liquid or its contaminants which disassociate
equipment	violently when current passes through
Capacitors	Lightning strike

High explosives. A high explosive is generally a material that releases a large amount of energy when its molecules break down (disassociate). When a high explosive detonates (the reaction occurs at a speed faster than that of sound), it produces a shock wave (blast) and shattering effect (brisance). High explosives vary in sensitivity, the energy required to set them off. Some, which require little energy, are called *initiating explosives*; others are very stable chemically and require an initiating explosion to set them off.

Low explosives. A low explosive burns rapidly (deflagrates) but at a speed less than that of sound. A shock wave will be created if the explosive and the gases created are confined and then the container ruptures. Black powder, smokeless powder, pyrotechnics, and most solid propellants for rocket motors are low explosives.

Gas explosions. More accidents, injuries, and damage are caused by explosions of combustible gases than by high or low explosives. Accumulations of such gases mixed with air or other oxidizer will explode when ignited. In certain instances the mixture will detonate ("go high order") when ignited, rather than deflagrate. Four percent hydrogen in air will burn, but when its concentration is between 18.3% and 59%, it will detonate. Between 59% and 74% in air it will burn and not detonate. Heated mixtures may also detonate since the amount of energy required to ignite it initially may be enough to bring the entire mass of gas to the reaction temperature at almost the same instant. This is what causes a hot automobile engine to "knock" (detonate). The presence of a strong oxidizer or a catalyst can speed up the reaction.

Commonly used gases (natural gas, methane, propane, and butane) explode when they leak into confined spaces where they mix with air and are ignited by sparks, pilot lights, lit matches, or other open flames. Because they are in confined spaces their concentrations are high enough to result in explosions. Hydrogen given off by car batteries caught under the engine hood or remaining in battery cells can ignite and explode. The resultant hot gases from hydrogen burning in the cells can cause the batteries to burst. Certain unstable gases, such as acetylene under a pressure of 15 psi or more, will decompose violently when heated or shocked and will explode.

Dust explosions. Solid materials in finely divided form in contact with air can deflagrate. The material occupies far less space as a solid than as in a gaseous mixture. When it ignites, it forms large amounts of gas. In a confined space this can cause bursting of the equipment or structure in which it occurs. Even metals which in massive form will not burn will ignite when finely divided. Factors affecting the explosiveness of dusts include: combustible nature of the material, size and concentration of the particles, temperature of the dust-air mixture, presence or absence of moisture, and presence of inert solid particles.

Explosive effects. Explosive effects are generally compared by results in open air since internal explosion effects, though much more severe, vary too much with the type of container in which they occur. Following are effects on external areas of structures, vehicles, and personnel which occur in open air:

Overpressure	Effect (psig)
0.2	Limit for uncontrolled area; no significant damage to personnel or facilities
0.4	Limit for unprotected personnel
0.5 to 1	Breakage of window glass
0.75	Limit for windowless, ordinary construction
1 to 2	Light to moderate damage to light vehicles such as aircraft
3	Exposed man standing face-on will be picked up and thrown; very severe damage, near total destruction to light industrial buildings of rigid steel framing
3 to 4	Severe damage to wooden frame or brick homes
4 to 6	Complete destruction of aircraft and other light vehicles or damage beyond repair
5	Possible ear damage; exposed man standing side-on will be picked up and thrown; complete destruction of wooden frame and brick homes; severe battering of automobiles and trucks
6	Moderate damage to ships
6 to 7	Moderate damage to massive, wall-bearing, multistory buildings
7	Possible internal injuries to human beings
9	Complete destruction of railroad boxcars
10 to 12	Serious damage and sinking of ships
12	Possible lung injuries to exposed personnel
20 to 30	50% probability of eardrum rupture
25	Probably limit of thermal injury

TNT Equivalency. TNT equivalency of an exploding material is the weight of trinitrotoluene (TNT) which will produce the same explosive effect (generally considered on pressures generated). Following are the increases in atmospheric pressure (overpressure) which will result when 1 lb. of TNT is exploded in air:

Distance (ft.)	2	4	6	8	10	20	40	100	200	400
Overpressure (psig)	320	70	28	15	9.6	3.0	1.2	0.35	0.13	0.05

Hazards Checklist—Explosives and Explosions

Possible Adverse Effects	Possible Causes
Rupture of container	Inadvertent activation by electric current, heat, electromagnetic radiation, lightning or other static electricity, impact or fire of:
Blast effects:	Explosives
Overpressures	Combustible gases in containers or confined spaces
Collapse of nearby containers	Fine dusts or powders
Damage to structures, equipment, and vehicles	Combustible gases or liquids:
Propagation of other explosions	In high concentrations
	In presence of strong oxidizers
Fragmentation effects:	At high temperatures
Holing of nearby containers, equipment, and vehicles	Afterburning of confined combustion products
Impact of pieces against personnel, equipment, vehicles, and structures	Delayed combustion in a cold firing chamber
	Ignition of hydrogen produced by battery charging
Dispersion of burning, hot, combustible, or corrosive materials	Warming a cryogenic liquid in a closed system
	Warming a liquid with a high vapor pressure in a closed container
Heat effects:	Ignition of sensitive gases, such as acetylene
Dispersion of toxic materials	Contact between water or moisture and a water-sensitive material such as molten sodium, potassium, or lithium; concentrated acids or alkalis; or similar substances.
Injury to personnel	

Flammability and Fires

General. For a fire to start, there must be a fuel (of which there are an innumerable number), an oxidizer (such as the oxygen in the air in which we are enveloped), the two of them in suitable proportions to burn and in contact with each other (conditions which generally exist), and an ignition source (of which there are many). Because the presence of each of these is not unusual, accidental fires are commonplace.

Combustion. In order to combine and burn, the fuel and oxidizer must be present as gases. When they are already in the gaseous phase, there is no deterrent to a flammable mixture being formed. Since the oxygen in air is always in a gaseous phase, generally only the fuel is required to complete a dangerous mixture. When the fuel is a liquid, it must evaporate to a gas in order to burn. Some liquids do this much more readily and at lower temperatures than others. The temperature at which the amount of gas given off by a liquid is adequate to ignite momentarily when ignited is called the *flash point.* There are numerous ways of determining and categorizing flash points and the hazards they represent. The National Fire Protection Association (NFPA) rates liquids with flash points of 20°F (–70°C) or less as highly hazardous, above 20°F to 70°F (–7°C to 21°C) as moderately hazardous, and above 70°F to 200°F (21°C to 93°C) as slightly hazardous. Above 200°F (93°C), a liquid would be rated "combustible." Once a liquid is heated so that it vaporizes, it is as dangerous as any other flammable gas and flash point has no significance.

Solids vaporize and burn in a number of ways. A few sublime and change directly to gas when heated. Some melt and then vaporize and burn like a liquid. When melting points are higher than flame temperatures, some solids undergo oxidation processes which create flammable gases. These flammable gases mix with more oxidizer and burn. The carbon in coal is this type of material. (Coal is a complex fuel which also gives off volatile materials when heated which then burns. This initiates the oxidation of the carbon, and the process continues.)

Avoiding fires. The best way to avoid fires is to use the least flammable substance that will accomplish the required mission of the product, keep the fuel away from any oxidizer, and avoid the presence of a source of ignition. The lower the temperature, the less tendency of a flammable mixture to ignite (since ignition requires more energy); therefore, the temperature should be kept as low as possible. Certain materials are far less reactive than others and have less tendency to ignite. These should be given preference over the more reactive materials.

Heat and Temperature

General. Temperature is the indicator of the level of sensible heat present in a body. The Second Law of Thermodynamics indicates that heat will flow from the region of higher temperature to one of lower temperature. Much injury and damage can be done by massive uncontrolled flows of heat in which there is a wide temperature difference.

Flow of heat. Heat can flow in three different ways or in combinations of the three: radiation, conduction, and convection. Any body will radiate heat to another body

Hazards Checklist—Flammability and Fires

Possible Effects

Injury to personnel:
    Burns
    Toxic gas and smoke inhalation
    Other heat and high-temperature effects
    Deprivation of oxygen for breathing

Destruction of material and resources:
    Carbonization and contamination of material
    Equipment rendered inoperative

Damage to the environment:
    Production of corrosive contaminants
    Destruction of wildlife and vegetation
    Production of airborne particulate matter

Possible Causes

Fuel/oxidizer mixture with ignition source:

Fuels:
    Heating fuels
    Engine fuels
    Paints and varnishes
    Solvent and cleaning agentsf
    Wood and wood products
    Welding and process gases
    Lubricants
    Rubber and plastics
    Furnishings and upholstery
    Clothing
    Refuse and trash
    Vegetation
    Other organic materials
    Hydraulic and coolant fluids
    Normally low-combustible materials in the presence of strong oxidizers or high temperatures
    Normally nonflammable metals in finely powdered form
    Grain dust and other particulate matter
    Hydrogen from charging batteries
    Products of incomplete combustion of organic materials

Oxidizers:
    Oxygen in air
    Oxidizing compounds
    Oxidizing gases

Ignition source:
    Open flames
    Arcs and sparks
    Hot surfaces
    Lightning strikes
    Spontaneous ignition
    Adiabatic compression
    Hypergolic mixtures
    Pyrophoric mixtures
    Water-sensitive reactive materials

at a lesser temperature with which it is not in direct contact by emitting thermal energy in the form of electromagnetic waves. Energy radiated is dependent on the temperature, area, and emissivity (the ratio of heat radiated by an actual surface to that of a perfect radiating surface or "black body") of the radiating body.

Conduction is the transfer of thermal energy from the molecules in one portion of a substance, or from one substance to another without physical movement of the substance itself. Of all the means of heat transfer, the most massive flows can occur via conduction. Convection is the transfer of heat through a fluid by movement of its molecules. The flow of heat may be from or to the surface of a solid, but the medium by which it takes place is a fluid: gas or liquid. Circulation caused by differences in density with the fluid because of temperature is known as *natural convection*; movement of the fluid created by such equipment as pumps, blowers, or agitators is *forced convection*.

Burns. Burns to the skin are generally categorized as first-, second-, or third-degree. A first-degree burn involves only a redness of skin; second-degree, sensitive blisters are formed and in severer cases fluid collects under the skin; and third-degree, destruction of the skin, subcutaneous tissue, red blood cells, capillaries, and sometimes muscle. Although third-degree burns are the most serious, second-degree burns are generally the most painful since nerve endings may be exposed. In third-degree burns the nerve endings are burned and deadened. Destruction of the capillaries can result in gangrene since the flow of

Hazards Checklist—Heat and Temperature

Possible Effects	Possible Causes

High temperature:

Burns to personnel
Reduced personnel efficiency and errors
Heat cramps, strokes, and exhaustion
Reduced relative humidity
Ignition of combustibles
Charring of organic materials
Reduced strength of metals and other materials
Melting of metals and thermoplastics
Distortion and warping of parts
Weakening of soldered seams
Peeling of finishes, blistering of paint
Expansion causing binding or loosening of parts
Decreased viscosity of lubricants
Increased evaporation and leakage of liquids
    (fuels, lubricants, toxic liquids)
Increased gas diffusion
Increased reactivity
Breakdown of chemical compounds
Premature operation of thermally-activated devices
Increased electrical resistance
Opening or closing of electrical contacts due to
    expansion
Changes in other electrical characteristics

Generation or absorption of heat from:
    Heat engine operation
    Fire or explosion
    Other exothermic chemical reaction
    Electrical heating
    Solar heating
    Aerodynamic or other vehicular friction
    Friction between moving parts
    Internal friction due to repeated bending or
        other work process such as repeated
        impacts
    Gas compression
    Biological or physiological processes
    Welding, soldering, brazing, or metal cutting
    Hot climate or weather
    Organic decay processes
    Nuclear reaction
    Immersion in hot fluid
    Lack of insulation from thermal sources
        Inadequate heat dissipation capacity or
        cooling system failure
    Hot spots due to coolant fluid circulation being
        obstructed

Low temperature:

Frostbite or cryogenic burns
Icing of operating equipment
Freezing of liquids
Condensation of moisture and other vapors
Reduced viscosity of liquids
Gelling of oils and lubricants
Reduced reaction rates
Increased brittleness of metals
Loss of flexibility of plastics and organic materials
Contraction effects, especially opening of cracks in
    metals
Jamming or loosening of moving parts due to
    contraction
Delayed ignition in furnaces and combustion
    chambers
Combustion instability in engines
Changes in electrical characteristics

Loss of heat because of:
    Mechanical cooling or refrigerating processes
    Heat loss by radiation, conduction, or
        convection
    Cold climate or weather
    Endothermic reactions
    Rapid evaporation
    Immersion in cold fluid
    Presence of cryogenic liquid
    Exposure to heat sink
    Gas expansion
    Joule–Thomson effect

Temperature variations:

Dimensional changes, especially in metals
Cycling fatigue of metals
Pressure changes in confined gases and liquids
Variations in stresses

Stopping and starting of heat engines and other
    powered equipment
Diurnal heating and cooling
Gain and loss of heat due to changes in radiation,
    conduction, or convection

blood to the affected area is stopped. The table below indicates some effects on skin in contact with surfaces at different temperatures.

Temperature (°F/°C)	Sensation or Effect
212/100	Second-degree burn on 15 sec. contact
180/82	Second-degree burn on 30 sec. contact
160/71	Second-degree burn on 60 sec. contact
140/60	Pain; tissue damage (burns)
120/49	Pain; "burning heat"
91±4/32 +	Warm; "neutral" (physiological zero)
254/12	Cool
37/3	"Cool heat"
32/0	Pain
Below 32/0	Pain; tissue damage (freezing)

Source: R.F. Chaillet et al., *Human Factors Engineering Design Standard for Missile Systems and Related Equipment*, U.S. Army Human Engineering Laboratories, AD 623-731, September 1965.

Other high-temperature effects. Work in a high-temperature environment can upset the metabolic processes of the body which must rid itself of the heat it generates. Radiation, conduction, and convection are three ways the body can do this but another means, generally the chief one, is by evaporation of the perspiration given off by the body. If these means of ridding the body of heat are inadequate, the person may suffer heat cramps, heat exhaustion, or heat stroke.

Temperatures elevated beyond a comfortable level, especially in the presence of moisture, will degrade performance so that the person affected will make errors. The exact points at which degradation will occur will vary with the intensity of the heat, the humidity, duration of exposure, tasks involved, physical and mental condition of the person involved and his or her training and acclimatization, and presence of other stresses.

High temperatures can cause fires or increase the susceptibility of materials to accidental ignition. The energy required to initiate a specific chemical reaction is fairly constant; the heat available when high temperatures are present can constitute part of that energy. The amount of additional energy required to initiate the reaction may then be small. Spills of liquid fuels are more hazardous in hot weather than in cold; not only will the higher temperature cause faster evaporation of the liquid, but less powerful initiation sources are required to ignite any resultant fuel-air mixture. High temperatures created by thermal radiation from hot surfaces, molten metal, or open flames can cause charring of organic materials, such as wood, paper, and cloth, and even their ignition. Contact with high-temperature steam lines, electronic equip-

ment, or an overheated bearing can also cause charring of organic materials and even ignition of volatiles.

Chemical reaction rates increase with temperature so that some fuel-air mixtures at high temperatures will explode when ignited rather than burn as they would at room temperatures. Normally nonreactive materials may react under higher temperatures, and normally stable chemical processes may go out of control. Corrosion, being a chemical reaction, increases with temperature. Gas or liquid pressure will increase with temperature so that the container might rupture or the gas or liquid is lost through overflowing or through a relief device. Reliability of electronic equipment and, generally, the strengths of metals will be degraded by heat and high temperatures.

Effects of cold and low temperatures. Three principal effects of low temperatures on the body are chilblains (a mild form of tissue damage); immersion syndrome (from immersion for long periods of time in water of less than 50°F (10°C); and frostbite (constriction of blood vessels in mild cases and freezing of the tissues and subsequent gangrene later in more severe cases). When wind is also present, heat loss from the exposed skin increases to produce a cooling effect and chilling. *Wind chill factors* indicate the equivalent temperatures at which evaporation from the exposed skin would be the same as the ambient temperature under windy conditions. (Freezing will not occur even if the wind chill factor is far below the freezing point unless the ambient temperature itself is 32°F (0°C) or less.)

Other adverse effects of low temperatures are freezing of water and bursting of pipes or other closed containers when expansion of the near freezing water is restricted. Ice or other congealed liquids can immobilize parts designed to move or can restrict the distance they can move. The added weight of ice can cause a structure to collapse. Skin will stick to low-temperature metal surfaces. At cryogenic temperatures "cold" burns can cause destruction of tissues as damaging as third-degree burns caused by high temperatures. Extremely low temperatures can cause loss of ductility in metals and brittleness which cause them to fail easily under shock.

Mechanical Hazards

General. Every solid product could have at least one type of mechanical hazard. If gases and liquids do not have mechanical hazards the containers in which they are processed, stored, or transported might. Therefore mechanical hazards can potentially be present anywhere, could exist in or with every product, and must be eliminated or controlled.

Sharp edges and points. Poor manufacturing processes or the desire to reduce manufacturing costs often result in sharp edges and points being left on a product. A person who inadvertently contacts or hits one can suffer a scratch, cut, puncture wound, or even an amputation.

Hazards Checklist—Mechanical

Possible Effects	Possible Causes
Part of body caught in pinch point	Guard or barrier not provided
	Guard removed
	Design of guard inadequate
	Lack of interlock
	Failure of interlock
	Interlock bypassed
Cuts, scratches, and puncture wounds	Sharp points and edges
	Rough surfaces
	Ejected parts and materials
	Broken parts
Bruises and crushed or broken bones	Fall from an elevated position
	Impact by moving equipment or part
	Falling objects, covers, or parts
	Toppling or overturning of unstable products
	Part of body caught in pinch point
Strain	Excessive weight for person to lift
	Awkward object to lift

Mechanical Hazards

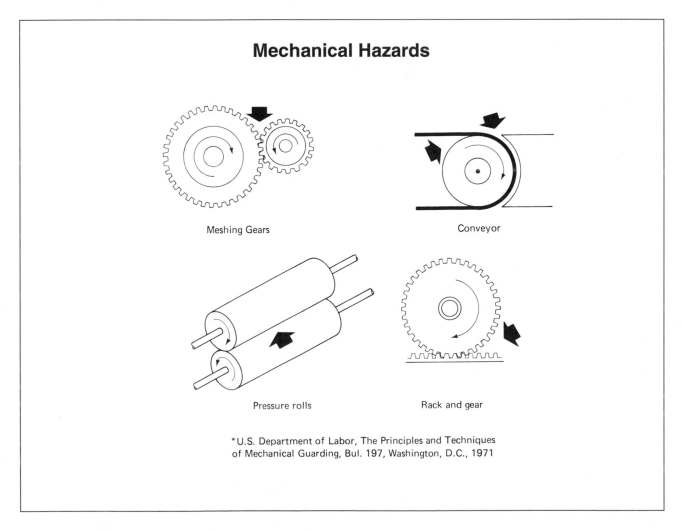

Meshing Gears

Conveyor

Pressure rolls

Rack and gear

*U.S. Department of Labor, The Principles and Techniques
of Mechanical Guarding, Bul. 197, Washington, D.C., 1971

Sharp edges or points or rough surfaces should be left only when required for specific purposes. When they are required, the means by which they are to be utilized should be examined to determine whether or not a protective guard is advisable and possible.

Rotating equipment. Fingers, rings, watches, neckties, and articles of clothing are a few of the things that can be caught in rotating equipment so that injury results to the wearer. Guards should therefore be employed wherever possible to eliminate contacts. In some instances, safeguards such as substitution of rubber blades for metal on fans will minimize possibilities of injury. Use of slip clutches which will stop motion if something is caught is another means of protection.

Pinch points. Where two moving or one moving and one fixed surface come together they create a "pinch point" in which a finger, hand, or other limb could be caught and crushed, mangled, or severed. A few examples of pinch points (or "nips" or "run-in-points") are shown on page A-12.

Weight. A product whose weight is too much for the person who might lift it can cause muscle injury or hernias. The amount which might be considered liftable or excessive varies with the height to which it must be elevated, the muscles used, and its bulk. For a normal adult male not trained or used to lifting, 35 lb. is generally a fair limit; for a woman, the fair limit is 25 lb. When the lift may have to be done in an awkward position, such as when emplacing an assembly in a product, the limit should be lower.

Stability. Equipment must be examined for stability to determine whether or not large units can topple or overturn and injure someone they hit. Small-sized containers of hot or corrosive liquids are especially vulnerable to overturning. Items which are tall in relation to the bases on which they rest may tend to tip. Extensions which might move the center of gravity of the product to a point outside the base will cause it to tip. Examples are loaded drawers which are pulled out of file cabinets and loaded end leafs on extension tables.

Ejected parts and materials. Certain operations throw off solid particles which must be guarded against. An example is the matter thrown off in a grinding operation which could injure the eyes or the skin. Matter inadvertently in contact with a high-speed rotating device can be thrown about. Breakage of a grinding wheel itself or of other rapidly rotating components can generate injurious missiles. For further information on injuries which can result from such missiles, see "Acceleration" at the beginning of this Appendix.

Impact. Moving equipment or moving parts of equipment can cause injury by impact. Reciprocating equipment may be hazardous in this respect. Hinged covers which can fall, hitting a person's head, body, arms, or fingers, should be examined for their hazardous potentialities. The section entitled "Acceleration" at the beginning of this Appendix presents additional information in impacts.

Pressure Hazards

General. Hazards are present at all pressure levels. A hurricane wind of 120 mph exerts a dynamic pressure of only one-quarter of a pound per square inch (0.25 psi), but it can drive a straw into a tree or lift the roof off or demolish a building. Pressures in any product should be kept to the absolute minimum which will still permit it to accomplish its function.

Ruptures. A rupture is a bursting of a pressure vessel when the expansive force of the fluid inside exceeds the vessel's strength. If the fluid is a gas, it continues to expand after the vessel ruptures, creating a shock wave. When the fluid is a liquid, it will expand no more than its normal volume at that temperature, but it will not generate a shock wave. A hydraulic system is therefore generally safer, from the pressure standpoint, than a pneumatic one. Increasing the temperature of the gas or liquid will increase its pressure so it may cause a rupture of the container. For this reason, pressurized cans have warnings against throwing them in a fire and some are equipped with relief devices. Also, for this reason, pressure vessels should not be left near hot surfaces or in the sun if absorption of heat will adversely affect them. Pressures need not be high for ruptures to occur. The Consumer Product Safety Commission reports that in 1974 there were 32,000 persons treated for injuries caused by exploding soft drink bottles.

Dynamic pressure hazards. The forces released when a valve or other fitting on a pressure vessel, such as a gas cylinder or pressure cooker, has broken off have produced some spectacular accidents. Unsecured gas cylinders have taken off like rockets. The exhausts from pressure vessels or from leaks have blown pieces of debris into personnel, injuring them. Persons working on pressure systems without relieving systems of their pressures have been injured by the gas jets themselves and by blown objects. Pressurized products should therefore be equipped with relieving devices if they are to be worked on. In 1974 a man in California was awarded damages after his eye was injured when a plastic cork in the neck of a champagne bottle he was trying to open was ejected unexpectedly by the gas inside.

Static pressures. Static pressures in tall liquid containers may be great enough to cause ruptures of the containers. Also, negative pressures may cause the collapse of vessels which are adequate for internal positive pressures. If steam or other vapor condenses in a closed vessel, the pressure inside may drop to less than the ambient. If the difference is great enough, the external pressure may cause crushing and collapse.

Whipping of hoses. A hose or line that has an unsecured end or one that breaks free when under pressure has a

Hazards Checklist—Pressure

Possible Effects	Possible Causes

High pressure:

Injury:
- Eye or skin damage due to blown dirt or other solid particles
- Whipping hoses hit personnel
- Lung, ear, and other body damage by overpressurization
- Cutting by thin, high-pressure jets

Container ruptured (internal pressure) or crushed (external pressure):
- Blast effects
- Fragments of ruptured container blown about

Overpressurization
- Connection to system with excessively high pressure
- Regulator failure
- Heated gases in closed containers
- Heating fluids with high vapor pressures
- Water hammer (hydraulic shock)
- Deep submersion
- High acceleration of liquid system
- Warming cryogenic liquid in a closed or inadequately ventilated system
- Excessively high combustion rate for boiler, evaporator, or other fired vessel

Pressure relief failure:
- No pressure relief valve or vent
- Faulty pressure relief valve or vent
- Relief inadequately sized

Failure at normal pressure:
- Deteriorated pressure vessel or lines
- Inadequate connection
- Failure or improper release of connectors
- Inadequate restraining devices

Leakage:

- Leaks in lines and equipment designed for lower pressures
- Blowout of seals and gaskets
- Release of toxic, corrosive, flammable, odorous, or high-temperature fluid
- Loss of system fluids
- Early fuel exhaustion
- Loss of system pressure
- Loss of lubricants
- Contamination and degradation of materials
- Slippery surfaces
- Short-circuiting of electrical circuits and equipment
- Displacement of air or other gas by liquid
- Vibration and noise
- Blowout of seals and gaskets
- Permanent deformation of metal containers
- Excessively rapid motion of hydraulically- or pneumatically-activated equipment
- Unsecured container propelled about by escaping gas

Reservoir losses:
- Overfilling of container
- Erroneously open drain or connection
- Inadequately fitted or tightened parts
- Worn parts and connections
- Fittings loosened by vibration
- Cracks caused by structural failure
- Porosity or other weld defect
- Contact surfaces inadequately finished or dirty
- Wrong type of gasket or seal
- Cuts in seals, gaskets, or hoses
- Hose holes caused by wear, kinking, or deterioration
- Hole torn by impact

Low pressure:

- System inoperable
- Implosion of pressure vessel
- Inadequate air for respiration
    - Physiological damage (atelectasis)

- Compressor or pump failure
- Condensation or cooling of gas in a closed system
- Decrease in gas volume due to combustion in a closed system
- Inadequate design against implosion forces
- Increased altitude

Pressure changes:

- Compressive heating
- Joule–Thomson cooling
- Physiological disturbances (cramps, the bends)
- Condensation of moisture

- High gas compression
- Rapid expansion of gas
- Rapid change of altitude
- Rapid rise toward surface from underwater
- Explosive decompression

tendency to whip unless it is secure and cause injury or damage. Even low-pressure water hoses will whip when unsecured.

Water hammer. Water hammer is a shock effect that results from the momentum of a liquid mass when the flow is stopped suddenly. The shock may be great enough to rupture a line, valve, or container. Water hammer generates noise and vibration which announces the problem. It can frequently be eliminated by avoiding use of quick closing valves or through use of accumulators. Another and similar problem occurs during startup in lines in which condensate from steam may have been caught in a pocket. When starting the steam coming into the lines picks up and propels the water forward so that it violently hits valves, bends, and other fittings and sometimes damages them.

Leaks. Leaks can be the source of numerous hazardous conditions. Escaping gases can blow debris in a person's eyes or, if the pressure is high enough, cut the fingers. The escaping gas or liquid could be flammable, toxic, corrosive, odorous, or slippery or it could contaminate nearby supplies or equipment. The loss of pressure can result in the system's becoming inoperative. Leaks can simply result in the exhaustion of fuel, cooling water, lubricant, or other supplies and stocks of material.

Radiation Hazards

General. Radiation is electromagnetic in nature, and the hazards involved depend on the frequency (wavelength) of each type. Generally, the higher the frequency (the shorter the wavelength), the more severe the problem. The ranges of various types of radiation sometimes overlap, but their characteristics are given briefly below. Other factors which have to be considered when radiation hazards are involved are: the magnitude of the radiation emitted, the distance of the person (or product) from the source of the emission, the existence and amount of shielding, and the time of exposure. The first three factors control the intensity of the radiation received.

Ionizing radiation injury. Ionizing radiation causes injury by dislodging electrons from the atoms that make up body tissue cells. When the injury is permanent, the effect is said to be *irreversible*. When radiation damage is rectified by natural processes, the effect is *reversible*. Ionizing radiation injury can be caused by x-rays, gamma rays, alpha particles, beta particles, neutrons, and other nuclear particles. X-rays and gamma rays are essentially the same and have identical properties, but x-rays are produced in a vacuum tube (which can be turned on and off at will). Gamma rays are produced by radioactive materials, natural or man-made. Alpha and beta particles are emitted from the nuclei of radioactive elements.

X-rays are produced by high-speed electrons striking a suitable metallic target. Electrical equipment operating at potentials over 15,000 V may be sources of x-radiation

and must be suspected until tests have shown otherwise. Other sources of radiation are radioactive materials such as were used for painting luminous dial and clock hands and numerals; devices to produce beta particles to neutralize static electricity; thoriated (thorium is radioactive) tungsten welding rods; and very small amounts in ionization-type smoke detectors.

Ultraviolet radiation. Ultraviolet (UV) is a nonionizing radiation, either from the sun or man-made, which can cause thermal or photochemical injury. Acute exposure to solar UV can cause first- and second-degree burns. More common are eye injuries since less intense radiation is required. Besides the sun, other sources of UV include ultraviolet lamps, electric arc welding, plasma torches, high-intensity lights in photocopying machines, sources of "black light" and, recently, certain types of lasers. Ultraviolet light can also cause deterioration of rubber and other sensitive materials. Light from arc welding causes color-perception difficulties.

Visible light. High-intensity light can cause injuries whose severities and durations depend on the intensity–time level of exposure. Especially severe are accidental exposures through optical magnifying instruments to the sun without proper light attenuation. Other overexposures can occur more gradually on snow, sand, or large bodies of water where there is strong sunlight. Intense lighting generally is inadequate to cause eye injury, but it may produce glare which makes instruments hard to read and which causes eye fatigue, discomfort, and headaches. Even a short exposure to a fairly high intensity light, such as an automobile's headlights, can cause momentary blindness which can result in accidents if it occurs at a critical instant.

Infrared radiation. Infrared radiation (IR) is given off by any body above absolute zero in the presence of another body of lesser temperature. Skin burns are the principal injury which can result if the radiation is intense. The injurious IR can be produced by heating elements, high-temperature furnaces, molten metal, fires and explosions, and lasers. Small but intense amounts of IR energy in laser radiation can injure the eyes.

Microwave radiation. Microwave absorption by a body increases the kinetic energy of the absorbing molecules, which manifests itself as heat and sometimes with an increase in temperature. The chief hazard is in the inability of an organ to dissipate the heat. In small amounts microwave radiation is used to warm muscles of the body. In excessive dosages, exposure can result in cataracts of the eyes. Sensitive areas of the skin will feel the heat and pain if the dosage is acute. In high-intensity microwave radiation, rings, watches and metal bands, keys, jewelry, and similar objects worn or carried can become so hot they can burn the bearer. Metal containers holding flammable liquids in strong microwave fields can become so hot that ignition can occur, and unshielded or otherwise unprotected electro-explosive devices can be set off by induction. Currents can be induced by strong microwave fields in metal equipment and electrical circuits that can result sparking, noise, and other problems.

Hazards Checklist—Radiation

Possible Effects	Possible Causes

Ionizing:

Tissue damage	Inadequate containment of radioactive materials
Degradation of electronic components and changes in their characteristics	Accidental exposure to ionizing source
Degradation of material strength	Inadvertent production of rays by radar, communications, or TV components operating at potentials over 15,000 V
	Use of x-ray equipment
	Nuclear reaction

Microwave:

Heating of metals and tissue by induction	Radar equipment operation
Cataracts or other eye injury	High power and microwave equipment operation
Interference with operation of other electronic equipment	Other microwave generator operation (ovens)
Activation of sensitive electro-explosives	

Infrared radiation:

Undesirable heat gain or temperature rise	Flames
Increased temperature in enclosed space	Solar radiation
Overheating	Infrared heaters
Skin burns	Highly heated surfaces
Charring of organic materials	Lasers
Initiation of combustion of flammables	

Visible light:

Temporary blindness	Strong sunlight
	High-intensity lights and flashlamps
	Electric arcs

Ultraviolet light:

Vision damage and other eye injuries	Sunshine
Deterioration of rubber, plastics, and other materials	Electric welding arcs
Ozone or nitrogen oxide generation	Germicidal lamps
Decomposition of chlorinated hydrocarbons	Lasers
Color fading of fabrics	Photocopying machines

The exact level at which microwave radiation can cause injury is a matter of debate. In the United States the safe limit is usually set at a power density no greater than 10 mW/sq. cm. for periods of 0.1 hr. or more (OSHA); in Russia it is one-tenth of that (1 mW/cm. sq.). The Bureau of Radiological Health has stipulated that microwave ovens must not leak more than 1 mW/cm. sq. of radiation at time of sale and no more than 5 mW/cm. sq. during the lifetime of the equipment when measured 2 in. from the oven door.

Toxic Hazards

General. A material which in small amounts can produce an injurious effect in the average, normal adult is considered to be toxic. Certain individuals are unusually susceptible to substances which have no effect on most other individuals; these persons are said to be "allergic" to those substances (allergens). Some toxic materials are harmful to the skin, but the most dangerous are those which enter into the body.

Method of entry into the body. Access of material into the body may take place in a number of ways. Strongly corrosive materials may injure or destroy the skin and permit their entry into the bloodstream. Entry through the skin can also be through cuts and wounds or, as in the case of tetraethyl lead, the agent can pass through the whole skin itself.

The chief route of toxic liquids and solids into the body is through the mouth; a less frequent mode of entry is through an injection or puncture wound. In some instances, food or hydrochloric acid in the digestive system may tend to change and detoxify harmful chemical compounds and render them harmless. This affords the body some degree of protection. In a few instances, more damaging substances can be produced. Methyl alcohol is metabolized to formaldehyde and formic acid which are highly irritating and cause inflammation and damage to the kidneys.

The chief route of gaseous toxicants into the body is through the nose and mouth and respiratory system. In some respects, it is the most dangerous route since small amounts of toxic gas can produce major effects. The respiratory system provides very little protection against entry in the way the digestive system does.

Asphyxiants. An asphyxiant is a substance that prevents the absorption of oxygen into the blood and causes high levels of carbon dioxide in the lung sacs and in the blood. Asphyxiants can be either "simple" or "chemical." A simple asphyxiant is generally one which dilutes or blocks inspiration of air to such an extent the lungs and blood receive an inadequate supply of oxygen (carbon dioxide and nitrogen are diluting gases). A chemical asphyxiant

enters into a combination with the blood so that the hemoglobin will not pick up molecules of oxygen (carbon monoxide, hydrogen cyanide, and hydrogen sulfide are chemical asphyxiants).

Irritants. An irritant will inflame tissues at the point of contact with the body. The most sensitive part of the body is the eye, followed by the respiratory tract, mouth, and throat. Different parts of the skin vary in susceptibility. An irritant can be a gas (such as ammonia or chlorine), a liquid (such as cutting oil or silver nitrate), or a solid (such as coal dust or tobacco smoke). Most of the irritant processes of gases and liquids are chemical reactions; solids irritate by mechanical means.

Systemic poisons. Systemic poisons cause injury to specific organs of the body after having been carried there by the blood. Such poisons interfere with the use of oxygen in the metabolic process or in other reactions which prevent the organs from carrying out their normal functions. Systemic poisons can injure organs such as the kidney or liver (halogenated hydrocarbons, alcohol); bone marrow, spleen, and blood-forming system (naph-

---

Hazards Checklist—Toxic

Possible Effects	**Possible Causes**

Injury to:
    Respiratory system
    Blood system
    Body organs
    Skin
    Nervous system
	Any substance whose presence in relatively small amounts will produce physiological damage or disturbance

	Gas which can be inhaled:
	    From leak or release from pressurized system
	    Evaporation of spilled liquid or from open container
	    Product of reaction between two or more chemicals
	    Product of combustion
	    Outgassing of gases in confined spaces

Irritation of eyes, nose, throat, or respiratory passages	

Asphyxiation	Liquid or solid which can be ingested or absorbed:
	    Fine metal or other particulate matter
	    Food or other material taken in by mouth

Reduction in personnel efficiency or capabilities	Lack of skin protection Inadequate personal cleanliness
Cancer	Injected by high-pressure spray Through an open wound
Destruction of vegetation and animal life	

	Inadequate oxygen for respiration due to:
	    High altitudes
	    Dilution by inert gases
	    Combustion that consumes all available oxygen
	        Insufficient ventilation in occupied, enclosed space
	        Atmospheric pollution by industrial, automobile, or other exhausts
	        Blockage of respiratory organs by particulate matter in air

	Use of food, cosmetic, or drug that is a carcinogen

thalene, benzene, phenol); and nervous system (methyl alcohol, carbon disulfide).

Anesthetics. Anesthetics cause loss of sensation, either local or general, in the body by depressing the nervous system and interfering with involuntary muscular action. This can result in respiratory failure. Anesthetics include halogenated hydrocarbons (frequently used as cleaning or degreasing agents) such as trichloroethylene, ethyl ether, ethylene, and nitrous oxide.

Neurotics. Neurotics depress or stimulate the nervous system, brain, or spinal cord. Ethyl alcohol is a depressant; caffeine in coffee is a stimulant.

Hypnotics. Hypnotics are sleep-inducing drugs. Hypnotics include the barbiturates, chloral hydrate, and paraldehyde. Certain drugs used for other purposes have sleep-inducing effects; for example, some proprietary drugs used for hypertension alleviation have a tendency to make the user drowsy.

Carcinogens. A carcinogen is a chemical that will cause cancer. Some of the carcinogens were discovered only by their effects after inadequately controlled use. Vinyl chloride is an example. Others are suspect because they have caused cancer in laboratory animals; whether they would have similar effects on humans is unknown. Substances known to be or suspected of being carcinogens can be gaseous, liquid, or solid in form. The list of suspected carcinogens is growing every year.

Rating Toxic Substances

1. *Time-concentration factors (Ct) and dosages (D).* The Ct (milligrams per cubic meter ö minutes) is used for gaseous toxicants entering through the respiratory system; D (milligrams) is used for solids and liquids. L or I indicates whether the concentration or dosage is lethal or incapacitating. The MLD (minimum lethal dosage) is the smallest amount that will kill the most susceptible in a group of test animals; LD_{50} is the median dosage, the amount lethal to 50% of the group.

2. *Threshold Limit Values (TLVs).* TLVs, primarily for rating toxic gases, indicate the *average* concentration of toxicant the average person can tolerate without injury for 40 hours per week over a lifetime.

3. *Emergency Exposure Limits (EELs).* Indicates the approximate length of time a person can remain without ill effects in an atmosphere contaminated with specific concentrations of toxic gas.

4. *Relative ratings.* Some handbooks rate the toxicity of substances on scales such as from 1 to 6 or from 1 to 10. These scales and the ratings of each chemical differ with the raters.

Vibration and Noise

General. Vibration and noise can produce adverse physiological and psychological effects on personnel and extremely damaging effects on equipment. Vibration and noise may be caused by sources outside the product being considered or may be generated by the product itself.

Injury. The most common injury caused by vibration is sound-induced hearing loss, including loss of hearing sensitivity and immediate physical damage (ruptured eardrums). Vibration can contribute to other disorders and result in Raynaud's disease. Vibration and noise can annoy and distract operators and others so that they make errors which could lead to accidents. A loud noise can startle a person into taking an involuntary action, such as dropping a breakable object or making a misstep. Noise can also interfere with communications. High-intensity, low-frequency vibrations can cause the skull, other bones, and internal organs to vibrate with annoying or injurious amplitudes.

Raynaud's disease. Raynaud's disease is the blockage of blood vessels in the hands from the use of vibrating tools. The reduction in blood flow makes the hands feel cold, skin pale, and often with decrease in feeling. The effects are especially noticeable in cold weather. It has been a problem for people who use pneumatic chisels and hammers and hand-held rotating grinding tools. The worst effects appear to be with impact tools which vibrate at 2000–3000 beats per minute. The most dangerous frequencies for rotating grinding tools are at 40–125 Hz, especially with amplitudes greater than 100_m.

Other effects on humans. Other effects on humans attributed to vibrating tools are arthritis, bursitis, and injury to the soft tissues of the hands of users. Vibration can degrade the coordination and visual capabilities of operators and workers. An operator of a piece of mobile equipment might have trouble maintaining control of a vehicle which in vibrating strongly. A person who must make delicate adjustments may find it impossible to accomplish them except by chance. A craftsman attempting to do fine work on a vibrating surface may botch the job.

Metal fatigue. Metal fatigue induced by vibration is generally a progressive phenomenon that can result in failures of rotating parts, steam lines, pressure vessels, and other mechanical and structural parts. Cantilevered parts are especially susceptible since vibration can reach high amplitudes at their unsecured ends and high stresses at their secured ends. Poorly manufactured parts that have places where there are high stress concentrations are also prone to initiation of failures at those points.

Noise. Noise is unwanted sound. Degradation of hearing can result from long-term exposure to sound of even moderately high levels, from a high-intensity noise, and from aging. Sound level is usually measured in *decibels*. The number of decibels = $10 \log I/I_O = 20 \log p/p_O$, where I is the intensity of a sound wave and p is the sound pressure. I_O is an intensity that corresponds to the faintest

Hazards Checklist—Vibration and Noise

Possible Effects	Possible Causes

Effects on personnel:
    Fatigue
    Inability to read instruments or to activate controls
    Involuntary reaction to sudden loud noise
    Injury to hearing ability
    Raynaud's disease
    Interference with communications
	Irregular motion of rotating parts
	Bearing deterioration and misalignment
	Irregular or cyclic motion
	Loose or undersized mountings
	Pump or blower cavitation
	Reciprocating motion
	Vibrating tools
	Misaligned equipment in motion
	Lack of vibration isolators
	Scraping of hard surfaces against each other

Damage to equipment:
    Metal fatigue and other changes in crystalline
        structure
    Loosening of bolts or other fastened parts
    Breaking of lead wires, filaments, and supporting
        parts
    Crazing and flaking of finishes
	Bottoming or failure of shock mounts or absorbers
	Fluid dynamics:
	    Escaping high-velocity gas
	    High-velocity fluid hitting a surface or object that
	        can vibrate
	    Pneumatic or hydraulic shock (water hammer)

Operational effects:
    Loss of calibration of monitoring and measuring
        devices and other equipment
    Chattering of spring-type contacts, valves, and
        pointers
    Possible false readings on pointer-type devices
    Static electricity generated between plastic surfaces
	Aerodynamic flutter or buzz
	Jet engine exhaust
	Sonic booms and other shock waves
	Highly amplified music or other sounds
	Explosions or other violent ruptures
	Lack or failure of sound isolation devices such as mufflers

sound detectable at a frequency of 1000 Hz, 10^{-16} W/sq. cm. The referent sound pressure at this intensity is usually taken as 0.000204 dyne/sq. cm. or 0.0002 microbar.

Because the effects differ with sound frequencies, devices used to measure sound can generally do so for three wide bands of frequencies: A, B, and C. The A band approximates the response of the human ear and is the most commonly used (designated as dBA). Tables and charts are available by which readings in the other bands can be converted to their dBA equivalencies. OSHA now requires that 8-hour exposures to personnel not exceed 90 dBA. The National Institute of Occupational Safety and Health has recommended this maximum be reduced to 85 dBA since exposures to 90 dBA can still cause hearing loss (exposures to noises at the 85 dBA level will not).

When a new piece of equipment that generates noise is to be added when other sounds are present, it is sometimes desirable to be able to compute the noise level that will result. To do this, the existing noise level and that of the product to be added must be known. When the difference in levels in decibels between the two is as shown in column A below, the corresponding value of column B is added to the higher of the two separate sound levels. Thus, if one level is 75 dB and the other 72 dB, the difference is 3 dB. Two dB (from column B) is added to 75 dB to make a resultant noise level of 77 dB.

A Difference in Levels (dB)	B Add to Higher Noise Level (dB)
0–1.5	3
1.5–3	2
3–5	1.5
5–9	1
More than 9	0

Miscellaneous Hazardous Characteristics

Below are some hazardous characteristics that do not easily fit into the categories discussed in the foregoing pages.

Contamination. Contamination can cause excessive friction and binding of moving surfaces and interference in movement, especially where close tolerances exist; clogging of openings, such as those in filters, valves, nozzles, regulators, lines, and orifices; scoring and abrading of

Hazards Checklist—Miscellaneous

Possible Effects	Possible Causes

Contamination:

Increased friction and binding between sliding surfaces

Clogging and blocking of lines, valves, regulators, filters, nozzles, orifices

Scoring and abrading of closely fitted moving surfaces

Erosion of lines and equipment by large particles in fluids

Spring contraction prevented by large particles between coils

Contamination of potable liquids

Destruction of vegetation and marine life

Source of odors

Interference in seating of valves

Flammable particles compressed in air could ignite

Accumulations of flammable contaminants could ignite

Deterioration of fluids

Resilient materials punctured

Electrical leakage through dirty insulation

Reduction in lubricity

Induces corrosion

Airborne dirt or other environmental particles

Leakage or spillage of petroleum or its products, solvents, or other deleterious material

Microbial or fungal growth

Polymerization

Wash water from oil and chemical process or storage tanks

Misalignment or poor fitting of parts

Discharge from industrial processes or plants

Internal combustion engine exhaust

Particulate matter from cutting and grinding

Cuttings and pieces of organic fibers

Plastic and elastomer fragments

Process residues

Filtration system overload or failure

Metal particles from moving surfaces in contact

Corrosion

Wind-borne particulate matter

Lubricity:

Slips and falls

Loss of control of a moving vehicle

Loss of friction for braking

Loss of friction for traction

Surface material hard and very smooth

Water, oil, or other lubricant on a smooth, hard, flat surface

Presence of water on a greasy surface

Ice on horizontal surface

Odor:

Annoyance, leading to tendency to make errors

Reduced ability to withstand other adverse environmental conditions

Nausea

Characteristic of a material

Leak or spill of an odorous fluid

Products of a chemical reaction

Breakdown of molecules when heated

Volatilization of material when heated

Rotting material

Release of a volatile material from a mixture

Outgassing from a porous material of a substance used in its manufacture

---

lines and moving surfaces by friction; corrosion of metal surfaces by chemical reaction with the contaminant; creation of a fire hazard if the accumulated contamination is flammable; degradation of fluids and other materials so they can become unusable; and destruction of vegetation and marine life.

- *Entry of contamination.* Contaminants can enter a product from an unclean environment, such as dirt carried in the air or salt from ice-melting chemicals; from spillage and leakage; and from failures of screens or filters.

- *Internal formation of contamination.* Contamination formed by or within the product can have the effects indicated above even in a closed system in which contaminants can be created. Contamination can be gen-

erated inside a product by polymerization, microbial or fungal growth, wear from metal surfaces in moving contact, chemical reactions between a fluid and material in which it is contained and with which it is not compatible, or from residues resulting from inadequate cleaning.

- *Discharge of contamination.* The product may discharge some of the contaminants it has created as products of combustion or other wastes from its operation, leakage of fluids due to product malfunctions, spillage or overflows of chemicals or other deleterious materials, discharge of dirty washer process-water and chemicals, and emission of smoke or soot.

Lubricity. Some liquids and semi-liquids are hazardous because they make a solid surface slippery. A person may slip and fall and injure himself or herself. Water on a smooth, flat surface, such as the bottom of a bathtub or a tile floor, becomes highly dangerous. On a surface where there is also a layer of oil or grease, the presence of water makes the situation even worse. Water, oil, and other liquids may be present because of leaks or spills, but water is also used intentionally to clean floors, sidewalks, and other locations over which people pass.

Odor. An odor can be detected only when a gas, which may come from the vaporization of liquids or outgassing of volatile materials from solids, contacts receptors in the nasal cavity. The exact mechanism by which this occurs is still not known, but it has been theorized that whether or not a gas has an odor, and the type of odor if it has one, depends on the shape of the gas molecule and on whether or not it is electrically charged. The molecule must be soluble in water and fat so that it can penetrate thin layers of those substances and stimulate the odor receptors. One researcher has postulated that there are five molecular shapes which fit into receptor cells, giving five odors. Two other types of odors can be detected because the molecules have either a positive or negative electrical charge. A molecule which fits more than one receptor cell will have a complex odor. Molecular isomers, which have the same chemical composition but different molecular structures, will have different odors.

Approximately one person in 1000 has *anosmia*, the inability to detect any odor at any time. Another two percent suffers from *paranosmia*, the inability to detect certain odors or odor groups. Anosmia or paranosmia may be permanent or temporary conditions which are affected by inheritance, illnesses, or desensitization of the olfactory sense by continued exposure.

Desensitization may mitigate the adverse effects of odor exposure, but before desensitization occurs a very small level of a disagreeable odor can cause a person to sicken or it may be so annoying that a person will make errors which in critical instances could lead to accidents. Unpleasant odors will also reduce a person's ability to withstand other adverse environmental factors, such as high humidity, heat, or both.

Another problem is that the gradual desensitization ruins a person's ability to detect a warning odorant. Ethyl mercaptan has been used as an odorant to warn of leaks of natural gas in heating systems. One part in a million can usually be detected easily, but a person who is exposed to small amounts of leakage over a long time may become desensitized and will probably not be able to detect a more massive and dangerous leak. Because of this desensitization, odorants have not been used more as a warning mechanism.

Notes

[1] C. S. White and I. G. Bowen, *Comparative Effects Data of Biological Interest* (Albuquerque, N.M.: Lovelace Foundation for Medical Education and Research 1959), p. 19.

[2] Trademark of the National Fire Protection Association.

[3] R. F. Chaillet et al., *Human Factors Engineering Design Standard for Missile Systems and Related Equipment*, U.S. Army Human Engineering Laboratories, AD 623-731, September 1965.

[4] U.S. Department of Labor, *The Principles and Techniques of Mechanical Guarding*, Bul. 197, Washington, D.C., 1971.

Appendix B

Postdesign Checklists of Hazards

Sometimes it is desirable to check a product or subsystem, or an operation or means of operation, for hazards after the design has been completed and before a prototype is to be tested. Sometimes a purchaser of a product might wish to check the product to verify that it is not unduly hazardous. The checklists on the following pages are provided for such postdesign uses.

Acceleration Checklist

1. Will the product or any of its parts be in motion and therefore subject to acceleration or deceleration effects?

2. If the entire product will be in motion, will there be any loose objects which can be translated (moved out of position) by acceleration, deceleration, or centrifugal force?

3. Does the product contain any spring-loaded or cantilevered object or device that could be affected by acceleration or deceleration?

4. Is there any liquid in the product that could be lost or that could adversely affect operations by sloshing? Is the container in which the liquid is held sealed? Is the container large enough to prevent any loss of liquid under acceleration or deceleration?

5. Is there any liquid in the system that can cause hydraulic shock (water hammer) by rapid closure of a valve or by other sudden stoppage? If this is a possibility, has an accumulator been provided?

6. Are springs and other shock absorbers designed to avoid "bottoming"?

7. Can structural members be overloaded by a sudden impact, stoppage, or dynamic load?

8. Are vehicles which can be subjected to bumpy roads or to sudden stops or turns provided with seat belts or other methods of restraint to prevent injury to the occupants?

9. In personnel-carrying vehicles that are subject to impacts or sudden starts or stops are cushioning materials used to prevent injury by safeguarding the riders from hitting hard surfaces?

10. In such vehicles have sharp points, knobs, and other hard protuberances against which personnel can injure themselves by impact been removed or safeguarded?

11. Will the vehicle be able to stop within a reasonable distance if the surface on which it is moving is wet?

12. Is the braking surface adequate for the vehicle's weight and expected operating speed?

13. Are surfaces of products on which persons might walk so slippery that they might fall?

14. Is the lifting or lowering device designed to start and stop smoothly to prevent dynamic overloading?

15. If there is a possibility that fragments could be thrown off rotating devices, such as from grinding wheels, are protective shields provided?

16. Is there a means by which the speed of a rotating device can be kept within safe limits?

17. Is the case in which a high-speed device is rotating strong enough to contain any fragments if the device fails in motion?

18. Has the product's circuitry been analyzed to ensure that there is no possibility of a single-point failure causing an inadvertent start by which someone might be hurt?

Chemical Reactions Checklist

1. Is there any material present that will react with the moisture in the air or with any other source of water or moisture?

2. Will the product to be marketed injure any skin which it might contact?

3. Will even a small amount of the product cause injury to the eye by chemical reaction?

4. Is a material that could cause injury, either alone or in combination with another material, provided with a suitable warning label?

5. Is there any special person who might be allergic to the material or a material used in the product?

6. If the material could cause injury if taken internally, is a practical antidote indicated or is the fact that there is no antidote indicated?

7. If the material is to be used in the home and might injure a child, is the container provided with a child-resistant means of opening it?

8. Is there any material present that will react with the oxygen in the air to produce a toxic, corrosive, or flammable material or one that will ignite spontaneously?

9. Is there any material present whose molecules will break down in the presence of heat or ultraviolet radiation to produce dangerous products when not so intended?

10. Is any electrical equipment present that could create ozone by sparking?

11. Are there two metals in contact, or which could come in contact, which could cause electrolytic corrosion?

12. Is any liquid or gas used compatible with the material of the container in which it is held?

13. Is there any place where leakage of fluid could have a dangerous reaction with a nearby material?

14. Is or does the product contain a material which is hypergolic (reacts to initiate a fire) with any other material?

15. Will the product to be marketed react with any other common substance to produce a toxic or flammable gas?

16. If the product is of such a material, is a warning provided about using it in an enclosed space or other location where it would be highly dangerous?

17. Is there any metal or other substance that will cause the materials to be used to break down and form dangerous products by acting as a catalyst?

Electrical Systems Checklist

1. Are the voltage and amperage levels high enough to cause shock injury?

2. Is there any point at which a person could touch a live conductor when the product is activated?

3. Is double insulation used in preference to a grounded system for an electrical tool or appliance?

4. How long will it take to discharge a capacitive circuit? Is there a warning to that effect?

5. Is cooling provided to reduce failures and dangerously hot surfaces?

6. Is there any surface, other than a heating element, hot enough to burn a person or ignite a material?

7. Are the voltage and amperage high enough to cause arcing or sparking which can ignite a flammable gas or combustible material?

8. Are there any points, such as motor brushes or open circuit breakers, where arcing or sparking can occur?

9. Are there any places where lint, grease, or other flammable material which can be ignited can accumulate?

10. What is the possibility of inadvertently activating the product while a person is in a position to be injured?

11. Are fuses, circuit breakers, and cutouts sized to protect the circuits and equipment they are supposed to protect?

12. Can the malfunction of a voltage regulator or other device cause damage to other components or equipment?

13. Is the insulation used suitable for the service to which it will be subjected?

14. Is there a means to cut off power while replacing or changing a piece of equipment, an assembly, or a component?

15. Is there an emergency button for this product? Is it necessary or can the hazard which could create the emergency be eliminated or better controlled? Can the button be reached easily by anyone who might have to use it?

16. Are shields provided to protect personnel against any components that could rupture violently?

17. Is a means provided for grounding any product that should be grounded?

18. Is an interlock which removes power provided on the access to any equipment interior where a person could receive a fatal shock?

19. Are contacts, terminals, and like devices provided with a barrier, guard, or insulation to protect a person from coming in contact with them?

20. Are wires and cables protected against chafing, pinching, cutting, or other hazard which could damage the insulation so that a person could get a shock or weaken or cut the metal conductor?

21. Are connectors so wired that no "hot" leads or pins are exposed from which a person could receive a shock?

22. Is the design of each connector such that the operator will not be exposed to electrical shock or burns when normal disconnect methods are used even on powered equipment?

23. Are fuses or circuit breakers in a readily accessible and safe location?

24. Are wires and cables adequately secured to the chassis of the product on which they are installed?

25. Is the insulation on wires and cables nonflammable or self-extinguishing except where there is no possibility of a fire occurring?

26. Are batteries firmly secured where they are to be used?

27. When batteries are to be used, is the location marked with the polarity, voltage, and types(s) of battery to be used?

28. When batteries are to be "jumped" for engine starts, are the batteries posted with instructions indicating the precautionary measures to be taken?

Explosions and Explosives Checklist

1. Does the product contain any explosive or any material that can act as an explosive?

2. Is the explosive suitably protected against inadvertent activation?

3. Is the explosive susceptible to heat and high temperature, electromagnetic radiation, mechanical shock, electrical current or a spark or arc, or other means of ignition?

4. If the main charge needs an initiating device to be activated, is the initiating device normally separated from the main charge?

5. Are the explosive and the initiating devices suitably marked with warnings?

6. Do cartridge-actuated devices take only cartridges of sizes intended for its use and not permit the use of oversize cartridges?

7. Does the cartridge-actuated device have a means of rendering it safe when not in use?

8. Does the cartridge actuating or actuated device come provided with safe operating instructions?

9. Does the product use or contain a container of liquefied gas, such as propane, butane, or natural gas, which can leak into a closed space, form an explosive mixture, and explode when ignited?

10. Does the gas contain an odorant that will permit detection of leakage?

11. Is there a piece of operating equipment that generates large amounts of carbon monoxide that will form an explosive mixture with air in a closed space?

12. Do instructions for lighting gas or fuel burners provide warnings on the need to, and how to, avoid excess gas or oil accumulations when starting a fire in a furnace?

13. Is there any possibility that a compressor could intake a gas such as acetylene that will explode when pressurized in the presence of air and heat?

14. Is there any large amount of explosive material present, such as nitrates, nitrites, and similar chemical compounds, which can disassociate violently in the presence of heat?

15. Is there any means by which ammonia or any liquid with a high vapor pressure in a closed container could be heated by proximity to a hot surface, exposure to the sun, or other heat source?

16. Is there any liquid present, such as trichloroethylene, which will explode when subjected to high-intensity heat, such as a welding arc or cutting flame?

17. Will any fine combustible spray, heated flammable gas, or fine dust be present which could be ignited in a closed space?

18. Is there any possibility of contact between liquid oxygen and a hydrocarbon to form a shock-sensitive explosive mixture?

19. Is there any possibility that a cryogenic liquid can be heated when it is in a closed or inadequately vented container?

20. Is there any possibility of condensing ozone because of the presence of a cryogenically cooled surface near a sparking electrical apparatus?

21. Is there any chemical present that could explode or form an explosive mixture when in contact with water?

Flammability and Fires Checklist

1. Does the product contain or use any combustible material?

2. At what temperature will the combustible material normally ignite?

3. Is there any condition, such as a broken product or the presence of another substance which acts as a catalyst, which will cause the combustible material to ignite more easily?

4. Is it practicable to substitute a nonflammable material for one that will burn?

5. Has the material been rated nonflammable or self-extinguishing by a testing agency? According to what standard?

6. If the combustible material is a liquid, what is its flash point?

7. Is there any source of ignition in the product which might be present during normal operation, for example, a source of high heat or of electric sparks or arcs?

8. What type of outside sources of heat, matches or other open flames, or welding arcs or flames would cause ignition of the material?

9. If the combustible material is a liquid, is it kept in a secure container from which it will not spill or leak and in which it would be protected from an ignition source?

10. Is the fuel container located where it is protected from damage which might cause it to leak if the product is impacted?

11. Is the fuel container located where it will not spill onto a hot surface if the product in which it is located is upset?

12. Does operation of the product involve the evolution of a gas that might be flammable, such as hydrogen when a battery is overcharged?

13. Does the product contain any monitoring and warning device to indicate the presence of a fire or conditions which might precede the occurrence of a fire?

14. If the occurrence of a fire is possible, has a means of fire extinguishing, either manual or automatic, been provided?

15. Have warnings been provided to alert personnel to the presence of a flammable material and the means to avoid fires?

Heat and Temperature Checklist

1. Is there a source of heat in the product that has a temperature high enough to cause burns?

2. Is there a surface hot enough to burn a person who comes in contact with it inadvertently?

3. If the product must be handled, will it be of a temperature that will permit continuous contact?

4. Is there any material present that would melt, warp, lose strength, or catch on fire because of a high-temperature heat source?

5. Will operating temperatures cause damage to paints or other finishes?

6. If there is any cold metal surface that can cause skin to adhere and freeze, is the surface protected against contact?

7. Is there any material that will become brittle and break easily when subjected to a low temperature?

8. Will changes in temperature cause undesirable loosening or binding of parts?

9. Is there a necessity for providing a fuel, coolant, or lubricant that is capable of operating either at an extraordinarily high or low temperature?

10. Is it necessary to provide freeze plugs or other safety devices that will prevent damage to a water system if the water freezes?

11. Is a relief valve necessary on a pressure system to permit venting of fluid if the temperature increases its pressure?

12. Can the temperature of electronic equipment be reduced to minimize operating failures?

13. Is there any place where an organic material might char in the presence of a high temperature?

14. Are containers of pressurized fluids that have high vapor pressures kept away from source of heat?

15. Are pressurized containers shielded from the direct rays of the sun?

16. Is a warning provided on small pressurized containers not to throw them in a fire even when they are empty?

17. Are persons who must work in a closed space protected against high environmental temperatures?

18. Are operators free from the anxiety of possibly touching a hot surface when working?

19. Are persons who must operate a moving vehicle protected from wind chill in cold weather?

20. Does an engine-operated vehicle or other equipment have a means of monitoring its operating temperature?

Mechanical Hazards Checklist

1. Have sharp points, sharp edges, and ragged surfaces not required for the function of the product been eliminated?

2. Have guards been provided to keep personnel from being injured by moving mechanical parts, such as gears, fans, belts, or other components in motion?

3. Does the product have any pinch points, rotating components, or other moving parts which must be guarded?

4. Are ventilation openings small enough to keep fingers away from dangerous places?

5. Are openings in or around guards small enough to keep persons from inserting fingers into dangerous places?

6. Is a warning provided against loading cables, chains, and hoists beyond their rated limits? Does the warning on hoists also indicate that loads should not be raised or lowered with quick starts or stops that will put high strains on the cable or chains? Is the equipment posted with rated load capacities?

7. Have lock nuts, lock washers, safety wires or cotter pins, or similar devices been used to secure fasteners of critical assemblies so that they will not loosen or separate?

8. Has equipment that might be damaged or that might cause damage by impact during operation been provided with bumpers, shock absorbers, springs, or other devices to lessen the effects of impacts?

9. Have critical moving assemblies or other sensitive parts of a product that could be jammed or damaged by dropped or loose articles been protected by screens, guards, covers, or other barriers?

10. Can large or heavy parts that have to be replaced be removed without damaging surrounding components or assemblies?

11. Do hinged covers or access panels that must be raised to open have a means of securing them in their open positions against accidental closures that could cause injury?

12. If a heavy product or assembly must be lifted frequently, are handles or other handling aids provided? Are lift points provided and labeled?

13. If a product or assembly can be damaged if it is turned to any but an upright position, is it so marked with a warning and a directional arrow? Is every container in which it might be transported similarly marked?

14. If reversed or rotated mounting or assembly of parts cannot be tolerated, is an arrangement, such as nonsymmetrical parts of pin or bolt patterns, used to prevent errors?

15. Has the product been designed and tested to ensure that it will not overturn or topple easily, especially if it is to contain a hot or otherwise dangerous fluid?

16. Do slide assemblies for drawers in cabinets have limit stops to prevent them from being inadvertently pulled out too far?

Pressure Checklist

1. Is the pressure vessel designed and manufactured in accordance with the applicable code?

2. Has the pressure vessel been designed in accordance with the legally required safety factor?

3. Has the pressure vessel been proof-pressure and/or burst-pressure tested?

4. Have all the lines and fittings been rated for the pressures they must withstand? Have they been pressure tested?

5. Are any flex hoses, their connections, and fittings secured in order to prevent whipping if there is a failure?

6. Is the pressure system located near or can it be subjected to an unintended high heat input that would raise the pressure excessively?

7. Is it possible to accidentally connect the system to a source of pressure higher than that for which the system or any of its components was designed?

8. Does the container or any line that might be overpressurized have a relief valve, vent, or burst diaphragm?

9. Is the relief valve, vent, or diaphragm set to operate at a pressure which is less than the pressure that can cause damage?

10. Will the exhaust from the relieving device be conducted away safely for disposal?

11. Is there any component or assembly in the pressure system which, if installed backward or to which a reversed connection is made, could cause an accident?

12. Is there any means of preventing a reversed installation or connection?

13. Is each container or line that holds a flammable, toxic, corrosive, or otherwise dangerous fluid suitably identified and marked?

14. Should the product, assembly or subassembly, or line be marked with a warning that it is to be depressurized before any work is started on it?

15. Is there a means of depressurizing the system without endangering the person who will work on it?

16. Is a safety-critical hydraulic system whose failure could result in an accident unless suitable action is taken by the operator provided with a warning light in a conspicuous location to alert the operator of a failure?

17. Is there any opportunity for compression of the fluid in a closed system?

18. Does the product contain or use a cryogenic or high vapor pressure liquid in a closed container that could inadvertently be heated?

19. Does the fluid line have a quick-closing valve or other shutoff device that could result in water hammer and a shock wave?

20. Is there a possibility of a closed pressure vessel collapsing because of condensation of steam or other gas, decrease in altitude, or excessive operation of a vacuum pump? Does such a product or pressure system contain a vacuum relief valve?

21. Do the direct pressure readout gages have shatterproof glass or plastic faces and blowout plugs?

22. Are lines that might be subjected to temperature changes provided with means to expand and contract?

23. Is flexible hose protected against chafing, twisting, or other damage?

24. If there is an accumulator, does it have a warning indicating the maximum operating pressure?

25. Are hydraulic lines located *below* electrical, hot, or other lines on which leaks could result in fires?

Radiation Checklist

1. Does the product use any radioactive isotope for any reason?
2. If it does, what type of radioactive emission does it generate?
3. Is the quantity used at any one time adequate to cause injury to a person close to it?
4. Is it possible to inhale or swallow the radioactive material?
5. Are the containers of such materials suitably marked?
6. If the product uses electricity, does it generate potentials of 15,000 V or more?
7. Is it possible that the components having such potentials could generate x-rays?
8. Have the prototypes of such products been tested to determine whether or not they can generate such x-rays?
9. Does the product generate high-intensity ultraviolet radiation, such as by carbon arcs?
10. Are warnings provided to alert persons who could be affected to the need for protective eyewear to prevent injury to the eyes?
11. Are products that will produce high-intensity microwave radiation protected to limit access to areas where such radiation will exist at harmful levels?
12. Is the level of leakage radiation within the allowable limits set by the Bureau of Radiological Health?
13. Is there a warning against rings, watches, and other metallic jewelry in areas where microwave radiation might exist?
14. Has the laser been categorized in accordance with the requirements of the Bureau of Radiological Health?
15. Does the laser require special safeguards, such as a key switch, because of the category in which it has been classified?
16. Is there a warning label on any laser that can cause eye injury?

Toxic Materials Checklist

1. Does the product contain any material which in small amounts could be harmful to a person if it is inhaled or swallowed or absorbed through or chemically reacts with the skin?

2. Can the material affect the nervous system, act as an anesthetic, or cause cancer?

3. Can the material have an increased toxic effect if it is mixed with another substance (potentiation)?

4. Can the material in a product react with any other second material to create a toxic material?

5. Does the container of the material provide a warning against mixing the material with anything else with which a harmful substance can be generated?

6. Can deterioration or combustion of the material result in a product (or products) that could be toxic?

7. Will use of the product generate carbon monoxide? Is it possible for the carbon monoxide to leak into an enclosed, occupied space?

8. If the toxic material is a gas, does it have a warning odor? Should an odorant be added to warn of its presence if there is a leak?

9. Have tests been made to determine if any new substance is toxic, how toxic it is, what the effects might be, and any antidotes or treatments?

10. Has the substance been tested by the Food and Drug Administration or by a qualified independent testing organization?

11. If the material is a gas, has a Threshold Limit Value (TLV) or other rating been established?

12. Have any Emergency Exposure Limits been established? Is this information used on any warnings?

13. If the product is for household use, is it clearly marked with a warning if it is hazardous and does it have a child-resistant closure?

14. If the material is hazardous in an enclosed space, does the warning so state and indicate the conditions under which it is safe to use?

15. Is there any history of the material ever having caused injury?

Vibration and Noise Checklist

1. Is the rotating or reciprocating equipment or its components mounted and secured in order to avoid or minimize vibration?

2. If vibration sources cannot be eliminated, is the product provided with vibration isolators or dampers?

3. Are the isolators, dampers, shock absorbers, or similar devices adequate for eliminating vibration? Have they been tested?

4. Is the handle of any power tool by which vibration could be transmitted to the user's hand provided with vibration isolators in order to avoid Raynaud's disease?

5. Has piping for fluids been fastened securely to supports so that it will not vibrate when in operation?

6. Have bolts and other fastened parts for safety-critical assemblies been tightened securely to prevent motion between parts?

7. Have safety-critical bolts and other fasteners been secured by devices in order to ensure that they will not loosen under vibration?

8. Is the metal or a product that vibrates such that vibration will not cause changes in crystalline structure and metal fatigue?

9. Are means available to ensure proper alignment of mated rotating parts so that there will be no vibration?

10. Are thin surfaces avoided in air streams where they could cause "flutter" and noise?

11. Are designs that could cause chattering of cantilevered or spring-mounted components avoided?

12. Is the possibility of water hammer in a hydraulic system in which there is rapidly flowing fluid avoided by using an accumulator or other protective device?

13. Can the use of high-speed rotating devices be minimized by use of slower operating devices in order to avoid vibration and noise?

14. Has a noise survey been made of the assembled product?

15. Is it practicable to reduce the noise in the product?

16. Is it possible to use sound-absorbing material to reduce noise emissions?

Miscellaneous Hazards Checklist

1. Will contamination affect the safe operation of the product?

2. If contamination might affect it, are the critical parts of the product hermetically sealed or otherwise protected?

3. If filters or screens are provided, are they easily removed for cleaning? Are the filters and screens of ample capacity or is it necessary to clean them often?

4. Is it possible to clean the product easily without causing damage or is it necessary to use a hazardous cleaning agent?

5. Have instructions been provided on keeping the product clean and on how often it should be cleaned?

6. If any of the contamination products that might accumulate be flammable, such as grease or lint, is the user warned of precautionary measures to be taken?

7. Is there any material in the product that will act as a nutrient for fungal or bacterial growth?

8. Would the contamination cause any electrical problem, such as short-circuiting, or loss of cooling air flow?

9. Could the product emit contamination that could injure vegetation or marine life it might contact?

10. Is it possible that a material, such as a fluid, used in the product could deteriorate or react with other substances to generate contamination?

11. Are flow passages in fluid systems and clearances for mechanical parts in motion such that contamination will not cause clogging or binding?

12. If the product is one on which persons would walk, is the surface so smooth and hard that they might fall? What would be the effects of water, waxing, or of spilled fluids on the slipperiness of the surface?

13. If the product is a vehicle, will it have the capability of stopping under foreseeable adverse conditions that might cause loss of friction for stopping?

14. What surface conditions could cause a vehicle to lose control?

15. Have operators been provided with instructions on the actions to be taken if such adverse conditions are encountered?

16. Do any of the materials used in the product have a characteristic odor that might be offensive?

17. Might any odorous substance used for and during the manufacture of the product remain after the product is completed?

18. Will any material used in the product break down or volatilize in the presence of heat so that odorous gases are given off?

19. Will a material react with another substance to produce a product that has an offensive odor?

Index

Triple Redundancy Incorporating Self-Adaptive Failure Exclusion (TRISAFE), 68. *See also:* Decision redundancy
TRISAFE. *See:* Triple Redundancy Incorporating Self-Adaptive Failure Exclusion
Troubleshooting and maintenance using fault-tree analysis, 183
Tye, W., on sneak circuit analysis, 195, 203-204

U

Underwriters Laboratories, 41. *See also:* Standards
    risk assessment methods used by, 235
Undesirable product conditions, 99-100
United States v *Carroll Towing Company*, 242. *See also:* Accident, avoidance, costs of
United States Air Force, 171. *See also:* Fault-tree analysis
United States Atomic Energy Commission, on fatal accidents, 234
United States Customs Service, 33. *See also:* Federal organizations concerned with safety
United States Supreme Court, 119
United States v Park, 119. *See:* Safety program management
U.S. Interagency Task Force on Product Liability, 45

V

Verification. *See:* Safeguard verification
Vertical standards, 44. *See also:* Standards
Vibration and noise
    hazards, 282-283
    postdesign checklist for, 298
Visual warnings, 108-109. *See also:* Warnings
Voluntary standards, 42-43
    defined, 42

W

Warning(s), 104, 108-110. *See also:* Failure minimization methods
    Clark Equipment Company's, 96
    defined, 92
    FMC Corporation's, 96
    labels, 91, 92, 96
    potential dangers of, 91
    standardization of, 91-92, 96
    symbols, 96, 97
Warranty(ies). *See also:* Product liability
    express, 10
    implied, 10
Weather problems, 76
Westinghouse Company, 141. *See also:* Critical Incident Technique
White, William, 30
Willis, Harold R., 167. *See also:* Mapping
Winterbottom v *Wright*, 9. *See also:* Privity
Worker's compensation, 11-13. *See also:* Third-party suits
Writers, technical publication, 123

Y

Yuba Power Products, 10. *See also;* Strict liability